The Assessment of Industrial Markets

First Published in 1968, *The Assessment of Industrial Markets* offers a quite different approach to the subject of industrial marketing research. It concentrates on the techniques of industrial marketing research and devotes a chapter to each major method. More space is also given to the mechanics of research. The author's purpose has been to set out clearly the salient factors and methodologies. Chapter demographics refer the reader to more detailed or advanced reading on any particular aspect of industrial marketing.

The book is essentially practical and contains an important innovation. Where appropriate, checklists have been developed for the processes and actions required in a number of industrial marketing activities. Also, the checklist which appeared in Industrial Marketing Research is included in the present work in a revised and extended form. This is a must read for students of marketing, business management and business economics.

The Assessment of Industrial Markets

Aubrey Wilson

Routledge
Taylor & Francis Group

First published in 1968
by Hutchinson & Co Ltd.

This edition first published in 2024 by Routledge
4 Park Square, Milton Park, Abingdon, Oxon, OX14 4RN

and by Routledge
605 Third Avenue, New York, NY 10017

Routledge is an imprint of the Taylor & Francis Group, an informa business

Publisher's Note
The publisher has gone to great lengths to ensure the quality of this reprint but points out that some imperfections in the original copies may be apparent.

Disclaimer
The publisher has made every effort to trace copyright holders and welcomes correspondence from those they have been unable to contact.

A Library of Congress record exists under LCCN: 66008652

ISBN: 978-1-032-87691-7 (hbk)
ISBN: 978-1-003-53483-9 (ebk)
ISBN: 978-1-032-87858-4 (pbk)

Book DOI 10.4324/9781003534839

The Assessment of Industrial Markets

Aubrey Wilson

(Managing Director, Industrial Market Research Limited)

HUTCHINSON OF LONDON

HUTCHINSON & CO (*Publishers*) LTD
178–202 Great Portland Street, London W1

London Melbourne Sydney
Auckland Bombay Toronto
Johannesburg New York

First published 1968

*This book has been set in Times, printed in Great Britain
on Antique Wove paper by Anchor Press, and
bound by Wm. Brendon, both of Tiptree, Essex*

09 088740 9

To my parents

Contents

Introduction

Management aids, systems and philosophies have proliferated over the years and have between them produced a higher level of performance but also acute managerial self-consciousness. This has led in turn to a commitment to the status-giving philosophy of 'scientific management'. The danger of a commitment of this sort is the acceptance without either belief or understanding of those management activities which have distinctly modish overtones.

Every few years there are certain prescribed postures which must be adopted if a manager is to merit the continuing good opinion of his superiors and colleagues. Not to claim familiarity with the concepts of corporate long-range planning or zero defects or value analysis would be admitting not to have kept pace with key advances in the field.

So with marketing orientation; this is now an accepted philosophy, if not necessarily the practice, of most companies concerned with industrial products and services. That the success of a company starts and finishes with the customer is no longer argued. It follows from this that it is necessary to know, or perhaps more importantly, to anticipate what the customer wants. The cost of wrong decisions and poor anticipation has become progressively higher; more decisions of increasing complexity must be taken more frequently and with greater precision.

The speed with which requirements and configurations of industrial markets change, the shortening of product life cycles, emergence of new industries and collapse of old ones, changing natures and climates of competition and the increasing internationalisation of businesses are accepted features of modern industrial life and spell out the need for more and faster information services. The stability of the industrial goods sector of the economy has always been compared favourably with the volatility of consumer goods markets. The distinction is no longer real and the ecology of the economy has demonstrated over and over again the realities of the interdependability of both sectors.

The hunger for certainty in marketing operations has ensured the emergence of industrial marketing research as a major management aid because the basis for correct decisions is derived from the collection and interpretation of marketing information.

Certainly industrial marketing research as a separate recognisable activity within companies is a relatively new phenomenon. This is not to say that it was not practised successfully by a great many people since commerce began, but the Emersonian idea of the world beating a path to the door of the best mousetrap maker is a philosophy for more leisurely times.

Whereas those firms and individuals who are using or undertaking industrial marketing research techniques are well aware of the very great advances which have been made in the last ten years, the exact nature of these advances is far from obvious in the literature on the subject and in the content of much that is taught in universities, technical colleges and by professional and private organisations. The insistence on rigorous methodology and a pre-occupation with gathering unrelated facts would seem to be only slightly less prevalent today than in the early days of industrial marketing research.

The existing gap between the elegant methods of users and practitioners of industrial marketing research and the published material available to those who wish to study its techniques remains vast. This is nowhere better typified than by the fact that the first book to be published anywhere in the world on the subject (and of which I was joint author)—*Industrial Marketing Research—Management and Technique* (Hutchinson, 1963)—remains, up to the time that this present book was written, the only book devoted wholly to the subject. In the intervening five years, consumer marketing research books have proliferated, a few even going so far as to indicate the existence of a separate activity concerned with industrial markets. It is true many more articles on industrial marketing research and many more courses are available today than five years ago, but none offers an integrated overview of the whole subject. The seeker of information must necessarily return to the 1963 state of the art.

For this reason, therefore, it was decided that a new book rather than a revised version of the old one was needed and that while covering the advances made in techniques, it should also recognise that it is no longer necessary to advise management to use industrial marketing research and to spell out the advantages it brings. Thus, the present book has a different approach from the previous one. It concentrates on the techniques of industrial marketing research and devotes one chapter to each major method whereas in *Industrial*

Marketing Research—Management and Technique they were grouped into a single chapter. More space has been devoted to the mechanics of research than was possible previously.

This book does not attempt to make the reader highly proficient in all the methods which are discussed. I would make no claim for an ability to do so. The purpose has been to set out clearly the salient factors and methodologies and to refer the reader onward for more detailed or advanced reading of any particular aspect; for example, while the chapter concerned with processing the research yield is complete in itself, the reader is referred to the appropriate texts for deeper study of, for example, scaling methods. I do not feel that this book can achieve its purpose if the broad sweep of the argument and explanations are limited by discussions of specialised aspects which are more adequately dealt with by experts in these fields.

It is hoped that the bibliographies for each chapter will provide a guide for further reading (see pages 387–94). However, producing a bibliography for each chapter has highlighted the paucity of literature on a number of aspects covered in the book; thus those chapters where published information is lacking are dealt with in greater depth in the present book in an attempt to at least partially remedy this deficiency. For example, no single authoritative reference could be located on the use of postal questionnaires in industrial surveys yet postal questionnaires are ubiquitous and an important part of the industrial marketing research mix.

It is now almost mandatory to bemoan the lack of published case studies in British marketing literature, and most of all in marketing research. Regrettably there appears to have been very little liberalisation of British managements' attitudes to publishing results of surveys as cases. Examples of studies have been given throughout the book to illustrate real-life situations but unfortunately few would qualify as workable case studies. One change all who are concerned with industrial marketing research would like to see over the next decade is the increasing availability of case-study material.

Product orientation now so much eschewed does tend to come through very strongly in a rather different context in the majority of marketing books. Almost without exception, these books are concerned with marketing of, and marketing research for, products rather than services. Yet expenditure on services, both consumer and industrial, has risen rapidly in the last decade and research into demand for industrial services has increased with it. Although the techniques for researching services as opposed to products does not vary in many aspects, there are some special areas which do require separate treatment. Throughout this book products and services are considered both together and separately although to avoid repetition the distinction is made specifically only when necessary.

The book is intended to be a practical one and to this end contains one innovation; that is, where appropriate, check lists have been developed for the processes and actions required in a number of industrial marketing research activities. The success of the 'Industrial Marketing Researchers Check List' in *Industrial Marketing Research —Management and Technique*, which has had ten reprintings separately from the book and which is included in the present book in a revised and extended version, has left no doubt in my mind as to the value of check lists in marketing.

As editor of *The Marketing of Industrial Products*, I was privileged to come into contact with perhaps the leading practitioners and teachers of marketing in Great Britain and my work as editor showed me the synergism that can be obtained by collaboration of this type so that I did not hesitate to call on many of the authors in that book to review individual chapters. In particular, I would like to thank Mary Griffin and Franklin Colborn. However, the major task of reading fell to Gordon Brand and Christopher West and it is to them that I must attribute the considerable improvement between the early drafts and the final version of the book.

I am, as with my previous publications, deeply indebted to my colleagues at Industrial Market Research Ltd. for their many helpful suggestions and inputs. I am particularly grateful to Helen Sasson and Hugh Buckner both for assistance with the content and ordering of the book and for drawing my attention to several important omissions which otherwise might not have been rectified. Their long experience in the daily operations of a busy industrial marketing research agency concerned with a very wide range of problems has been reflected in the many suggestions which they have made to keep the book on a totally practical level.

The task of preparing the manuscript from badly typed and illegibly written draft was undertaken cheerfully, accurately and with astonishing speed by Marie Tucker.

Although authors think they suffer in preparing a book none are so deprived as their families and friends. For the fifth time therefore my thanks are due to those closest to me for tolerating for so long my pre-occupation with this book and for willingly accepting my acute withdrawal symptoms as a necessary pre-condition of writing and preparing this book for publication.

Prefaces usually exonerate manuscript readers and others who contributed from responsibility for the inadequacies and errors in it. This is most certainly true in this case. If the book is received with the same enthusiasm as its predecessor it will be a tribute to the combined knowledge and help of my very many collaborators. Its deficiencies are solely the result of the author's obstinacy.

AUBREY WILSON

London, August 1968

CHAPTER 1

Characteristics of Industrial and Consumer Markets

The high level of acceptance and use of industrial marketing research in the majority of industrially mature countries is due to a number of factors related to the advent of the large corporations. These corporations substituted scientific management techniques for entrepreneurial flair and flexibility and in so doing created a demand for formalised management information systems. It was also the large companies which were the first to appreciate that the marketing concept was as applicable in industrial markets as in consumer markets. Because the marketing concept looks outwards from the firm to the market, its adoption reinforced the requirement for better and faster information and greater accuracy in forecasting the direction and needs of industrial markets. The giant corporations were able to devote some of their financial and intellectual resources to experimentation and to the development of techniques which would provide a flow of control information for their operations and planning.

The initially slow acceptance of industrial marketing research by the medium and smaller firms reflected their hesitance in moving from traditional product orientation towards the marketing concept, often a resistance to any change at all and a belief in the infallibility of the entrepreneur's *nous*. Some time was to pass before it was appreciated that entrepreneurial skill was not superseded by industrial marketing research but enhanced by it. Arguments rejecting research tend to centre around some highly idiosyncratic and unexplainable findings which appeared in some of the early projects. These occurred not only in the pioneer studies undertaken in the late 1940s but also in more recent research. An evaluation of these and other surveys almost invariably shows that less than satisfactory results occurred because of the use of techniques more applicable to assessing consumer markets than industrial markets.

As industrial marketing research advances there have been many pleas that no dichotomy should be created between it and consumer marketing research. They are, after all, it is argued, two parallel branches of research. The analogy should be taken a little further: parallel lines meet only at infinity. Consumer and industrial marketing research are in some ways similar but certainly not in the application of techniques, and most particularly not in sampling methods.

There is no demand whatsoever for industrial goods and services which does not stem in the ultimate from the demand for consumer goods and services. The links may be remote and tortuous or they may be direct. The demand for magnesite stems ultimately from a demand for consumer goods but there can be many stages in the demand process as Figure 1 clearly shows. The demand for electric motors for the washing machine shown on the diagram is much more direct, being only one step removed from consumer demand.

Marketing research in consumer and industrial goods markets can be closely linked because many of the results obtained from consumer research will contribute to accurate findings in industrial marketing research. For example the market for elapsed timers which are sold to manufacturers of cooking appliances can be calculated by simple correlations from the cooking appliance market share data which is provided by research among consumers. But it is here, and only here, where the link between the two disciplines exists. Although the techniques are basically similar their application varies widely. A consumer marketing research approach is likely to be as fatal to an industrial marketing research project as it would be to attempt to assess consumer markets using industrial marketing research methods.

Unless this most fundamental and indeed vital consideration is accepted there can be little chance of success with an industrial marketing research project without a degree of good fortune which no researcher ought to rely on. Luck is not an element which can be built into a research plan.

It is not sufficient merely to state and illustrate that a difference exists between the two activities. A convincing reason must be advanced if the distinction which is being made is not to be regarded as mere sophistry—an attempt to form a new and exclusive club—to raise the researcher and his special field of study in management's esteem.

The differences however are real enough and stem from the essential differences in the characteristics of industrial goods, industrial services, industrial markets and industrial buyers.

It is necessary first, before examining these differences, to define 'industrial goods and services'. Even here it is possible to get lost in research, economics and semantic polemics. The simplest definition will nevertheless suffice. 'Products and services purchased for organisational purposes.' These can then be classified. 'Primary materials, fabricated parts, fabricating materials, process materials, packaging materials, capital equipment, accessory equipment, operating supplies and general and specialised services.'

The definition has the virtue of cutting straight through the 'problem' area of an industrial good which is also a consumer good. For example, typewriters are sold to consumers and to commercial and industrial users and therefore, on a product basis, can be regarded as a subject for both industrial and consumer marketing research. Swimming pools might be sold to institutions as well as 'A' group consumers. Small power tools, private and commercial vehicles, carpets, space heaters and a whole host of products fall into the 'double' category. If the market is seen in terms of characteristics of the buyer and the buying situation rather than the product, then each item drops neatly into the industrial or consumer slot, as the case may be.

The situation has been summed up succinctly. 'The broad basic differences between types of goods arise not so much from variations in their physical characteristics as from differences in the ways in which and the purpose for which they are bought.'[1]

It is pertinent to examine in detail some of the areas of difference which are encompassed in the definition.

DERIVED DEMAND

The example in Figure 1 draws attention to the fact that the source of demand in an industrial market may be very far divorced from the product or service being researched.

It is a basic exercise in economics to establish the effect of demand for one product upon another. The demand for capital goods is wholly derived from the demand for the goods they produce whether they are industrial goods or consumer goods. Thus, demand for capital goods and the materials and components from which they are made is dependent in the ultimate upon consumer demand and also upon the confidence of buyers in the prospect for their profitable use, upon the buying power of business enterprises needing them and upon the availability and cost of credit. Demand for a wide range of consumer goods is independent of most of these imponderables and only in a few cases is it dependent upon one or two of them.

[1] R. S. Alexander, J. S. Cross and R. M. Cunningham, *Industrial Marketing*, Irwin (Homewood, Illinois, Revised Edition 1961), p. 3.

B

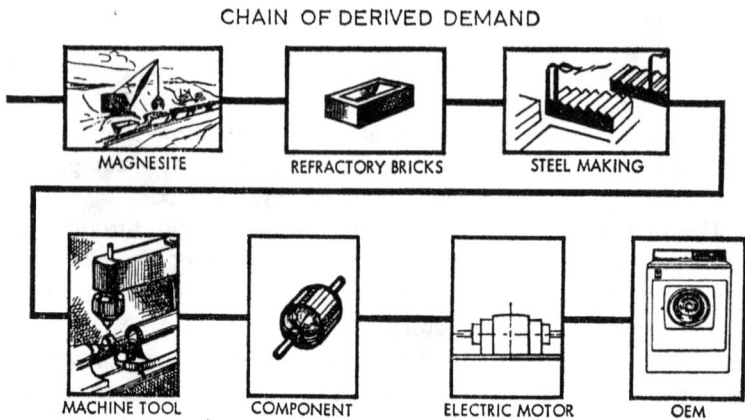

MAGNESITE   REFRACTORY BRICKS   STEEL MAKING

MACHINE TOOL   COMPONENT   ELECTRIC MOTOR   OEM

Fig. 1

Derived demand in general has less price elasticity than direct demand, always assuming the existence of substitutes. This implies that industrial goods manufacturers as a whole are rarely able to expand their markets substantially through price reductions. However, a distinction must be made between the price elasticity of an industry and that of the individual manufacturer. A manufacturer of producer's goods may hope to increase his turnover, if only temporarily, by price reductions below current market levels.

In most sectors of the consumer goods industries, direct demand is highly responsive to price changes. For this reason it is as possible for an industry as it is for a firm to substantially improve its share of consumer spending at the expense of the other industries' or manufacturers' products by judicious price reductions.

One of the greatest problems in assessing an industrial market and particularly in forecasting its future is the large number of variables caused by the interaction of the various activities which comprises the chain of demand. In the example given in Figure 1, if the demand for washing machines declines it will impact, however lightly or distantly in time, on the demand for magnesite. If the demand for industrial actuators, business machines, pumps and medical equipment which use fractional horse-power motors declines while washing machine demand remains high, the situation may nevertheless result in a fractional horse-power manufacturer postponing a purchase for machine tools, thus impacting down the line on the demand for magnesite. In both examples, however, the demand induced or inhibited for magnesite may be infinitesimal—total demand being an aggregation of many small parts.

It can be seen at once that assessing markets at this distance requires quite another approach from the consumer market where it is common practice to seek to identify market characteristics and demand in terms of demographic and motivational terms.

DURABILITY OF PRODUCTS

Just as consumer and industrial markets are separate and distinct so there is a further subdivision regarding the latter, as between capital goods markets and other industrial goods. Research into capital goods markets resembles that for other industrial goods, but different additional characteristics exist demanding separate evaluation. In particular, the durability of capital goods which leads to their spasmodic and infrequent purchase is an important market characteristic not applicable to many other industrial goods such as materials, operating supplies and components.

Historically, the market for capital goods has been much more volatile than for certain other goods, especially non-durables. It is durability that forms the basis of the classification of demand for capital goods into two types. These are 'replacement demand', for the same product or for an improved product capable of increasing efficiency or reducing costs; or 'expansion demand', which is for new products or processes for increasing the capacity of existing plant. The central demand characteristic in capital goods is the ability to postpone either types of purchase—either by extending the useful life of existing plant (possibly at the cost of reduced efficiency) or by not expanding output. This implies that a proportion of capital goods buyers are only actively in the market intermittently and, more important, that the periodicity of demand is determined by conditions outside the control of the sellers and can be subject to rapid readjustment—without warning to unwary sellers.

Capital goods can and do last a considerable period of time. Moreover even when they approach the end of their useful life they can often be made to continue to operate, perhaps at far less than optimum efficiency, but sufficiently well to justify postponement of replacement. Indeed, many old capital products have a 'second-hand' life, being purchased either by less prosperous firms which cannot afford new equipment or else shipped overseas to countries less industrially developed.

A census of machine tools in 1961 revealed that 22 per cent of all metal-working equipment at that date was over 20 years old.[1] By 1966 this figure had risen to 26 per cent.[2] A search for historic machinery still preserved on site brought to light a large number of items over fifty years old, and a still surprisingly high number over seventy-five years.

Many examples can be found of various forms of lifting devices of up to and exceeding 100 years old. In fact, centenarian machinery in industry is sufficiently common as not to be necessarily remarkable.[3]

The problem of longevity in assessing industrial markets is two-fold. First to estimate accurately the life cycle of a product so that replacement demand can be assessed, and second to appraise precisely what product will replace the old one. A thirty-five year replacement cycle for a steam-raising boiler will not necessarily give the point in time when a new steam-raising boiler will be bought. At the moment of replacement steam power may be substituted by hydraulics or pneumatics, and where demand thirty-five years ago was for a boiler, today it could as easily be for a compressor or an electric motor. In fact, products bought at one period may readily be replaced by other products utilising a totally different concept, for example, the substitution of traditional metal-forming methods by explosive forming.

Consumer goods too can have a long life, particularly works of art, houses and furniture and, to a very much lesser extent, consumer durable goods such as radios, washing machines and vehicles. But taken over the whole range of consumer purchasing, most products have a very limited life and are replaced either because they no longer work or work very inefficiently or, more usually, because they have become psychologically obsolescent—for example clothing and interior decorations.

LONG MANUFACTURING CYCLE

With few exceptions, such as housing and wines and spirits, consumer goods are manufactured in a relatively short period of time often to be counted in minutes or hours, and only occasionally days. For example, even such a complex piece of equipment as a motor vehicle takes only twenty-one hours to assemble while a television set requires only one hour on the production line. Production of very

[1] *First Census of Machine Tools in Britain*, McGraw-Hill (London, 1961).

[2] *Census of Machine Tools in Britain*, McGraw-Hill (Maidenhead, 1966).

[3] Aubrey Wilson, 'Industrial Archaeology in London', *Industrial Archaeology: Journal of History of Industry and Technology* (Bristol, May 1966).

many industrial products, particularly capital goods and plant, but often materials too, such as seasoned timbers, celluloid and vulcanite sheets, complex organic compounds and other chemicals may be counted in weeks, months and years. Major plant such as a sea water distillation plant or a refinery will require perhaps three years from site preparation to coming on stream while the months and indeed years of preparatory work must not be forgotten. A continuous laundry machine can take up to six months to manufacture and a walking drag line fifteen months. These are not exceptional in any way and are typical of a very large number of industrial products.

These differences are important for the industrial marketing researcher as they assist him to distinguish between the appropriate techniques and to identify realisable objectives for the varying circumstances, as market assessments must often be made well in advance of the end-products becoming available. But products, industries, economies and governments can change beyond recognition in the time a plant might come on stream. For example, a decision by a West African government encouraged and supported by overseas interests of one political colour, to build a sea water distillation plant made good sense at the time. Such a plant would have reduced that country's dependence on imported salt and the drain on its foreign balances. Various political and other factors delayed the decision and by 1966 when the plant might have been expected to come on stream the government had fallen, support of the overseas interests had been withdrawn and priorities had necessarily changed. The viability of the plant became dubious to an extreme.

Again it is true that a consumer market can rise and fall with astonishing rapidity—hula hoops are the classic example, and women's clothing the classic industry. But the capital goods needed to make hula hoops and dresses can be adapted easily and quickly to make rainwater goods and skirts. The sea water distillation plant lacks almost any flexibility.

Because industrial products frequently have a longer manufacturing cycle than the majority of consumer goods, greater weight must be given to questions relating to quantities produced and the timing of production effort. Where production precedes, rather than follows, demand—as it must with a wide range of industrial goods—adjustment to demand is difficult and can be costly. Longer term rather than short-term demand estimates are needed for judging the likely volume of consumption.

MARKET CONCENTRATIONS

Three types of concentration are generally distinguishable in industrial markets. Geographical, industrial and purchasing.

Geographic concentrations are well-known and documented. Useful innovations in cartography[1] have made the geographic identification of the location of an industry a simple matter, both in terms of national and local concentrations and in terms of industrial and commercial products. Certain major classical concentrations are well known—such as metal-working industries in and around Birmingham, pottery in Staffordshire and cotton textiles in Lancashire. However, many other important industries are more widely and evenly dispersed throughout the British Isles—for example electronics, pharmaceuticals, man-made fibres and clothing.

A comparison with consumer market dispersals shows the differences at once. In consumer markets certain geographical concentrations are recognisable insofar as geographic factors have some impact on the consumer's purchasing pattern; but in more general terms consumer markets are widely spread with concentrations covering the whole range of densities.

Industrial concentrations result from the nature of the capital goods, materials or components being marketed. For example, an image orthicon tube can find no application except in television cameras. Thus their sales are concentrated in this industry. An optical comparator must be marketed in a much narrower field than, say, measuring instruments. However, further variations in concentration can occur. The markets for measuring instruments become larger as the instrument becomes cruder.

There also exist wide variations in the degrees of concentration in various industries. It is the inter-relationship between the industrial concentrations making a particular product and the industrial concentrations using the product which contribute one distinguishing feature of industrial, as against consumer, marketing research.

In industrial markets *purchasing concentrations* arise when the markets are dominated by, or consist of, large users only. Plant for the manufacture of oxygen and other industrial gases constitutes such a market and the most extreme example is that of Post Office equipment where purchasing presents a monopsonistic situation.

[1] *Industrial Markets of Great Britain*, Geographia (London, 1962), and E. B. Groves, *Basic Sales Grid—United Kingdom* (Marketing House Publications, London, 1968).

The importance of these distinguishing concentrations becomes obvious when the concept of market segmentation is considered— that is the division of large disparate markets into smaller homogeneous segments each with one or several common characteristics. The segmentation criteria are however totally different in consumer and industrial markets. Consumer markets only concentrate *geographically* in the sense of numbers. Similar microcosms can be found in each concentration. For example by age, sex, socio-economic group, ownership of certain consumer durables. By comparison the concentration of the natural fibre textile industries in Lancashire, Yorkshire and parts of Scotland and the West Country cannot find its equivalent in any form in London where there is an absence of such industries.

The dissimilarity applies also to *industrial* concentrations. An economic concentration of the type encountered in telephone equipment and cable markets cannot exist in consumer markets.

The equivalent of *purchasing* concentrations found in industry only occurs in a limited range of super luxury items—jewellery, furs, some types of housing and travel. In consumer markets the concentration of purchasing power in a few hands produces a propensity to save rather than spend.

It is the combination of the three factors of concentration— *geographic, industrial* and *purchasing*—that expresses one of the fundamental differences between consumer and industrial marketing research. As a result of these characteristics it becomes feasible in industrial markets to use highly selective marketing research techniques through the existence of one or more of the three concentration factors and the inter-relationships between them. Individual markets are more easily located and it is simpler to determine the needs of such markets. It is not, however, as some commentators have suggested, easier to measure them. The relevance of marketing research in relation to concentrations is not so much their location as the charting of shifts within them. A stereotyped approach to market averages, based purely on past performance and current data, soon proves highly unrealistic in industrial markets.

DISTRIBUTION METHODS

A distinction between consumer and industrial marketing research embraces the methods by which the goods reach the consumer or user. The vast structure of the consumer goods distributive trades fulfils this function; but the needs of industrial purchasers are frequently met by direct contact between supplier and purchaser and where intermediaries exist these are often highly specialised.

Where users are widespread, geographically and industrially, where the value of units purchased tends to be small or the periodicity of purchases irregular, a formal wholesaling/stockholding service becomes economic and desirable. This is of course a generalisation to which exceptions can be found; but in industrial markets products tending to move through intermediaries are those such as standardised engineering components and tools, for example nuts, bolts, washers, springs and drills, building materials and some electronic components and chemicals. Investigations have shown that manufacturers of non-acid descaling plants, steel flooring and closed circuit television equipment, for example, find no advantage in distributing other than direct to the actual user.

Consumer marketing research concentrates more heavily than industrial marketing research on distributive channel analysis, if only because the industrial distributive channels are shorter and less tortuous. The measurement of the velocity and volume of goods passing through the various types of distributors has long fascinated economists and marketing researchers in the consumer goods sector, although it would be going too far to suggest that such studies have always been accurate and useful. Industrial distribution has been comparatively neglected as a subject worthy of research and analysis. Such studies as exist are almost invariably confined to industrial goods which are stock items, those which require little technical skill to use, are easy to install and maintain, and where the need exists for producers to find finance for stockholding and distribution.

But if the structural differences are great so are the functional differences of industrial and consumer goods distributors. The role of the retail distributor can be summarised in an over-simplification: 'to merchandise his goods and services'. The industrial distributor, while he should certainly be concerned with merchandising his goods, has a far wider responsibility. For many products and in many industries the distributor's activities include the provision of technical advice in the choice of products, the study of applications, installation, loan and repair of equipment and a problem-solving capability. Examples of these backing facilities can be found in high vacuum equipment, power transmission belting, industrial paints and laboratory glassware. This wider responsibility has important implications, as will become obvious later in this book.

RECIPROCAL TRADING AND IN-FEEDING

A phenomenon rarely encountered in consumer goods markets but which has very important implications in industrial markets is reciprocal trading and in-feeding; that is an agreement between firms and departments of firms to purchase each other's products or services. Reciprocal trading in industry can mean that certain large users of some types of industrial products are never in the market to purchase, except from the chosen partner under a reciprocal agreement. At one time such purchasing agreements were regarded as the antithesis of scientific purchasing but a far more tolerant attitude has developed towards them in recent years. This changed attitude stems largely from increased recognition of the interdependence of industry, advantages of in-feeding, standardisation of products, intensified competition among sellers and occasional corporate or personal relations between buyers and sellers.

An example can best serve to illustrate the implications of reciprocal trading. In 1963 the United Kingdom market for fractional horse-power motors was 10·5 million units. Further investigation showed that of this amount some 7 million units were in-fed or reciprocally purchased. That is, manufacturers of fractional horse-power motors were purchasing from within their own organisations or with cross-trading firms just under 70% of total demand. This 70% was never open to competitor manufacturers. It requires little marketing expertise to appreciate that the marketing strategy and scale of operations for a manufacturer operating in, or seeking to penetrate, a market of 10·5 million units would be very different from that in a market of only 3·5 million units.

The consumer goods equivalent of this situation does not exist. If the local greengrocer chooses to supply the local grocer at cost in return for similar facilities, its impact on both local and national market is nil. Even when such large organisations as House of Fraser or G.U.S. permit their many thousands of employees to purchase from them at a discount the total impact on local and national markets is still barely calculable.

In consumer marketing research it could not be a worthwhile exercise to estimate the number of consumers who at any one time might be out of the market because of reciprocal shopping arrangements. In an industrial research project the size of a market, however accurately estimated, could be completely misleading if a significant purchaser or a number of medium-size purchasers were permanently out of the market due to reciprocal trading agreements.

An American study showed that among a representative group of manufacturers almost half of the respondents agreed that reciprocity was a factor in buyer-seller relations in their companies and in certain reciprocity-prone industries—e.g. chemicals and petroleum—respondents were unanimous in citing reciprocity as a factor in purchasing or sales.[1]

BUYING PRACTICES AND MOTIVES

Purchasing in industrial markets is for the furtherance of organisational rather than personal goals. 'This is not to imply that they (industrial buyers) are immune to the influence of personal considerations in performing their organisational tasks. It is rather to stress the duality of their motivations in their purchasing activities.'[2] This distinction accounts for yet another major area of differentiation in the characteristics of the two markets.

Consumers have been called 'economic imbeciles' but such a view overlooks the fact that the consumer cannot be an expert in the many products and services he buys and that amateur buying ability is pitted against the professionalism of sellers. This disability does not usually apply in industrial buying since it is expected that the purchaser will be as expert, and possibly more expert, than those who solicit his business.

However, an even more fundamental difference exists between the organisational and consumer buying. Research has shown that it is extremely rare in industry, except in the case of small entrepreneurial organisations, for a single individual to be responsible for a purchasing decision. This is usually shared by several people. This group is known as the Decision Making Unit (DMU) and can be defined as a number of individuals who are participants in a decision-making process, who share common goals, which the decision will help to achieve, and the risks deriving from the decision. Thus it embraces all those who initiate, specify, control and purchase.

However, the Decision Making Unit tends to be neither formal nor fixed. It will be highly unstable varying between each purchase, each

---

[1] D. S. Ammer, 'Realistic Reciprocity', *Harvard Business Review* (Cambridge, Mass., January-February 1962). L. Sloan, 'Reciprocity—Where does the P.A. (Purchasing Association) Stand', *Purchasing Magazine* (New York, November 20th 1961).

[2] Jacqueline Marrian, 'Characteristics of Industrial Goods and Markets', *The Marketing of Industrial Products*, Aubrey Wilson (Ed.), Hutchinson (London, 1965), p. 11.

reason for purchase and each time of purchase. This is not only because personnel themselves change, moving into and out of firms, but also because of changed responsibilities within firms. For different purchases different types of expertise and job functions may be called on to advise or act. The buyer himself may remain stable but he is almost invariably limited in his freedom to purchase by the decisions taken by others in the DMU.

In a recent study of buying in British industry,[1] it was discovered that responsibility for any stage of purchase is typically shared by more than three groups of specialists with basic decisions being made by each group. These groups may comprise a company's Board, Operating Management, Production Engineering, Finance, Sales, or another eight or ten designations. The study showed that the final choice is frequently composed of a consensus of individual decisions rather than a single decision following a discussion of facts. Thus the research problem resolves itself into a two-dimensional one: first to identify the constituents of the DMU and then to isolate the decision-forming factors.

By comparison in consumer purchasing the decision is more often than not that of a single person purchasing for herself or himself or for the family unit, which remains relatively stable. Moreover, these decisions are frequently 'impulse' rather than considered, particularly as between one make of product and another.

Nevertheless it must not be assumed that purely rational motives are always present in industrial purchasing. It is only now that the problems presented by industrial buying situations are being probed and an old canard that industrial buying is entirely a rational process is being broken down.

The industrial buyer is no less human in his domestic purchasing role. His psychological drives, desires, ambitions, urges and biological needs do not change. For this reason the classical conception of industrial buying as being wholly rational and dispassionate must be qualified in the face of new information to the contrary.

'A characteristic which has enjoyed considerable vogue in marketing regarding the industrial and ultimate consumer markets is that of the former consisting of buyers who are rational, expert and possessing complete knowledge of values and substitute products. By contrast the buyer in the ultimate consumer market has been characterised as irrational, prone to impulse, inexpert and imperfectly knowledgeable regarding values and products available . . . it cannot be ignored that the designated organisational buyer, while he is

[1] Hugh Buckner, *How British Industry Buys*, Hutchinson (London, 1966).

constrained by organisation policy, is subject also to personal goals and aspirations in executing his organisational role.'[1]

The differences that do exist between consumer and industrial buying are largely, but not wholly, in the organisation of the buying function. In terms of buying motives there are many similarities which can be researched by the same psychological techniques. It is the impact of the industrial purchaser's *milieu* which conditions him to express his needs and desires in a certain but perhaps more restrained way because of his vocation and training.

KEEPING THE DICHOTOMY

The examples which have been given will suffice to show that the differences between consumer and industrial markets are indeed wide and fundamental. If this assertion is accepted the concept of industrial marketing research differing in its essential features from that of consumer marketing research will also be accepted. The dichotomy is real and must be preserved while recognising the interdependability of the two markets and even the domination of the consumer markets. The interdependability does not, however, imply a similarity in the application of techniques which are, and must remain, separate, at least until the present state of the art is much further developed.

[1] 'Characteristics of Industrial Goods and Buyers', *The Marketing of Industrial Products*, op. cit., p. 14.

CHAPTER 2

Objectives for Profitable Research

As recently as five years ago it was necessary to write: 'Between the *need* for marketing research and the *use* of marketing research lies a deep gulf. As industry becomes increasingly complex and the knowledge and memory of individuals decreasingly reliable as a guide to decision making, executives can no longer try and solve intricate problems solely on the basis of training and personal experience. The days of the brilliant empiricist have gone. Theoretically, management can turn to formal techniques for collecting, analysing and interpreting data in order that knowledge and accumulated experience can supplement opinion and intuition and improve the quality of decisions. For the most part, however, this is not done, for few managers are prepared to acknowledge their inability to solve their own problems or are willing to be the first to call for assistance. Fewer still will accept that the marketing researchers' "witchcraft" will produce a panacea when their own experience, judgement and knowledge have failed.'[1]

A minor revolution has overtaken management since those days and while it is true there still remain firms which cannot see the relevance of industrial marketing research to their operations, there is a large and growing number of companies who, with the zeal of a proselyte, have embraced marketing research and are now preoccupied with the collection of information which sometimes has either no relevance, or only a marginal relevance, to the firm's current and planned activities. On the basis that 'it might come in useful', complex systems of information gathering are devised and ingenious retrieval methods practised. But looked at from the viewpoint of the firm's total operation it can often be seen that the cost of acquisition cannot equal, let alone surpass, the value of the research material's use to the firm.

[1] N. A. H. Stacey and Aubrey Wilson, *Industrial Marketing Research—Management and Technique*, Hutchinson (London, 1963), p. 86.

It is axiomatic that no marketing research—industrial or consumer —is good research in the sense of the contribution made to the organisation's operations unless it can be used or applied. One criteria of good industrial marketing research is 'is it profitable?'

Industrial marketing research provides an aid to management, through the use of research techniques and analytical methods, in making decisions relating to the production, sale and distribution of the firm's products in order to reduce costs and increase the profitability of the firm. The vital corollary is that research is not a substitute for top management's judgement, but it is an aid to that judgement.

For years marketing men called for better tools to help them to understand and solve their problems. Now many of these tools are available an increasing knowledge and ability is required to put them to work effectively in the decision-making processes of business organisations.

It has been pointed out[1] that psychology, sociology and cultural and social anthropology have made a significant contribution to knowledge of human behaviour, and advances in concepts and techniques for identifying and measuring behavioural factors have been achieved. This work has a special relevance to marketing since a new insight has been provided on perception, memory, attitudes, learning, personality, motivation, communication flow and opinion leadership. Statistical decision theory has been developed to show how both judgement and statistical evidence can be combined in decision-making. In marketing, when evidence is often as much qualitative as quantitative, this is an important advance. Mathematical models designed to describe the functioning of economic units or systems and to predict the outcome of given inputs into the system are now commonplace. Operational models are being successfully applied to problems of sales forecasting, advertising, sales and inventory management. The speeding up process has been the result of interdisciplinary movement that has led marketing to draw increasingly on other fields for new ways of thinking and new methods and skills for obtaining and interpreting data.

Such a proliferation of tools, however, has led to some confusion in the selection of the right ones, poor identification of the most profitable informational objectives and serious bottlenecks in using the research yield.

---

[1] Joseph W. Newman, 'Put Research into Marketing Decisions', *Harvard Business Review* (Cambridge, Mass., March/April 1962).

THE NEED FOR RESEARCH

The need for research will be obvious enough in stress situations, for example the failure of a new product, the sudden emergence of a strong, competitive situation or the collapse of a market. The continuing need for research is, however, better seen against the environment in which the firm operates and its corporate objectives whether these are stated formally or not. All firms are in one or more of the situations shown in the diagram.

EXISTING PRODUCTS NEW PRODUCTS[1]

	EXISTING PRODUCTS	NEW PRODUCTS[1]
EXISTING MARKETS	1	2
NEW MARKETS	3	4

Fig. 2

Existing products or services   New products[1] or services
Existing markets   New markets

1. Existing products in existing markets. Except in the rare circumstance of marginal costs, for most firms the most profitable form of expansion is to exploit existing markets with existing products or services. This maximises a firm's skills, resources and knowhow. It gives a higher utilisation of factories, equipment, machines, tools, offices, transport, and personnel and often places the firm in an improved position to effect procurement economies. Industrial marketing research can, in most circumstances, indicate if exploitable opportunities remain in the existing market for the current ranges or services.

2. New products in existing markets. A firm's markets are as much one of its resources as are its physical, financial and managerial possessions yet in the non-marketing orientated firm they are rarely seen in this way. The 'industries we serve' concept—'what are our customers buying that they could buy from us?'—offers a company

[1] 'Existing' and 'New' refer to the firm. A 'new' product or market to the firm could be an established product or market for other companies.

opportunities to generate new product or service ideas and to launch them into a favourable environment created by past successful fulfilment of customer needs. Marketing research can be used to identify new opportunities arising from existing customers' requirements.[1]

3. Existing products in new markets. Management often remains blind to the opportunities of selling an existing product range or a service, perhaps with some adaptations into totally new industries. Studies of product applications and service needs, frequently reveal a market segment new to the firm. An example of this in relation to a spring balancer is given later in this chapter. This is an appropriate area for the use of marketing research, particularly in export markets.

4. New products in new markets. Marketing in this situation is clearly the most difficult and in which a 'blue skies' approach can be extravagantly wasteful. Typically firms will have little information on which to base product, production and marketing plans when they propose a development of this sort. Of the four situations outlined this is the one in which the research function has the most vital role to play.

DECIDING TO CONDUCT RESEARCH

Because firms are always in one or more of the four segments outlined, it is apparent that there is always a use, if not a need, for research. Allocating a research problem to any of the four sectors does not necessarily provide a go, no-go indication to the would-be research sponsor. It is very necessary therefore to scrutinise each research objective to ensure that it is not only feasible but that it accords with the total corporate plans of the company. Objective checking thus becomes as vital as objective setting. As in most aspects of marketing, it is possible to reduce the process to a standard procedure or 'check list'. Certainly one of the most efficient methods of checking objectives is contained in a simple six-question process devised by the Long Range Planning Service of Stanford Research Institute. This list simply asks:

● Why is some kind of action required?

● What action is required?

● What resources will the action require?

● What will be accomplished by the action?

[1] Mary Griffin, 'Generation of New Product Ideas', *Marketing of Industrial Products*, op. cit., p. 31.

- When can the results of the action be expected?
- What conditions must be met?

Ideally there is little that industrial marketing research cannot achieve given unlimited appropriations and time, neither of which are ever, or ever likely to be, available. The researcher has to work within the limitations set by the organisation, the environmental conditions and the resources available. This is dealt with in more detail in the following chapter. For the moment it is useful to categorise the areas of research objectives which should be considered, even if not actually researched. Knowledge of what is not known is at least as important as knowledge itself.

In the feature already referred to[1] a useful six-point categorisation was suggested to provide generic areas for investigation. These are:

- What is going on? The function of keeping management informed so that they can exercise control. Sales estimates, market shares and sales potential are examples. The figures reflect what is happening but do not in themselves explain it.

- How do you account for it? This is the idea-getting or hypothesis formulating function. It can involve any number of steps designed to reveal more about the nature of people, things and relationships.

- Is the explanation valid? The function here is that of checking on the validity and importance of ideas and tentative explanations.

- What, then, should be done? This step involves the reasoning from the evidence obtained as to the nature of the situation being studied and prescribing the alternative courses of action which appear to be appropriate.

- What results can be expected? Tests can be instituted to predict the outcome of the suggested alternative courses of action.

- How successful was the action? The function here is that of evaluating how well the chosen course of action achieved its purpose. It may include examination of sales figures, or tests to measure advertisement exposure or changes in knowledge or attitudes.

Under all these headings industrial marketing research has a substantial contribution to make. However, generic headings do not necessarily assist in becoming specific as to requirements. Asking: 'How do you account for it?' does not automatically produce the required specific questions such as: 'What contribution did pre-start

[1] 'Put Research into the Marketing Decisions', op. cit.

C

up services make towards the decision to invite quotations from only a limited number of firms?' There is clearly a vast range of questions which could be asked under each heading.

A framework of such questions is contained in the Marketing Researchers Check List in Appendix A, but a second grouping which is not interrogative assists in relating the contribution of industrial marketing research to the total business organisation.

The work of marketing research can be said to embrace: evaluating general business conditions and factors influencing the volume of sales and profits; determining the needs (idealised and realised) of the market in order to modify existing products and services or to create new ones that will fit most profitably into the pattern of demand, estimating that demand and determining the most effective distributive methods for the product; analysing the effectiveness of marketing methods and their costs relative to meeting and increasing demand for products or services; appraising the relative position of the firm in its industry and analysing the reasons for improving or deteriorating performance; product research for existing products and the development and introduction of new products or services.

It will be found that the sections in the Check List in Appendix A group easily under these headings, but a more detailed examination of some of the major headings can provide an insight in specific terms of the contribution which might be expected.

MARKET SIZE

Market size data provides a quantitative framework into which the major part of a project and the total marketing plan can be fitted. It gives a benchmark to measure progress, assists in the development of realistic sales targets and marketing budgets, guides the equitable division of sales territories and enables an industry-wide comparison to be made. It can give short-range warning of 'top out' conditions described later in this chapter, enables an evaluation of the competitive climate to be appraised and makes a substantial contribution to the development of both pricing policies and the price setting.

Because of these and other contributions that an accurate knowledge of market size can provide, it is not surprising that almost always the first question a research sponsor asks in a proposed enquiry is the size and trends, in quantitative terms, of the market under consideration. It is not, however, necessarily always the most important question to an individual firm. For a firm offering a narrow product range of say air compressors as a subsidiary product interest to a considerable machine tool business, the size of the market may be of less immediate relevance than their 'image' as air compressor manufacturers seriously committed to this business.

A sense of proportion on market size is needed both in terms of requiring market size data at all, and then in terms of accuracy tolerances needed. It is here that the greatest economies can be made in research costs and time. However, having established a need to assess market size, it is something that can usually be achieved with a high degree of accuracy for many products and in many markets. It is probable that 60 to 70 per cent or more of all industrial marketing research appropriations are directed to uncovering market size and important segments within the market; for example by product characteristics.

IDENTIFYING 'TOP OUT' CONDITIONS

All products which reach the market are subject to the life cycle. That is a growth curve from introduction to maturity, eventually reaching saturation and then declining. This is shown in Figure 3.

The curve may be both narrow and steep for a product which is subject to the forces of fashion or which is found to be unsatisfactory

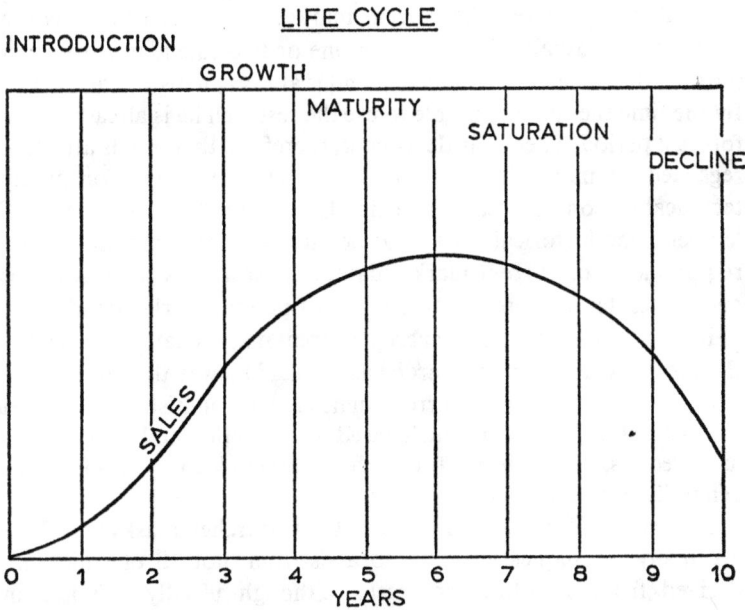

Fig. 3

after an initial trial period. It can be a long shallow curve for a stable relatively unchanging product.

In either circumstance the saturation point will eventually be reached. The peak of the curve is the 'top out' position from which maximum point sales will decline. Top out conditions of course also apply to profits and these may not necessarily follow the sales curve.

One purpose of research can be to attempt to identify a top out situation in time to either effect an extended product or service life or feed in a new product or service. Industrial marketing research can do this by identifying general danger signals and also by isolating significant warnings which have particular relevance for the individual firm. Industry-wide over-capacity or declining unit price may be obvious enough warnings (although they can often be mistaken for temporary phenomenon), increased imports or greater durability may not be so easy or obvious to trace. It is possible that within an individual firm analyses will reveal a series of criteria which provide clear top out situation warnings. It is part of the industrial marketing researcher's role to identify these.

MARKET TRENDS

In industrial marketing research there is really no such thing as a 'current market' size. The current market in research terms is the latest period, usually the preceding one or two calendar years from the date the research is conducted, and is always an historical market. By the time the sponsor is able to use the research he is already in the forecast period. There is little wonder, therefore, that trends are often regarded as more significant than 'current' markets. For purely technical reasons, forecasting demands as accurate an assessment of 'current' and historical markets as possible so that even if there is no requirement for current market data, almost always the researcher and forecaster are forced into a study of present market conditions.

Research sponsors tend to accept current market data more readily than forecasts, since it is regarded as factual in a way that forecasting can never be. Although current market data or historical market reconstructions can be as much based on deduction and assumptions as forecasts, nevertheless for perhaps psychological reasons they generally have a higher credibility.

Forecasting is an essential part of the researcher's tasks and there are many techniques available to assist him, not all of which are derived from statistics. Forecasts, although usually confined in industrial marketing research to predicting the direction and shape of the market in the period under review, will include assessments of other factors such as technical trends and the emerging climate of competition in terms of both products and firms. The entire marketing strategy is likely to rest on the forecast and therefore its place within a project is of paramount importance as it will provide the basis for all that follows in the implementation of the report.

DESIRABLE PRODUCT OR SERVICE FEATURES

Many products fail because they have been developed in a marketing vacuum although they are themselves excellent. Research to determine the most desirable product features or, conversely, the most suitable market for a given product is an insurance, not against failure but against the consequences of failure. The profile of a product in its ideal form can be drawn. This does not preclude it from containing technical incompatibilities and commercial impossibilities. For example, a frequent need among users of open metal floorings is for greater strength but lighter weight. The first characteristic can only be obtained at the expense of the second unless aluminium is used instead of steel or cast iron, and aluminium is far more costly. Thus both technical and commercial irreconcilables occur in the ideal profile for a single product. Without attempting to reconcile them, a knowledge of the ideal presents clear guidance for product development.

To move an existing product closer to the user's idealised conception of it can have considerable implications for the firm since, as it has already been shown, any increase in sales of an existing product in an existing market is almost always a highly profitable development as this enables the full resources and skills of the firm to be further exploited. Under these circumstances the need to acquire new resources and skills is minimal. It is surprising therefore that the determination of desirable product features is not more frequently seen as one of the most relevant of short-term research objectives.

PRODUCT APPLICATIONS

As with product adjustments, the development of new applications for existing products can more fully exploit the resources and skills of the firm but at the same time open up new market segments for the company. In developing new applications the emphasis is reversed. That is, it is possible to obtain customers in new industries while at the same time often widening sales in existing customer industries. An example of this is apposite.

A manufacturer of spring balancers, used to enable power tools to remain in a given position while the operative is not holding them, found that his sales in the engineering industry were poor. A study was undertaken of the market but was sufficiently wide to embrace other industries besides power tools. A substantial new market for holding carcasses was uncovered among abbatoirs and butchers—an area not previously considered by the spring balancer manufacturer. The penetration of this area required only an adjustment in the holding device and spring tensions.

Industrial marketing research can often reveal new and unsuspected applications for products, frequently with a minimum of product adjustments. Such applications are provided from the fertile imaginations of users who see the purchase and adaptation of products they buy, only in terms of their own personal needs. These needs projected can frequently open up totally new market segments.

PRICING POLICY

Clearly one of the most important questions facing manufacturers of industrial goods is that of price policy, both in relation to their own and to their distributors' sales. Inevitably the price policies of industrial goods manufacturers produce an impact on the final price of consumer goods and services which are the prime determinants of the manufacturers' and industries' future levels of activity. The constituents of final price are in all cases broadly similar but of course the proportion which each constituent forms varies. Some of the constituents are predetermined and some are largely unpredictable but several can be manipulated.

The manufacturer of industrial goods seeks to obtain a price which will yield him the greatest net return. Unfortunately, once this price is found it will not remain the best optimum price for very long. Shifting conditions of demand and adjustments in the manufacturer's cost constituents are daily occurrences. Three facts which the industrialist needs to know to ensure intelligent pricing decisions are first, the type of competition faced; second, the nature of costs; and third, the behaviour pattern of demand for the products. The industrial marketing researcher has here an important contribution to make and one for which an economist's training is particularly suitable.

Competition

The actions of competitors are of concern to every firm and nowhere more relevant than in the field of pricing policy. The ability of firms to initiate and maintain price competition is often a vital factor in a marketing situation. The 'loss leader' is not a phenomenon of the supermarket alone. Discounts can be manipulated in a large number of ways. For example, a 'skimming' pricing strategy can be adopted when a proprietary position exists. Such a policy sets out to achieve the highest price possible at the outset but has a built-in regulator to reduce price progressively as competition intensifies. A new entrant to a market, presuming that margins are high and therefore vulnerable, can rapidly find himself in considerable difficulties. Another pricing strategy is to offer basic equipment at a very low capital cost or even free, and recover costs on higher priced consumables or services—a situation common in the office machinery field and some chemical processes. A knowledge of the price strategy is vital in assessing competitors' ability to sustain, attack or avoid any particular pricing situation.

Another aspect of pricing policy in relation to competition is the problem of ascertaining the real price of a product. In many industries quoted prices are not easily available or are largely meaningless; the chemical industry is a good example of an industry operating under these conditions where obtaining prices and data relating to prices such as credit and discount policies occupies a considerable proportion of marketing researchers' time.

Nature of costs

The nature of costs is one which has for long been the subject of argument between businessmen, accountants and economists. Manufacturers are not concerned with niceties of cost or price, only with arriving at the correct price for the product. Probably competitor costs are the most difficult item to estimate because, traditionally, these are a well-guarded secret in most firms. Even in relatively well-charted technological processes and stable industries the development of new methods and the installation of new machinery can make significant changes in cost structures. Cost intelligence, perhaps by the use of business ratios, makes a real contribution towards pricing policy and its adjustment to competitive conditions.

Pattern of demand behaviour

To ascertain the pattern of demand behaviour it is necessary to study the market both historically and currently. The demand for many industrial goods is inelastic and price reductions by one firm can lead to a downward spiral with no commensurate increase in sales. On the contrary, price cutting in many instances can and does lead to a considerable falling off in demand while purchasers hold off in anticipation of the next round of price cuts.

Another important aspect of demand behaviour is to determine how the market will react to any given price level. This has proved to be extremely difficult to probe and, as has been pointed out,[1] the pitfalls of this type of research are so great that most research specialists have abandoned it altogether. Research into acceptable price still has a long way to develop but it can nevertheless provide very practical assistance in arriving at a suitable price.

The role of the marketing researcher is to bring to management's attention the various facts upon which pricing policy decisions are made and the analyses that will enable the creation of a dynamic and responsible pricing strategy to be developed. Policy makers can be presented with a rounded and objective picture of the whole situation. In aiding management to achieve rational price policies, the industrial marketing researcher acts as a catalyst between management functions.

RANGE VARIABLES

Over a whole range of industrial products, manufacturers are faced with producing not a single type but a range—prime movers of different ratings, containers of different capacities, valves of varying output, chemicals with alternative formulations. How extensive should this range be? What is the 'spread' of demand likely to be over the entire range? What is the optimum-minimum range? Which complementary products would it be profitable to introduce? In what depth should spares be stocked? What services must be provided to ensure correct ordering by customers, correct installation, use and maintenance? How far can these functions be abrogated without affecting sales?

'Product mix' and the ancillary services that go with it are a major element in marketing strategy. Not only are the varying features of individual firms' products important in decision-making, but the extent and depth of the range and service comprising the 'total line' is of equal relevance. In markets where product differentials are more illusory than real, for example in industrial chains and 'V' belts, it is often the depth of stock, range and excellence of the service which finally decides a purchasing action.

The job of marketing research in this context is to determine

[1] A. B. Oxenfeldt, *Pricing for Marketing Executives*, Wadsworth (Belmont, California, 1966), p. 64.

demand as yet unfulfilled for products and services; to evaluate competitive ranges and services and to determine the areas in which market advantages are held by the firm or its competitors.

In most ranges, sales tend to be concentrated over a few sizes or capacities. The oft-quoted 80-20 rule applies; that is 80 per cent of sales are transacted over 20 per cent of the range. No formula has yet been devised for finding out under what circumstances a firm can be more profitable by either increasing or decreasing its range of products and depth in which they are offered.[1] So far only an empirical approach can provide indications; moreover it is usually impossible to assess what would have happened had the opposite decision been taken. The basic problem is to assess the potential of a currently poor selling product. Instances are plentiful of products arriving on the market too soon.

It is also difficult to assess if the presence in a range of a product with a poor rate of sale makes a contribution towards the sales performance of better products. In order to be seen by customers to be seriously in a business, firms often have to offer a far wider range than in fact the viability of the product range justifies. Nevertheless the 'image' impact of a full line is frequently an important decision-making factor in the choice of one firm's products rather than another. Management trained in accountancy rather than marketing disciplines normally find this difficult to understand.

SALES COVERAGE

Industrial marketing research can make a considerable contribution to establishing the effectiveness of sales coverage, not only in the obvious geographic dimension, but also in industry and time terms. The concept of segmentation in marketing is one of the basic strategies and must necessarily be formed on knowledge of the characteristics of the segments or market structure, current and potential markets must be assessed, penetration levels estimated and substitution factors considered. The example already cited of the spring balancer is typical of uncovering new and important markets in sections unrelated to the present activities of the company. Thus analyses of sales by user industry is of vital consequence. But within the context of these analyses there are other characteristics to be

---

[1] Range width can be defined as the number of different options of products of the same genre; for example, plywood, chipboard, hardboard. Range depth would be the alternatives available within any one type; for example chipboard of different densities, panel sizes, thicknesses, finishes.

considered: for example, stratification by size of purchasing company, in specific applications and by key user requirements. Both these latter factors can open up new potential sales for a company.

In producing information on sales coverage in relation to the time dimension industrial marketing research can provide data both on seasonal and other factors which impact on demand and indicate whether the firm is obtaining the maximum share possible at both the peaks and troughs. More important, however, by tracing and correlating the seasonal and time movements (which may also be climatic) it is possible to develop an anti-cyclical product and marketing policy, thus ensuring that the efforts of the company are applied in those areas and at those times when the maximum return can be obtained.

SELLING METHODS

There is often a built-in assumption that past and present methods of selling are the only suitable ones for the firm. The fact is that no matter how marketing orientated a firm may claim to be, it rarely asks if the selling methods are appropriate and acceptable to the customers. It may be argued that if they were not, then sales would not be made. This, however, is not correct since the choice of supplier may be between firms using identical methods but the conditions of market leadership could well emerge when a firm breaks away, perhaps only subtly, from the pack with a method of selling which is more acceptable than those currently used by their competitors.

Selling can be at one extreme the 'hard sell', with a high call frequency or at the other the 'soft sell' which is a gradual building up of favourable conditions before an attempt is made to close the deal. Selling can be on a 'cold calling' or carefully pre-arranged basis. Salesmen can vary from highly technical to non-technical. Sales can be achieved through the medium of application and systems engineering or through maintenance and other services. Agents can be incorporated into the system of selling, or selling might be entirely on the firm's own premises and the sales effort directed to getting customers to call. Exhibition selling may figure high or demonstrations—static and mobile—may represent the spearhead of the selling attack. All these and many more variations are feasible and industrial marketing research, correctly used, can indicate which will be the most suitable and effective for any particular product, market, industry or time.

The productivity of an industrial sales force is immeasurably improved if an element of precison can be introduced into sales operations by the accurate designation of the best areas of potential sales opportunities. Measurement of markets developed on a geographical basis makes it possible to develop realistic sales targets and to divide territories on an equitable basis which in turn permits maximisation of the salesmen's efforts.

The uncovering of good potential sales areas, the equitable division of territories, the setting of sales targets cannot be accomplished without first establishing criteria for measuring salesmen's performance. The intensive study of salesmen's reports (and indeed, the study of the formulation of the reports themselves) is a marketing research job which yields positive results out of proportion to the effort expended. If, as unfortunately is sometimes the case, internal company barriers prevent the analyses of salesmen's reports by marketing research departments, then at least marketing research can set up the analytical procedures to enable the information to be obtained. There is little doubt that analytical work of this type can be extremely profitable in many industrial sales management situations.

A reason for the apparent reluctance of industrial selling departments to permit the study of sales reports and salesmen's activities has been assigned by one authority[1] to the fact that many sales managers have been promoted from the ranks and are not by temperament analytically minded individuals. In part, it also stems from fear, endemic in many management structures, that such investigations will disclose inefficiencies which may be used in judging the sales manager's performance or, to use a more highly flavoured term, in doing 'a hatchet job'.

It is perhaps in the area of industrial sales management in particular that so much else which the industrial marketing researcher contributes is welded together for the execution of sales strategy. The industrial salesman is, in most firms, the front line behind whom all the effort and munitions of marketing have been gathered. The product, the product mix, distribution and transportation, stocks, delivery cycles, prices, advertising, public relations campaigns and all other aspects of the marketing effort are utilised and personified through the salesman. In this context the industrial marketing researcher sees the fruition of his work through the effectiveness of the salesman responding to 'overall' marketing policy.

Just as the salesman represents the physical expression of the end-product of the researcher's work, so he is also the forward element of the communications systems. By reporting back, the salesmen often

[1] *Industrial Marketing*, op. cit., p. 140.

bring to the researcher information often not otherwise obtainable. If the salesmen cannot always be objective then they can always be informative, and the effective and fully operational sales force is one that can implement policy, acquire orders and transmit back information. Considerable amounts of useful information can be derived with the minimum amount of effort by salesmen from their continuous circulation among customers.

SALES PROMOTION

The measurement of advertising effectiveness is, in the final analysis, the assessment of the contribution advertising makes to net profits. This is an analysis that still cannot be made with precision as there are always factors, other than the obvious one of sales promotion, determining the level of sales. Nevertheless, even if it is not possible to measure advertising effectiveness in terms of profits derived, it is always possible and important to ensure that all sales promotion is having a positive effect. This can be determined in a number of ways and one aspect of the assistance the industrial marketing researcher can render to management is to create methods of evaluation that are meaningful within a firm.

Basically, the information that marketing research places in the hands of the advertising department is the means of making a more effective choice and use of media and promotional methods as well as facts for the development of advertising strategy and copy. These include: location of markets by area and function; measurement of market size; analysis of industrial structures; studies of purchasing patterns; influence-forming criteria of existing and potential customers; information on competitors' activities and identification of the Decision Making Units. The evaluation of media claims in industrial markets is something which needs penetrating specialist study. Industrial media and advertising effectiveness analysis are still in their infancy; and they are sometimes limited by the intransigent attitudes of technical journal and other publishers in refusing to disclose circulation data, and by some publicity managers and advertising agents in producing and obtaining acceptance of copy based exclusively upon an intuitive approach.

It is possible for the marketing research department to develop with the advertising department the means to assess and, at least, partially measure the effectiveness of campaigns thus forging a link between these two sub-functions of marketing. However, advertising is not the end of sales promotion. Other methods must also be assessed—trade shows, product sampling, public relations campaigns, educational programmes and even entertainment of customers, are examples. Here again the marketing researcher can provide data to assist in the evaluation of the usefulness and the effectiveness of the proposed promotional method.

In industrial sales promotion methods, unlike consumer advertising, the emphasis is on purchasers' profit rather than their personal gratification, although this latter is now gaining acceptance as a factor of importance. The most fundamental problem faced by industrial advertisers is the manner in which the product can be shown to increase the buyer's profitability. The industrial product which does not hold out the prospects of benefits and eventual improved profit is difficult, if not impossible, to sell. The marketing researcher, while accepting 'profit' as the rationalised basis of a purchase,[1] can also help to determine the unconscious decision factors. A press brake may make a significant contribution to profits but between Smith's and Jones's press brakes there may be no observable difference. How and why does the buyer decide? It is in the isolation of the decision factors where the marketing researcher can provide the greatest aid to the advertising departments.

A now classic study[2] and later studies of the same type have produced a reliable check list of information needed by industrial purchasers in order to make intelligent purchasing decisions. Among the important items are the price, nature and distinctive characteristics of the product; advantages of competitive products; suitability and adaptability to the buyers' specific needs; other buyers' experience as users; benefits to be derived by its purchase; reliability of the supplier in relation to claims for the product; delivery and contract fulfilment; and continuity of service or repair and replacement facilities.

In all these areas the industrial marketing researcher can offer vital information that will in turn contribute to the construction of the advertising story, the product and company images and the background to the market. After acquiring the appropriate data, relating the purchasers' information needs and the decision-forming factors to the firm's products is the function of the advertising department.

From all this emerges the conclusion that if sales promotion, however difficult its evaluation may be, can be measured or assessed

[1] It is known that there are as many emotional factors in industrial purchasing as in consumer purchasing although these factors may differ. This is discussed in Chapter 8, 'Interviewing'.

[2] Virgil D. Reed, *Advertising and Selling Industrial Goods*, Ronald Press (New York, 1936).

for its effectiveness, the way would be pointed towards given promotional techniques to be used under specific circumstances. This is a desirable improvement on much of the present-day intuitive approach used by firms in deciding their promotional policy and appropriation.

MARKET STRUCTURE

The configurations of a market can be of key importance in developing both marketing and product strategies. Certainly without this knowledge segmentation becomes largely meaningless. The structure of a market will comprise the disposition of the major firms competing for business in the market; firms manufacturing different but substitutable products; the division of the uptake of the products under consideration by the various user industry segments; the division of the market by regional, seasonal and size strata of firms; the extent to which demand is met from imported, locally licensed foreign products, and home manufactured products and the value and direction of export trade. Without these last data it is impossible to calculate the net home market size.

Other important aspects are the extent to which distributors are involved. For example, many building materials can only be sold through builders' merchants who are of paramount importance in any marketing plan for a building materials manufacturer.

One vitally important aspect, often neglected in industrial marketing studies, is probing reciprocal trading and in-feeding practices, referred to in Chapter 1. At the other end of the spectrum the source of materials, operating supplies and components can also provide valuable information on competitors' activities and the climate of competition. To take an example, feldspar is used in ceramic manufacture. Any ceramic company with its own feldspar concession may well have a strong price advantage reserve and thus is well placed to meet new competition or to enter a new market. A knowledge of supply conditions can be as vital as a knowledge of demand conditions.

Other structural factors are related to key user requirements. 'Discrete' differences in these requirements create segmentations within a market which can be used effectively in developing marketing strategies.

DISTRIBUTION METHODS

If anything reveals the bias of a researcher towards consumer research techniques, it is the emphasis so often placed on distribution channel research which is generally cited as one of the primary objectives of industrial marketing research. The truth is very different. While the whole edifice of the consumer goods industry rests on over 500,000 outlets, in industry the distributor or other intermediary has no role at all in the movement of a very wide range of industrial goods, while his role for very many other products is minimal or marginal. Thus distribution analysis is only a primary research objective in a limited range of products, for example fuel oils, building materials, fastening devices and automotive equipment.

Apart from a small number of privately undertaken research projects, the whole field of industrial distribution remains largely uncharted. There has been no pioneer to accomplish for industrial distribution what James B. Jefferys has achieved for consumer goods distribution in his two informative volumes which clearly charted the movement of consumer goods from producer to final consumer.[1] Without this basic data it follows that there could have been no analysis of distributive channel dynamics.

If it came as a surprise to businessmen and economists that the distributive channels for consumer goods, thought to be largely static, were in fact changing, and changing rapidly,[2] there is perhaps an even bigger surprise in store for industrial goods producers. It has been suspected for some time that the changes now taking place in the structure of distribution of industrial goods are considerable and fundamental.

The end result of distribution channel studies, the general lack of which has been noted, is the provision of factual information which may be used by management in making rational policy decisions. The decision framework is predicted upon the assumption of the availability of the facts, and the transition from theory to practice founders, for many manufacturers, on the absence of these facts. Examination of the requirements for sound channel decisions should serve to stimulate increased research activity in order to produce the requisite factual background.[3]

The very lack of ready-made reference emphasises the importance of distributive data especially tailored to the individual requirements of the firm. In this respect the industrial marketing researcher is in a

[1] James B. Jefferys, *Distribution of Consumer Goods*, Cambridge University Press (Cambridge, 1950). James B. Jefferys, *Retail Trading in Britain, 1850-1950*, Cambridge University Press (Cambridge, 1954).

[2] Nicholas A. H. Stacey and Aubrey Wilson, *The Changing Pattern of Distribution* (Revised Edition), Pergamon Press (Oxford, 1965).

[3] William T. Diamond, *Distribution Channels for Industrial Goods*, Ohio State University (Columbus, Ohio, 1963).

position to provide invaluable and perhaps original and exclusive market data for the formulation of distributive policy. Further, in providing such information on distribution the value of marketing research can impress itself more readily upon management than it would perhaps in almost any other field of marketing activity.

The importance of using the most efficient distributive system is amply shown when it is realised that the distributive on-cost between factory and industrial user is in a significant number of cases in excess of 15 per cent on the ex-factory price.

One American estimate gives the cost of physical distribution as the third largest component in the total cost of business.[1]

A study carried out in the United States[2] showed that selling and distributive functions combined claim roughly a fifth of the domestic unit cost dollar. Comparisons with the United Kingdom, Common Market and Latin America indicated that although the proportion of final price these costs accounted for was smaller (about 12 per cent) in those areas, the difference stemmed largely from smaller sales and promotional effort. From this it can be assumed that the distribution costs alone in the United Kingdom are as high a proportion, if not higher, of total cost as in the United States. For years businessmen and economists have looked with mixed feelings on the increase in distribution costs in the economy. Over the past fifty years significant strides have been made towards reducing the cost of production but these feats have not been duplicated in the distribution of goods.

The elements of distribution effectiveness analyses have yet to be set out as a formula. Although not all-inclusive, six areas have been suggested in which marketing research can provide vital management aid in this particular aspect of marketing policy development.

First, analysis of sales data to determine the homogeneity of the markets served by the distributive channels. These are: geographical-purchasing patterns; products-purchasing patterns; quantities-purchasing patterns; timing; distribution of sales among customers; relationship between high stock-turn and low stock-turn items and their distributors. In this particular context, the study is to determine how business in low volume sales items with relatively high distributive costs should be transacted, as opposed to high volume sales items. This is a study rarely, if ever, carried out by manufacturers but it is one that can provide valuable cost analysis data.

[1] John F. Magee, 'Logistics of Distribution', *Harvard Business Review* (Cambridge, Mass., July-August 1960).
[2] T. R. Gates and F. Linden, *Costs and Competition*, National Industrial Conference Board (New York, 1961), p. 75.

Second, analysis of sales characteristics of the products related to sales fluctuations. The importance here is to establish sales *variability* rather than sales *average* beloved by business managers. The significance of variability in this context cannot be over-emphasised. The answer to many questions vitally affecting decisions about the distributive system and the assessment of its effectiveness depends on the characteristics of sales variations about the average. These movements can be extremely wide and short term in character but in other cases steady and predictable. However, it is the characteristics of the variations which determine how a distributive system will work and, thus, how it should be designed to operate most economically.

Third, analysis of sales variations in terms of time, size, location and volatility. The most obvious purpose of this type of analysis is the determination of replenishment lead time,[1] to assess how large the pipeline stock of an item must be to maintain a desired delivery period. In attempting to produce a correlation between sales variations and replacement the researcher makes a distinctive addition to marketing policy.

Fourth, analysis of stock functions in relation to companies' needs. Stocks are not merely reserves to meet customer demand. They fulfil many functions, for example stock in transit, reservoirs from periodic shipment, reserve (or safety) stock, take-up pool to even production fluctuations.

Fifth, analysis of costs of physical distribution. Although costs, in the firm, might truly be said to fall into the province of the cost accountant, the industrial marketing researcher can legitimately research in this area to analyse cost elements for the purpose of measuring distribution efficiency. He is more than likely to find that most companies' accounting records or studies do not reveal direct unit costs for each type of product in relation to, for example, stock-holding and handling. This type of analysis can create impetus for improved and refined cost studies and by carrying out internal and comparative analyses.

Sixth, the analysis of alternative distribution channels and methods. An unfortunate tendency common in distribution problems is to regard channels and methods, once accepted and working, as permanent. A constant review of new methods and new channels is both desirable and necessary. Alternative methods should be assessed and measured, so far as possible, by the same criteria adopted to check existing channels. Changes in manufacturing techniques and products

---

[1] 'Replenishment lead time' can be defined as the period between placing an order and the receipt of the goods.

D

(quantitatively and qualitatively) also need to be examined in relation to the effectiveness of the distributive channels to cope with these changes.

The problem of distribution analysis can be developed at considerable length and holds the fascination which the unknown must always hold for the researcher. The choice of distributive systems by a company will have a significant impact on the type and location of buildings, on product design, on investment in plant, on the provision of services and on corporate organisation. The industrial marketing researcher has a key role to play in providing the information upon which accurate, effective and profitable distribution can be based.

CLIMATE OF COMPETITION

In business conditions of today it is unwise, and indeed usually impossible, for any firm to ignore competitive aspects of the market place. Even the largest firms are vulnerable to attack from relatively small companies. Indeed, large and small firms manage to exist side by side only by virtue of the fact that 'bigness' does not necessarily provide an in-built advantage. Loss leading by a company with considerable resources may eliminate small competitors at any given moment in time but it cannot maintain a competition-free environment. Automotive battery manufacturers have been under attack from small firms for several years which has put great pressure on the margins of the large companies. Almost any firm with metal-working facilities can compete, and compete successfully, with large companies undertaking relatively simple fabrication work.

The assessment of the competitive climate is usually concerned with the study of prices, products directly and indirectly substitutable, and processes which compete. However, these are only some of the components of competition. The firm's activities such as promotional efforts, provision of services, environmental and economic advantages and guarantee policy, all require probing if the total picture is to emerge.

It has been suggested that to probe competitors while undertaking a survey is to take marketing research up to and perhaps beyond the acceptable ethical boundaries. This is wholly untrue. No ethical problem arises always provided that no request to competitors for information is made without making it quite clear that a study is being carried out. The ethics and methods of competitive interviewing are set out in Chapter 8, 'Interviewing'.

Some firms will refuse to contribute information, as it is their right to do. The majority are, however, prepared to co-operate on an exchange of information basis. In any event, it is possible to acquire a considerable volume of information on the competitive position from desk research, from users and suppliers and from competitive firms' knowledge of each other's activities. For example, the average sales per salesman in the packaged steam generator field has been found to be £100,000 per annum—a figure a research sponsor was well able to validate as approximating to his own sales records. Thus a correlation could be established between numbers of salesmen employed by competitors and sales of packaged steam generators.

Although information on industrial advertising media and expenditure is an onerous but simple calculation, as indeed is estimation of exhibition expenditure, all of this can be obtained by desk research.

Users, however, make a major contribution to knowledge of competitors' activities. They can provide data and will do so freely on numbers and periodicity, of salesmen's calls, sales organisation, product ranges, delivery periods, discounts and prices, and can in addition give valuable assessments of the quality of management and the sales force. In the same way, material and component suppliers are in a position to reveal detailed information on their customers who may comprise the competition to the research sponsoring firm. This is dealt with and illustrated in Chapter 11, 'Processing the Data'.

Sources of information on firms' competitors are many and varied and there is certainly no need to have recourse to espionage. If a particular piece of information cannot be obtained from normal research sources then it must be accepted that the project must proceed without it. Under no circumstances can the acquisition of information except by normal techniques and from ethically acceptable sources be countenanced, since industrial espionage is inimical to the long- and short-term interests of research and can only lead to a complete loss of co-operation.

LIMITATIONS AND PROSPECTS

In setting out a number of research objectives which can usually be achieved within the present state of the art for most products and services and in most markets, the fact cannot be ignored that there are still aspects of industrial markets which will not as yet yield to the techniques currently available. For example, it is difficult to provide a validated segmented market size estimate for reduction gears, industrial flooring or fusible interlinings; in monopolistic or oligopolistic situations uncovering all facets of competition is often impossible; the pure illogic of many pricing decisions defies analysis; it is as yet quite impossible to measure the effect of most types of advertising. For both the sponsor of research and the researcher, the need to have knowledge of what can and what cannot be achieved is vital.

The Check List in Appendix A, although of considerable length, is nevertheless by no means exhaustive. It shows, however, how wide the boundaries of industrial marketing research can be and how much the researcher can offer as an aid to management decision-making.

The important thing is for companies to correctly identify their informational requirements and then to assess accurately how feasible it is to achieve these by industrial marketing research. The limitations which the research parameters place upon the objectives is dealt with in the next chapter.

CHAPTER 3

Parameters of Research

It is rare in a market research project for sponsors seeking answers to the same problems to approach their informational needs in precisely the same way, to devise their briefs in similar form or to allocate comparable resources. Thus research with similar objectives and with similar methods is often productive of dissimilar results. These will in fact reflect the variation in the inputs as well as the quality of research. This is not to say that higher inputs or narrower objectives are always productive of better, more detailed and accurate research.

The essential skill in the use of industrial marketing research as part of the total marketing operation is to optimise what is available. This in turn means that the research sponsor and the researcher must have an appreciation not only of the available resources and the objectives of the study, but must also see them against a background of the total corporate policy of the company. The key to profitable research is to devise the programme so that it contributes useful knowledge for short-term marketing needs and also helps in the development of a long-range departmental programme. However, any attempt at optimising the research effort must be preceded by an understanding of the parameters of research.

There are many factors impacting upon industrial marketing research decisions but they can all be encompassed under four headings: (a) time available, (b) physical resources available, (c) finance available, (d) research objectives. Every research decision is conditioned consciously or unconsciously by these factors and every decision is affected by each one of them in varying proportions. Conversely any changes in any one of them reacts upon the others.

TIME AVAILABLE

It is true to say that ill-timed research is often useless research, most particularly when a management decision deadline is involved. A second factor on timing is that research which has to be completed in an unrealistic time span is generally either bad research or unnecessarily expensive research. As will be seen in Chapter 4, 'Preparing for the Project', the timing of a research project is dependent upon many factors, some of them outside the control of the researcher. Moreover the link between two of the parameters, time and cost, becomes obvious if the impact of environmental factors is considered.

For example, a study of the impact of natural gas on the British economy proposed in early 1966 was deliberately postponed until after the World Power Congress later in that year when a volume of new information became available from the papers presented at that Conference. Although the survey time was lengthened by the delay, the cost saving achieved through the avoidance of research into areas covered by some of the conference papers was considerable. This enabled the appropriation to be re-distributed over other less well-documented areas.

Studies required late in 1967 which could be reasonably delayed benefited from the publication of the preliminary 1963 Census of Production information during 1968. Until 1968 researchers were working with figures ten years out of date.

The relationship of time and cost are direct and obvious. The link with 'resources' is less so. Nevertheless, resources which are at the firm's command can materially shorten a research project or lack of resources lengthen it. Thus if it is possible to build into the project available resources such as data processing equipment, there will be a clear and measurable impact on the time schedule.

So far as objectives are concerned, here again adjustments might lead to considerable lengthening or shortening of research time. A study requested for information on the use of polyester yarns in shirts, raincoats and curtains required a 16 working week programme. The basic problem for the firm was to assess the priority of their needs and to measure it against the parameters. That is, they could leave the objectives alone and agree on a longer time schedule—an unacceptable proposition because of a fixed date for 'go no-go' decision on plant investment; they could have 'doubled-up' on the survey having the shirts and raincoats surveyed in one study and a second study, with a separate team simultaneously researching the curtain market—again unacceptable because additional costs involved were as much as 50 per cent higher; they could adjust the objectives to meet the time and cost limitations.

This last course was decided on and curtains were dropped from the research objectives because this segment is a largely undocumented and highly fragmented industry. The time schedule was cut from sixteen to ten weeks. For the firm, information on the curtain market would have been extremely useful but in realistic terms it was recognised that the decisions to be taken could be made without this data.

The problem of time is the one which appears to receive the least attention. Sponsors press too hard for unrealistic schedules and researchers are often unwilling to oppose them—a fault found more often in the research agency than with the internal researcher. This situation need not arise if the researchers give their time calculation to the sponsor to show precisely how realistic it is, how outside events impact on it and perhaps delay it, and how it relates to the other inputs. (See Figures 5 and 6 in the following chapter.)

RESOURCES AVAILABLE

Most firms have some resources which they can contribute to an industrial marketing research project whether the project is conducted wholly within the firm or by an outside agency. Some of the resources are obvious enough, such as the availability of a computer or other electronic data processing equipment. However, in large and dispersed firms there are often many forms of resources whose immediate application in a marketing research project is obscured by the primary purpose for which they were obtained. It really requires a management audit to identify all the resources which might be available and, indeed, there is no reason why such an audit could not be taken. The danger of becoming pre-occupied with the gathering of unrelated facts exists, however.

It is possible to group non-financial resources under three headings: personnel and their experience, accumulated records and machinery.

The specialist human skills within a company cover a very considerable range, particularly when both scientific and technical knowledge and experience are often requirements for an industrial marketing research project. For example, the presence of an occupational psychologist in the personnel department might make use of motivational research techniques practical and relevant in a study of buying attitudes. The psychologist, apart from piloting the interviews, can brief the other field workers and assist in interpreting the results. The use of visual research techniques as shown in Chapter 10 can be greatly enhanced if a member of the operational research team can be brought in to direct the researchers.

In both these instances there can be considerable cost saving in relation to the use of outside consultants. Moreover if management wills it, it is often possible to obtain internal assistance more quickly than assistance from outside. Finally, research objectives which might not be within the ambit of a research department can be accomplished once additional specialists are made available. Thus it can be seen that the utilisation of personnel resources impacts on the other parameters.

Accumulated records are perhaps the most accessible of a firm's resources to the research department and here the human problems of secondment, overloading of duties and the development of personal preferences and loyalties which are inherent in the adaptation of human skills are not involved.

Accumulated records stem from the existence in the firm of previous marketing research on the subject to be probed or else related to it, trade and professional association collected and disseminated data, inter-firm comparisons, and a whole host of analyses (some of which are detailed in Chapter 5, 'Use of Secondary Sources'), which can be taken in isolation or in conjunction with external data.

Accumulated records can often be the source list for devising samples or filling sampling frames. Returned guarantee cards, service department records, salesmen's call sheets, purchasing dockets and complaints records in the relevant circumstances and with due regard to the question of bias, can save a considerable time in sampling procedures.

Needless to say, both the technical and commercial library of the firm is likely to be a treasure house for data and, since all good research begins by uncovering what has already been done in the field, the existence of a specialised library which is also a well indexed one is of inestimable value to the researchers in saving both time and money. Many firms maintain indexed collections of newscuttings or abstracts, perhaps only for public relations purposes. Such collections, provided the information is easily retrievable, are one of the most important sources available to the researcher.

In considering the problem of accumulated records it is necessary to emphasise again that the primary purpose for which the resource was acquired may obscure its value to the marketing researcher. Thus in considering the input of accumulated records into a research project a balance must be struck between the effort required to retrieve the data from the records and that required to generate it anew. Certainly where the advantage lies in the former circumstance, there can be an appropriate adjustment in time and cost estimates for the total project and possibly even a widening of research objectives.

The third sector of physical resources is concerned with machinery. There is usually far less difficulty in identifying the existence of this type of resource within a company although it often requires an awareness of an exceptional type to relate the machinery to the research need. Electronic data processing equipment is sometimes so expensive and complex that its existence is constantly thrust upon the researcher. But relatively simple equipment has a contribution to make too. A massive postal questionnaire handled by clerical staff is of a totally different and higher order of costs than one which can be put through a mechanised mail room with collating, folding and addressing machinery.

A hard-pressed switchboard can make telephone interviewing slow and expensive, lack of transcription facilities for taped interviews or interview reports can often hold up a project. Simple hand-operated or complex electronic punched card equipment can both make considerable contributions to a project and thus impact upon the other parameters.

FINANCIAL RESOURCES

The cost of research is obvious enough when it is either bought from outside or else conducted by a department operating on its own budget. However, an element of cost falls outside both the agency and the internal department although it is real enough. That is the amount of time spent by the sponsor in preparing his research requirements, briefing the researchers, liaising with them and reading and interpreting the report. Moreover, in this context the sponsor is usually not a single person but a unit comprising several people. Indeed it has been found in practice that the sponsor's time (and thus money) costs are often higher than the total research costs, a factor often overlooked in computing the cost of a survey.

In considering financial inputs to a research project, therefore, there lies yet a further parameter; that is the savings in cost which might be obtained by either a 'package' research deal, which reduces sponsor's time input, as against the sponsor taking on part of the research activity. The most satisfactory situation would be one in which the sponsor stated a research objective and had no more involvement until the report in pre-digested form with built-in decisions was delivered to him. The reality is a far cry from this.

Clearly the amount of money available for a project will impact directly on time, the use of resources and the objectives, as has already been demonstrated. More money will not necessarily reduce the cost of the sponsor's participation since in many surveys such participation is vital. Thus cost considerations are not necessarily paramount in any specific project.

Nowhere in industrial marketing research does the clash between its theory and practical considerations of everyday business life become more intense than in the decisions which lead to compromise between the most suitable techniques for obtaining research results and the budget for so doing. In pure research, and in an ideal world, there would be no compromise in the search for truth. Industrial marketing research however is business, and business, like life itself, is essentially an area of compromise. If the choice is between a compromise in technique (and thus in the accuracy of results) and no research, the theoretical approach might well settle for 'no research'. Certainly one respected authority[1] has suggested that budgetary reasons can sometimes make 'no research' the right answer. The practical marketing research approach is to establish what type of research can be executed within the limits of the appropriation and which will contribute more than its cost in solving the marketing problem under review. There can be little dispute that judgement based on facts is better than judgement alone. The concomitant is that almost any good research is better than no research, but the same is not true of bad research.

Since profitability is the end object of all industrial marketing research it follows that the research results must be capable of profitable employment. This will only be measured by the financial cost of the project as compared with the business results achieved as a result of the research yield. It is not surprising, therefore, that all the parameters of research tend to be transferred to money terms and to provide a common standard of comparison both between the research inputs and the end result of the project.

OBJECTIVES

Finally, in discussing research parameters it is necessary to look at objectives. The simplest and to many firms most devastating question a researcher can put to his sponsor is to ask: 'How will the information be used when it is obtained? All too often the answer is evasive, platitudinous or facetious. By seeking a clear statement as to the use of information required, it is usually possible to assess if the proposed research is over-dimensioned or if the opposite is true.

[1] Richard D. Crisp, *Marketing Research*, McGraw-Hill (New York, 1957), p. 93.

A common research question is 'How large is the European market for X?' The West European market in fact comprises some fifteen countries, almost all of them different in characteristics and outlook and hardly any of them offering comparable statistical data. There are few, if any, firms capable of absorbing and using in a reasonable time information in depth from all these markets in a single report. In fact what usually happens is that the most promising market is dealt with first so that by the time the last country is reached the information is almost invariably out of date. Clearly in requests of this type there is a strong practical case for a more clearly defined geographical study. The implications of such restrictions in terms of time and cost are obvious.

However, the question of practical research objectives is three dimensional since objectives need appraisal not only on a geographical basis but also on depth and validity basis. A firm making a wide range of paint spraying equipment might, ideally, like to know the size of market for each piece of equipment. The question here is whether information on market size for groups of equipment rather than for individual items would not be just as useful in devising both product policy and marketing strategy. Similarly, for a manufacturer of packaged steam generators who looks upon liquid phase heaters as a marginal but competitive piece of equipment to products at one end of his own range, is the cost and time involved in surveying demand for liquid phase heaters commensurate with the value of the data yielded? Firms must decide individually on the equations; the plea is that these factors should be considered in deciding the correct research inputs.

In terms of accuracy in attempting to discover the size of a market and a firm's share, the ideal situation is a complete census of the market. This could give a wholly accurate result. However, the researcher must ask if a wholly accurate result is warranted for the policy decisions to be made. It is not unusual for a research project to achieve a 90 per cent accuracy at a cost of x while the attainment of the next 5 per cent can easily be 3x and the last 5 per cent 10x. Is the final 10 per cent accuracy justified by the expense and time involved? If the product is made by continuous production techniques such as in the manufacture of paper, it might well be that greater accuracy (if as much as 10 per cent were involved) would be justified when profitable working hangs on narrow margins. A market study of abrasive materials cannot possibly demand so critical a margin of accuracy. The researcher, and indeed the research sponsor, must take a realistic view of the research needs and decide the optimum between acceptable precision and a realistic time and cost.

SELECTION OF TECHNIQUES

It has been demonstrated that there exists a real and direct inter-relationship between time, cost, resources and objectives, and that the researcher and his sponsor are constrained by these factors. The form of this constraint in practical terms is directly concerned with the selection of the appropriate research techniques.

For example, agreement on research costs acceptable to the research sponsor and research department or agency clearly sets limits to the extravagance of the sponsor's demand and the researcher's enthusiasm.

In measuring available funds against techniques it is necessary to have some knowledge of the order of magnitude of costs for the various techniques. It is, however, a meaningless exercise to put price tags on research methods. Prices and values change with the cost of inputs of labour and the availability of accumulated research material and with the varying levels of demand on services. Costing methods are however dealt with in detail in Chapter 4, 'Preparing for the Project'.

Considering the time parameter, it is obvious that different techniques vary both in their elapsed time to complete and their yield. No hard and fast time element can be computed for any methods because the variables are too great. It is generally accepted that postal questionnaires are a slow method of gathering information. A realistic time assessment for getting the first replies including the necessary preparation time is about four weeks, or twenty working days. A telephone interview can be completed, including preparation, in a matter of hours. If the numbers are increased, three weeks to obtain perhaps 500 or more replies by a postal questionnaire is extremely quick compared to the time that would be needed to complete 500 telephone interviews.

Another variable for consideration is the managerial level and job function of the respondent. It can take a very long time indeed to obtain access to Board members of large firms by telephone, while at the other end of the scale, salesmen can be just as difficult to interview.

Thus each technique will have to be considered in relation to the objectives, the typical respondent, the numbers of respondents, their geographical spread and even the time of year.

Bearing in mind the variables which can be introduced, the following time assessments will provide at least a crude guide to the time inputs likely to be required.

Postal questionnaires: twenty working days from preparation to completion of analysis.

Telephone interviews: seven to ten valid calls per day. This allows for call backs, misconnections, wrong respondent identification and the time required to write up or record the interviews.

Personal interviews (non-structured): two to three per day, depending on geographical spread.

Personal interviews (semi-structured): seven to ten per day, depending on geographical spread.

Personal interviews (structured): fifteen to twenty per day, depending on geographical spread.

All these timings are necessarily subject to considerable adjustment but it can be seen that if a survey result is wanted in six weeks and involves ninety personal unstructured interviews, it will require at least two if not three interviewers working simultaneously, if there is to be enough time for analysis and writing.

So far as the personnel resources are concerned, useful generalisations can be made to relate the required skills to different field techniques. In almost all field work a statistician or at least a researcher with knowledge of statistics and industrial sampling techniques is needed. Despatch and analysis of mail questionnaires require clerical talents or possibly higher grade technical skills if the processing of returns is complex. The services of an industrial psychologist to formulate the questionnaire are also a valuable addition to the team.

Personal interviewing of the structured or semi-structured 'question and answer' type requires little more than a pleasant manner and personality combined with a certain amount of drive to obtain the interviews and to keep the respondent moving through the questionnaire. Non-directive interviews need skills of a very high order indeed and employ the talents of expert interviewers. Under no circumstances can an unskilled interviewer be used to obtain reliable results for this type of interview. Depth (or focused) interviewing requires equal but very different ability and group interviewing cannot be undertaken successfully except by an expert, almost always a psychologist trained in clinical techniques.

Observations such as are undertaken, for example in product application studies, stock checks, machine loading, plant and vehicle utilisation and movement, can sometimes, but not always, be carried out by well-briefed but unskilled researchers. There are special qualities required for this type of work rather than special skills. Telephone interviewing also requires expertise, but it is perhaps one which can be acquired fairly rapidly.

Resources other than human to be found within or available to a marketing research department or agency must also be considered in relation to decisions on research techniques; it is more difficult to generalise here. The uses of machinery are increasing daily and the very existence of machinery, whether it be the latest equipment for data processing or an office duplicator, usually generates its own use. The danger is perhaps that of building 'machine time' into a survey when it is not warranted or when it displaces a more appropriate technique.

The demand for abstruse statistical calculations and cross-tabulations does not occur in industrial marketing research with the same frequency as in consumer research when the entire project usually rests upon the application of statistical techniques to numerical data. Nevertheless 'hardware' in industrial marketing research is relevant. When it exists or can be hired (as with computer service centres) it should be used especially when it is an adequate substitute for resources not otherwise available.

Finally in considering the selection of the appropriate techniques against the background of the research parameters, it may appear paradoxical that of all the factors which govern the selection of research techniques, that of the research objectives which are paramount, has been left for comment till last. The reason for this is to show first the modifying forces at work when techniques are to be decided. This approach is essentially a plea for emphasising the practical as against the ideal. In most business situations compromise is necessary and the pressures of time or lack of resources must in turn frequently lead to a modification of the original plan or to the 'no research' decision. The crucial decision is how far research objectives can be adjusted.

In the final assessment it is only the likelihood of satisfactory research results being obtained from the use of any particular techniques that enables the decision upon acceptable modifications to techniques to be made. Commencing with the research objectives, the modifications that stem from availability or otherwise of time, money and other resources must be measured. Good research is almost certainly handicapped from the start if the sponsor asks: 'What objectives can be achieved with the resources available?' Rather than this there should be a statement by the research sponsor on the ideal and minimum acceptable objectives and degree of accuracy needed. The decision can then be made as to how far the available time, money and other resources can be made to fit the needs of the project.

There must be, inevitably, areas in which no compromise is possible. Some surveys can only be successfully undertaken by a given technique. For example, an attitude study of industrial buyers requires focused interviewing; a survey of competitive products' technical characteristics requires 'desk' research and visual techniques. The situation can arise when, for various reasons, the only suitable techniques cannot be adopted. To compromise under these circumstances would be wrong. There is no advantage in undertaking a survey by means known in advance to be ineffectual. The only decision in these circumstances is not to do research.

Thus the background to decisions concerning techniques is first and foremost the research objectives, then comes the consideration of the modifying factors and finally, the decision to undertake or not to undertake research and, if the answer is to pursue research, the means of so doing.

CHAPTER 4

Preparing for the Project

'Management's job is to decide what needs to be done, to specify who is to do it, to see that it gets done and to evaluate how well it was done. Business operations run on facts and the effectiveness with which these are carried out depends on the intelligent and purposeful use of the reporting process which, in turn, determines the quantity, quality and relevance of the information available for planning and control purposes. The lack of essential information, the use of irrelevant or inaccurate information as well as the misuse of any information can seriously impair a firm's competitive performance.'[1]

This summary of the relationship of the information supply function and the role of management pinpoints the first vital step and all that follows from it . . . 'to decide what needs to be done'. Its very simplicity is deceptive since deciding 'what to do' in any given set of circumstances often provides as many versions as there are personnel involved. Nevertheless, if the final research yield is to be of maximum value to its sponsors it must have clearcut objectives. These ought also to be agreed objectives although, as has already been pointed out in the preceding chapter, the four research para-meters may force a modification from the 'ideal'. Thus in considering an industrial marketing research project the very first stage is to isolate the problem—what needs to be known.

The stages before the fact-finding commences range from obtaining a clear and precise statement of research objectives from the research sponsor to the beginning of the phase in which the related data are collected. Thus the initiation stage of a marketing research project is itself spread over four areas of activity.

These activities can be defined as:

1. Brief—an initial statement by the research sponsors of the desired research objectives.

[1] Leslie Rodger, *Marketing in a Competitive Economy*, Hutchinson (London, 1965), p. 75.

2. Work-plan and research design—planning the actual research operation and a restatement to the research sponsors of the objectives in a form which indicates the scope and depth of the research and the methods to be adopted.

3. Timing and costing—the research schedule, and appropriation.

4. Initiation—the allocation of resources and responsibilities for the research.

GO, NO-GO

Before the initial stages of a marketing research project are entered there is an important and fundamental decision to be taken jointly by the would-be research sponsors and the marketing researchers. That is, should research be done at all? For industrial marketing research to be of value, it must have either a long- or short-term profit motive or both. In securing or improving the position of the firm in the market there is neither time nor justification for marketing research that only satisfies the curiosity of the researchers without contributing to the firm's overall performance. Given then that the end-object—increased profitability—is not forgotten, there is a research equation to be worked out. The variables are many, but can be stated simply as the components of the cost of research and both direct and indirect profits expected from the research. The figures are related to the size and nature of the market to be evaluated.

There are, however, besides profit objectives other factors which may alone, or in combination, determine if the project should be undertaken. Clearly availability of various types of resources and the position of the project in the company's cost/benefit list of priorities will be two such limitations. The feasibility of achieving reliable and usable results within the present state of the art will be another. More important perhaps will be the commitment of management to the use of industrial marketing research as a reliable tool in decision-making. If research is undertaken either in a spirit of cynicism or because it is fashionable to do so, there is little chance of its findings being applied successfully. Management reactions, which can be summarised as 'We knew that already', or else 'I don't believe it', are usually indicative of insecurity and a situation in which industrial marketing research, if it is used at all, becomes a talisman to keep away the evil eye.

Clearly managements' views on what is wanted will vary in accordance with the purpose for which the data is intended. A sales manager may be content with an accurate assessment of market share,

E

while the advertising manager seeks advice on the effectiveness of certain media and the transport manager may confine his interest to the logistics of his competitors.

Research embracing a single objective such as these is rarely economic, since costs rise not in proportion to the number of questions asked but in relation to the types of techniques used, the numbers of interviews, the volume of data needed to be obtained and time element. Generally it costs no more to ask two questions from a single respondent than one. Thus research objectives can often be extended in scope without increasing costs.

The acid test of research objectives is a simple one and has already been stated. 'How will the information be used when it is obtained?' This question can reduce a research objective from 'What is the size of the European market for self-locking nuts?' to 'What is the size of the French market for self-locking nuts?' Similarly, a request for data on the size of the various market segments for a multi-industry product such as convoluted tubing or closed circuit television will often reduce itself to a demand for information on a limited number of sectors. Few firms, it was pointed out in the previous chapter, have the personnel to use market information on many markets or segments simultaneously. Frequently the answer to a question as to the use of information will indicate that research is not required, management is not yet ready to receive and use the material, or that the problem has not been completely thought out.

There is however the opposite reason for deciding not to undertake research—that is when the objectives cannot be achieved with a degree of accuracy necessary to make the information usable. A study to determine the demand for floor treatment materials for all types of flooring at a confidence level of, say, the ± 5 per cent order of accuracy would be a wasted effort. Such a level of confidence cannot be achieved in this market at the present time using the techniques currently available.

The researcher and sponsor at the outset need a coarse screen through which the research objectives as first conceived should be passed to ensure that further consideration of the research is worthwhile.

● How will the information be used?

● What profit contribution will it make in both long- and short-term?

● Are the accuracy tolerances reasonable and achievable?

● What are the alternatives to doing research?

● Is the time element a practical one?

● Are the resources necessary to complete the research likely to be, or to be made, available?

This check list is intended only as an approximate guide to the decision to continue through the preliminary stages. In detail, time and resources will require investigation in depth but at this very early stage 'rule of thumb' approaches will suffice to establish the viability of the project on grounds of time and cost.

SETTING THE OBJECTIVES

The research will never be any better or more useful and profitable than that permitted by the objectives. Clearly if these are not correct the research, no matter how excellently carried out and presented, can never yield its full value. The importance of clearcut and agreed objectives cannot be over-emphasised.

Ideally everyone would like to know everything. Practical objectives, however, are those in which the information will make a clearly definable contribution to the company's operations.

The nature of a marketing research problem, when subjected to critical analysis, may, and sometimes does, turn out to be something entirely different from that which was originally supposed. One of the skills of the marketing researcher is a highly developed ability to strip problems of their non-essentials and bring them into sharper focus. But it is not sufficient to produce a clearcut research objective. It is also necessary to apply human and social skills to obtain mutual understanding with the research sponsors and others in the firm to achieve an acceptance of a clarified definition and agreement on the best means of attacking the problem.

Setting the problem is not the work of one man. Many departments of the firm may be involved: Buying, Production, Finance, Commercial, Sales, R & D, as well as the full complement of the marketing research department's skills and talents. Each individual and each group has specialised knowledge and special problems as well as a different viewpoint to contribute. Each may demand different types of information and each may be able to utilise information obtained for the others. Nevertheless the individual specific needs must be subordinated to the overall strategy, and must fit into the main scheme.

Several dangers arise at this stage, not the least of which is a presumption of understanding between sponsor and researcher. Requests for information on the role of distributors can be interpreted in many ways. Their importance in quantitative terms—the volume of goods passing through these particular channels; their importance in strategic terms—the inability to obtain distribution without them as is the case of many building materials and components; their importance in service terms—the availability of pre-start up and maintenance services; their economic importance—stock-holding, bulk breaking, provision of credit, forward purchasing, levelling of price variations. To probe these different interpretations takes the researcher to different groups of respondents and by different routes with different techniques. Thus the importance of defining just what is meant by a request to provide information on distributors takes on a particular importance. This example could be multiplied indefinitely for other marketing operations.

A better way of ensuring that objectives are clearly understood between sponsor and researcher is to return to the approach which asks the purpose for which the information is required. If, to take the example already given of distribution channels, information is needed to devise a franchise system, then the research emphasis falls clearly upon an examination of the distributor's value to his customers, his merchandising ability and physical and service facilities. A study of the quantitative aspects of operations of distributors is of less immediate or no interest to manufacturers if a decision has already been taken to use distributors. Thus it would be possible to concentrate the research and to produce a study in depth of the aspect of operations of immediate concern to the manufacturer. If a change of distribution methods is contemplated, that is to circumvent the distributor, then the major interest of such a study would centre on the strategic aspects of distributive network and the extent to which distributors fulfil their economic functions which must then be taken over by others in the distributive pipelines.

Thus an understanding of total objectives provides the researcher with an insight into the practicability and desirability of any particular research objectives. Indeed, by providing information on the total objectives it is possible that the researchers may well suggest that the distributors, in the example being used, need not be studied at all but that the reaction of users is of primary importance and their attitudes and activities in relation to distributors are the factors on which marketing decisions should be based.

But this particular approach is perhaps micro-marketing research since most study objectives are far wider, and rightly so, than a simple examination of one type of agency in the total marketing system. It is used here only to illustrate the dangers of mis-communcation in discussing *information* objectives as opposed to *marketing* objectives. If this distinction is made then the chance of an early misunderstanding is reduced, although never wholly eliminated.

The very complexity of marketing research problems, their broad scale and wide-ranging implications are in part the reasons for difficulties of definition. When problems are defined by sponsors they tend to be all-embracing and attempt to cover every eventuality. Defined in this way, the objectives seek to both alleviate the need for later research by covering everything in a single major effort, and to provide the sponsors with a wide range of alternative courses of action. Conversely problems defined for investigation by marketing researchers are frequently so circumscribed that the resultant findings concern too small a segment of the total problem or cannot be related to other aspects of the total problem. Viewed from the position of the top marketing executive they appear to lose their link with reality.

It has been said that anyone other than a legal draftsman would find it impossible to frame even simple rules for a tennis club with such clarity and unambiguity that a skilful lawyer could not fault them. It would be surprising, therefore, if the researcher and sponsor could reach total agreement and understanding. In developing the research objectives it should be accepted that there will be areas which lack clarity. It is a favourite indoor sport of businessmen and management executives to prove that it is impossible to define either basic research or research problems. The concomitant is that it is foolish to spend time studying something not knowing what the something is. There being a certain amount of apparent logic even in a syllogism of this type, it is not surprising that some distaste has developed for the semantics of research. Difficulties do exist, and it should be recognised that there are limitations to what can be achieved by marketing research. But as Winston Churchill once pointed out: 'It would be an inconvenient rule if nothing could be done until everything could be done.'

It has been suggested that the only way to define problems in a sufficiently concrete form to make them manageable is to formulate a comprehensive, long-range research programme so that individual studies are designed to contribute not only to the short-term marketing needs but also help in the development of the corporate long-range programme. Undoubtedly this is an ideal aim, but the marketing research needs of the majority of firms are not seen in this light. There is a danger in the selection of the wrong long-term research objectives because the errors multiply in ratio to the length of the complete programme. On single studies the scale of errors must be smaller. Nevertheless this is not an argument for setting aside the broader concept of research and again compromise may be necessary. Since the plea must always be for a *practical* approach to marketing research it is as well, without losing sight of the desirable, to adjust marketing research practice to current needs and the current ethos.

A check list,[1] although devised for applying the 'marketing concept', gives a framework within which an order for immediate needs for industrial marketing research can be discerned.

● Decide on long-term marketing objectives.

● Enumerate in detail the policies, plans and programmes needed to attain the objectives.

● Identify blocks barring progress towards goals and specify areas where further information is necessary.

● Define what and how the marketing research function can contribute to information gathering and problem solving.

● Obtain the agreement of all members of the marketing team to objectives, plans and programmes.

● Set up a priority order and time-table for the research projects.

● Allocate the necessary budget, personnel and facilities for implementing the programme.

It is against this background that the research objectives should be identified and viewed. A distinction, however, is required between 'objectives' and 'goals'. 'Objectives' are general aims and 'goals' specific aims whether these are related to the research effort, the marketing activity or the total corporate activity of the firm. However, the distinction is rarely made in the majority of companies manufacturing industrial goods or providing industrial services because 'goals' and 'objectives' are not often defined except in the most nebulous terms. 'Objectives' as loose as 'boosting sales', to mention one of the more frequent ones, are useless for the purpose of preparing specific and precise proposals for a project. The statements of sales targets, for example, should be refined and practical. A logical grouping which contains actual figures would be:

● Increase unit sales to ....

● Sell the range as a whole rather than individual items.

[1] Lee Adler, 'Phasing Research into the Marketing Plan', *Harvard Business Review* (Cambridge, Mass., May-June 1960).

- Improve share of market to........................ per cent.
- Identify and concentrate on key accounts.
- Introduce new products to account for..............per cent of sales by 19.........
- Reduce unit sales cost by........................per cent.
- Gain greater immediate profitability and open new territories.

In a subject in which generalisations are dangerous it is nevertheless worth stating that research objectives should always be 'grass root' enquiries. Supplementary, more sophisticated information will invariably also be forthcoming in a well-conceived and executed research project, aimed at resolving fundamental problems and satisfying basic information needs. 'What share of the market can we anticipate obtaining? What return should we seek on investment? Are we going after the best and most suitable markets? Should we be in this business in the first place?' Answering such questions contributes towards making practical and profitable business decisions.

Before preparing the work plan, one final factor needs to be considered by sponsor and researcher alike. This is the degree of confidence the sponsor requires in the final results. It is important to achieve a high level of confidence in surveys relating to large-scale plant and very high unit cost equipment such as an electron microscope. For fuel oils in, for example, one particular Standard Industrial Classification, relatively low confidence levels will usually be acceptable and usable, bearing in mind the great saving in research costs. Objectives, however clearly stated, will not on their own be sufficient to enable the researcher to prepare his project. In setting objectives, sponsors should also give consideration to the level of confidence they require in the results.

THE BRIEF

The discussion so far has centred on correctly identifying research objectives and although these may be the *raison d'être* of the research, the sponsor will also wish to indicate both the general scope of the study, the product, market and other definitions, and possibly some of the detail which he is hoping to achieve within the mainstream of the research activity. The most efficient preliminary method of shaping the research requirements is by discussion, frequently at a technical as well as commercial level, with those who will ultimately be responsible for applying the research findings. These early discussions will provide not only indications of what is needed by the sponsors but also what might reasonably be achieved by the research-ers. Even at this early stage the sponsor can make quite clear the minimum requirements which would be acceptable and which would decide the research 'go, no-go' decision. Conversely the researcher can from the start disabuse any optimistic sponsor of any ideas that research can be purchased at bargain-basement prices. Thus at the end of the discussion common ground will have been found between sponsor and researcher.

The next stage, however, is to set down in writing the research brief. This is important if misunderstandings are to be avoided in the work plan. Language is a poor tool for conveying information. A term can mean this to one person and that to another. 'It is some-times too great a mental effort for the sponsor to devote himself to definitions and to the terms of reference. In such circumstances there is only one way out of the situation: the marketing researcher him-self has to attempt both definitions and terms of reference and submit them to the sponsor.'[1] If the brief is to be written by the researcher—being his view of what is required—it is vital that this should be studied, modified and agreed by the sponsor. 'When this rule is not observed the great danger exists that the sponsor may complain after the completion of the survey that he really meant something else; the research covers too narrow a field and the researcher omitted to delve into one or several important problems.'[2]

However, it is more usual and generally more efficient for the sponsor to write the brief. He can do so far more meaningfully than the researcher who naturally tends to write a brief which fits his research experience and resources.

Writing a brief has the effect of making the sponsor re-examine yet again his requirements and the researcher his approach to the project. Objectives agreed across a table, set down in black and white, often strike the sponsor as inadequate or in some other way unsatis-factory. This is an experience common to anyone who has attempted to record meetings or conversations.

Thus, whichever way it is arrived at, the written brief will contain the essential ingredients to which the work plan can be geared. This will generally comprise:

● Statement of the research objectives.

● Internal information available to assist in the development of the research design.

[1] Max K. Adler, 'Industrial Marketing Research—Techniques', *The Marketing of Industrial Products,* op. cit., p. 71.
[2] *Ibid.*

- The purpose for which the research will be used.
- The product, industry, geographical area and other relevant definitions.
- Information segments (e.g. market size, structure, competitive climate).
- Required time schedule.
- Cost limitations.[1]
- Any exclusions or facets of the research requiring special considerations.
- Need for anonymity.

With this, or as much of it as possible before him, the researcher is ready to move to the work plan. A check list of information which should be provided by the sponsor is illustrated in Figure 4.

WORK PLAN

Once the objectives have been agreed the researcher must reconcile himself to several days', perhaps weeks', work in devising the optimum research approach, deciding on the research 'mix' against the background of the research parameters and on the feasibility of achieving the results within the level of confidence limits required.

The first step, as with so many other aspects of industrial marketing, is to devise the ideal research project. This might be one in which money and time are no object. To arrive at the acceptable it is useful to have some idea of the desirable. To understand what 'too much' is, it has been said, a man needs to know what is 'enough'. This is as true for facts as for food.

The ideal research brief will set out a series of headings specific to the project and the information yield to be obtained. Typical headings might be: market size estimate and breakdowns, configurations of the market structure, forecast, user industry attitudes and activities, competitive climate, product comparison, governmental factors. Each of these main headings will now need to be further subdivided to show the section goals. For example, in studying the configurations of the market information might be sought under the following headings: division of market between main suppliers, uptake of major user sectors, extent of imports and exports, volume of

[1] It is not usual for research sponsors buying research from agencies to indicate cost limits.

Department	Enquiry No. ....
Address	Date ....
Enquirer(s)	No. of copies of Design.........................
....	By (date)...

Product/Service Definition
Survey Limitations
Market Size Information Required
Market trends Information Required
Definition of Users and Potential Users and Information Required
Identification of Competitors and Potential Competitors and Information Required
Identification of Raw Material Suppliers and Information Required
Governmental Factors/Standards, etc.
Competitive Products or Substitutable Products
End User Industries and Information Required
Geographical Areas to be included
Yield and Accuracy Required
Description of relevant internal data or analyses available
Guidance on Method
Time Requirements
Cost Indications
Miscellaneous

Fig. 4

SURVEY ENQUIRY FORM

products passing through intermediaries, regional and cyclical variations in demand, extent of in-feeding and reciprocal trading practices.

Even finer detailing should occur at this stage and the sub-heading reduced to outline check lists to indicate both depth and direction of probing. Within the user industry section questions relating to the following might be found: location of purchasing decision (composition of the Decision-Making Unit); decision-forming factors, e.g. security of supplies, services available, reputation of supplying firm, price, quality, availability of related products; users' information sources on products, history of last change of supplier.[1]

With this ideal project profile, preliminary desk research can commence to see what information is immediately available. Official statistics, trade association data, past surveys, salesmen's reports and a host of other sources which are described in the next chapter may indicate at once that certain questions need not be asked or that their answer can be derived from sources other than field work. The feasibility of reaching some or all of the research objectives will certainly become much clearer at this stage.

For example, the classifications into which hydraulic jacks fall, all-embracing as they are, will nevertheless provide a clear maximum market figure beyond which the market for any sub-group cannot extend. This is a useful order of magnitude which, apart from aiding in the decision whether to do research at all, will enable a relationship to be established between the research costs, the maximum possible potential market and a reasonable share which the sponsor might obtain.

The desk research associated with the work plan should reveal the extent of the research problem and provide all readily accessible data on the subject of the research. For even the most intensive desk research not still to leave many questions unanswered as to the feasibility of the project is quite exceptional. By detailing the main research segments as suggested, it is then possible to identify most of those questions where an answer will, or might be, obtained by desk research. The questions which have been listed and which do not look like being resolved by desk research will then require consideration for investigation by field research.

Only with this examination will it become possible to check the feasibility of achieving the objectives and the time and the cost. It has been said already that it costs little or nothing more to ask additional questions of the same respondents. However, there is a law of

[1] The Check List in Appendix A will indicate the wide range of questions which can be asked under each heading.

diminishing returns in that the longer the questioning, the less reliable or informative the answers become until respondent fatigue or irritation reduces the value of the information to nil. Thus there is a very practical reason for not asking more questions than are absolutely necessary.

The researcher at this stage must make a preliminary decision on how long an interview might reasonably last and on how many, and which questions can be asked. Experience will tell a researcher a great deal on these points. Unfortunately for the inexperienced, there are only commonsense rules to guide researchers. It cannot be said that Managing Directors of large firms are less likely to devote time to an interview than foremen in small firms. The only certain way for an inexperienced researcher to assess how long an interview might take, what sort of questions can be asked and how they should be formulated, is to adopt an empirical approach. At the work plan stage it is possible to pilot interviews personally or by telephone. This will provide a sufficiently accurate guide, until the research begins, as to how practical the questions are. This is not to suggest that the pilot work in the main survey itself should be undertaken at this stage, only that there must be at least a preliminary hypothesis on the usefulness and yield of the approach suggested.

There is generally not sufficient time in the preparation of the work plan to pilot a postal questionnaire and therefore an assessment of how much data can be obtained by this means is usually based on experience of postal questionnaire yields in previous surveys. For the inexperienced researcher, certain rules of thumb have been detailed in Chapter 7, 'The Postal Questionnaire'.

It is a useful exercise to go through the work plan section by section and in great detail, indicating how it is proposed to obtain the answers to the various questions. To do this is valuable not only to show which questions will apparently not be answered at all, but also how much cross validation can be obtained by the use of various techniques, the depth to which answers might be expected and the accuracy tolerances which can be achieved.

At this point it is necessary to consider the question of the sample. As a first step, at the work plan stage it is important to establish universes. That is the total population of the groups to be researched, number of manufacturers of similar products (e.g. rubber, textile or plastic conveyor belting), numbers of manufacturers of different but competitive products or methods which can be used for the same purpose as the product being researched (e.g. pneumatic conveyor systems, vibration methods, encapsulation techniques, pipelining), numbers of establishments of actual or potential users, numbers of distributors, numbers of other informed sources (e.g. trade associations, trade press, consultants, government departments).

Universes alone will tell only part of the story. Their configurations are of importance too. That is, some stratification by significant sample criteria will be needed (numbers employed, numbers of establishments, share of the market, geographical location, etc.). Details of the sampling procedure are given in Chapter 6, 'Sampling in Industrial Markets'. Here it is only necessary to indicate that the sample problem must be considered and resolved. Thus in preparing the work plan which is still in its idealised form, the researcher will have devised a sample to achieve the ideal objectives.

It is now necessary to begin work within the research parameters; that is, to take into account the time, resources and money available, and see how these can be mixed to achieve the objectives. If, at this stage, the researcher feels that because of the configurations of the respondent segments he must have information in *depth* from at least half of his universe, he will probably abandon the use of postal questionnaires and consider a different approach. Similarly if it is found that the numbers involved are few, and the information needed is detailed, non-directive interviewing will offer itself as the most appropriate method.

Thus the researcher can juggle with the allocation process of distributing resources among alternative uses. All available resources are not necessarily directed to one use even if it is, in one sense, the most efficient use. Rather, the resources available are balanced among competing uses in a way that leads to the greatest yield for the informational objectives.

TIMING

Before the final allocation of resources can be made it is necessary to examine in depth the proposed time schedule. There are four considerations which require phasing and reconciliation:

* The time for the whole study from conception to completion.

* The period between acceptance of proposals and commencement of survey.

* Perishable information.

* The inter-relationship of parts of the project and outside events.

The research year, like most working years, comprises less than 235 days allowing fifteen days for annual holidays and an average of five days sickness each year. With this in mind the technique for the overall timing is simple. Each section of the research must be separately timed and then the sequential and concurrent sections designated. Desk research into the location of producers and users can be carried out concurrently with the perusal of other published data. Desk research into location of producers and users carried out concurrently with the field interviews of these groups is unwise for a number of reasons. An obvious one is the probable necessity of having to return to an area to carry out interviews as the desk research proceeds and reveals new firms. With careful planning going back over the same geographical ground is usually unnecessary. These two activities, identification of firms and field interviews, should be sequential. Identification of firms and analysis of published data should be concurrent.

Research Time

The length of time of each activity is, of course, a function of the numbers and availability of researchers to carry out the work and also the extent to which work on any one project can be dovetailed with that of another. Just so long as the elapsed time for each section of the research is accurately estimated, and the concurrent and sequential activities correctly assessed, then the total research timing —that is from initiation to report presentation—can be estimated.

The simplest way of ensuring a correct alignment is to illustrate the various methods and their approximate timings and relationship with outside events in graphical form. It will become obvious immediately if any sequence has become disjointed. Not only can the timing of the whole project be seen at once, but also and importantly, how it interlocks with the existing and anticipated programme.

Figure 5 illustrates a typical research timetable from the beginning of the bibliographical research and technical consultancy to the presentation of the final report. This covers a period of eighteen weeks with the field research cutting across the Christmas holidays which must lengthen the period required for some activities. It can also be seen that the collection of competitive prices and product information is timed to take in a trade exhibition during which time competitive interviews begin but, for obvious reasons, spread well beyond the end of the exhibition.

The flow diagram, while showing the sequence of events, does not give any guide to the effect of any holdups which may occur irrespective of their source. Thus although the bar chart may provide, for the purpose of the work plan, an elapsed time estimate, it is not a good guide for the day-to-day operations of the survey. This is better monitored on a critical path basis.

Figure 6 shows the same sequence of activities set out as a critical path. Events 12 and 18 have been timed to coincide with a relevant exhibition. To do this the critical path has revealed the need to commence the research seven weeks ahead of the exhibition, not two weeks as shown in the flow diagram. This brings the research into the Christmas period (weeks 13 and 14) at a point at which minimal activity is occurring in the field. The interim report and preliminary hypotheses shown on the bar chart would, of course, be incorporated in the network; these conclusions would be based on the pattern of events which emerged as regularly 'updated' information was added to the diagram.

The same eighteen week elapsed time is shown but the research has been moved to a different sequence of eighteen weeks to optimise both internal and environmental factors, such as the availability of research staff and the impact of outside events.

Commencing time

The second factor in timing is the period required to initiate the project. The time-lag between acceptance of the research design and the commencement of work depends mainly upon the work load of the department or agency and to a lesser extent upon the degree of similarity between the new project and the work in hand or proposed.

It is an unusual and probably an unfortunate department or agency which can begin a project the day the research design is accepted. It is usual and useful for researchers to quote a likely time required for initiating the survey when presenting the research design so that the research sponsors can make an estimate of the time which will elapse before the report is received. For the outside agency a new hazard appears at this point. In the period between the submission of a design and its acceptance, other designs may have been commissioned; this will have a significant effect on the time-lag factor before the initiation for a further new project. Thus when the later project is eventually authorised it is necessary to inform the sponsor of a longer starting delay, and possibly an adjustment in the total timing. The converse could occasionally be true, that is the acceptance of a parallel non-competitive project which enables both to progress with greater rapidity.

Within the marketing research department of a firm the need for

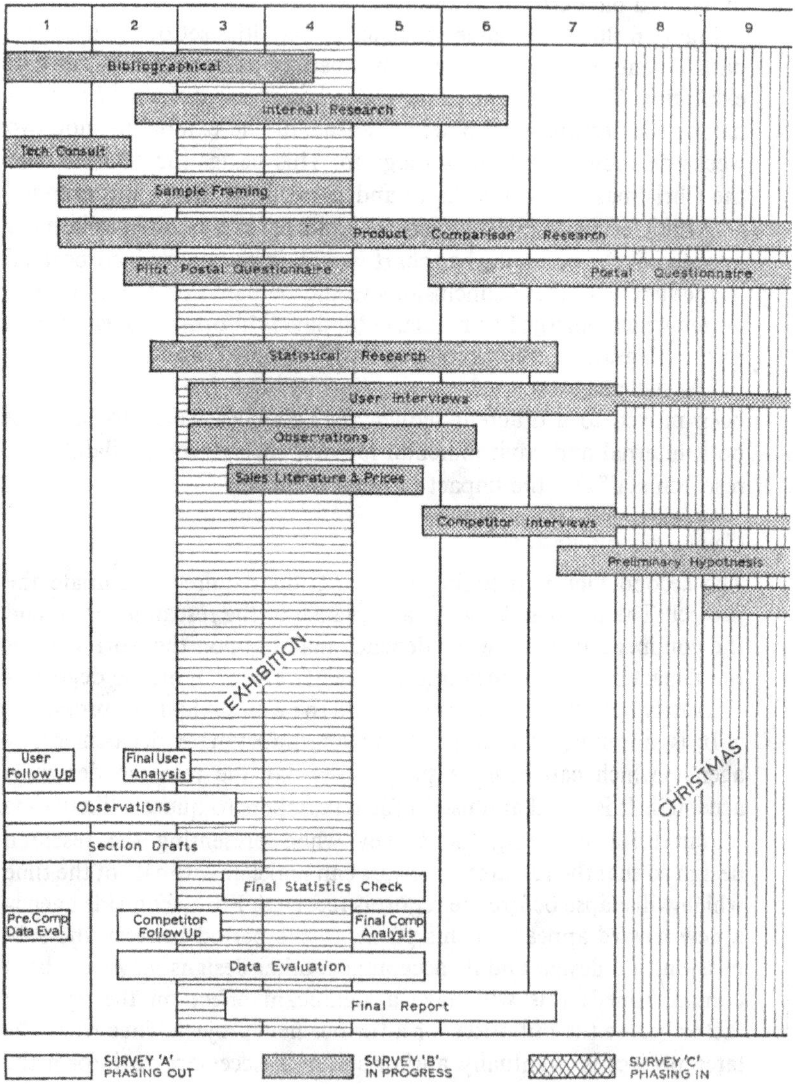

	1	2	3	4	5	6	7	8	9

Bibliographical

Internal Research

Tech Consult

Sample Framing

Product Comparison Research

Pilot Postal Questionnaire

Postal Questionnaire

Statistical Research

User Interviews

Observations

Sales Literature & Prices

Competitor Interviews

Preliminary Hypothesis

EXHIBITION

CHRISTMAS

User Follow Up

Final User Analysis

Observations

Section Drafts

Final Statistics Check

Pre.Comp Data Eval.

Competitor Follow Up

Final Comp Analysis

Data Evaluation

Final Report

SURVEY 'A' PHASING OUT   SURVEY 'B' IN PROGRESS   SURVEY 'C' PHASING IN

Fig. 5

SCHEMATIC TIME DIAGRAM

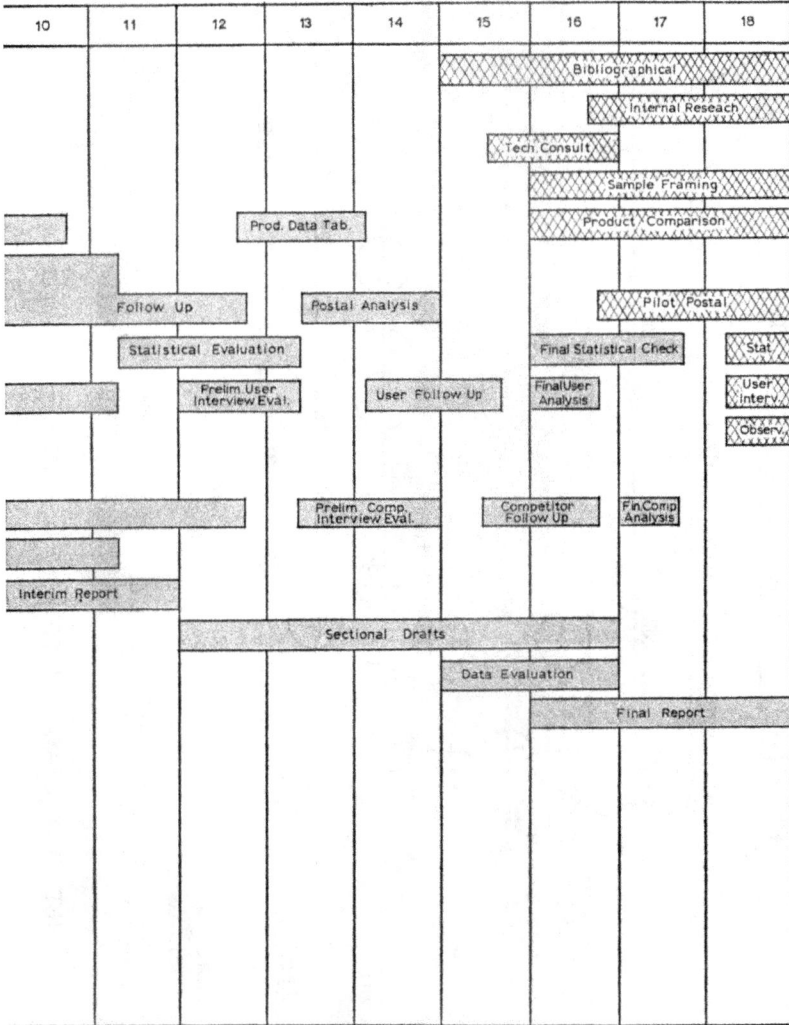

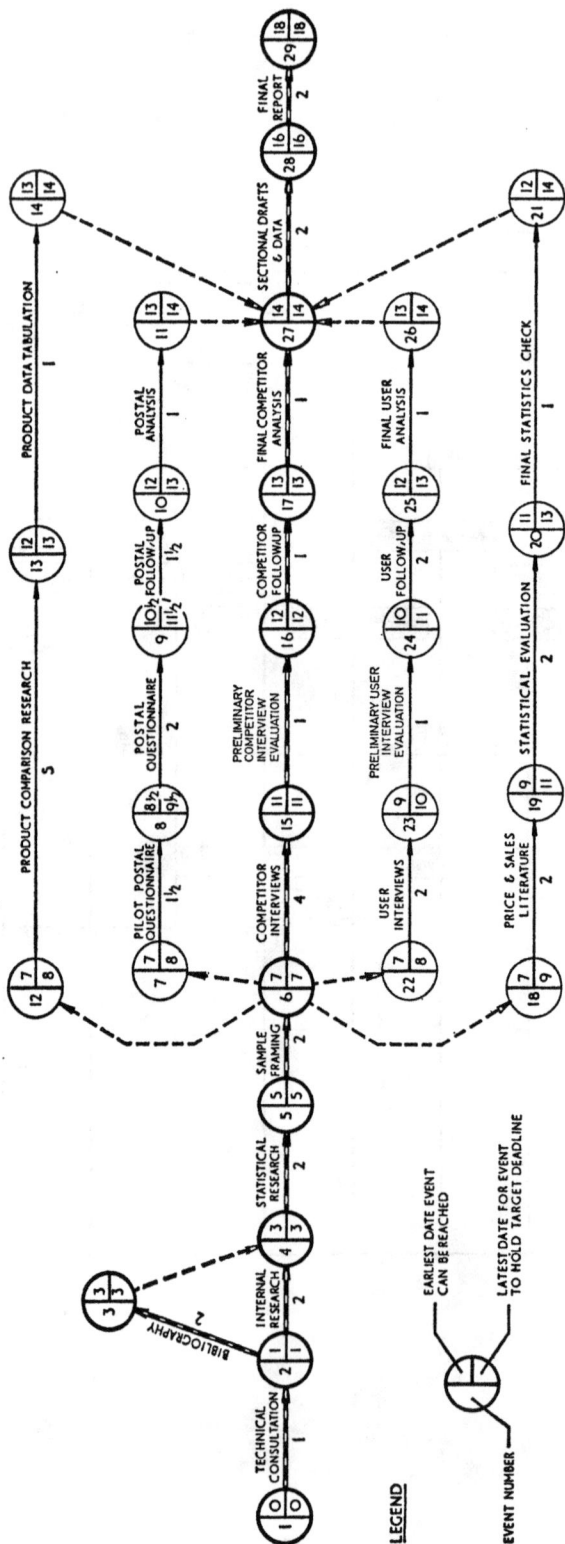

Fig. 6

NETWORK DIAGRAM OF MARKETING RESEARCH PROJECT

sudden adjustments of initiation timing is likely to be less frequent than it is in an agency. It is often possible to forecast the demands on the department and when they become too great, to obtain authority for establishing degrees of priority or to commission work outside.

The initiation date is finally decided on the basis of the availability of the researchers allocated to the project. This, once again, is not necessarily a formal completion of previous work and an equally formal beginning of the new project. It is more in the nature of a 'phasing in' and 'phasing out' of old and new as the bars in the bottom left and top right-hand corners in Figure 5 show.

New research does not generally start as an attack on a broad front, involving the talents of all the researchers all the time. It is more in the nature of preliminary skirmishes occupying the researchers for limited but extending times as the project gathers momentum. As an example, a survey into industrial distribution channels can commence with a preliminary postal enquiry to non-competitive firms distributing through similar channels, fixing appointments with trade associations and distributors for personal interviews, bibliographical research and the gathering of directly relevant and related data. The first of these activities occupies an intelligent clerk for a short time while the other activities demand increasing periods of time from more skilled and experienced people. Researchers, technical consultants and specialists in certain research functions—statistics, economics and industrial interviewing—join in at later stages and for increasingly long periods.

Initiation begins when the first person starts work on the survey. The research proper, however, is not under way until the skills of researchers are called into play. The time-lag between the commissioning of the project and the beginning of the research needs calculation for internal organisational purposes and it is this time-lag which the research sponsors will need to know. There is rarely an excuse for late starting and this start-up period can, and should, be accurately stated and adhered to.

Perishable information and interim reports

Some industrial markets are fast-moving and the information, to be of value, cannot be held for long. Pharmaceuticals often provide an excellent example of this situation. It is not unknown for a branded pharmaceutical to complete its life cycle in as short a period as two years which in turn means that the constituent chemicals and the plant involved will also be affected. Markets for specific brands are highly volatile. Even as short a reporting period as four to six months, not an unusual timing for a marketing research report, may see a significant change in marketing dispositions caused by the introduction and publicisation of one brand of product at the expense of another or by hitherto hidden defects becoming obvious while the product is in use. The withdrawal of the first Salk vaccines and of thalidomides are examples of the latter circumstance. Chemical and machinery manfacturers are as much the victims of these changes as the pharmaceutical producers themselves.

It is a responsibility of the researcher to identify vital and 'perishable' information and transmit it to the research sponsors before its value is lost. The problem of discounting the future is changed if the competition has already had opportunity to act upon the information before it reaches the research sponsor. In allocating research work the time element in relation to the acquisition of material upon which action is needed immediately requires special attention. The terms of reference may make no distinction in time between the different research objectives—the researcher must.

Interim reports are the subject of diverse opinions. Arguments can be advanced for and against such reports. There is, however, no case for withholding information which requires immediate consideration by the research sponsors in order to produce a *tour de force* on the report's presentation. An example of the type of information requiring immediate processing can be found from a study on the market opportunities for a plastic laminated textile. The research was indicating quite clearly that the market would not be important unless a certain technical deficiency could be overcome—an achievement which until then had defeated all the manufacturers. In the course of the survey information came to hand of the development of a process by a Japanese firm which claimed to have achieved the required effect. Before the survey proper was completed negotiations were far advanced between the research sponsors and the inventors of the process for the United Kingdom rights to the process. Had the information about the new development been left to form part of the final report, the action of the manufacturer might have been forestalled by a competitor.

It is possible, of course, to give an instance of a contrary effect. A coated paper manufacturer received an interim report at the first stage of a product diversification study. This interim report indicated an apparent potential market for contact paper in a specific industrial application not hitherto used. Before the report could be completed the manufacturer was purchasing plant for its manufacture and preparing plans to penetrate this market. However, the final report showed quite clearly better and larger markets for products made on the machinery already in the plant. The premature action, in market terms, was only a limited success; in comparative profit terms, a failure.

Faced with valuable information which time is likely to erode, the researcher must make an important value judgement—whether or not to submit an interim report. The golden rule, however, is if in doubt, always give an interim report.

Impact of outside events

One reason why marketing is not regarded as a science is because of the as yet unsolved difficulty of formulating testable hypotheses. It is impossible to produce a controlled laboratory condition in a constantly changing environment which itself defies measurement. This has held back quantitative analysis. The changeable, largely uncontrollable and unmeasurable environment has important implications for the researcher. Attempting to probe users' reactions to a given product is made more difficult by a competitive product being suddenly subjected to intensive promotion during the research. This is because respondents contacted at the end of the project will have been exposed to a different series of information and persuasive messages than those interviewed at the beginning of the project.

Similarly, market phenomena can impede or assist research work. It is essential to try and identify environmental factors and then attempt to avoid or to exploit them. The simplest situation are national holidays which are known well in advance of the research and which imply clearly defined hold-ups in the research work in the field. Similarly, exhibitions can greatly assist certain research activities such as product comparisons. Both these circumstances are illustrated in Figures 5 and 6. Conversely a survey preceding or concurrent with a Restrictive Practices Court hearing is likely to meet with little co-operation from firms under investigation. The hearing itself might, however, provide vital new information not previously available.

The only ways current developments can be related to current research timing is by a constant surveillance of sources of market information, by a lively imagination and a grasp of business and research essentials. The information that a trade, professional or financial journal is seeking advertising for a specialised supplement on a subject related to a topic under research is usually sufficient indication to a good researcher that there will be new information available or information leads appearing, and also that many firms will already have had their fill of granting interviews and giving information. Both are important points in time scheduling.

Because industrial market developments often affect all companies within an industry simultaneously (if to varying degrees) it sometimes happens that similar research may be carried out by different firms at the same time. The coincidence is unlikely to stretch to similar work plans so that the actual order of the research of the different firms will not necessarily coincide but many of the firms selected by the different researchers for interview almost certainly will. This means that the researchers who seek later interviews are liable to receive less than enthusiastic co-operation. In these circumstances it is sometimes wiser to consider postponing the project or, alternatively and where possible, to reshape the work to take in interviews less likely to be used by competitors.

These are the imponderables of timing. They can only be met by the astuteness of the researcher—a quality that can neither be instilled nor communicated.

Overall time

With all the timing information available it is now possible to provide a time estimate but this must be compared with the research requirements to ensure that it comes within the schedules specified by the sponsor. If it does not, it is necessary to return to the work plan to see whether by an adjustment of the mix or the objectives the schedules can be met. If they cannot, then the sponsor must be consulted on whether the enquiries should not be terminated at this point or else reconsider his timing requirements. Sometimes an interim report on one aspect of the study alone may permit the work plan timings to be acceptable.

A study of the demand for freight containers was required in four weeks, an impossible time to set up the field work interviews let alone obtain quantitative results. However, the first basic decision required was related to the fabricating materials and not the market size. A crash research enquiry was set up probing the single aspect of material. By attacking information concentrations it was possible to establish a consensus in favour of one of the materials where users appreciated the relationship of gross and net weight to bulk (containers are usually physically filled before the maximum weight is reached). The heavier fabricating materials were not seen as a real disadvantage in this respect and additionally were recognised as having considerable strength and wear resistance advantages. With this attitude information confirmed, the quantitative research was able to proceed within its original time limits.

COSTING

For the research design to be meaningful to management it must contain an estimate of cost. This is perhaps one of the most difficult of the researcher's tasks since, although it is possible to put price tags on each technique, the imponderables are many and often have considerable financial influence on the project.

The basic cost elements are: time, travel and subsistence, cost of using (or hiring) equipment, purchase of books, analyses, telephone, postage, reproduction costs, stationery and report production. This is, however, a deceptively simple series of headings. 'Time' is the aggregation of the cost of researchers of various skills and experience. It is relatively easy to cost 80 visits[1] for personal interviews but more difficult to assess how long it will take to analyse the interview findings since they may be copious or meagre. It is easy to cost the acquisition of some types of statistical data but difficult to estimate how long it might take to correlate it with other information. It is possible to state that a presentation meeting will take one day of three researchers' time but impossible to say how many days' additional work might evolve as a result of questions asked at a meeting.

It is little consolation to the researcher to be told that experience will provide indications of cost or that a 'swings and roundabouts' costing philosophy will make his department viable or his agency profitable. Both these factors are, of course, true but something more precise is needed for guidance. It is necessary to get the predictable elements of cost as exact as possible. To do this the research techniques must be broken down as finely as possible. Interviews must be stratified according to the skills of the researchers who will conduct them and the volume of information likely to be yielded and, most important, the form in which it will be yielded. Thus structured interviews (typically used in consumer research) require only limited skills and the information yield is completely predictable so that analysis time is also predictable. Semi-structured interviews require rather a higher degree of skill which is commensurately more expensive and the yield tends to be greater but less easy to extract from reports.

---

[1] A 'visit' should be distinguished from an interview. A 'visit' represents a field call on a company and may in fact include several interviews during the single 'visit', or produce no interviews at all.

Here analysis time will be proportionately greater, to which must be added editing time to sift out the various categories of information.

Unstructured non-directive interviews require a high order of skills. Reports are less direct than in other types of interviewing and intensive skilful editing and analysis is needed. Thus unstructured interviews, having a high unit cost, must be used with discretion and where they will be most effective.

But to the interview costs must also be added the cost of getting the interviews. As a rule of thumb, a telephone interviewer of average skill can fix appointments for visits at the rate of about ten per day. Thus for each interview arranged, whether structured, semi-structured or unstructured, must be added 1/50th of the week's salary plus overhead costs of a telephone interviewer.

Postal questionnaires are fairly easily estimated. Their formulation is not usually more than 2 or 3 days' work for an experienced researcher but sampling and sampling frame filling can extend from three to four days per thousand names to several weeks. The time involved in physically preparing and despatching a questionnaire is easily calculable by any office manager since this is a straightforward typing/clerical job. The final imponderables are the time required for analysis and report writing.

Total cost has to be spread over the response rate, not the numbers despatched. Given a cost of £100 per thousand despatched, the true cost is £1 per reply for a 10 per cent response. At £1 per reply the cost of telephone interviewing compares most favourably and gives a much higher information yield. Thus in estimating costs of the postal questionnaire it is important to forecast the response rate before deciding just how practical it is to use this technique. This is dealt with in detail in Chapter 7.

Travel and subsistence costs are fairly easily calculated once the sampling frame has been filled. Allowance must, however, be made for recalls, interview failures, poor travel facilities which lose interview time, national and other holidays, especially overseas, and all factors which might make an interviewer non-productive in the field.

It is pointless to place money values on techniques since the variables are far too many to make them meaningful. For example, the cost of a telephone interview will depend on whether the telephone call is local or long distance, if the caller is on STD or operator dialling and, of course, upon the current telephone rates. It is more meaningful to translate cost items so far as possible into time and then to attempt to establish the individual costs. A good telephone interviewer will not expect to complete more than seven valid calls per day. This allows for a high number of calls in which no contact is made. In a 5-day week some 35 completed calls can be expected at the basic cost of the interviewer's salary.

No rule of thumb can be given for the cost of analyses of the various types of interview as so much depends upon the questionnaire and the format of the interview reports. Ten dichotomous questions without cross runs can be analysed in minutes with the correct machinery but may take a week using clerical labour. Given multiple choice questions, open-ended questions and a large number of cross runs, the time required for analysis can mount astronomically. The questionnaire illustrated in Figure 14 in Chapter 7, was analysed in four working days by a clerk. That in Figure 15 took a team of three people two working weeks. The questionnaire in Figure 16 was pre-coded and analysed on a computer at a total cost of £250.

Report writing time and cost is even more difficult to calculate. Some people can write with journalistic speed while to others it is a slow, painstaking and painful process. The work plan will certainly give accurate guidance on the ground to be covered. This combined with the analyses which are known to be required will provide at least an order of magnitude on time. Most surveys covered by the headings referred to in Figure 4 can be written by a researcher of average speed in about twenty to thirty working days for first draft. Editing and second draft may require a further three to four days.

The final time element is checking the report itself in its completed typed, litho-ed, duplicated or printed version. Report production costs are perhaps the easiest item to calculate. Typing speeds are known variables, the cost of paper, reproduction, checking and binding are simple calculations.

The last group of costs are clerical and administrative and, in the case of marketing research agencies, include items like introduction fees which are often payable to intermediaries such as advertising agencies and fees to international and research consortia headquarters. Again, depending upon departmental or organisational practice, these costs may require to be uplifted.

To the grossed up figure must now be added the bought out charges such as computer time, technical consultancy which may also require an uplift.

The cost elements can now be drawn together. An example of a cost sheet of the type an agency might use is given in Figure 7 and an actual costing form of an internal department in Figure 8. The

CLIENT	DATE		STUDY No.	
	Days	Nos.	Rate	Total
PRE-START UP				
Client Meetings				
Preliminary desk research				
Telephone, postage				
Design preparation				
Clerical/typing				
Others				
SUB-TOTAL				
DESK RESEARCH				
Bibliographical				
Statistical				
Sample construction				
Sample filling				
Telephone				
Postage				
Books and Statistics purchases				
Others				
SUB-TOTAL				
PREPARATION				
Appointment fixing				
Coding				
Field arrangements				
Briefing				
Purchased consultancy				
Others				
SUB-TOTAL				

Fig. 7
SURVEY COSTING SHEET

Fig. 7 continued

	Days	Nos.	Rate	Total
FIELD RESEARCH				
Field salary				
Travel and subsistence				
Postage				
Telephone/telegram				
Field checking				
Bought in interviews				
Others				
SUB-TOTAL				
ANALYSIS				
Editing				
Punching				
Tabulation				
Analysis				
Writing				
Report editing				
Clerical/typing				
Telephone				
Others				
SUB-TOTAL				
MECHANICAL/PRODUCTION				
E.D.P. Time				
Typing				
Clerical				
Stationery (inc. photocopying)				
Postage				
Binding Report				
Report delivery charges				
Others				
SUB-TOTAL				

Continued on the next page

Fig. 7 continued

	Days	Nos.	Rate	Total
GENERAL				
Typing				
Telephone				
Sponsor meetings				
Clerical				
Translations				
Postage				
Travel and subsistence				
Contribution to overheads				
OTHERS				
SUB-TOTAL				
GRAND TOTAL				

summation of the total research costs provides the first basic costing figure. To this must be added the appropriate margin for overhead and, in the case of an agency, profit.

The final summation brings the research cost figure. As with timing, if this figure exceeds the appropriation available then the research mix has to be re-examined and the appropriation re-allocated. The alternative is to seek a change in timing, allocated reserves or objectives which might enable the appropriate figure to be met.

RESEARCH DESIGN

The work plan is now ready to be transferred to a 'blue print' form— the research design—for submission to the research sponsor. This is to be the document, if necessary with modifications, on which the research, go, no-go, decision will be made and against which the results will be compared. It is important, therefore, that the document should be precise, unambiguous and detailed. The research design is a double insurance policy—it ensures that the sponsor gets what he pays for and it also ensures that the researchers are not asked for information at the end of the project which they were not instructed to obtain at the beginning.

The document therefore should summarise the major parts of the

JAMES A. JOBLING Ltd.
PROJECT COST SHEET

INDUSTRIAL MARKET RESEARCH DEPARTMENT.

Survey:

Internal Sponsor: Completion date:

Costing

	Days	Rate	Estimated Cost £	Actual Cost £
Salaries				
Market Research Officer				
Market Research Assistants				
Secretarial and Typing				
Other				
Total Salaries				
Desk Research				
Books and publications				
Stationery				
Telephone				
Postage				
Purchased Statistical Data and Research				
Incidental Travel and Entertaining				
Total Desk Research				
Field Work				
Questionnaires—Printing				
Postage				
Telephone Interviews				
Personal Interviews—Travel				
Entertaining				
Other				
Total Field Work				
Report Preparation				
Printing				
Covers and Binding				
Total Report Preparation				

Estimated
Salaries £
Desk Research £
Field Work £
Report Preparation £
    Total Cost £

Actual
Salaries £
Desk Research £
Field Work £
Report Preparation £
    Total Cost £
Calculated by.............................

Fig. 8

work plan but omit all those sections which are purely concerned with the mechanics of the research, other than a summary of the method.

Thus the design will provide the following information:

Background. Why the research is being considered. Not everyone who will read the design is likely to know all the ramifications surrounding its initiation.

Objectives. Brief statement of the major research purposes.

Definitions. Descriptions of products, markets, geographical regions, etc.

Research approach. Statement on research strategy to be adopted.

Report coverage. Major headings of each section with brief lists of section contents.

Method. Explanation of methodology. At this stage only an outline will be given.

Research yield. Results expected and accuracy tolerances. Ideally these should equal the objectives but in practice this will not be so. The yield represents the minimum return the sponsor might expect against the agreed objectives.

Time. Starting time and research time.

Cost. Fixed price or cost range.

This 'blue print' can now form the final 'chopping block' for discussion between sponsor and researcher. The sponsor may require more details in one section, another section may be eliminated or reduced in importance. Whatever changes are introduced, the total project must be retimed and costed on the basis of the changes introduced.

Once the final revisions have been agreed the Research Design which remains as a point of reference, becomes the Terms of Reference for the project and will in fact usually comprise the opening pages of the final report. The research yield may dictate changes in the design which are not obvious at the outset. Any departure from the agreed design ought always to be agreed in advance with the sponsors. These changes will be added to the Terms of Reference as quoted in the report, giving both date and authority of the changes.

INITIATION

Once the work plan has been agreed the researcher is free to give full play to his specialist skills since the next stages of the enquiry are strictly researchers' business.

The preliminary work carried out for the preparation of the research design will have already given the researcher guidance about the general approach to adopt concerning techniques. It is now necessary to provide for the division of the work and the co-ordination of the various units and individuals concerned. The project itself may be all desk research or largely field work. Postal and telephone questionnaires may be involved. Responsibility for each section must be allocated and timed. If limited personal interviews are also to take place as a pilot survey for a postal questionnaire, then clearly the interviews must be completed before the questionnaire can be formulated and possibly before the sample can be drawn.

Personal interviewing in industrial marketing research is a very much slower process than in consumer research. For a specific project there can rarely be substitution of respondents within firms and often substitution of firms is also undesirable. For this reason the allocation of personal interviewing must be carefully planned both as to timing and to ensure that an interviewer with the appropriate training and possessing the necessary experience is available. It is uneconomic to use a first-class interviewer on desk research when this type of work can be given to someone less adept at interviewing.

A marketing research department or agency is rarely just waiting for a project to begin and therefore has to schedule new work to interlock with other work. Consequently both the timing and division of work call for great skill if all its resources are to be economically deployed.

Self-interlocking programmes are frequently possible within a firm, but the independent agency is rarely fortunate enough to combine parallel but non-competing projects. In an internal department or in an outside agency, the need for economy is always important and therefore the research leader has a responsibility to apply his talents to discovering at the outset how his resources can best be utilised.

The skilful deployment of resources can be most usefully applied at the initiation stage. Initiation of the project should be accompanied by a thorough investigation into the internal information available and a review of useful and easily accessible contacts. In this respect the chief researcher should, when allocating the work, be sure that the knowledge he has acquired of internal research information is available to the research executives and assistants who may need it. It happens far too often that a researcher will spend a considerable time gathering information already in possession of the firm because he, unlike the chief researcher, rarely knows the whole picture within a department.

One way to make sure that information is not collected which is already in possession of the firm is to prepare a sponsor data sheet. This will cover a number of salient points to which answers will be sought from the sponsor, to check his available knowledge and its validity. For example, it is usual for sponsors to know who their direct competitors are. A listing of these will save the researcher perhaps a day's work or more locating these firms.

In practice it has been found that with modifications it is possible to develop a single form of data sheet which will meet most circumstances. Although it may take several months and several surveys to structure this correctly, the effort is always worthwhile. The marketing researchers Check List in Appendix A provides the first rough basis by eliminating obviously inappropriate questions. The sponsor data sheets when properly constructed can avoid 're-inventing the wheel' and can thus be instrumental in saving a very considerable sum of research money.

One warning is needed, however. Sponsor data may not be validated information but based on opinion, hearsay or out-of-date information—industrial folklore. Only that which can be proved as accurate should be accepted, all else must be tested as any other information yielded by the research.

The qualities of good research leadership are never better displayed than in the allocation of work and resources and the dissemination of internal information. Good leadership always achieves a balance between allowing the researchers to stand on their own feet while not being afraid, or reluctant, to consult. Unless consultation takes place freely at the initiation stage the possibility of wasteful and time-consuming activities is always likely.

All research projects involve the use of secondary material—that is research findings gathered by others; government, trade associations, trade and professional journals, private research and the many other sources referred to in the next chapter. At the outset, the likely secondary sources of information should be clearly listed and the researchers should be expected to contribute to this list. Furthermore, keeping the researchers working as a team is an insurance against one researcher discarding material and sources of value to another engaged on some other aspect of the project.

The initiation stage is essentially a division into the component parts of the agreed research design—from here on generally referred to as 'terms of reference'. Not until the writing of the report are all the pieces reassembled into a whole. Thus it is always possible that a fundamental error of research direction or allocation at the beginning of a project will not come to light until a very late stage. Similarly, in any analysis of a completed project it is a frequent experience to find that uneconomic operations and unduly high costs have stemmed from an unsuitable initiation procedure.

G

CHAPTER 5

Use of Secondary Sources

The glamour of field work beckons enticingly once the basic problems and definitions of the research have been cleared. The preparation stage of a research project will unquestionably have indicated how far it will be necessary to generate primary information and how far the work can rest on data derived from secondary sources. It is an unnecessary extravagance to begin field work until the many possible sources of secondary data have been checked for accessibility, relevance, accuracy and topicality. It is not an overstatement to say that premature field work is almost invariably the major cause of wastage in a marketing research study.

Information sources can be divided into two classes: primary (or original) and secondary. The term 'original research' tends to have a very different meaning to scientists and technicians, and this can result in some misunderstanding when representatives of the two different disciplines—technical and marketing research—meet. For the marketing researcher it is necessary, therefore, to use the term 'original research' with care if understanding between members of the management team is to be complete.

Secondary sources can be defined as those that have been collected previously and reported by some individual or organisation other than the present researcher. In this category therefore come all forms of government and other official statistical and bibliographical data, and published and unpublished reports, surveys, comments and, most important, data derived from the internal records of the research sponsoring organisation. All these provide a useful frame of reference and sometimes confirmation in many marketing situations.

The relationship between primary and secondary information can best be seen against the background of the cost and time element in marketing research. Assessing the relationships between these elements and the data sources in the research project before initiating the project is a study of material importance for the marketing researcher.

Differences of opinion exist as to the role and importance of secondary sources of information, and the ease with which it can be generated. Two eminent American authorities have considered that the use of internal data requires 'relatively little formal technique' and that it is 'largely a matter of knowing the company's operating procedures and establishing systematic methods for recording the desired information.'[1] Setting aside the fact that 'knowing the company's operating procedures' can be a major task requiring much skill in itself, the statement by implication writes down the value of internal data. Using internal data calls for an inter-disciplinary approach since, apart from statistical methods and accountancy techniques (of various types) a degree of technical competence in the products or services of the firm will probably also be needed, as well as above the average satisfactory relationships with the guardians of these data in the firm.

An opposite view[2] and one which experience would indicate to be more valid is that: 'It is surprising, considering how many records exist in the accountancy and other departments of the company, that so little effort is made to make use of these records for the purpose of marketing research. Perhaps this situation exists because it is not always easy to obtain the internal data for analysis purposes.

Even when free access is assured, the information is very often available only in a form which makes it unusable to the research team. They must, therefore, transform it for their own purposes and this can take a long time and need considerable effort. Whether the effort is invariably worthwhile depends upon the skill of the research team in extracting the vital information in the shortest possible time.

For internal records a competent statistician is a necessity. Statistics is the art of comparison. One figure does not mean anything at all. Only when it is brought into contact with another figure does it come to life and often reveals a most interesting and important story. One of the characteristics of a good marketing researcher is that he can see trends and correlations where the layman sees only a forest of figures and that he has the skill of showing these connections in a form which is easily understood and recognised.'

In advocating the use of internal research and analysis and other types of secondary research for industrial marketing research pro-

[1] H. W. Boyd and R. Westfall, *Marketing Research: Text and Cases*, Irwin (Homewood, Illinois, 1964), p. 252.

[2] 'Industrial Marketing Research—Techniques', *Marketing of Industrial Products*, op. cit., pp. 72–3.

jects, it should not be presumed that these types of activity alone will provide all the answers required in any particular research enquiry. In only the most unusual circumstance will any one technique produce all the data required. The results derived from secondary research will therefore generally represent one research input, or will provide control or regulatory data for the survey. In the case of market size investigations, internal research for example can possibly only reveal the lower limits of the market, its segmentations (and then by no means all of them) and possibly throw some light on its configurations. But combined with data derived from, say, input-output analysis, it can easily reveal areas where greater penetration is possible with high profit yield or conversely where additional penetration will only be obtained at a sacrifice of profitability. For these and other reasons, secondary research of any type should no more be considered in isolation than field research should be undertaken prior to the completion of secondary information examination.

INTERNAL DATA

A most useful source of secondary data is usually provided by the firm's own records. For marketing research purposes, however, existing records often need radical adjustment to make them useful. The difference between ad hoc and continuous research is highlighted by the need, the cost and the usefulness of adjusting business information for the purpose of marketing research. It is rare that a firm's records or its record-keeping methods can be altered economically to meet the needs of a single project. Where continuous marketing research is carried out, however, a case can be made for new methods of obtaining the relevant marketing statistics by using the record-keeping activities of the firm. From the compilation of such new statistical material, information can be obtained for other projects which will serve the firm well on future occasions.

Comparative statistics of production, sales and overhead costs are typical examples of information to be found within the internal records of most firms. It is common practice, in large businesses at least, to maintain detailed statistics for the purposes of control of all forms of marketing expenses, production costs and occupational and administrative overheads. Data for marginal costing exercises, for example, can be used in other ways than pure cost accountancy—ways which produce additional meaningful information for the marketing researcher.

However, stating that internal data exists, or can be derived from the records of the company, in no way solves the problem of obtaining access to it. There is in many firms a reluctance to reveal, even to the firm's own staff, information when its direct relevance to the enquirer cannot be understood or established; divisions and departments in companies tend to be autonomous and resent enquiries by personnel from outside the section concerned; staff specialists such as accountants, surveyors and costing clerks frequently resist any attempt to wrest information from them or to adjust their information collection or retrieval systems for purposes not immediately applicable to their activities.

The easiest and most efficient way of assuring access to internal data is to commence the project with agreement by the sponsor that these data will be made available to the researcher. This can be obtained relatively easily at the initiation stage but is much more difficult to achieve towards the end of a project. That this should be so is easy to understand. Many sponsors unsure of themselves in an industrial marketing research *milieu* will use their known internal and validated data as control material to check the accuracy of the research. Thus if their own sales are kept a secret they can then compare these against the market size offered by the researcher which cannot by definition be smaller than the company's own achievement. Faced with either an unnecessary research cost to obtain information already known by the sponsor or a refusal by the researchers to begin the work without important internal information, most sponsors can be brought to see that their attitude is likely to prove as expensive to the firm as it is futile.

If the request for information is left to the end of a survey the sponsor may well remark, with some truth, that if the researcher has managed to acquire information without the internal data, then it would be useful to check this against the knowledge within the firm since no additional research cost is involved.

In order to see what types of internal data can be successfully used in an industrial marketing research project, it is better to consider the wealth of material inside most firms from the point of view of the analyses which can be accomplished with the raw data. These analyses, which are now considered, fall into five groups: (a) sales analyses, (b) ratios, (c) correlations, (d) historical trends, (e) actuarial methods.

(a) *Sales analyses*

Useful internal information can be derived from an analysis of sales records. Data from this source are capable of providing a considerable volume of facts needed for marketing research and in the smaller firm it is frequently the only source of information. An organisation's own sales figures are the raw materials of sales analyses. These figures generally exist in a form capable of being assimilated easily. Analytical work of the type needed to process internal sales records does not call for a very high level of technical skill and can often be delegated with a minimum amount of supervision. For this and other reasons sales analyses can be both the cheapest and one of the most effective elements in a marketing research study.

The first activity in any marketing research project is defining the nature of the problem. Sales analysis used at this early stage can make a very considerable contribution to the enquiry as it can be instrumental in reducing the magnitude and thus the cost of external research.

Sales data classified in various ways provides management with information on sales accomplishments. Sales volume is one of the most important marketing factors affecting profits. Three other important determinants of profits earned by the marketing effort are—gross margins yielded by sales, expenditure incurred in selling and sales promotion. For planning research and future marketing operations, thorough-going sales analysis fulfils an important but often neglected function.

The main types of analyses which can be extracted from internal sales records are—geographical division of sales, industrial (by classifications) division of sales, sales by size of order, sales by type and size of customers, sales by type of product, seasonal sales, sales by order source or type, costs per sale, the most profitable sections of the business, the economics of small orders and shipments, evaluation of the impact of external events and internal adjustments and an analysis of complaints. Each of these admits of a separate analysis and will produce answers to problems affecting various facets of the research.

Some firms regard all record keeping, financial and statistical, as a function of accountancy because there is a confusion between the accountant's and the statistician's use of figures. This is quite wrong except in the rare case where the accountant has also made a study of statistics. There is very little common ground between accountancy and internal marketing research, and in order to keep both departments running smoothly, while it is essential that they should liase, they should not overlap.

(b) *Ratios*

One technique of marketing research, particularly in the industrial field, is the use of criteria as measures of performance. The establishment of appropriate criteria is a frequent objective in research and in many instances the only form of reliable measurement available to the researcher. These criteria can be established by the use of percentages or of time ratios. Their use enables a standard of performance to be empirically established and, in many industries, allows the production of indices of efficiency for the industry as a whole to be constructed. On this basis it is sometimes possible to quantify a market and its segments by projecting internally generated data.

The following have been suggested as being the most important ratios that can be established within a firm. Financial marketing ratios—those which though of a financial nature have a direct bearing on the marketing and sales functions of a business. For example: *stock-turn*, the relationship between sales and stock normally held; *capital-turnover*, the relationship between net sales and total investment; *profit per pound invested*, the relationship of earnings and every pound of investment; *fixed assets*, the relationship between fixed assets and total investment; *gross margin*, the relationship between the cost of sales and total net sales.

Cost ratios—profit is directly related to costs and one of the most important functions of managements is to control costs. There are certain ratios which can be established as representing standards of cost for a business. These are: cost of goods per sales pound; profit per sales pound; direct selling costs; general overhead expenses; publicity costs; physical distribution costs; and total operating costs.

Studies of ratio-analyses have isolated over 400 ratios and suggests the development of others for the specific use of firms.[1] There is little doubt that the all too frequently unrelated mass of facts and figures drawn from companies' operations can be made to reveal important data for marketing research.

A major contribution to ratio analysis is the publication of *Business Ratios*[2] by Dun & Bradstreet. *Business Ratios* provides a regular series of main statistical indices of business performance

[1] Spencer A. Tucker, *Successful Management by Ratio Analysis*, McGraw-Hill (New York, 1961), and *Efficiency Comparisons With Large Organisations*, British Institute of Management and the Centre for Interfirm Comparisons (London, 1962).

[2]*Business Ratios*. Published three times a year by Dun & Bradstreet and Moodies Services (London).

derived partly from published accounts and partly generated by the Dun & Bradstreet group. These are presented as means, upper quartiles and lower quartiles of the major industrial groups from 1963 onwards. The indices can be compared with each other, with similar indices for individual firms and with those of equivalent industry groups in other countries.

(c) *Correlations*

The use of correlation techniques is most frequently a post-survey function rather than one carried out at the first stages of internal research. Nevertheless in some circumstances such an analysis is possible and desirable. For example, in attempting to forecast equipment expenditure it is possible to make use of such known variables as can be obtained from the Census of Production and relate them to the experience of the firm. Knowledge of one variable leads to more accurate estimates of a second variable than is otherwise possible.

Correlation analysis is thus a method of measuring the relationship between two or more variables, the analysis indicating whether or not a relationship exists, the degree of relationship, time relationships and the reliability and thus the practicability of the relationship for the purpose of forecasting.

For example, the demand for capital goods and their constituents is dependent upon confidence of their buyers in the prospects for their profitable use, upon the buying power of business enterprises and upon the availability and cost of credit. These factors together reflect the general business climate but the degree to which industrial goods expenditure is dependent upon them varies considerably; hence correlations between industrial goods expenditure and gross national product, for example, are not in themselves necessarily meaningful.

Given a lack of direct relationships it is still possible to make use of other indices in selected parts of the economy which, roughly, tend to correlate with the incoming orders to an industry and possibly in some instances to the firm. Examples of this are investment expenditure of nationalised industries, steel production, motor vehicle production, machine tool orders, demand for artificial fibres, defence spending, stocks and sales of radio and television equipment, output of chemicals, agricultural production and subsidies. All these provide means of determining the economic outlook for a firm's industrial products which may be related to these markets. In addition to these specific indicators, there are also indices of prices, stocks, employment, wages and note issues—to mention some of the more important.

The inter-relationship of consumer goods and industrial goods demand can be most clearly seen when correlation analysis techniques are examined. Rapidly changing consumer concepts of leisure are impacting heavily on some services such as the cinema and garages. These in turn are leading through the chain of derived demand (see Figure 1) to a diminution or stimulation of the demand for the goods which these consumer services require. A coarse correlation exists between the fall in cinema admissions and the demand for cinema furniture and equipment. Similarly a correlation can be seen between the growth in vehicle ownership (in turn correlated with socio-economic groupings and income growth) and the demand for partial or full diagnostic vehicle testing services.

There is certainly no alchemist's stone capable of transmuting official or other statistics into a comprehensive index that will yield dependable relationships. A particular relationship is based on economic and social conditions and is subject to change over a period of time. Relationships can be real, spurious or coincidental. The work of the researcher is to establish which of the relationships are dependable and not to reject correlation techniques because they are not all-embracing or always reliable.

(d) *Historical trends*

It is an oft-repeated censure that many economic predictions are based on nothing more than extrapolations of an historical curve. If extrapolation were the only method of making business forecasts, the censure would be deserved. The faulty or limited use of historical trends does not, however, mean that they are useless or without significance. Indeed much valuable material can be obtained from a perusal of the historical statistics of a firm for investigating marketing problems and preparing long-range forecasts, provided the investigations and forecasts are not based solely upon these statistics. The use of historical trends are not a substitute for training, judgement and experience which modify and adjust the story emerging from the records. Besides historical records, knowledge of the firm, the industry and the factors underlying general economic conditions are the ingredients of accurate marketing investigations and forecasting.

Historical trends do, however, tell a story and for the marketing researcher an important one. Their usefulness is nevertheless restricted to long-term planning because margins of error inherent in such projections can be disastrous if used for the day-to-day operations of a firm. Two important conclusions that can emerge from a study of a company's records over a number of years are long-term growth trends and cyclical business fluctuations. Capital expenditure, calculated at constant prices, related to historical growth trends and to gross national product data to determine the present position of the capital goods industries, is a good example of the correct use of this type of material in a marketing research study.

(e) *Actuarial methods*

The analysis of company records using actuarial methods can also provide marketing research data. This method attempts to apply the techniques used in predicting human life expectancies to the problem of life expectancy of physical equipment in order to arrive at more accurate estimates of a replacement market. Applications for this method of analysis are limited to certain types of products and to specific circumstances; for example where, historically, firms have manufactured a significant proportion of the total replacement of their own equipment and where the sales task is essentially one of meeting a replacement market, and therefore they have accurate knowledge of the product's performance under specified operating conditions.

There are, of course, limitations to the application of actuarial methods to equipment life which have been discussed in Chapter 1, 'Characteristics of Industrial and Consumer Markets'. Nonetheless, if the internal information is available, and always bearing in mind that purchases of equipment can be deferred and that replacement can be either for scrapped or down-graded original equipment, important inferences can be drawn. Once a 'life expectancy table' for equipment has been constructed, specific replacement rates can be computed and applied to units of existing equipment in different age groups; this then makes it possible to forecast the extent of probable replacements (due to deterioration and obsolescence) over a period. It is also possible to use the 'life expectancy table' together with returned guarantee cards and maintenance and repair records to determine volume of replacement and level of stocks of equipment —for example a stable stock, that is when a given age of distribution of equipment is maintained, or a stationary stock, that is a stock where removals are balanced by replacements.

The National Institute of Economic and Social Research has carried out and published valuable studies on the life of capital goods and another contribution to the use of actuarial techniques are the surveys on the age of machine tools. Apart from the value to the machine tool and related industries themselves, these exercises also enable marketing researchers developing actuarial techniques to check their validity and to adjust them for even greater accuracy. A volume of information on 'life expectancies' and 'actual lives' of a wider range of industrial goods would bring the actuarial techniques into the prominence they deserve in marketing research and provide many firms with an effective and inexpensive method of obtaining reliable material for forecasting levels of demand.

The examination of these analytical approaches has sought to indicate their relevance to internal research. It should not be thought that they are inapplicable to data generated externally to the firm. A fuller discussion of analytical methods will be found in Chapters 11, 'Processing the Data', and 13, 'Industrial Marketing Research as an Aid to Forecasting'.

USE OF EXTERNAL SOURCES

It would be a remarkable firm in which it was possible to pursue all secondary research internally. Inevitably the researcher will need to consult external secondary sources if only to visit specialised libraries from which material cannot be borrowed. The number of external providers of information, like the sources themselves, are myriad. In each survey it will be necessary to identify the appropriate and relevant contacts.

The majority of industrial marketing research enquiries will be in the domain of commercial information so that it is possible to list a number of generally used sources.

OFFICIAL SOURCES

Library research may or may not include the examination of government publications which represent an important and often the only authoritative source of information. In the United Kingdom H.M.S.O. is a storehouse of information on an extraordinarily wide range of subjects. An index of H.M.S.O. publications is issued annually and provides a complete guide to the material available. In this will be found such invaluable information sources as Monopolies Commission reports, Restrictive Trade Practices Court reports, White Papers and *Hansard*, which can contribute not only to the factual armoury that industrial marketing research calls for, but also enables the researcher to acquire rapidly the feeling and mystique of the technical, commercial and political background of an industry, a firm or even a product.

Publications by international organisations and foreign governments have a considerable relevance to research matters both overseas and within the United Kingdom. Many researchers have, for example, noted a frequent similarity between West German statistical data and that of the United Kingdom which in turn has led to some accurate deductions concerning United Kingdom markets which are not officially documented.

The fact that such comparisons can be made, as in this example with West Germany, stems not only from parallel circumstances in the manufacturing and user industries but also because of basic economic similarities. West Germany is 96,000 square miles. The United Kingdom 94,000. The population in 1965 in the United Kingdom was just over 54·5m., in West Germany 59m. The average income per head in both countries was £517 in 1965. The proportion of gross domestic product supplied by manufacturing industry, agricultural and services are approximately the same in both countries.

Studies of American exports of diesel engines to Latin America provide another example of the use of data provided by an overseas government to determine salient factors about a market.

The work of such organisations as the European Productivity Agency, World Health Organisation, Organisation for European Co-operation and International Monetary Fund will be familiar to most researchers. Less well-known are the publications of, for example, the U.S. Department of Commerce and the U.S. Small Business Administration which cover a very wide range of subjects, often in considerable depth.

At local government level such ubiquitous information sources as rating and valuation lists, reports and minutes of local and area planning, health, education, finance and other committees can all provide valuable information. Statutory reports of other authorities, for example police, fire service, weights and measures inspectors and many others are frequently very revealing in their content.

SEMI-OFFICIAL SOURCES

Falling just outside the sphere of government are the important sources that lie between government and trade and professional association data—these might be termed semi-official sources. There cannot be many researchers who are not aware of the work of the

National Institute of Economic and Social Research. Similarly the activities and reports of the British Standards Institution are well-publicised and well documented.

Within the group of semi-official sources might be included research reports and information provided by the universities and bodies such as Industrial and Commercial Finance Corporation and the National Research and Development Corporation. Reports of public corporations and authorities, particularly concerning investment plans, are obvious examples of useful data with application to a considerable area of industrial research. More important perhaps, many of these organisations—the Gas and Electricity Councils for example—will have their own research departments which in turn will be able to direct researchers to information sources relevant to the industries, or to provide data on a researcher-to-researcher basis which may require no further processing.

TRADE ASSOCIATIONS

For far too long, but perhaps with some justification, trade associations have been accused of obstruction and unnecessary secrecy in their dealings with outside organisations and researchers. Adam Smith's dictum that 'People of the same trade seldom meet together even for merriment and diversions but the conversation ends in a conspiracy against the public or in some contrivance to raise prices' sums up the public image of trade associations. There are, however, associations which undertake research for use by their members and which encourage a more enlightened approach to research enquiries.

'Trade associations have an essential role to play as regards both the circulation of information on European markets and the sponsoring and financing of basic surveys. Only collective action can provide small and medium-sized firms with an opportunity to study the possibilities offered by the new European markets.'[1]

Unfortunately, while it is true that Trade Associations 'have an essential role' in relation to research, it is also often abrogated in favour of government or else, at best, as an internal service for members only. Tapping into trade association information can be difficult if not impossible and yet when the data they so rigorously attempt to hide is examined, it will often be found that it can be

[1] *Market Research on A European Scale*, Organisation for European Economic Co-operation (Paris, June 1960), p. 9.

obtained by other methods. All of these alternative methods will be far more expensive and most will incur duplication of previous work which is a drain on the economy and an irritation to respondents. For example the British Compressed Air Society collect and publish total sales figures which are available only to their members. This information can, however, be obtained with equal accuracy by the use of normal industrial marketing research techniques. The figure of £41·8m. for the sale of air compressors in 1965 may be regarded as a high-level secret by members of that association but it is common knowledge to anyone who has researched the field.

Now that price agreements, the *raison d'être* of many trade associations in the past, are comparatively rare, a new and enlightened attitude to the provision of trade statistics and other data is developing. Such an attitude will yield far greater advantage to their members than most associations have yet comprehended, for example, by providing control and comparative data both within their industry and inter-industry.

Despite the difficulties and obscurantist attitudes adopted by some associations, they can nevertheless prove to be among the most valuable sources of secondary information. The principal problem is to know of and locate the work that has been done by them and then, of course, to obtain access to it. However, even if no printed data are available, discussions with trade association officers can provide valuable general information or they may make helpful suggestions as to sources—especially regarding their members —who have information on the subject of the researcher's enquiries.

SCIENTIFIC AND TECHNICAL RESEARCH ASSOCIATIONS

Whereas it is possible to be in two minds as to the usefulness of trade associations in industrial marketing research, there can be no doubts about the value of scientific and technical associations. Invariably within these organisations there will be information on the latest development in the industries concerned and, since they are very practical organisations, information will frequently embrace related commercial matters.

There are several types of research organisation to be considered. Government research organisations such as the Building Research Station and Tropical Products Institute; Grant-aided Research Associations, partly financed by public funds and partly by subscriptions from members, for example the British Cast Iron Research Association and the Rubber and Plastics Research Association; industry research associations not supported by public funds such as the Institute of Brewing; development associations—usually formed to sponsor members' products, the Aluminium Development Association and Natural Rubber Producers' Research Association are typical examples; private organisations undertaking sponsored (commissioned) research such as International Research and Development Ltd.; private research by firms with their own R and D departments; university research which is largely paid for by public funds from various sources and sometimes by industry or individual firms, for example the Gas Chromatography programme at Birmingham University.

Most of the organisations of the types listed will make information freely available. Research wholly financed by public funds, other than Defence and other classified material, is available to researchers as of right. Thus enquiries covering the work of the Water Pollution Research Laboratory will bring answers to any questions within their capability. Grant-aided research is available only to members of the association but officials are always helpful on a *quid pro quo* basis. Most university research results are published eventually, either as theses or reports. Development Association research findings are usually freely available since the objective of the associations is to give a wider knowledge of their products and a greater utilisation. Needless to say, it is not easy to obtain access to private and privately sponsored research although, as with many other aspects of industrial marketing research, much can be gained by informal discussions and exchanges of information.

The bulk of the information which can be obtained from scientific and technical research associations will be concerned with developments in the field of interest of the associations. Its major use to industrial marketing researchers will be to provide an insight into technical developments in the industries involved and to assist in identifying emergent threats and opportunities caused by technical changes. These data are needed to provide 'best judgement' to modify the quantitative factors of a forecast. It may be relatively simple to forecast vehicle population but forecasting the share of the total vehicle population of 1985 held by the electric car will depend upon obtaining information on technical factors concerning not only the development of the car itself but also of the batteries to power it. Typically it is here that technical research associations can guide the researcher in his assessment. A classified list of technical research organisations of all types and the category of research conducted forms a most useful source book.[1]

PRIVATE RESEARCH ORGANISATIONS

Not usually regarded as likely sources of information, marketing research organisations of other firms in an industry can be of value. Between firms as well as within industries, information is exchanged, particularly when there is a reciprocal basis for so doing. The wealth of material in the archives of companies' market research organisations and departments is difficult to obtain acess to and it is not always ethical to do so. If access can be obtained and there is no breach of the normal professional standards of marketing research practice, there is little doubt that this particular source of secondary information can be of very great value, both in the collection of facts and in pointing the direction of further research or contacts.

So far as marketing research agencies are concerned, few will refuse information which they are at liberty to give to an enquirer because there is every chance the agency will in its lifetime want to obtain information from the enquirer's firm. Agencies above all should give freely of their knowledge since it is they who most frequently request such facilities from industry.

There are, however, other bodies besides agencies providing research facilities which are often invaluable sources of information. High on this list will be research officers and departments of Banks, Stockbrokers, Foreign Governments in Britain, Chambers of Commerce and Trade, Trade Unions, political parties and insurance companies.

TRADE PAPERS

Articles from trade and professional journals can contribute to most research enquiries. The main problem here is eliminating inevitable duplication caused by highly competitive publishing within each trade. For example, currently in Great Britain there are twenty-nine journals covering electronics, twenty-three chemicals and forty textiles.

The trade press staff are generally well informed on conditions and circumstances within their own trades. In addition to providing quick references to information which has actually appeared in their papers,

---

[1] *Industrial Research in Britain*, Harrap (London, 1964).

they can also give other useful leads on the subject desired, or refer a researcher to well-informed persons within the trade. The degree of co-operation given by trade papers to researchers is always high and it is a rare editorial or technical department that is not prepared to spend some time in assisting research enquiries. In addition, many trade papers maintain their own research departments and some publish valuable reports on various aspects of the industries they cover. A further facility is that a comprehensive index of the contents of journals often exists.

COMPANY REPORTS AND INVESTMENT PLANS

Company reports taken in conjunction with reports which appear from time to time from other sources, such as the *Board of Trade Journal*, trade associations, professional bodies, trade and professional journals, government departments, official and private research organisations and ad hoc or periodic reviews of intended investment plans of firms or industries, can provide valuable information for forecasting. While announced investment plans are only suggestive of the course of economic activity, evidence indicates that their use in industrial marketing research, and in forecasting in particular, is meaningful. It is particularly helpful in relation to capital goods if only because of the long-range programmes which must be prepared for investment in many types of plant and equipment.

It is not suggested that company or industry investment plans can be used as a substitute for other factors responsible for the level of capital investment—such as the total demand for goods and services, public works programmes, tax structures, the economic outlook or long-term growth trends. What is suggested is that the intention to install much plant and equipment does, by the nature of the long manufacturing cycle of the plant or equipment, require the placing of firm orders well in advance of requirements. These purchases, once committed, are unlikely to alter appreciably—except under the impact of violent economic changes leading to significant shifts in sales and profit prospects or in the cost of finance. In this last respect because of the lead time—that is the delay between placing orders and their delivery—next year's economic conditions are not, for many industrial product items, indicative of next year's orders.

H

OTHER SOURCES

In this miscellaneous group are such publications as directories, manuals, year books, handbooks and exhibition catalogues, firms' catalogues and advertising material. Even out-of-date directories can produce useful information, for example business mortality rates and withdrawals from trades.

An example of information stemming from a study of sales literature is given by certain sections of the storage equipment trade. A survey of the catalogues of the main firms indicated quite clearly that sales organisations were based on agency selling and that the division of sales area followed a repetitive and geographically distinctive pattern giving a vital clue to market locations. This same literature, in almost every instance, included lists of well-known firms who were customers, thus providing reliable indications of important user industries. The converse—an indication of the industries in which the product being investigated was not currently acceptable—was of equal value in directing sales and promotional effort.

USE OF LIBRARIES

Whether from internal or external sources, bibliographical research is the backbone of secondary information sources. It is from such research that the published information available from libraries, trade and professional papers, government sources, trade associations and others, is derived.

It is usual, but not always imperative, to study these types of secondary information sources at the beginning of a research project, to enable them to be assembled for the researchers. This step is often taken while the work plan is being devised, or else at the initiation stage when the allocation of resources, the division of the project and the timing is being decided. Bibliographical research—or 'library research'—is one of the most neglected activities in industrial marketing research. It is difficult to understand why this should be so since it is one of the cheapest of all research techniques when used in an orderly and planned way. Research activity of every sort is expensive in both money and time. It is always wasteful to repeat work done elsewhere. Without knowledge of information sources, duplication and repetition are inevitable.

Facilities for bibliographical research are plentiful, and accessible to the smallest firm. In the principal population centres in the United Kingdom there are well-endowed public reference facilities.

Through the operation of the Library Association schemes the most esoteric published works are brought to researchers in a matter of days and sometimes hours. Subject specialisation by libraries and the co-operative purchasing of books are well developed so that even small local public libraries have rapid access to the specialised collections within regional or larger groups which also often include university libraries.

Commercial libraries, such as those operated by many Chambers of Commerce, Trade Associations, Universities, Technical Colleges and Institutes are available to members and can also often be used by non-members on application.

More important, perhaps, are the highly specialised private libraries which many firms have built up to cover their own areas of interest. Such libraries frequently include indexed newspaper cuttings, a source of information rarely available elsewhere. Access to these libraries is not open to everyone but it is often possible to use their facilities either through personal contact or by the offer of reciprocal facilities. It is certainly true that many firms are proud of the completeness of their libraries and are delighted to extend facilities to outside researchers, be they independent research agencies, non-competing or even rival firms.

Bibliographical research should not be sparked off by a single research enquiry but should be a continuous programme of scrutiny of material likely to be useful for current and future programmes. Clearly an appreciation of what is likely to be useful and what is merely interesting is needed, and the smaller the research department or firm, or the more widespread its activities, the greater the necessity to discipline the squirrel mentality of hoarding in the hope that 'it might come in useful'.

SOURCE SOURCES

Because of the vast range of bibliographical material available to researchers, attempts have been made to provide a single reference book for information sources. Many of these efforts have been defeated by poor classification and thus difficult retrieval and their mechanics are often more complex than the normal search for the sources. The only suitable approach for bibliographical research guidance is to relate the guides themselves to at least broad subject headings. Thus, although now much out of date, Kendall's *Sources and Nature of the Statistics of the U.K.* was a thorough and monumental coverage of statistical sources.

Perhaps the best source of sources available are four small books but which synthesise the very considerable experience of their authors and which deserve a place on every researcher's shelf.[1] They are in fact far more valuable than many directories and other reference books so often found on library shelves since source sources are required more frequently than any individual directory. Indeed one of the most valuable things a researcher can do is to build up such lists for bibliographical research. Care must be taken, however, that these are not more complex than the data they purport to lead to. Above all retrieval must be simple and quick.

The diversity of sources can nowhere be better appreciated than by an examination of the literature on information sources such as those already referred to. These books pinpoint sources which themselves have their own source books. For example, Bagley[2] refers to the use of Abstracting Services, details of which can be found in lists in Ulrich's *International Periodicals Directory*.

ASLIB AND OTHER SERVICES

The wealth of material available creates its own problem in terms of deciding how much time can be devoted to the secondary information searches. Fortunately some corners can be cut by services available either on a membership or fee-paying basis. By far the most important of these are those provided by ASLIB (Association of Special Libraries and Information Bureaux). Its command of specialised information on scientific, industrial and commercial matters is unrivalled. Membership of ASLIB gives access to the information services. On receipt of an enquiry from a member, ASLIB will provide a list of reference sources drawn from a huge range of books and periodicals. Obviously the more tightly defined the enquiry the better the response will be. The purpose of the service is to locate sources—the researcher must obtain his information from these and not expect ASLIB to answer the research enquiry.

In addition to locating sources ASLIB will arrange the loan of books from other libraries and specialised collections, provide translations and translators. Its publications include its directory of

---

[1] D. E. Davinson, *Commercial Information—A Source Handbook*, Pergamon (London, 1963). W. A. Bagley, *Facts and How to Find Them*, Pitman (London, 1962). R. J. P. Carey, *Finding and Using Technical Information*, Edward Arnold (London, 1966). B. Houghton, *Technical Information Sources*, Bingley (London, 1967).

[2] *Facts and How to Find Them*, op. cit., p. 66.

specialised subject library collections and their locations, and an index of theses accepted for higher degrees in Universities in Great Britain and Ireland.

An important lead to information sources is the Library Association's *British Technology Index* which is a monthly publication indexing about 400 journals under an extremely wide classification system. Using the index it is possible to identify in a matter of minutes the most recent publication of information under any particular heading. An annual cumulative volume enables the researcher to save a considerable amount of time tracing older publications and information.

Far more comprehensive and therefore that much more time-consuming to use is the *British National Bibliography*. The Bibliography has listed each work published which has been lodged at the Copyright Office of the British Museum under the Copyright Act of 1956. These publications include documents of any type available to the public, that is books, pamphlets, reports, first issues of new periodicals and also local and central government publications. Publication of the Bibliography is weekly and cumulative volumes appear at three monthly, yearly and again five yearly intervals.

Another service of inestimable value to researchers is that provided by the non-profit European Long Range Planning Service of the Stanford Research Institute, Zürich, Switzerland. Subscribers to this service, apart from receiving the large number of technical, commercial and planning reports, have access to a most comprehensive information service which, as well as locating sources of information on any given subject, as does ASLIB in the United Kingdom, also provides copies of publications and provides direct answers to questions which ASLIB does not.

There are also many commercial services available to subscribers, Moody's Industries and Commodities service; Exchange Telegraph Company's daily statistical service; Bradstreet's *Register of Commercial Credit Ratings* lists details of over 170,000 firms broken down by region. This register can provide a most useful and accurate source for filling sampling frames. *Daily List of New Companies* describes its function in its title.

There are many services providing information specifically for individual industries. For example, *Industrial Daily News* gives details of calls for tenders and contracts let in the building and civil engineering field.

ABSTRACTING SERVICES

The vast amount of available material makes abstracting services of particular value to many researchers. These are short summaries containing all the salient points of articles from periodicals. Some are published as regular features in periodicals, while others are published separately in what are usually termed 'abstracts journals'. Most abstracts also provide full details of the publication they are drawn from to assist in location of the entire article or book, should the reader require it. The majority of abstracts are scientific or technical, although some business ones are available, for example *Management Extracts* published by the British Institute of Management.

CLIPPINGS

It is possible to devise a type of personal abstracting service by subscribing to a newspaper clipping agency. These agencies, given a subject heading, will peruse a very wide range of British and foreign journals and cut any feature or reference to the subject, sending the original or photocopy to the subscriber. The service is not cheap but will often pay for itself by providing items which might otherwise be missed. However the services do not operate satisfactorily on an *ad hoc* basis and require continuous operation to achieve any degree of efficiency. Moreover, the readers are not skilled abstracters and cannot always identify with accuracy what would be of interest to the subscriber. For example, it would be unrealistic to expect an agency to distinguish references to consumer marketing research from those of industrial marketing research. Further, although many remote and esoteric items are located in obscure journals, it is not unknown for a leader page feature of a national paper to be missed. Nevertheless, while recognising the drawbacks of clipping services they can still save considerable research time.

OBTAINING THE INFORMATION

Having located sources of information the problem still presents itself of obtaining the actual reference. So far as books are concerned, most can be obtained from the public library services either from within their own resources or through the special library schemes which most public libraries participate in. The ASLIB Directory gives full details of the special resources of British libraries of all types and therefore can guide the enquirer straight to the most likely place where a book can be obtained.

Journals are rather more difficult to obtain, particularly if back numbers are not available or the researcher does not wish to purchase them. Most journals can, however, be obtained by a postal loan service organised by the National Lending Library for Science and Technology, Boston Spa. Here literature from all over the world is collected—over half a million volumes being available currently. The main function of the library is to lend to other libraries. The cost is as little as £4 for 50 loans or £10 for 50 photocopies of features. The services of the National Lending Library can be obtained directly through firms' libraries or the public library service.

A STANDARD OPERATING PROCEDURE

Faced with the many sources of information, a considerable loss of time is likely to ensue in using the material unless some logical sequence is adopted. Clearly the 'logic' of any system will be related to the research objectives. It is possible, however, without suggesting that any one operating procedure will fit all circumstances, to suggest a sequence of research which will in most circumstances provide a quick and efficient way through the sources available. The research steps and associated secondary information are given below in the form of a check list.

- Establish the subject area(s):
  Define the product, market and other areas to be included in the standard search. Identify the relevant Standard Industrial Classification (S.I.C.) numbers.
  Determine possible main topics and sub-topics which may be pertinent in searching the various literature indexes.
  Make use of research design and client data (if any) and expand the definitions if the remainder of the literature search indicates it to be necessary.

- Review internal files for information already collected:
  Contact internal personnel familiar with subject under investigation.
  Scan titles and contents of previous reports.
  Scan library subject index.
  Scan newspaper and cuttings files.

● Gather information on important manufacturers' product lines:
  Review buyers' guides and trade directories, establish manu-
  facturers' and relevant product lines.
  Send for product catalogues and obtain price lists.
  If appropriate examine manufacturers' advertising in recent
  technical journals. Obtain appropriation details from *The
  Statistical Review of Press and TV Advertising.*
  Obtain annual reports of competitors which are public
  companies.
  Obtain status reports on companies which are private com-
  panies.
  Scan *Board of Trade Journal* reports for investment plans.
  If needed, obtain Moody's or Extel Card and stockbroker
  reports.
  Look up company affiliations in *Who Owns Whom.*

  Following the competitor search a list should be drawn up
  showing for each firm:
  Number of employees.
  Assets.
  Profit record.
  Turnover.
  Names of directors (if required).
  Affiliations.
  Product range manufactured.

● Determine periodical reference sources and review their
  published information:
  Identify appropriate articles in periodicals through indexes
  and by scanning recent issues of periodicals if not covered
  by an index. Use:
  (a) *British Technology Index.*
  (b) Research Index.
  (c) ASLIB.
  (d) Stanford Research Institute Long Range Planning
      Reports.
  (e) Individual trade journal indexes.
  Review identified articles and obtain copies from the National
  Lending Library for Science and Technology.

● Review Government and official and semi-official publications
  including the following. (Note: often more detailed analyses of

Government figures are available for a small charge.) Initial ones include:

Census of Production.
Census of Distribution.
Monthly Digest of Statistics.
Annual Abstract of Statistics.
National Income and Expenditure.
Overseas Trade Accounts of the United Kingdom.
National Institute Economic Review.
National Economic Development Office Reports.
Monopolies Commission Reports and Restrictive Practices Court Hearings.
British Standards Institution Reports.
United Nations reports and statistics.
International Monetary Fund reports and statistics.
Organisation for Economic and Commercial Development (O.E.C.D.) reports and statistics.
Nationalised Industries: Annual Reports.

● Obtain and review industry surveys that are pertinent:
Moody's Industries and Commodities Service.
Business Monitor (Board of Trade).

● Contact sources of additional quantitative and qualitative information. The intent here is to obtain published information and literature—personal interviews with associations and magazines and others are considered part of the field research and should not take place at this point.

Trade Associations (*Directory of British Associations*).
Trade Publications (*Newspaper Press Directory*).
Export and import information (Customs and Excise, Embassies, Trade Commissioners, foreign Chambers of Commerce).
Board of Trade market intelligence library (especially overseas statistics).
Companies House (company information).
ASLIB's *Directory of Specialised Libraries.*
Bank reviews.
Technical or Commercial Research Organisations (*Industrial Research in Britain*).
H.M.S.O. (all government publications).
Political parties (reports).

Trade unions (Research Departments).
Professional Associations (Technical Libraries).

● Compile lists of names, addresses and telephone numbers of users, suppliers to competitors, distributors and professional advisors (e.g. architects, insurance companies, etc.). If all addresses are in one or two directories simplify identify directories and make sure a copy is available. If addresses are to be compiled from several sources this should be done at this stage. Geographical factors should be watched. See Trade and business general and specialised directories, e.g. Dun & Bradstreet *Guide to Key British Enterprises;* Dun & Bradstreet *Middle Market Directory; Kompass;* Kelly's *Directory of Manufacturers and Merchants; Basic Sales Grid—U.K.*

CHAPTER 6

Sampling in Industrial Markets

Sampling in industrial and consumer marketing research is the process of selecting the respondents to be interviewed or otherwise contacted, or the phenomenon to be observed. The purpose is to ensure that those selected are representative of the entire universe to be measured and that the information is obtained from as small a number as possible consistent with reasonable accuracy. Thus a sample in marketing research terms has precisely the same meaning as in everyday parlance. In other words, just as a sample of material or a product is taken to be typical of the whole of the material or the product line, so in the same way a true sample would be a miniature of the whole population (not necessarily human) or universe being surveyed.

It is perhaps in sampling procedures where the greatest and most fundamental divergence occurs between consumer and industrial marketing research. As will have become obvious from the comparative examination of these markets in Chapter 1, the composition of an industrial market or segment is essentially different in its characteristics from a consumer market.

UNIVERSE CHARACTERISTICS

In simplest terms the majority of industrial markets can be described as pyramidical. That is the companies which compose a market or segment will tend both to have a skew distribution in terms of turnover and to comprise different strata of information sources. At the top of the pyramid in a typical market may be a very limited number of material or component suppliers whose aggregated output correlates in some way with the output of the researched product. Beneath this will be a few manufacturers of the actual product being researched whose output less exports plus imports represents the total home market. Beneath them, now in larger numbers, could be a stratum of original equipment manufacturers purchasing the specified product and incorporating it in their own products, thus permitting another correlation. Down still further there could be a substantial number of distributors or other intermediaries handling the items which incorporate the researched product. Beneath them again there may be yet another group purchasing and installing products in the premises of the actual users. Next come the actual users of the product, by now running into large numbers and finally, the users of the product or services of the previous group. Such a pattern, of course, is unlikely to apply to any one good but the market pyramid may be composed of several of these strata and indeed the last stratum might well start another cycle. Diagramatically the position might be shown thus:

ONE FACE OF THE MARKET PYRAMID

COMPONENT OR MATERIAL SUPPLIERS

MANUFACTURERS OF ACTUAL PRODUCT

ORIGINAL EQUIPMENT MANUFACTURERS

DISTRIBUTORS OF ORIGINAL EQUIPMENT

INSTALLERS OF ORIGINAL EQUIPMENT

USERS OF ORIGINAL EQUIPMENT

THEIR CUSTOMERS

Fig. 9

ONE FACE OF THE MARKET PYRAMID

An actual pyramid for indicating instruments is shown in Figure 10.

The second dimension of the pyramid is the distribution of turnover among firms comprising each strata. As a generalisation it will be found that most industry patterns conform to what has been termed the '80-20' rule. That is, 80 per cent of turnover is transacted by 20 per cent of firms within an industry; 80 per cent of demand is accounted for by 20 per cent of customers; 80 per cent of sales are concentrated on 20 per cent of the range offered. In statistical terms this conforms to a Lorenz curve. Typical industries where the 80-20 rule will be found to apply are building supplies, electric motors, adhesive tapes, machinery rollers and hydraulic jacks.

Yet a third dimension is provided by geographic clustering caused by certain industries and activities being linked to an area historically or by virtue of restricted sources of energy, labour or raw materials or markets. Examples abound: cotton textiles, shipbuilding, fishing, whisky distilling.

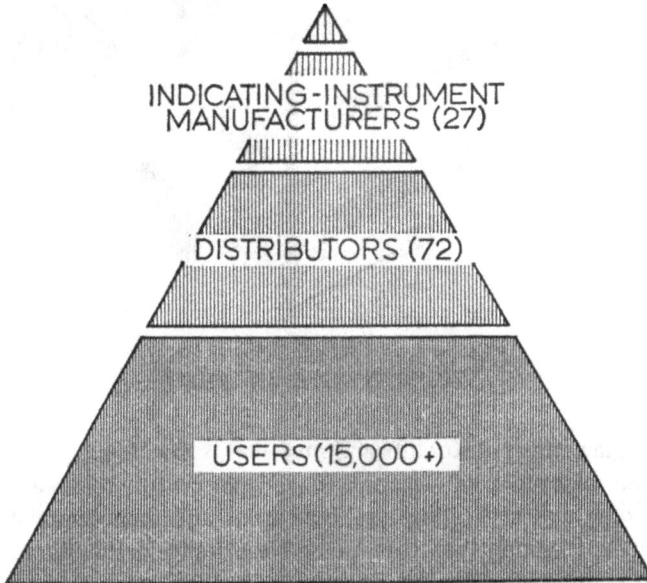

MARKET PYRAMID - INDICATING INSTRUMENTS

SUSPENSION SUPPLIERS (4)

INDICATING-INSTRUMENT MANUFACTURERS (27)

DISTRIBUTORS (72)

USERS (15,000+)

Fig. 10
MARKET PYRAMID—INDICATING INSTRUMENTS

The various faces of the pyramid and the segments which compose it are illustrated in Figure 11. The front face of the pyramid shows the various strata illustrated in Figures 9 and 10 but this time the 80-20 rule is illustrated with each stratum broken up to show 80 per cent of firms control only 20 per cent of the market. The second face which comprises the regional clusters illustrates that the 80-20 rule in general terms will also apply to the regional clustering.

Because of low populations in certain industries and in certain strata, it is often possible to take a complete census of that industry or stratum or to take a census of the important units within the stratum and then sample the remainder. For example, in the mecha-

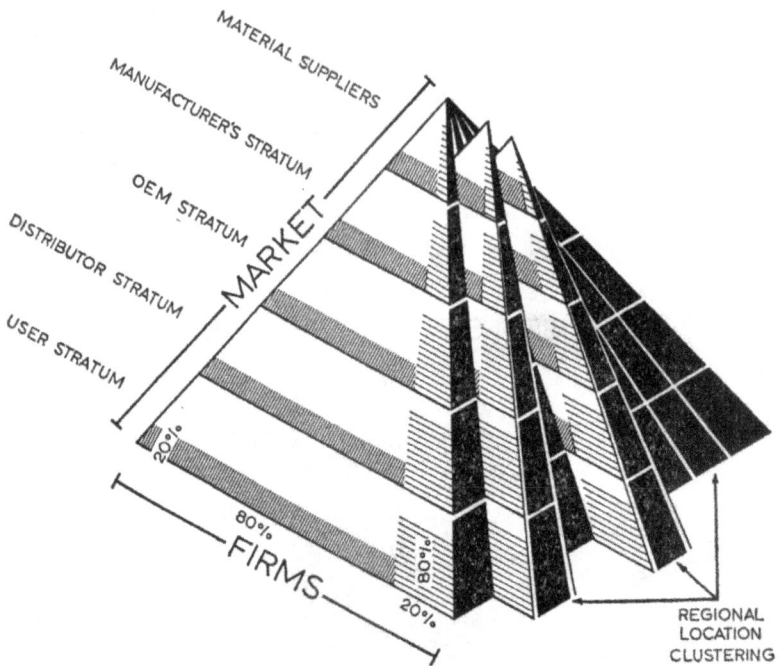

Fig. 11
THE MARKET PYRAMID

nical engineering industry fifteen firms—that is less than 1 per cent of the total of over 4,000—account for 35 per cent of total sales. By identifying and separating out these firms and then sampling the remainder it assures that there are no large 'lumps' left in the residue which might distort the final results. A hundred per cent coverage of the leading firms is thus included within the total sample.

There is no gainsaying, however, that selecting a universe comprising an arbitrarily selected upper stratum appears to preclude any possibility of constructing an unbiased total sample. Accepting that a representative sample, in the consumer research sense, cannot be drawn, the technique of varying the sample fraction based upon size assessment can be incorporated into the sample design to produce results far more meaningful than would otherwise be possible.

Virtually each universe for industrial marketing research sampling is divided between two major strata, that requiring hundred per cent coverage and the stratum for sampling in the more accepted sense of the word. The results suitably weighted, combined and projected have been shown to produce an answer that is both reliable and within an acceptable degree of accuracy for the purpose of the majority of research projects.

A negative example is apposite. A survey of the use of industrial gases in South Wales given even a 95 per cent response from a census (not a sample) could still be highly inaccurate if Steel Company of Wales were in the 5 per cent of non-respondents. Their consumption of industrial gases in this geographic area alone accounts for a very substantial part of the total.

Thus it can be said that a major part of any sampling process in the industrial field is to identify the significant firms first to ensure the typicality of the sample group or, to put it another way, to extract the untypical from the universe using whatever criteria are required to decide on untypicality—e.g. size, location, use of re-searched products or services.

SAMPLING TYPES AND METHODS

A sample, however, remains a microcosm and the likelihood of it having exactly the same characteristics as the population being surveyed cannot be assured. At best it can be said that a sample is accurate within certain limits. There is a bewildering array of sampling methods but the two basic concepts from which they all stem are probability and non-probability designs.

According to statistical theory, a sample should be so drawn that every element in the whole has a known positive chance of appearing. Knowledge of the probability of each element's selection permits the probability to be calculated of the results being correct, within stated limits, as an estimate for the universe from which the sample is drawn.

But if each unit has an equal or known chance of being selected the opposite is also true—that it has an equal chance of *not* appearing. To continue with the example already quoted of Steel Company of Wales and industrial gas consumption, in a universe of industrial gas consumers SCOW represents one unit and may or may not on a probability basis be selected. Its omission, however, will distort the survey to the extent of making the quantitative results relating to consumption meaningless because in an industrial market, unlike a consumer market, each unit is not equal. The lack of equality can stem from many reasons: size, consumption, possession of certain types of equipment, geographical location, form of organisation and others. The untypical units in a universe must be identified before sampling can be carried out.

This situation is typical of an industrial market and emphasises the importance of non-probability sampling. A non-probability or 'quota' sample is a form of sampling which depends upon the stratification of the sample in terms of certain known characteristics of the universe. It is an attempt to secure equal representation by dividing the universe into more homogeneous segments than the aggregate, selecting units at random from each of those strata and combining them to form a total sample.

'The crucial issues in stratified sampling are dividing the population into appropriate strata and obtaining accurate information as to the distribution of the relevant characteristics in the population (though random selection within strata is still of major importance).'[1]

Within these two main sampling approaches there exists a range of alternative methods which require consideration in deciding on the sampling method for a survey. These sub-methods can best be considered in tabular form[2] and are shown in Figure 12.

The groupings and methods listed are by no means mutually exclusive and a combination of two or more methods would be both permissible and commonplace in many types of studies.

Unfortunately, nomenclature in sampling is by no means standardised and it is possible to become confused by varying titles for the same methodology. Even the basic concept of non-probability can be described with several names, 'quota', 'qualitative', 'judgement', 'purposive', 'controlled' are just a few of a wide selection. The only way to avoid confusion is to compare the various definitions given to these and other titles by their authors and to work to the definitions rather than the titles.

It is possible to theorise at considerable length on sampling methods and to argue about the use and relative accuracy of probability and quota samples and on a methodology for using them. No hard and fast rules can be made which would be applicable in every case and indeed which would yield identically accurate results in similar cases. Before a decision can be made on the optimum sampling technique other factors besides that of the sample design have to be considered and these considerations weighed against the research parameters.

DEFINING AND IDENTIFYING THE UNIVERSE

Throughout an industrial marketing research study it is necessary to define objectives; the research objective, the questionnaire objec-

[1] Robert Ferber, *Market Research*, McGraw-Hill (New York, 1949), p. 71.

[2] The tabulation is partly based upon the analysis contained in J. F. Rummel's and W. C. Ballaine's *Research Methodology in Business*, Harper & Row (New York, 1963), pp. 68-77.

tive, the interview objective and many others. Not the least important where sampling exercises are involved is the sampling objective. By sampling objective is meant the definition of the purpose of the sample and from this the definition of the universe to be studied. This is a fundamental exercise on which the validity of the survey largely depends.

In consumer research it is often only a question of studying published demographic and other material to both define and locate the universe to be studied. In industrial research the opposite is true. Industrial boundaries are rarely clearcut and in any event many firms are often active in several different industrial classifications at once. It is not, on consideration, a simple task to allocate a Standard Industrial Classification for ICI. Although chemicals obviously come to mind first, the output of that vast industrial complex crosses many boundaries and the same is true for the giant 'electrical' firms. Even the administrative and organisational pattern of a firm adds to the confusion. The large industrial holdings companies might be regarded as providers of financial services but equally they might be said to be engaged in the activities of their many subsidiary companies.

Thus if the problem is to determine the demand for vitreous enamel pipes it is first necessary to establish whether research will be conducted among buyers (that is construction companies), or purchasing influences (that is architects and consulting engineers), or end-user specifiers (that is local authorities, estate developers, river boards and sewage authorities), or suppliers (that is firms actually making the pipes). These are all fairly simple and homogeneous groups.

When, however, a universe is defined as 'the electrical industry' it may be difficult to draw a line where that industry ends and the electronics industry begins or, using another example, where the electronics industry ends and the optical industry begins. Obviously the more homogeneous the universe defined, the sounder will be the sampling base because at least one source of error is reduced.

An example will illustrate both the point and a methodology. A survey was required to establish the level of demand for an industrial overall leasing service in the food processing industry in the Registrar General's Midland Standard Region among firms employing more than 100 people. 'Firms employing more than 100 people in the Midland Standard region in the food processing industry' is a tight, homogenous definition.

In order to establish the size of the universe, the total number of

I

Sample Type	Sample Method	Description
PROBABILITY	Random	Every unit in the universe surveyed has an equal (or known) chance of inclusion.
	Systematic	A sample interval (every nth element) is chosen which will yield a predetermined percentage of the entire roster.
	Stratified	Predetermined number of samples drawn at random from defined stratum, each domain or sub-sample being treated as if it were the population itself for the purpose of random sampling.
	Area	Samples drawn to be representative of selected geographical areas.
	Multi-stage	The population is regarded as a number of first stage units each of which comprise second stage and later stage units. The second stage frames are drawn only from those units selected from the first stage.
NON-PROBABILITY QUALITATIVE	Purposive	Identification of controls as representative characteristics. Selection of units with control characteristics proportionate to the total number of cases with which such characteristics appear in the universe.
	Quota	Using purposive sample controls a quota of cases are selected bearing each of several predetermined characteristics.
	Multi-phase	Information is collected from an original sample then from segments of the original sample. (Note in *multi-phase* sampling the sample microcosm are units of the same type—in *multi-stage* sampling the units are of different types at different stages.)
	Replicated	Two or more sets of sample units are selected from the same population.

Fig. 12

SAMPLING METHODS

Lottery method. A list is made of all units or elements in the universe and the numbers are assigned to each unit consecutively. The numbers are then put on slips of paper or 'chips' of equal size, mixed thoroughly and drawn. (Technically speaking the randomness is lost since after each 'chip' is withdrawn the chances of the remaining chips being drawn are improved. For practical purposes, however, the method can be considered unbiased.)

Random numbers. All units in the universe are numbered serially so that each has the same number of digits. A table of random numbers (which is constructed so that any digit from 0 to 9 has an equal chance to appear in any given position in the table) is used by selecting any point in the table and then reading off consecutive numbers in any direction. The numbers read indicate the assigned numbers of each case to be selected for the sample.

From the microcosm one (k) is drawn at random. Then counting from k every nth (fixed interval) is drawn for the sample.

Different sampling methods may be required for different stratum, once the stratum have been selected.

Each sample area, say *countries*—England, Ireland, Scotland, Wales—is broken down into block areas, say Registrar General's Standard Regions, North Midland, Midland, London and South East. A random sample is drawn of these regions to divide them into segments, say *local authority areas*—Salford, Hanley, Camden—and another random sub-sample is drawn of these segments.

Stratification and proportionate sampling can be used at any stage.

It is usual to develop a master design in which the number of cases with the 'control' characteristics to be selected as a sample is proportionate to the total number of such cases with such characteristics in the total population. Weighting can be applied to particular strata of interest for which the sample size may be increased proportionate to strata of less known importance.

Researcher is given freedom to select, within a proportioned quota, units with predetermined characteristics.

Information from the second sample is usually collected at a later time than the original sample and the samples are usually selected on the basis of information obtained in the first phase.

Data from each sample is collected by different researchers and analysis made to determine whether any differences between the samples were significant because of differences between investigators.

persons employed in the industry in the selected region had to be extracted from the Summary Tables of the Census of Production. These tables provide detailed information by Standard Industrial Classification (S.I.C.) order and minimum sub-headings giving stratification for the United Kingdom as a whole and in the Standard Regions.

Accurate information as to the required breakdowns was also obtained from a build-up by Standard Region of the Ministry of Labour records. However, an estimate of the numbers of firms and employment was derived by simple percentage calculations for each region on the assumption that, although the employment patterns and structure of industries by size of firm varies between industries, little variation would be found within one industry in these respects between the various regions selected for the survey. The confidence levels required by the terms of the survey permitted the application of the national situation to the regional position. This was done and estimates made of the establishments employing over 100 persons by S.I.C. in the Standard Region selected.

These estimates were further qualified by calculations of the number of operatives (as opposed to administrative and clerical personnel) employed, based on information in the Census of Production Summary.

One further issue in relation to establishing universes requires consideration; that is the time dimension. A universe may not remain valid for the same project at different moments in time. In an attempt to estimate an industry's capacity—say pre-formed concrete kerbs and flags—it is possible to aggregate the total number of installed machines and to estimate the extent of their usage. Any quantification derived from this exercise may have no relationship to the following or previous years when acquisitions, closures, rationalisation, proliferation or any other industrial/commercial phenomena might have occurred and changed the total market picture.

Clearly unless the 'universe' is defined and established with accuracy, the likelihood of the sample being accurate is remote and fortuitous. Thus in any sampling exercise the first task is to probe the characteristics of the 'universe' before any discussion on sampling method and size occurs.

CONSTRUCTING THE SAMPLING FRAME

Two approaches can be used for constructing the sampling frame. These are formalised and sequential framing.

Formal framing leads to the assembly of a complete list frame, that is, complete in the sense of a turnover or other significant criteria, of each unit in the frame in terms of the product or service researched. Only in this way can a properly stratified sample be drawn which does justice to the turnover distribution characteristics. However, for the moment at least and until companies must perforce give information on their turnover, to generate the information on which to construct the frame is likely to take the entire research appropriation, if it is possible at all.

Sequential framing permits the researcher to start the field work without any preliminary frame knowledge, choosing his respondents in an entirely pragmatical way; perhaps the largest respondents or the most co-operative, and include in the interviewing some questions on market structure. By evaluating this secondary information with the insight and knowledge of the project, the researcher can progressively adapt his sample to the market structure as it is gradually revealed. This procedure generates a kind of self-building sampling process, much in the way a jigsaw puzzle is put together.

The choice between the two techniques will depend upon the circumstances surrounding the research project and the configurations of the markets. There is little doubt that the formalised framing is more efficient but also more time consuming than sequential framing. Moreover, when many types of companies must make an annual declaration of turnover, as will be the case when the legislation concerning company activities comes into effect, it will also be more practical to carry out formal framing. For the present at least it is difficult to use in the majority of markets.

Sequential framing exposes the researcher to more methodological risks but is quicker and produces good samples provided all pointing and gauging information is thoroughly cross checked.

'The sequential method carries the specific risk of deteriorating into a time honoured method of industrial marketing research, that is pumping friends and talkative insiders without putting the information obtained in a wider frame of reference. Some journalists operate in this way, they cover various sources regardless of bias, looking down their noses at statistical reliability and validity. Against this journalist type of researcher has been pitted the die-hard statistician type who distrusts the "latticework" of unclassifiable information and insists upon quantified measures of accurate information as is good practice in advanced consumer research.

The danger of this state of affairs is that an artificial controversy is created. Indeed industrial market populations usually fall apart in a sparsely populated top group of large enterprises which require a personal approach and densely populated tail group of small enterprises of which buying behaviour can only be measured statistically.

A stratified sampling plan is called for, coupled to a differentiated form of approach; in sampling the statistician's viewpoint must prevail (since only he can guarantee the statistical generalisation of results), whereas in the method of approach the journalist's technique is worth consideration.'[1]

FILLING THE SAMPLING FRAME

The esoteric problem in industrial marketing research sampling is essentially the difficulty of identifying the microcosm of the sample. In consumer research a number of important fundamental questions are answered even before the respondent has spoken; certain facts are known—sex and approximate age, whether he or she is a house or flat dweller, and his or her probable income group or social class. In addition marital status and ownership of certain products can often be ascertained by observation. In the industrial microcosm the most basic facts may be difficult or impossible to ascertain. 'J. Smith & Co. (Engineers) Ltd.' on the sign or in a directory and an outer waiting-room can give no indication, or the wrong indication, of the type of activity carried on, the size of the firm, the type of equipment it is using or any other important facts needed to fit the firm into the sampling frame. Indeed even such basic information items as these may themselves require intensive research to establish.

Other important facts often needed for an industrial sample refer to the extent and nature of use of the products which are the subject of the enquiry and which must necessarily involve a wide variability between firms. The differences that do exist may stem from the fact that firms are within different industries but also from the fact that even within firms in the same industry technical experience and manufacturing practices differ widely.

Summarising the work of a study group on sampling in industrial market research, it was stated: '. . . one of the most difficult problems of sampling in industrial market research is to develop the knowledge, use and usefulness of published sampling frames.'[2]

Almost all books on market research give as the basic source for filling sampling frames directories of one type or another. Certainly

[1] Co de Konig, 'Effective Techniques of Industrial Market Research', *Journal of Marketing Research* (Chicago, April 1964).

[2] Max K. Adler, *Sampling in Industrial Market Research*, an unpublished paper (London, 1966).

experience would indicate that this is the most common source, perhaps because it is also the easiest one to obtain access to. There is no doubt that directories are not only most frequently likely to provide the best basis for filling sampling frames but they may often be the only method available. However, as with internal analyses, reliable and accurate sources can be generated from within a firm and represent a valuable market research asset inasmuch as they are not immediately accessible to other companies.

There is no virtue in attempting to list where information for sampling frame filling can be obtained as each survey will tend to be of the 'one off' variety and will also tend to need a frame specially constructed for it. Directory lists can be easily obtained from many sources[1] but most directories suffer from the usual deficiency of being out of date before they are in print.

Once a familiarity is obtained with the appropriate directories the researcher will find a profitable investment of his time would be to consider other sources, both internal and external to the firm. Internally: returned guarantee cards, shareholders' lists, abortive quotation lists, complaints and servicing records are, without being specific, the types which can be considered. Externally: application for various types of licenses (to store petroleum and other inflammable materials, road hauliers' licenses); registrations (employment agencies, certain types of retail establishments such as chiropody, pet shops); planning permission applications; publications under statutory notice; rating lists and membership of professional and trade groups are among the more obvious sources. It is possible, however, to develop unique sources. Unfortunately pressures on researchers are often too great to permit them time to research into areas from which they can obtain information for frame filling. Indeed the Paper previously referred to did not, despite its depth and coverage, reveal what might be termed a 'novel' sampling source although the contributors included the leading experts on sampling.

An industrial marketing research agency tends to generate a wide-ranging list of sample sources for the varied assignments they undertake. Within a firm concentrating its research efforts along fairly narrow channels there is every justification for spending time and money investigating sampling frames specific to their needs. The investment cannot fail to yield a satisfactory result.

A word is necessary on purchased lists. That is the lists provided by specialist firms or list brokers, usually direct mail houses, who

[1] G. P. Henderson, *Current British Directories*, C.B.D. Research (London, 1967), is quite the best single guide to directories.

can offer 'packaged' groups. For example, 18,515 architects, 3,500 publishers, 200,000 company directors. The complete list of groups runs to many pages. As a quick and simple way of filling a frame it has much to commend it. However, there are major drawbacks and for the marketing researcher often the ones which eliminate the possibility of using these lists. The groups offered are rarely more than 'block' groups. There are, after all, many ways of categorising architects, publishers and company directors. Moreover, there is every chance that the lists will have originally been drawn from directories so that they can be no more accurate than their sources and often less accurate because of transcription errors and erosion.

So far as mailing houses are concerned a third and very important deficiency is the fact that the original lists will not be given to the researcher; they remain the property of the mailing house. Thus apart from having to take the accuracy of the listing and mailing on trust, it is not possible to code for identity, compare respondents with non-respondents or to check for duplication, eliminations or use other refining processes.

The most frequently used sources for filling sampling frames in the United Kingdom are:

> *Guide to Key British Enterprise*
> *British Middle Market Directory.*
> *Kompass Register.*
> Classified Telephone Directories.
> Kelly's *Directory of Manufacturers and Merchants.*

Within certain industries some directories will take prior position over the general directories listed. For example, for metalworking Rylands directory and for the textile industry, Skinner's *Cotton and Man-made Fibres Directory of the World.*

Trade Association membership lists contain many dangerous omissions. There are 170 members of the Textile Machine and Accessories Manufacturers Association listed but the Census of Production shows 686 firms active in this industry. The British Federation of Master Printers has 4,000 members but there are 9,400 firms in the printing and publishing industry. While it is true the Association may represent the bulk of the industry on a volume basis (a claim usually made but not always substantiated), it is hazardous to an extreme to attempt to fill a sampling frame from what is basically a sub-section of the industry. Both randomness and accurate stratification are at risk.

A further discussion on sources will be found in Chapter 5.

THE SELF-SELECTED SAMPLE

In Chapter 7 on postal questionnaires, a reference is made to the risk of 'self-selected' samples, that is returns from companies who have replied because of a common characteristic which makes them untypical of the non-respondents. This danger can on occasions be turned to good account by devising a survey in which the sample will in fact select itself. For example, using a multi-stage approach and a short simple questionnaire, almost certainly by post, to obtain a large number of wide-ranging contacts, the first stage can be the self-selection process. A simple identification question will divide users from non-users and also a third group, potential users. The user group can then be taken as the second stage. Non-response bias is, of course, inherent and becomes more intense at each stage, but this problem can be attacked by both the use of other techniques (for example telephoning a sub-sample of non-respondents) and other sampling approaches.

ERRORS IN SAMPLING

All sampling investigations are subject to experimental error. Careful consideration of the sample design and frame filling keeps the errors to a minimum but no sampling investigation can give a result, except in terms of probability. It is the order of probability which must be decided. The confidence which can be extended to final results depends both on the magnitude of the interfering effects and on the sample size.[1]

The words 'accuracy' and 'precision' are often used rather loosely and interchangeably but there are important differences between the two concepts. Accuracy means freedom from error; precision refers to the reproducibility of the sample results. That is, if many samples of the same size were taken from the same population by the same methods the consistency of the results obtained from the various samples would indicate the precision of that particular result based on samples of this type.

Statistical Sampling Errors

'The statistical "sampling error" of probability sample results is often mistakenly used as a measure of accuracy. Actually it is virtually

[1] M. J. Moroney, *Facts from Figures*, Pelican (London, Revised Edition, 1965), p. 123.

impossible to measure the accuracy of sample results whether probability samples or not.'[1]

Statistical sample errors have been classified into two groups. First inherent sampling error. This cannot be avoided but it can be measured and controlled at a tolerable level of known risk by probability design. Thus while a certain percentage of samples of a given design will lead to wrong conclusions about the population, the analyst must rely on the low probability of occurrence of such aberrant samples and act on the assumption that his particular sample is not one of them.

Second, errors of procedure. In practice these are more serious than the inherent sampling error. If they are part of the design they tend to occur in all samples which that design yields. In effect the difference between the target population and the population actually sampled is an error of procedure. Poor field work which is an error in execution, not design, will lead to inconsistent biases that are hard to allow for. Elaborate control procedures can minimise errors in execution.

Non-response is the most important source of errors arising in procedure. Contact with the target sample using personal interview techniques rarely reaches 90 per cent and by telephone techniques 75 per cent might be considered a good response. For postal questionnaires 50 per cent is likely to be a good average response. In these cases the companies actually sampled will only be reasonably similar to the target population if the factors accounting for non-response have no influence on the subject studied. How probable this is depends entirely upon the sample itself, the market, the product or service and the questions.

There are several methods of reducing non-response errors, the first prerequisite being to establish that an error exists at all and then, if it does, identifying its cause. In this respect very often the experience and records of the research sponsor will provide an accurate body of control data for comparisons to be made.

A check list for dealing with the problem of non-response can systematise the approach to the problem:

● Classification of cause of non-response:
    not available
    correct respondent not identifiable
    establishment moved

[1] Thomas T. Semon, Reuben Cohen, Samuel B. Richmond and J. Stevens Stock, 'Sampling in Market Research', *Marketing Research—Principles and Readings*, Parker M. Holmes (Ed.), South Western Publishing Company (Cincinnati, 1966), p. 299.

       company or unit ceased to exist
       change of company activity.

● Pre-stratification of samples based on stratified sampling frames immediately offer some basic data about non-respondents. Clustering of non-response can be significant.

● Post-stratification based on data collected during those contacts at which partial information was obtained (e.g. reasons for refusing interview).

● Development of check questions which provide an implicit answer to basic questions (e.g. information on operating experience can lead straight to an accurate deduction of the make of installed machines).

● Attempt to re-interview. It is frequently possible to obtain contact and information by change of respondent. Thus a refusal by a design engineer to provide data might be overcome by first establishing the composition of the decision-making unit and then interviewing others in it. (In the study *How British Industry Buys*, this technique was found to be highly successful.)

Non-response in industrial samples is much more likely to stem from refusal than failed contacts. This means that call-back is not a technique often open to the researcher to adopt but it also means that weighting for non-contacts on a time and recall basis is not necessary. In these circumstances it is once again important to return to the possibility of using a different approach to obtain the information sought. One worth adopting is to confine enquiries with 'refused interview' contacts to seeking reasons for refusal to be interviewed than to provide data on the subject under review. Most respondents in the 'refused interview' group are more than willing to give the reason for not wishing to be interviewed—mostly as a personal justification for apparent discourtesy. This opportunity should not be lost.

A survey of the market for galvanised iron tanks produced a high refusal rate among fabricators. Investigation of the reason for refusal revealed that the price agreement in the industry had been referred to the restrictive trade practices court and members of the trade assocation had been unofficially advised that while the matter was *sub judice* no discussion of their markets, prices and practices should take place. The significant differences between respondents and non-respondent fabricators was, in fact, membership of the price ring, an important fact for the researcher.

Non-statistical Sampling Errors

Awareness of sources of error is important in sampling if the extent of the error is to be measured or at least assessed. It is, however, important to distinguish errors which arise from faulty sampling and those which stem from poor questionnaire design, faulty coding, tabulation, miscommunication, poor field work and any other aspects of research. The research chain is as strong as its weakest link and it does not matter where in the project that link is placed.

Errors in sampling occur as often from non-statistical sources as from statistical sources. These can be identified in seven groups:

* errors in criteria used to measure the phenomenon being studied.
* errors in identification and classification of the universe from which the sample is to be drawn.
* errors in identification of the correct respondent within the selected firms—that is correct in the sense that he has the requisite knowledge, responsibility and authority to speak for the firm.
* time biases—that is changes occurring between the first measurement and the final analysis.
* errors of computation and grossing up errors.
* measurement errors (incorrect information given by respondents).
* non-response.

As an example of incorrect identification of respondents, a common and often undetected error is that the respondent company may be carefully selected to meet the sampling criteria and the respondent himself identified as the correct member of the DMU but he may well be talking of his experience derived from work in another company which slots into another stratum of the sample. This is a problem of role perception[1] and thus interviewing technique.

Each of these aspects is dealt with in the appropriate places of the book. The inter-relationship of methodology with the actual application and the control of the techniques to be used is illustrated by the fact that these same problems can be identified in desk research, field work, analysis and presentation of the research results.

[1] An individual's or group's interpretation of their own or other's role in a specific situation. In an industrial marketing research situation a typical example might be whether a respondent regards himself as answering for his department, his firm or even his industry, or whether the interviewer is seeking information or assessing the respondent's performance.

SIZE OF SAMPLES

Given that a census can be taken in some of the industrial stratum or that the sample fraction can be high, it nevertheless still leaves high populations with a small degree of homogeneity. For example, such segments as users of polythene film, retail shops, diesel engine users and vehicle fleet operators. Some industrial groups can be very large indeed. There are, for example, 4,061 firms classified as mechanical engineers, all of whom might very well be buyers of lubricating oil; 507,000 retail shops, any of which could use window lighting control units; and 6,643 printers and publishers with a potential requirement for ink. Assuming size, rather than activity or equipment owned, to be the criteria, then when the largest 15 mechanical engineering firms which account for 35 per cent of mechanical engineering activity, the largest 200 chain store operators with 10 per cent of the nation's shops and the largest twenty-five printers and publishers turning out 20 per cent of total print requirement have been removed, this still leaves populations of 4,064, and 506,800 and 6,618. True enough these can be re-stratified again by the significant criteria or by region but by any standards the universe remains large.

How then is size of sample to be judged? It is easy to say the sample should be adequate and representative, but those are both meaningless and pious expressions. It is only slightly more helpful to say that sample size depends partly on the objectives of the study and partly on the nature of the universe to be studied.

The amount of variation which can be attributed to chance elements varies inversely as the square root of the number of cases drawn in the sample. In two samples, one of which is four times the size of the other, it would be expected that the sampling error—if all other error sources were held constant—would in the larger sample be only half of that in the smaller sample. It follows logically from this that the greater the heterogenity of the universe in regard to the characteristics being investigated, the larger the sample must be to give an acceptable degree of accuracy. It is possible to apply sample error formulae if there is some prior information on the universe being studied.

The ingredients of the 'mix' in deciding sample size are:

The extent to which the individual units are representative of the universe (local authorities of similar size and responsibilities are homogeneous; retailers heterogenous).

The inclusiveness of the sample.

Types of groups involved.

Number of categories of data required.

Method of analysis of data.

The size of the sample must be large enough to permit a valid analysis of the sub-samples used in the smallest breakdown of data to be made. In practice it must be considerably larger because this rule ignores the fact that there will not be 100 per cent response from any sample. Thus if the expected yield is 50 per cent response the sample will require to be double that which would suffice in statistical terms.

One authority has suggested that the minimum 'rule of thumb' number for a sub-sample analysis must be twenty-five to thirty. 'Thus the minimum number for each small breakdown could be multiplied by the number of sub-categories of breakdowns and this product could be multiplied by the number of categories and so on for an estimate of the total sample. However, this process assumes that a random selection of cases in each sub-category will be uniform throughout the population—an assumption that does not hold for many human characteristics of populations. Probably the researcher should plan for a size of sample much larger than this process would indicate to ensure a satisfactory number of cases in the smallest category.'[1]

There is a danger, however, of being bemused by sample sizes. The truth of the statement that a large sample is better than a small one, other things being equal, is accepted without question. However, other things, least of all in industrial marketing research, are rarely equal. The key consideration is sample error rather than sample size as the criterion for sample accuracy. 'That is in fact substitution of reality for a symbol, since, to the extent that sample size is important at all, it is important for its effect upon sampling error. The concept of sampling error as a criterion of sample adequacy is in fact easier to grasp than the concept of sample size.'[2] A sample is required which will resemble the (unknown) population and the sampling error is a direct measure of the extent to which the sample result is likely to differ from the population.

One way of determining if enough cases have been obtained is to keep a record of the answers to selected questions, making cumulative tabulations as the replies are received. When the proportion answer-

[1] *Research Methodology in Business*, op. cit., p. 68.
[2] Eli S. Marks, 'The Fetish of Sample Size', a paper read to the American Association for Public Opinion Research in Berkeley, California, May 1961.

ing in a specific way tends to stabilise, there is a fairly clear indication that the number has become adequate in respect of size.

In the following example[1] the question was: 'Who is most likely to initiate a project leading to new equipment purchases for expansion of capacity?' The table shows the per cent answering that Boards were most likely to initiate such a project.

Table 1

STABILITY CHECK

Cumulative number of cases (respondents to questionnaire)	Respondents saying Board is the most likely to initiate a project leading to new equipment purchased for expansion of capacity %
100	71
200	64
300	62
400	65
500	63
600	63
700	64
800	63
900	63
924	63

Only minor variations occur once a total of 500 cases has been reached. If only an answer to this one question had been desired, the research could have stopped after 500 replies had been received. However, the additional questionnaires permitted the analysis of the data by various sub-samples and for this reason the additional cases were valuable.

SAMPLING LIMITATIONS

The deficiencies of industrial marketing research sampling have been neither understated nor overestimated; they are just facts to consider. There are other problems than those stemming from the difficulties of obtaining data on the sample. Firms are an agglomeration of individuals and it is individuals who are respondents, not the corporate

[1] *How British Industry Buys*, op. cit., p. 93.

bodies they represent. Location of the right person both in terms of job definition and possession of authority to speak for the firm is important and difficult. A consumer respondent is never (or ought never to be) asked to speak for anyone but herself or her family. An industrial respondent speaks for his firm, his department, his job function, possibly even his industry and last but by no means least, for himself. These varying representational loyalties in a spokesman can often be conflicting.

Another obstacle, it has already been pointed out, stems from industrial definitions. Even if the Standard Industrial Classification were more precise than it is, firms do not always indicate their classification and, in many cases, are involved in several activities simultaneously which are covered by different classifications. Only a few industries tend, traditionally, to have single function activities.

The census approach to the sampling problem which can be adopted when small stratum exist has its own special limitations. Contradictory as it may sound, it could be possible for the sample to be larger than the universe to obtain accuracy. A typical case where this could occur is where there is a high substitution factor. Some therapeutic effects can be achieved both by pharmacological means and by the use of electronics. A census of major pharmaceutical firms in the particular field will not reveal the realistic market situation.

There is the eternal problem that dogs the majority of researchers in the natural and physical sciences, just as much as in marketing—that of conflicting or irreconcilable information. To validate or invalidate conflicting information too often would lead the researcher down byways which can make relatively little contribution to the final accuracy of the results; yet the sample must be constructed upon reliable data.

Because of the characteristics of industrial markets, the emphasis tends to be largely upon qualitative aspects of research—rather than quantitative—so far as sampling and projections are concerned. This is not to imply that quantitative significance cannot be adequately represented to show major tendencies within markets. Sampling techniques, despite the deficiencies shown, can still produce a reliable guide to market dimensions, structure and trends. They cannot produce absolute figures, except in the most unusual circumstances. The researcher should therefore be cautioned not only in his use of sampling techniques but in the conclusions to be drawn from their results.

A number of authoritative studies[1] of sampling techniques exist

[1] See Bibliography p. 389.

and have established themselves as standard works on the subject so that it is fortunately no longer necessary to provide a full discussion of sampling theory in a book devoted to industrial marketing research, of which sampling represents only a small part. Sampling is certainly one of the most complex sectors of marketing research and warrants the concentration and specialisation which many writers have devoted to it. Within the framework of this book comment has been limited to those aspects of sampling which clearly constitute the basic tools for the industrial marketing researcher. Where sampling is concerned the marketing researcher will tend to be a general practitioner and not a specialist.

K

CHAPTER 7

The Postal Questionnaire

The first of the field techniques to be considered is the postal questionnaire. It is one of the most frequently used methods of industrial
marketing research because everyone believes they can conduct a
postal survey, and the price of failure is thought to be relatively low.
There is, however, more skill in postal surveys than their apparent
simplicity suggests. Although, for example, the actual construction
of the questionnaire obviously requires expertise, less obvious but
nevertheless requiring equal skill is the actual format of the questionnaire, a vital factor determining the success or failure of a postal
survey.

Postal questionnaires can never be used successfully without an
understanding of their inherent advantages and disadvantages. In
order to decide when the use of a questionnaire is appropriate, these
should be considered and weighed against each other and the alternatives available.

ADVANTAGES

Economy is generally regarded as the dominant advantage of the
postal questionnaire. This is certainly true on a material and postage
basis which is approximately £50 per thousand questionnaires despatched plus researchers' time. But as already illustrated in Chapter 4
'Preparing for the Project', the real figure must be taken against the
rate of valid responses. If there is only a 10 per cent response then the
material and postage costs alone rise to £500 per thousand or
approximately 10s. per valid response. A second benchmark for
assessing economy is the information yield. Even with a 25 per cent
or higher response the cost per valid reply may still not be economic
if the numbers of questions answered is perhaps only three or four
and the validity of the answers cannot be established. Thus pure
mechanical costs are not necessarily a good guide to the economy
of the technique.

Nevertheless, the postal questionnaire can be a low cost research method and, with certain provisos, economy can safely be regarded as one of its advantages. Within wide limits, geographical dispersal of the sample does not affect the cost of a postal survey. There is, therefore, a far greater likelihood of the sample being representative than if cost considerations limit the geographical area of operation.

A further advantage is that certain types of respondents who might normally be difficult to interview can be induced to reply. For example, export sales managers involved in a heavy travelling schedule, maintenance and service engineers who cannot be called from the plant to see interviewers and executives not prepared to become involved with an interviewer for any length of time, are often willing to answer a few questions at a moment convenient to themselves.

When questions cannot be answered without consultation with others or without reference to records, a mail questionnaire gives the respondent the opportunity to obtain the information if he so chooses. Ill-considered replies are often avoided by this method.

The presence, particularly the silent presence, of the interviewer will often induce a quick reply or reaction when a more carefully considered answer is required. The postal questionnaire enables the respondent to move at his own pace.

A postal questionnaire can, if so phrased and laid-out, offer complete anonymity to the respondent—something which cannot be obtained in personal or telephone interviewing. This anonymity does not prevent some degree of identification detail being secured since questionnaires can be grouped according to Standard Industrial Classification or other codings which are frequently sufficient to provide information on the respondent's industry or background. The aggregation of questionnaire results will usually reveal a trend without the necessity of microscopic examination of each respondent. For many purposes this will suffice. Anonymity encourages many respondents to give more considered replies and replies which might be regarded as difficult to give directly to an interviewer. A natural courtesy and politeness is a form of distortion and bias in all question-and-answer type interviews which can be avoided to a certain extent by a mail survey.

Questions requiring visual presentation, particularly those concerned with the respondent's reaction to some specified stimuli or requiring the consideration of a number of options can usually be presented far more effectively by a postal questionnaire than across a table in a face-to-face confrontation.

A further advantage which could be peculiar to individual firms is the possibility of the existence of a 'natural' source of particularly suitable potential respondents such as were listed in the previous chapter.

Yet another advantage is the elimination of interviewer bias and the reduction of time bias which are inherent in other techniques. That is, interviewers consciously or unconsciously can slant replies and interpretations towards given answers; respondents react to external environmental factors prevalent at differing times during the total period of the interviewing process of a survey. Both these factors create bias.

Certainly for most types of questions analysis of postal questionnaires is far simpler than for many interviews and as historical records they can be more easily exploited for other purposes at a later date.

DISADVANTAGES

The first major disadvantage is in identifying respondents. The fact that a questionnaire may be directed to Managing Directors does not automatically guarantee that his assistant or some other member of the firm may not reply. To complicate this still further, there is the problem that job titles may well mean different things in different firms. Yet another difficulty connected with identification is ensuring that the selected firm fits into the sample frame. Asking respondents to identify themselves does not always produce accurate information for the researcher.

The second disadvantage stems from the assessment of typicality. Returning a questionnaire requires positive action and effort. This fact alone may single out the respondent as particularly interested in the subject, a buyer of the product, or in some other way untypical of the non-respondents who generally form the majority of the sample and who may be disinterested because they are non-buyers. Yet non-buyers' reactions and replies can be vital. The measurement of non-response bias has received scant attention by marketing researchers. Most researchers are primarily concerned in achieving as high a response rate as quickly and cheaply as possible.

An example of this will illustrate the point. In a survey probing the use of magnetic tape for computers the immediate response brought in a total of over 20 per cent replies, every one of which indicated that magnetic tape was not used. On the first assessment it might have appeared that magnetic tape consumption was non-existent or low. What in fact was happening was that those computer managers not using magnetic tape were able to reply immediately without consulting records, whereas those who were of major interest to the researchers—that is the magnetic tape users—needed time to produce a reply. Thus the non-respondents were the very group which were of interest. Later returns in this survey brought in magnetic tape user's replies but throughout the study non-user response remained higher than users, and a sample of non-respondents had to be probed by other techniques.

Another disadvantage is that the number of questions which can be asked in the hope of obtaining a useful total response is finite. It is said that 5 per cent of potential responses can be deducted for each question asked. Thus twenty questions will produce a nil response. While this is not correct it is a reasonable 'rule of thumb' that the response rate dips as the number of questions increases even when such questions are of a relatively simple nature. Maintaining a respondent's interest, as can be done with personal interviewing even of an extended nature, is almost impossible with a postal questionnaire and therefore the questions must be succinct and not require sustained effort by the respondent in order to answer them.

The problem of ambiguity or questions whose meaning is not understood by respondents is also a major one. There is no interviewer present to give further information and only the slightest sense of irritation in the respondent will result in the questionnaire not being returned. It is difficult, even in the most carefully formulated questionnaire and no matter how well it is 'piloted', to avoid the respondent who answers ambiguously or who accidentally misses or deliberately refuses to give relevant information. Even apparently straightforward questions can produce unsatisfactory results from a respondent who is trying to co-operate. For example: Question: 'What were the reasons for choosing the make of partitioning installed?' Answer: 'Because it was the most suitable.' This tells the researcher nothing. The question might have been better worded to ask about the technical and commercial aspects of the respondent's partitioning requirements and then to probe how far the choice made supported these. Any discrepancy between the two sets of factors indicates either an inconsistency in the respondent's opinions and activities or else a market requirement not met by suppliers at the time of the respondent's choice of equipment.

Omissions, refusals or conflicting replies might well be satisfactorily dealt with by an interviewer but the postal questionnaire approach is a 'take-it-or-leave-it' method so far as the researcher is concerned. It is, of course, possible to make re-calls or follow-ups but this is expensive and the law of diminishing returns is one that cannot be denied or ignored.

Another difficulty which can create its own series of biases is the fact that the respondent can see the whole of the questionnaire before completing any part of it. Knowledge of later questions can easily bias replies to earlier ones since it provides a means whereby the respondent can adjust his answers to give consistency. This rules out cross checking by asking the same question in a different manner, which can be practised in personal and telephone interviewing.

The difficulties which ensue from 'position bias' also require consideration. In the use of multiple choice questions there is a discernible tendency to choose the first or the central position. To cancel out this effect the order of choice (and the questions themselves where possible) should be varied and equal numbers of each variation distributed evenly throughout the sample.

Finally there is the problem of inability to adjust the survey direction or the questions without a complete re-circularisation. This can be illustrated by an example from the postal survey to determine buying factors for steel partitioning. The survey results indicated that 'mobility'—the quality of being able to dismantle, move and re-erect easily—was the principal decision-forming factor. It also showed that the respondents had between them installed every make of partitioning despite the fact that the 'mobility' characteristics clearly varied between the different types of partitioning. Further, steel partitioning manufacturers' literature emphasises the 'mobility' of their products as a primary advantage. This weight of evidence on the 'mobility' factor had, however, then to be appraised against a second factor revealed by the survey, namely that hardly any of the respondents had in fact ever moved their partitions. The question for the researcher to resolve was, therefore, why all the emphasis was on mobility when the partitions were rarely moved. This point could have been probed by personal interview but not by a mail questionnaire. The inconsistency between the two factors was only revealed as a result of the questionnaire and to determine the real decision factors then required further investigation. Had the research been conducted by interview it would have become obvious fairly quickly that a discrepancy existed between the reason for purchase and the actual use of the product. It would have thus been possible to investigate this point by re-orientating the interviews still to be carried out.

DECIDING TO USE POSTAL QUESTIONNAIRES

The researcher in deciding to use a postal questionnaire will have considered the question of the research parameters of time, resources, cost and objectives. In relation to these and the detail of the survey, he will also have to consider if the expected response will yield the answers either alone or in combination with other techniques. This in turn will lead him to deciding whether he can overcome or compromise on the problem of identification of the respondent, assessing his typicality and the validity of the responses. The answers to these questions cannot be known in advance of the research but there is a framework of both theory and practical experience to give indications of likely results.

The contribution of the behavioural sciences towards the improvement of postal questionnaire techniques has been very considerable indeed, and it is by using the information derived from these sources and combining it with knowledge of commercial practices that the postal questionnaire can be shaped into a reliable, economic and useful tool of industrial marketing research.

In deciding to use a questionnaire it is as well to go back to first principles and to ask a number of pertinent questions concerning the yield required.

'First principles' in this context is to look at the survey objectives and see what contribution might be made by a mail survey under normal conditions. It is then necessary to examine the postal questionnaire objectives themselves to assess their practicality (in postal questionnaire terms) within the limitations set by the techniques and money resources available. From this point a number of detailed questions require answers. A procedure might be as shown in the check list in Fig. 13.

This check list provides an outline guide to the factors which should be considered when undertaking a postal questionnaire. There will, of course, be other factors specific to the project and the firm which must be incorporated. For example, it is necessary to study how a questionnaire might be interpreted in general terms by respondents. An enquiry among a firm's distributors concerning their ability and willingness to supply services to their customers might easily be taken by them as a preparatory move to justify a change in distribution channel policy. Thus their replies may be deliberately biased to produce a given effect or, more than likely, these firms may immediately seek an alternative supply source in case of the eventuality they fear occurring. There could therefore be a panic in the

What contribution to the total survey objectives will the postal questionnaire make?	original information cross validation
What alternatives are there to achieve the same information yield?	bibliographical research telephone interviewing personal interviewing visual techniques statistical analysis test market operations operational research
What degree of confidence is required in the results?	high medium low
How do other techniques compare in confidence tolerances?	better same worse
Is the postal questionnaire objective clearly identified?	yes no
How many questions can it be achieved in—is this number satisfactory?	too high of the right order too low
Is the product or service concept researched understandable to respondents?	yes partially no
If 'no' can it be made comprehensible in postal questionnaire terms?	yes no
Is any explanation to make it comprehensible likely to divert potential respondents from replying?	yes no
Are questions formulated in a way which implies there is a 'right' and a 'wrong' answer?	yes no
What degree of confidentiality is placed on the information requested?	high moderate low non-confidential
To what extent is the respondent expected to identify himself?	by name by job definition by job title not at all

Fig. 13

CHECK LIST FOR A DECISION TO USE A POSTAL
QUESTIONNAIRE

Fig. 13 continued

With what degree of detail is the firm expected to identify itself?	name activity location S.I.C. numbers employed capital employed physical size commercial links not at all
Is the amount of work required from the respondent to read and complete the questionnaire reasonable?	yes no
Is the respondent offered any tangible or intangible benefit?	yes no
Could the same benefit be obtained by the respondent in a more satisfactory way?	yes no
Is it quite clear to the respondent what is expected of him?	yes no
Are the terms used likely to be familiar to him?	yes no
Are the number of options in multiple choice questions sufficient to give a range of answers or too great for a reasoned distinction to be made by respondents?	too few sufficient too many
Are the technical aspects of the questionnaire correct in every detail?	yes no
Do any questions conflict with alternative nomenclatures which may be preferred by some respondent groups?	yes no
Are there any current technical, political, sociological or other controversies likely to affect rate or form of replies?	yes no
Are any questions capable of more than one meaning?	yes no
Have external factors which might affect day or rate of despatch been considered?	yes no
Have external factors which might affect response rate because of inappropriate date of arrival been considered?	yes no

distributive pipe-lines and a major flight away from the firm's products. Conversely, a well-devised questionnaire, while not intended as a public relations vehicle, can in fact reassure distributors that the supplier is not only 'on their side' but actively engaged in improving his own operations to provide more and better assistance to distributors. It can be seen, therefore, that a postal questionnaire can be a two-edged weapon instead of a tool. All these factors must be considered.

THE PROBLEM OF COMMUNICATION

The greatest problem in all work which involves human beings is that of communication. Most words of every language are ambiguous and people misinterpret questions which seem at first glance perfectly simple and straightforward. It has been pointed out that to devise a proper sample, a researcher needs to be a statistician; to put a research problem in its correct setting, an economist or sociologist; but to construct a questionnaire the researcher needs to have both a gift for language and a psychological insight into people's minds, imagination and experience.[1] But all these virtues are unlikely to be available in a researcher and therefore it becomes even more important to develop methods which will at least avoid the major pitfalls.

These major pitfalls are words with more than one or, more importantly, with a special meaning within a given industry or trade. This is particularly true of technical descriptions. 'Retail sales' to some oil companies are sales of fuel ultimately destined for the consumer markets, whereas in most industries retail sales are those which are transacted with consumers. Refrigerated containers for shops are known by this name and also as refrigerated display equipment. To the trade as a whole, however, they are refrigerated merchandising equipment, and the difference between 'display' and 'merchandising' is not just semantic. A 'gyp' in the garment industry is a crook or cheapjack while in the motor accessory business he is someone operating outside the trade associations and trade agreements, and includes the largest and most respectable organisations.

But everyday words are equally imprecise. Some words are ambiguous in themselves and in their everyday context—an ambiguity that can be clarified in a personal but not in a postal interview. For example, 'service', 'use', 'capacity'. Then there are words which,

[1] *Modern Market Research,* op. cit., p. 104.

while having clear meaning, can produce a different effect in importance of magnitude. How high is 'high' or how thin is 'thin'? These are two obvious examples.

Another pitfall is the use of emotionally loaded words which can produce an untypical or untrue answer. Words such as 'waste', 'dirt', 'soiled', 'poor', 'inefficient', 'extravagant', however innocently used can sometimes be taken as an implied criticism or even personally.

The third aspect of interpretation concerns words with varying degrees of meaning and nuances which will change from individual to individual, across industry and across educational and class groupings. A word such as 'nice' has totally different meanings varying from that of strong approval to sarcastic criticism depending upon the educational and social group of the user of the word.

Other words defy allocating any precision at all. To revert to the check list earlier in this chapter, the question on 'confidentiality' gives four choices of answer—'high', 'moderate', 'low' and non-confidential'. Only 'non-confidential' is an absolute, the others represent degrees of confidentiality and will vary considerably. 'Highly confidential' in marketing research, important as it may be, is unlikely to achieve the same degree of importance as that same designation in military intelligence. A question using a quantitative indicator in isolation—'Do you use your calculator frequently'—provides nothing to which 'frequently' can be related. It could as easily mean once a day as once a month. Phrased within a code an order of magnitude can be perceived. 'How often do you use your calculator— frequently, occasionally, rarely, never?' This does not give a precision which might be desirable but it does at least provide a quartile to which the response can be allocated. Further precision can be obtained by giving the respondent a choice of alternatives, e.g. 'once a day', 'once a week', 'once a month'—the applicability of the variations in use being tested at a piloting stage.

This then leads to the question itself. Obviously it must be comprehensible as a question and equally obviously the answer must not be self-evident if a meaningful reply is to be obtained. Some questions lead inevitably to a pre-determined answer when the question is posed on a 'right' or 'wrong', 'desirable' or 'undesirable', 'good' or 'bad' or 'acceptable' or 'unacceptable' basis. For example—'Do you consider the prices of silver mica capacitors could be lower?' The 'desirable' answer is obviously 'yes'. 'Would you be in favour of a major promotional effort to increase productivity?' To be on the side of the angels, where most people desire to be, the answer must be 'yes' again. 'Have you ever left your occupation without giving the requisite period of notice?' To leave a job without notice is 'wrong', answers therefore strongly tend towards 'no'.

But bias can appear as much for purely mechanical reasons as for commercial, emotional or sociological ones. In multiple choice questions, it has already been noted, there is a tendency to choose the first or central item: early questions on a long questionnaire receive more consideration than later ones. Questions requiring effort to answer them, for example by consulting records, will invariably over a whole survey be less adequately and accurately answered than those only requiring opinions.

All these factors must be considered in formulating the questionnaire and all can be dealt with effectively if care is taken in the construction of the questionnaire. This will be demonstrated later in the chapter.

THE PROBLEM OF IDENTIFICATION

The second major problem in the use of questionnaires is that of identifying respondent and firm. There is nothing to prevent the researcher from having this on the questionnaire when it is despatched but the concomitant is that the response rate will fall by a significant amount. In any event, some will be returned with the identification removed. A number of split runs of questionnaires identified in plain language, open coded and unidentified, showed an almost consistent pattern of non-response. The plain language identification generally has the highest non-response rate followed by the coded question-naires and the non-identified group giving the highest return. The implications of these facts are too important to be ignored and it poses the question for the researcher which he must answer at the outset: 'Is high response rate more important than detailed identification?' The answer will provide him with the course of action to follow.

However, the issue of quantity versus detail is not always black or white. Often the identification of the firm and not the respondent will do; similarly other identification criteria may suffice—numbers employed, Standard Industrial Classification (S.I.C.), activity, loca-tion. The rule is that to sustain a high response rate the minimum identification should be sought as is compatible with the survey requirements.

The alternative of open coding can, however, be unpredictable. There are certainly some classes of respondents which feel that a coding does not identify them. These people will adopt precisely the same attitude to a coded questionnaire as to one without an individual identification on it. Others, however, may regard the code as a key to total identification down to the personal details of the respondent. Since they cannot know how much the researcher knows, this view is not without some logic and leads to a high non-response in this type of contact.

Yet another approach is to ask the respondents to identify themselves, personally or by some agreed criteria such as those already referred to. This has the disadvantage of producing a percentage of replies with full identification and the rest with amounts varying down to none.

Hidden coding, which is not difficult to introduce, must be avoided since this is quite rightly regarded as unethical. Hidden coding by body or edge punching of questionnaires is not uncommon and with the increasing sophistication of respondents such primitive attempts at concealment can only lead to a reaction against all postal questionnaires, to the detriment of research.

From the point of view of the questionnaires themselves, the more homogenous the respondent group the less necessary identification becomes. This of course tends to be a function of the sample and the sampling frame filling. The question of identification and the degree of identification required should be viewed against the sample composition.

One problem which arises, however, where identification is not sought is that connected with problems of the characteristics of the non-respondents. On a probability basis, with a 30 per cent response on an unidentified questionnaire, 30 per cent of contacts in search of non-respondents will be wasted ones. The equation then becomes the cost of secondary probing, wastage and the higher response rate as evaluated against each other.

A final difficulty to be considered on identification is whether the respondent is in fact the correct person to have completed the questionnaire. Probing buying decisions doesn't necessarily take the researcher to the buyer. Interests may well lay in the pre-procurement activities, that is with the Design Engineer, Financial Director, Production Engineer or others. The questionnaire may be transferred by one of these to the buyer and the reply returned giving the buyer's viewpoint and information on the original respondent *as seen* by the buyer. This problem is one of the most intractable but it can partly be met by the introduction of control and check questions into the questionnaire design which is dealt with later.

FORMULATING THE QUESTIONS

Until both stratification and frame of the sample are known, it is pointless to formulate the questions as they must be orientated towards the average type of respondent the frame includes, and based on a common linguistic standard.

The questions can be classified into three groups: Dichotomous, that is questions which will only produce a 'yes' or 'no' answer; multiple choice questions where alternative answers are listed, and 'open end' questions in which the respondent can express himself in a way of his own choosing. The three types can be illustrated:

'Does your company operate a staff location system?' This can only be sensibly answered by 'yes' or 'no'.
  'Which method is used?
    Public address
    Flashing light
    Sempahore
    Pocket paging
    Others (specify)'.

This multiple choice question will produce one or more answers from the choice given plus any system not listed.

'What are the most satisfactory and least satisfactory aspects of the system installed?' This is an open-ended invitation to comment exactly as the respondent sees fit.

Figure 14 shows the three types of question in an actual questionnaire. Question 1 is dichotomous, Question 4 multiple choice and Question 12 open-ended. All questions will fall into these three categories. The dichotomous question is the preferred one since they are the easiest to answer, easiest to code and easiest to analyse, producing no gradation and are therefore least likely to suffer with ambiguous interpretations in the replies. The possibility of a 'don't know' answer, of course, turns a dichotomous question into a multiple choice question. However in factual enquiries 'don't know' is usually synonymous with 'no' and can be generally counted as such.

The multiple choice question (or aided recall) ensures that the respondent considers all relevant aspects of the question but sometimes tend to block other alternatives which might emerge. If multiple choice questions are too wide, particularly when ratings are involved, it is unlikely all ratings will be meaningful. For example, if a respon-

MOTOR VEHICLE TESTING

1 Do you ROAD TEST motor vehicles ?   YES ☐ NO ☐

2 IF YES, how many vehicles do you test per week ?

	0-50	50-100	100-200	200-300
a OVER 200 b.h.p.				
b UNDER 200 b.h.p.				

3 Is the total number of road tests :

increasing ☐

same ☐

decreasing ☐

4 WHAT PERCENTAGE of your road tests are carried out to determine :

ENGINE performance ALONE	
BRAKE performance ALONE	
BOTH engine and brake performance	
Other (please state)	
TOTAL	

5 ON AVERAGE, HOW MANY man-hours are spent road testing per week ?

0-20	20-50	50-100	100-200

6 Does the presence of other traffic interfere with your road testing ?   YES ☐ NO ☐

7 IF YES, what fraction of your present time spent road testing would you save if Roads were TRAFFIC FREE ?

1/4	1/3	1/2	2/3	3/4

8 Do you own a roller dynamometer?   YES ☐ NO ☐

9 IF YES, what make is it ? When was it purchased ?
....
....

10 Is it adaptable for brake testing ?   YES ☐ NO ☐

11 If you do not own a roller dynamometer, have you ever considered the purchase of one ?   YES ☐ NO ☐

12 Please indicate the conditions required for vehicle testing.

(1) *Originally international paper size A4.*

Fig. 14

POSTAL QUESTIONNAIRE

dent is asked to rate ten suppliers on a ten point scale there are 100 options involved. It is quite impossible for the human mind to consider the total span of so many options all with fine distinctions between them. On a matrix of this size only the strongly positive and negative aspects have any real chance of coming through. Thus rating questions should take into account the limitations of respondents and be scaled down accordingly. A six point scale is efficient but the reliability falls rapidly with more than this number. However, with semantic scales giving degrees of approval, even six points can be too many when the meanings of the words themselves are not specific.

> Excellent
> Very good
> Good
> Fair
> Poor
> Very poor

There will be little confusion between the polar words 'excellent' and 'very poor' but distinguishing 'good' or 'fair' category is very difficult. Thus attempts at refinement on 'approval' scales may lead to a loss of usable research data. Simple 'good', 'intermediate' and 'poor' are likely to be far more meaningful than a 'rainbow' spectrum. A more detailed discussion of scaling techniques occurs in Chapter 12, 'Assessing Advertising Effectiveness'.

It is always easier for a respondent to tick squares than write in answers. Thus if a question lends itself to ticks rather than words, this choice should be used. Questionnaire design must always be directed to producing the maximum research yield for the minimum number of questions framed with the maximum simplicity compatible with the information requirements and respondent type.

THE ANATOMY OF THE POSTAL QUESTIONNAIRE

The questionnaire itself falls into four distinct parts:
   (a) qualification questions
   (b) check questions
   (c) main questions
   (d) identification questions.

(a) *Qualification questions*

First the qualification questions. It is important to ensure that the respondent or his firm are qualified to answer the questionnaire. There is little point in getting a person to complete a postal questionnaire on oil consumption experience if the firm is using coal-fired apparatus. Similarly an enquiry into the reading habits of Managing Directors can be misleading if the answers are provided by secretaries.

Thus the qualification question will usually be a simple dichotomous one. 'Do you use oil for process or space heating?' 'Do you decide how many firms will be asked to tender for a contract?' 'Which of the following activities come within the scope of your responsibilities?'

Qualification questions are specific to each enquiry and will have to be generated anew in each study. The rule is that they should indeed be specific and, wherever possible, cross-check with other questions in the postal questionnaire to give a degree of validation to the respondent's claim.

(b) *Check questions*

The second group of questions are check questions. This can be incorporated in a number of ways. For example, including in a multiple choice list of firms a non-existent one as in Figure 15 where MOTRAM is a made-up name. Respondents identifying this firm as known from experience can then be assessed as giving misleading information, whether from carelessness, ignorance or malice. Another method is by a quantification or weighting. If in a questionnaire a buyer of magnetic materials is highly critical of dimensional accuracy and consistency of batches but is revealed in another question to be a very small or sporadic purchaser of these materials, his replies can be weighted accordingly. A quantity check gives a clear insight into the depth of experience of the respondent which wherever possible should be included in a questionnaire.

(c) *Main questions*

The third group of questions are the core of the document; that is the questions designed to provide the data sought. These should be as few in number, as short in length, and as productive of as few interpretations and alternatives as possible. Above all they must be completely neutral in their formulation. There are certain rules which must be observed, many of which are self-evident.

It is an old saying if you ask a silly question you get a silly answer. Nowhere is it more true than in postal questionnaires. Every sample

L

Please mark x in these columns the frequency with which the operations occur in your contracts.

WHICH OF THE FOLLOWING OPERATIONS COME WITHIN THE SCOPE OF YOUR ACTIVITIES ?

		OCCASIONALLY	REGULARLY	WE SPECIALIZE IN	EQUIPMENT USED
ROCK DRILLING	Blasting				
	Plug and Feather Splitting				
	Fixing of Stay Bolts, Anchor Bolts, Tent Pegs.				
STONE DRILLING	Erection of Posts, Flag Poles, Fences				
	Erection of Crash Barriers, Enclosures.				
BRICKWORK DRILLING	Erection of Temporary Structures { Exhibitions, Agricultural Shows / Open Air Meetings, Rallies				
EARTH DRILLING	Gravel Pit Drilling				
	Soil Sampling, Earth Probing				
	Surveying, Prospecting				
	Fixing of Road Studs				
	Drilling for Gas Leakage Searches.				
Concrete Breaking Stone Breaking. Pavement Breaking. Brickwork Breaking Concrete Cutting Brickwork Cutting Asphalt Cutting.	Road and Pavement Maintenance				
	Demolition Work				
	Slit Cutting				
	Channel Cutting				
	Hard Core Breaking				
EARTH DIGGING	Road and Earth Trenches				
	Drainage and Irrigation Trenches				
	Forestry Trenches and Ditches				
CLAY DIGGING	Trenches and Channels for Pipe and Cable Laying				
	Foundations				
	Pits				
TAMPING.	Permanent Way Maintenance				
	Tie Tamping.				
	Backfill Tamping				
	Earth Compacting.				
DRIVING	Nails, Piles, Posts, Pegs, Rods				

(1) *Originally international paper size A3.*

Fig. 15

MATRIX TYPE QUESTIONNAIRE

Which of the following contracting equipment do you know

by name?
By reputation?
From your own experience?

HEARD OF BY NAME
KNOWN BY REPUTATION
HAVE DIRECT EXPERIENCE OF
PERFORMANCE
RELIABILITY
SERVICE & SPARES

Please assess the EQUIPMENT by marking in these columns.

5 - very good
4 - good
3 - average or fair
2 - poor
1 - very poor

Motor Drills Motor Breakers							
	COBRA						
	MOTRAM						
	PEGSON						
	PIONJAR						
	WARSOP						
Portable Compressors	Air Pumps						
	Atlas Copco						
	Bristol						
	Broom Wade						
	Consolidated Pneumatic						
	Holman						
	Ingersoll Rand						
	Joy Sullivan						
	Thor						
	Worthington						

WHAT WEIGHT OF MOTOR BREAKER DO YOU CONSIDER ACCEPTABLE FOR OPERATION IF IT HAS A BREAKING CAPACITY EQUIVALENT TO THAT OF A 45lb. OR A 60lb. PNEUMATIC BREAKER.

Capacity of MOTOR BREAKER equivalent to	45 lb. PNEUMATIC BREAKER	60 lb. PNEUMATIC BREAKER
Acceptable weight of MOTOR BREAKER	90lb ☐ 75lb ☐ 65lb ☐	100lb ☐ 90lb ☐ 75lb ☐
Would YOU use such a MOTOR BREAKER	yes ☐ no ☐	yes ☐ no ☐
For what OPERATIONS would you use such MOTOR BREAKERS		
How many MOTOR BREAKERS would you use		
Should MOTOR BREAKERS be convertible to DRILLING ?	yes ☐ no ☐	yes ☐ no ☐

Fig. 15 continued

contains a number of humorists just looking for an opportunity to be amusing at the researcher's expense. No encouragement should be given by formulating questions which invite sarcastic, facetious or even witty replies. These replies are not usable for the project.

It is also true, but not said so often, that if you ask an indiscreet question you get no replies at all. Questions can sometimes be indiscreet because the researcher is not aware of their significance. For example, correlation analysis will often give a valid relationship between output or costs and some other quite innocent factor. Thus to ask the output of a firm may be obviously indiscreet but to ask the number of lorries they maintain might be just as indiscreet if the management is aware of a correlation. It is up to the researcher to establish in advance what may be indiscreet. Any question in this category will often result in the questionnaire not being returned so it is important to clear well in advance precisely what can and what cannot be asked.

No respondent is likely to want to sit an examination for the researcher. If questions are given in a way which makes it appear there is a 'right' and 'wrong' answer, and failure to get the 'right' one will make the respondent look silly or ignorant in the eyes of the researcher, it will inevitably result in a high wastage factor.

It is not the purpose of a questionnaire to draw attention to the inadequacies—real or imaginery—of the respondent. The use of unfamiliar words is one way of doing this. Another is requesting the respondent to adopt techniques to answer questions with which he is not familiar (for example the use of accountancy techniques to provide details on production input) drawing attention to the lack of essential records which the respondent might feel he has been deficient in keeping (sales analysis by industry uptake) or underlining some actions that should have been, but were not, taken. (Too long an interval between machine servicing.)

Questions which may put the respondents in an unfortunate light or expose him to criticism must always end with a high non-response, particularly on questionnaires which are identified. It is a very human attribute not to want to expose oneself to risk of criticism by superiors or inferiors and for the most part no one is going to help a researcher to do this. Thus there is a need to understand the implications of the questions for respondents as well as their meaning to the researcher.

The law of diminishing returns must also be regarded in questionnaire formulation. The total number of questions must be kept down if the respondent is not to lose heart at the beginning. A busy executive faced with a six-page questionnaire might well be excused for feeling that the time devoted to completing it could not possibly be compensated for by any improvement in product or service promised in return for this co-operation.

(d) *Identification*

The last group of questions is concerned with identification of the respondent and firm. These may be simple requests to identify themselves or their job or the firm or more complex questions such as price cut-off responsibility (at what price level purchasing responsibility shifts from one individual to another). An answer which brings the respondent under the unit price of the product or service being researched will indicate that the whole return is likely to be invalid.

It is essential, however, that despite the four distinguishing groups of questions all of them should interlock. Maximum cross-validation can only be obtained if questions support each other. Examples have already been given; quantities purchased support or refute validity of opinions on the products themselves. Questions on purchasing responsibility throw an important light on price changes needed to move a firm from one supplier to another. Energy demand information may cross check with claims for installed machinery. The list is a long one. The questionnaire must be seen as a mesh with as many threads as possible touching.

CODING

In the preparation of postal questionnaires, and indeed with the other techniques, there must be considerable and continuous anticipation of what is to be done with the data collected. Obsession with techniques can blind the researcher to the need to end with his material in a form that lends itself first to analysis and then interpretation. These aspects of the research problem are dealt with in Chapter 11, 'Processing the Data'.

The purpose of coding is to assist in the tabulation and therefore in devising the codes both the tabulation method and ultimate analysis techniques will need to be considered.

If it is intended to hand tabulate the result of the questionnaire no complex system of pre-coding will be needed and indeed it is not difficult to work without any coding at all. However, the more complex the questionnaire, the more cross analyses needed the greater will the importance of coding become. For the use of computers

B. TIME RECORDERS AND/OR JOB COSTERS

If you do NOT use:—
*Do you use any other method for *recording* time keeping ?

    YES ☐ 1   NO ☐ 2   (27)

*If YES, please indicate briefly the method

. . . . (28)

. . . .

*Are you likely to install time recording apparatus in the next 5 years ?

    .YES ☐ 1   NO ☐ 2   (29)

Please now turn to Section C

If you USE:—

13 How many do you have IN USE ?

	Time Recorders	Job Costers	
0	☐ 1	☐ 1	
1	☐ 2	☐ 2	(30)
2 - 5	☐ 3	☐ 3	
3 - 5	☐ 4	☐ 4	(31)
6 - 10	☐ 5	☐ 5	

Over 10
(please state) . . . .

14 How many Time Recorders and Job Costers did you buy *last year* ?

	Time Recorders		Job Costers		
	Replacement	Extension	Replacement	Extension	
0	☐ 1	☐ 1	☐ 1	☐ 1	(32)
1	☐ 2	☐ 2	☐ 2	☐ 2	(33)
2	☐ 3	☐ 3	☐ 3	☐ 3	
.3 - 5	☐ 4	☐ 4	☐ 4	☐ 4	(34)
6 - 10	☐ 5	☐ 5	☐ 5	☐ 5	(35)

Over 10
(please state) . . . .

Fig. 16
EXTRACT FROM A PRE-CODED QUESTIONNAIRe
(1) ORIGINALLY ON INTERNATIONAL PAPER SIZE A3

coding is absolutely necessary. An example of a pre-coded question-naire for computer analysis is shown in the extract in Figure 16.

Codes can be either entered on the actual questionnaires, which are the small and the bracketed figures in the example shown, or else incorporated into a coding sheet. The latter course is often preferable, not only for reasons of clarity of the postal questionnaire but also because only a few of the questions asked will be dichotomous or multiple choice, which lend themselves most easily to coding.

When the question of coding is considered it will be realised that it is extremely difficult to establish categories and thus codes for open-ended questions, which is another factor to be considered when the actual questions for the questionnaire are decided. Analysis of open-ended and multiple choice questions is described in Chapter 11.

FORMAT

Design is always important but never more so than in a questionnaire on which the researcher is depending upon the goodwill of his respondent to complete. It must fulfil exactly the same functions as all merchandising methods: to attract, to inform, to persuade. The design must attract the reader sufficiently for him to discover what the questionnaire is about, it must inform him not only what is wanted from him, but also what he gets in return. It must persuade him to co-operate.

It should be clear that 'design' and 'layout' are not the same thing. The former is the province of the researcher, perhaps with the assistance of a 'visualiser' who can translate the questions into attractive formats. 'Layout' will generally require the skills of a printer or print designer.

It is possible by good design to disguise a large number of questions incorporated into a single questionnaire. The matrix form such as that shown in Figure 15 succeeds in doing this although it must be remarked that a massive matrix can be at least as offputting to some respondents as several pages of questions.

'Gimmicks' in design are not to be eschewed, particularly in the attention-getting stage. The greater the ingenuity which can be injected into the questionnaire, the more chance there is to achieve a high response rate. Attention must be caught as the first step to obtaining the respondent's co-operation.

It helps in deciding actual design of the questionnaire to consider how the results will be presented in the report. If in graphic form, this form may suggest the layout of the questions. Consideration of types of presentation lead back to the questionnaire itself and may well assist the researcher in developing an attractive format.

For layout it goes without saying that questionnaires must be neat and clear but it is an added advantage if it also has balance and symmetry. The majority of people, and most particularly those who are technically orientated, have a visual preference for these attributes. But the other verities of design are equally applicable. Texture: only good quality paper should be used, and certainly if it is to be printed on both sides the paper must be thick enough for the print not to show through. Colour: this adds an attraction to the questionnaire and sometimes makes explanations of the questionnaire itself simpler. Rhythm: the questions should flow easily and unforced in a logical sequence and, where possible, question length should be varied to avoid monotony. Harmony: the total design should be integrated so that the overall impression is favourable and appealing, and typefaces, colour, spacing, enclosures all harmonise. For example, an accompanying letter on a dead white paper can make a buff questionnaire look dowdy and cheap.

Questionnaires should ideally be on one sheet of paper, even if it is a large one. Respondents are more willing to complete a single sheet than a booklet of questions, or one that appears to go on for a number of pages. It is a common mistake to send eight sides of quarto or even smaller paper when the total questionnaire could be fitted easily on to a single sheet of A3 international size paper.

ENCLOSURES

It is important to consider the other documents which may accompany the questionnaire. These will generally be an explanatory letter and an envelope for reply. Occasionally when the subject of the questions is a particularly difficult concept for the respondents to grasp (although under these circumstances other techniques may be more appropriate), explanatory literature may also be enclosed. In the case of advertising evaluation studies, copies of the advertisements under consideration or the journals in which they appeared may also be sent. Very occasionally an incentive to reply may be offered.

The explanatory letter, which can be part of the questionnaire itself, serves the multiple purpose of explaining who the enquiring firm is, why they are carrying out the survey, what they want to know, what is expected of the respondent and what benefit he will receive in return.

Identification of the enquirer, even if the name is not known to the would-be respondent, is an implicit assurance that the enquiry is a straightforward and open one. The purpose of the enquiry, which may not be obvious from the questions themselves, will be of concern to the respondent. The instructions to the respondent (in the form of a request) should make his task easier and the benefit he will receive must be a justification for the time he will spend completing and returning the questionnaire form. From this it can be seen that the accompanying letter forms a vital part of the total questionnaire package. Examples of covering letters are given in Figures 17 and 18.

The second enclosure will generally be the reply envelope. The despatch of the questionnaire and its accompanying pieces is always in an envelope large enough to take the package but the reply envelopes are frequently too small to permit the questionnaire to be slipped in easily. For preference the questionnaire return envelope should accept the document using the same folds as are made to despatch it. It is usual to enclose pre-paid envelopes. Stamped envelopes, however, bring a higher rate of return although the cash wastage on stamps is also higher. However, a number of split runs have shown that despite the higher stamp wastage the total cost is significantly less than a follow-up letter while the response rate is much higher. More people will respond with a stamped envelope than a printed pre-paid envelope because a cash element is involved in the form of the stamp which creates an implied obligation to reply.

It is not usual in industrial marketing research for the incentive to reply to take the form of a gift or favourable purchasing situation. The benefit is usually expressed in broader terms. Incentives can be the offer of some of the salient research results, where this is possible and applicable. The result of a survey among computer users already referred to, to establish the footage of magnetic tape consumed is not very likely to be of concern to the majority of respondents; while a survey of trade associations to establish the extent of joint marketing activities by their members is certain to be of interest to most respondents. The possibility of improved products or services is always an attraction to industrial purchasers and the opportunity to express their needs or dissatisfaction with the existing situation an additional incentive. Incentives, to be effective, generally have to appeal to self-interest of the individual or the firm, although appeals on the basis of national benefit, e.g. improved exports, higher productivity, are not without effect.

PATRON: H.R.H. THE PRINCE PHILIP, DUKE OF EDINBURGH

BRITISH PRODUCTIVITY COUNCIL
VINTRY HOUSE
QUEEN STREET PLACE
LONDON, E.C.4
CENTRAL 9613
PRODCOUN LONDON E.C.4

DIRECTOR:
SIR NIGEL POETT, K.C.B., D.S.O.

September, 1967.

Dear Sir,

The end of QUALITY AND RELIABILITY YEAR is now approaching and we think it useful to have an objective and independent inquiry made to assess how useful it has been, and in what ways it has chiefly benefited British Industry.

The inquiry is being conducted on our behalf by Industrial Market Research Ltd., 17, Buckingham Gate, London, S.W.1. We should be most grateful if you would complete the enclosed questionnaire and return it direct, in the stamped addressed envelope provided, to Industrial Market Research Ltd.

All replies will be treated as confidential to Industrial Market Research Ltd.; the BPC will not have access to them, and will receive only the statistical results. Such information will not be associated with any one firm or person.

Industrial Market Research Ltd., and ourselves would be most grateful if you would reply as early as possible.

Yours faithfully,

Nigel Poett,
Director.

Fig. 17
EXAMPLE OF AN ACCOMPANYING LETTER

DIRECTOR:
A. F. COLBORN, M.A., B.Litt (Oxon)

SECRETARY:
D. A. CHATT, F.C.C.S.

THE INSTITUTE OF MARKETING

(INCORPORATED AS THE INSTITUTE OF MARKETING AND SALES MANAGEMENT)

PATRON: H.R.H. THE PRINCE PHILIP, DUKE OF EDINBURGH K.G.

MARKETING HOUSE, RICHBELL PLACE
LAMB'S CONDUIT STREET, LONDON, W.C.1
Telephone: HOLBORN 2651-5

April, 1965.

Dear Sir,

We are undertaking an inquiry into buying practices in British industry as a whole, in preparation for a study to be published later this year.

The questionnaire is in two parts and we would ask you to complete the few questions on the back of the last page. If you would be willing to help us further and complete the remainder of the form on the middle pages, we would be most grateful to you. This has been addressed to you by your specific job function; please complete it yourself to preserve the accuracy of the selected sample. In order that this study should be truly representative, we hope that you will return the questionnaire to us.

To reduce our demands on your time, the questionnaire is designed to be filled in on first reading. Please rely on your experience — it is not necessary to check your answers in your records, since, when all replies are analysed, trends will become apparent.

All replies will be treated as confidential, and will be used for statistical purposes only so that information contained will not be associated with any one firm or person. Please do not write your name or company.

Yours faithfully,

A. F. Colborn

Encl. Stamped, addressed envelope.

PLEASE TURN TO THE LAST PAGE

Fig. 18
EXAMPLE OF AN ACCOMPANYING LETTER

THE PACKAGE

The whole package, questionnaire, covering letter, accompanying literature—if any—and reply envelope needs to be ordered so that the respondent sees each piece in the correct sequence. He should no more be expected to find his way through a mass of paper than through a muddled questionnaire. If he reads the material in the wrong order there is every chance the questionnaire will be discarded before being studied because patience will be lost, irritation induced and a feeling of being exploited exacerbated. Moreover, if the package is folded so that it comes out of the envelope with many creases, is difficult to hold flat and generally looks uninteresting, there is an additional chance of it being thrown away.

It is advantageous if the package looks important. This can best be achieved by good quality paper and envelopes and by a wide fold. This in turn entails large envelopes which, despite the extra costs, will be an economy if it assists the response. Every business is inundated with direct mail shots, many of which get no further than the post room. The questionnaire must look like a document that demands attention, not one which can be put in the wastepaper basket by the post clerk, with impunity. Giving the package an impressive appearance is as important for its successful penetration of the internal communication channels as it is for attracting the ultimate respondent to study it. This is yet another reason why the sequence of papers in the envelope is important. Literature on the top will tend to get the postal questionnaire relegated to a direct mail shot level. Poorly reproduced duplicated letters will suffer the same fate. Individually addressed letters are at least assured of more careful consideration by the inward mail handlers than the anonymous 'Dear Sir'.

DESPATCH

There are many conflicting views on the best time to despatch a postal questionnaire. A Monday arrival for most commercial concerns is regarded by many researchers as unsatisfactory since respondents working a five-day week have both Saturday's and Monday's mail to cope with on that day. Equally Friday tends to be more rushed for most people than the rest of the week because of attempts to clear off problems and paper before the week-end. This can, however, be used favourably as, if people do tend to clear paper on Friday, it is as well the postal questionnaire should be at hand for dealing with at this time. The majority of researchers favour a Tuesday or Wednesday arrival date but there is little evidence to support this preference. There are, however, certain exceptions; many small businesses lack secretarial or clerical assistance and the proprietor often leaves administration matters to the week-ends. Clearly the best day for despatch will be governed by the general practices of the respondent group.

On a wider time scale obviously holiday periods are to be avoided as far as possible, Christmas, for example, because of the large volume of non-business material moving at that time. The end of a financial year, a period devoted to stock-taking and budget preparations, are all times to watch and avoid so far as a general practice exists in an industry.

From an internal point of view, the despatch timing should be checked carefully in case any other heavy mailings are contemplated at that moment. These may delay all or part of the despatch, which can be important in relation to the date on the accompanying letter. If there is a wide discrepancy between the date on the letter and its arrival, some respondents may decide not to reply at all as it would appear to be too late for the postal questionnaire to be of value to the researchers.

Once despatch begins it should so far as possible be concluded quickly. The time span of despatch is important in reducing any bias which may be caused by changes in outside events.

Getting out a postal questionnaire can be a complex business and like much else in marketing research it can be simplified and errors avoided by developing check lists and standard procedures. One such check list of 'vital actions' will be found in Figure 19.

FOLLOW-UP

It is usual to give a postal questionnaire about twenty-one days (fifteen working days) before closing it, although replies can be accepted so long as it is practical to include them in the analysis. It is also usual to adopt some follow-up technique to step up total response rate. These follow-ups can be less costly than the original wave since the sampling frame will be the same (less the replies received) but they are nevertheless still a heavy expense item. Follow-up responses are generally low and their worth must be measured against the importance of the response rate.

Follow-ups, to be of value, must assume that the respondent intended to reply but had not yet done so. They must also assume he

Procedure	Required Date	Last date for Completion	Initials
POSTAL QUESTIONNAIRE			
Sampling frame constructed			
Sampling frame filled			
Questionnaire constructed			
Accompanying letter devised			
Envelopes checked in stock or ordered			
'Reply paids' (if to be used) checked in stock or ordered			
Outwards envelope typing: (i) typing pool notified ...... (ii) allocated .... (iii) completed			
Stamps cash requisitioned			
Stamps bought			
Instructions for questionnaire printing issued			
Questionnaire ready			
Accompanying letter ready			
Additional questionnaires requisitioned for inclusion in report and master file			
Specimen letters requisitioned for inclusion in report and master file			
Despatch date fixed and cleared with mail room			
Post staff notified			

Fig. 19

CHECK LIST FOR PREPARING AND DESPATCHING
A POSTAL QUESTIONNAIRE

has misplaced the questionnaire. This means sending a second questionnaire with a tactfully worded reminder that a reply is awaited. The appearance of hectoring must be avoided, however, and the basic statements of the covering letter repeated: 'Who we are', 'what we are doing', 'what we want', 'what you will get' and a 'thank you'.

Follow-ups can also be conducted by telephone interviews with either the respondent or someone who might progress the questionnaire. This approach is dubious to an extreme, since for very little extra cost a telephone interview can be conducted and the research yield is much higher. At least one firm has conducted mail surveys by preparing the ground with a preliminary call to the respondent or his secretary, saying that the questionnaire is coming and requesting co-operation and then following it up with another telephone call after despatch. That a high response rate can be achieved is not in doubt. The key question is whether the information could not have been obtained either more cheaply or in greater depth for the same cost.

TESTING THE QUESTIONNAIRE

There is no better way of ensuring that a questionnaire will achieve the results required than by testing it. Two forms of test are advisable. The first is a straight copy test: that is the questionnaire should be 'copy tested' by personal interview with personnel of the calibre of those expected to respond to ensure that they are technically correct in their format and wording. It must be ascertained that the mystique of the particular trade or profession being surveyed will not result in reading into the questionnaire interpretations of what is required different from that which is actually intended. This is another way of saying that researchers must have an insight into the minds of their respondents.

Copy testing can also be conducted internally on a 'brainstorming' basis. Each question is subjected to criticism and internal respondents deliberately attempt to misconstrue the meaning and to provide answers which are relevant but not meaningful. To return to an example already given: the reply that a product was chosen because 'it was the most suitable' would immediately lead to a reformulation of the question to avoid this type of response. It is also quite useful in internal copy testing to attempt to find the 'funny' answers. This will at least avoid encouraging the humorists among respondents.

The second test is more in the nature of a market test. That is to actually despatch a trial shot of the 'package' and evaluate the form, rate and quality of response. This type of test or pilot will give a first indication of response rate, clarity of replies and acceptability of the package. If it is practicable, it is also useful to interview respondents *after* they have returned the postal questionnaire to check their reactions to it. Similarly a group of non-respondents should also be probed to establish why the questionnaire was not returned. Many valuable clues will be given from this exercise for re-ordering, re-designing and other changes.

This approach is necessarily an ideal one and will not be practical for cost and time reasons in many instances. It should nevertheless be followed where possible, and certainly where the postal questionnaire reaches massive proportions and a survey is heavily dependent upon its results.

Over a period of time it is possible to develop a series of specific criteria for questionnaires which will provide accurate guidance on aspects of formulation, format and mechanics. It is advisable to keep all questionnaires successful and unsuccessful, with an analysis of their results, criticism of their performance and an evaluation of the reasons for any particular characteristics revealed. This build-up of case studies of questionnaires can save a company a very considerable sum of money in the long run and possibly eliminate the need for test runs.

THE PROBLEM OF NON-RESPONSE

The problem of non-response in postal questionnaires is greater than for other techniques because of the difficulty of identifying the non-respondent. Respondents, it has been pointed out, will in some way be untypical of the total sample by very reason of the fact they replied. Because of this it is important to obtain some knowledge of the characteristics of the non-respondents. The methods for doing this rely upon sampling the non-respondent group which, of course, is a contradiction by definition. The purist can argue that a follow-up will only produce another series of respondents who will also differ in some way from both the first respondents and from non-respondents and so on until the whole sample finally replies. Conceptually this is true and for this reason the use of postal question-naires has limitations in sampling the non-respondents. Follow-up questionnaires can reduce the number of the tardy or the careless but cannot induce the unco-operative to respond.

The most efficient method of obtaining information on non-respondents is to adopt some of the alternative techniques of personal and telephone interviewing. It is comparatively easy by this method to isolate either the reasons for not responding or any common characteristics of non-respondents. This approach also illustrates the essential overlap in industrial marketing research techniques where one technique can (or in some cases, must) be used to improve the efficiency of the other.

There has been little radical or prolonged experimentation with postal questionnaires because of the risk of effects on response rates. However, one most detailed and thorough enquiry into the question of non-response bias has been conducted and reported on; it makes rewarding reading.[1] Although referring exclusively to social surveys, it is worthy of careful study by industrial marketing researchers using postal techniques.

[1] Christopher Scott, 'Research on Mail Surveys', *Journal of the Royal Statistical Society*, Series A, vol. 124, part 2, (London 1961).

M

CHAPTER 8

Interviewing

Because the interview, whether personal or by telephone, will in most industrial marketing research surveys provide the bulk of the data needed for completion of the research project, its role within the total research activity assumes the primary place. Although very considerable work has been done in the field of human communications there is very little information available on interviewing *per se* and interviewing for industrial marketing research purposes has barely been investigated.

Industrial marketing researchers frequently bemoan the lack of time and funds to research their own techniques. The industrial interview would rate high for consideration for researching, since such data as is available is almost entirely empirically based and widely scattered.

The term 'interviewing' is used glibly in most circumstances to indicate a formal question and answer confrontation, usually between two people. In fact the interview is much more than this and can be structured on many levels. An embracing definition of an 'interview' is useful therefore; 'discussions between two or more people, structured, semi-structured or non-directive, in which information is exchanged, values and attitudes explored and standards established'. Such a definition covers almost all situations in which the researcher is likely to find himself.

Throughout all the aspects of industrial marketing research a high degree of skill is required but it must be conceded that interviewing requires probably the greatest spectrum of skills because of the problems of communication which are so wide-ranging and complex. The variables which can be introduced into an interview defy classification and each one can produce differing results and emphasis.

Thus the first essential in preparing for field work involving interviews is to assess the method through which the information required will be yielded in the most useful form. Some types of interview can, for example, reduce interviewer bias to a minimum (it can never be wholly eliminated) whereas others, while being much more productive of attitude data, are particularly prone to this form of bias.

Basically the interviewer has a range of four types of interviews and a number of sub-types which can be used although all four types might well be used in a single interview if the circumstances are suitable.

STRUCTURED INTERVIEWS

The structured interview is one in which the questions to be asked are devised in advance of the interview, perhaps by pilot studies. The questions are formulated in a specified manner and in a given sequence. The interviewer is directed through the questionnaire by specified rigid procedures. By anticipating a range of answers for any single question the interviewer can be instructed to proceed to the next point. Thus 'if the answer to Q. 4 is "no" move to Q. 8'. In short, the interviewer has no discretion whatsoever in the conduct of the interview. Every respondent is asked the same questions in the same form and in the same order. Each question is worded as far as possible so that it will have the same meaning to each respondent, and so that the question itself will not bias or influence an answer.

It is obvious if the wording is changed there is a risk that the meaning might also be changed and thus replies will not necessarily be comparable. 'Do you expect your requirements for conveyor belting to change in the next year?' is not the same question as 'Do you expect your requirements for conveyor belting to go up?' or even 'Do you expect your requirements for conveyor belting to follow the pattern of this year?'

Similarly any change in order will produce non-comparable results as some questions will influence the answers to others. 'Would you, if re-equipping, install identical machines?' preceding a question such as 'Has the installation of ABC type machines been considered?' would tend to produce a 'yes' to the second question whether it were true or not, where the first question received an affirmative reply. This is because most respondents would seek to justify the decision relating to the earlier question, based on a total market knowledge. In reverse order the question on ABC type machines could draw respondents' attention to lack of total market knowledge and therefore produce a perhaps unjustified 'no' answer in the second question. Either way biases are inherent which suggests that the questions themselves require reformulation.

The structured interview is essentially a tool of consumer marketing research and is effective and cheap to use where massive interviewing is taking place, where the quality of interviewers is highly variable and not always assessable, and where respondents are subject to a relatively superficial examination. In an industrial situation the structured interview can rarely take in all the information needed at an interview where *expert* opinion is being probed; its use tends to block off the respondent when additional remarks are of value, and can be extremely boring or frustrating for them. It is essential in industrial interviewing to hold respondents' interest since the time they devote to granting interviews will be assessed by them against other work which might have been accomplished in the interview time. This situation occurs far less often in consumer research when interview time tends to come from unscheduled activities, usually not under time pressure.

The structured interview in industrial marketing research has only the advantage of reducing interview bias and of cheapness. Neither of these advantages are to be eschewed but related to the overall project they will rarely offset the numerous disadvantages of this particular interviewing method.

SEMI-STRUCTURED INTERVIEWS

The semi-structured interview is one in which a piloted check list of questions is used, as in a structured interview, but a greater degree of freedom is left to the interviewer to obtain the answers. That is, question formulation can be changed as well as the order of asking. Moreover probes can be used to elucidate obscure or incomplete answers.

The moment the interviewer uses his or her discretion, however, biases will develop. This can only be limited by the use of skilled interviewers using carefully arranged interview procedures and techniques and by an intelligent anticipation of the adjustments in the interview which may be needed.

Pilot research will indicate precisely how difficult or easy questions may be to answer, variations and qualifications in respondents' replies which may emerge, and prompts or transition statements[1] which may be needed. Not all combinations and permutations can be

---

[1] A transition statement is an interpolation by the interviewer to assist respondents to move easily from one subject of the interview which has been completed to the next. A transition statement avoids respondents answering on the new topic within the same frame of references as the previous topic.

anticipated but it is possible both by pilot studies and reference to previous work to prepare for a large number of diversions from the set questionnaire.

In probing decision-forming factors in a purchase a reply referring to 'quality and design' will often emerge, and yet 'quality' and 'design' have many different meanings. The latter can refer to aesthetic characteristics, technical characteristics of the product, the system or equipment in which it is incorporated, or even the advertising and packaging. Because it is possible to anticipate all-embracing terms of this type, it is also possible to brief the interviewer to probe the meaning of the terms used. By standardising these secondary probes the element of interviewer-bias can be reduced. 'Do you mean its appearance?' is a near-neutral question which will assist respondents to distinguish the factors which in his own mind comprise design factors.

Any cross validating of answers can be incorporated into the questionnaire design and within the limited freedom given by the semi-structured interview it is possible to develop additional validation factors. For example, probing the history of machine breakdowns by a structured interview must necessarily be limited to major causes of failure which can be incorporated into an 'aided recall' list. To set out and read through all possible causes of machine failure is as impracticable as it would be tiresome. However, in a semi-structured interview it is possible for an engineer interviewer to pinpoint failure causes by technical enquiries rather than an 'aided recall'.

The semi-structured interview also makes interview fixing simpler where respondents are antagonistic or refuse to be interviewed. By the use of key questions likely to interest the respondent, irrespective of what the order of questions might be, it is possible to lead respondents forward into the main questionnaire. Probing the reasons for refusal to be interviewed and allowing the respondent to express his resentment, fear or anger, can lead to a calmer more reasoned approach, and finally agreement to be interviewed.

Thus the semi-structured interview has many advantages in industrial research over the purely structured interview and these advantages are not outweighed by the problem of bias. The semi-structured interview is nevertheless not commonplace in industrial marketing research. Although the skills needed are less than those required for non-directive interviewing, they are still of a sufficiently high order for most researchers to regard the use of interviewers capable of conducting semi-structured interviews as wasteful. A circumstance in which such interviews might be used is where fairly heavy repetitive interviewing, usually of a low managerial or even at shop floor or clerical level, is required. For example interviewing operatives on attitudes towards brands of tungsten tipped drills, typists' choice of carbon paper, lorry drivers' preferences for cargo retaining systems.

NON-DIRECTIVE INTERVIEWING

The non-directive interview is by far the commonest and most useful method used in interviewing in industrial marketing research. These types of interviews are known by various names—'open ended', 'unstructured', 'free-ranging'. Each title describes a facet of the interview method. Non-directive interviews are, in fact, a free discussion between interviewer and respondent orientated towards, but not directed along certain channels.

The unstructured interview can begin at any point which the interviewer can successfully introduce and can be worked round the whole subject, crossing and recrossing some avenues of enquiry, validating, directly and indirectly, statements already made, probing, clarifying, developing interesting new lines of enquiry and abandoning unsuccessful ones. Such an interview can proceed on a much more informal basis than is attainable by a structured or semi-structured interview. It permits the interplay of personalities and ideas between interviewer and respondent and the researcher is far freer to observe the effect and reaction to questions concerned with the respondent or his firm. One of the great advantages of the unstructured interview is that the respondent, under the stimulus of a good interviewer, frequently produces ideas, comments and suggestions which might never have occurred to him in the course of a structured interview.

The informality and freedom of the interview creates a more relaxed atmosphere and reduces any anxiety arising from the interview situation. It also enables the interviewer to change ground quickly and approach subjects which the respondent is finding difficulty in dealing with, from a different direction.

The advantages of the non-directive interview are thus very considerable while the disadvantages are not significantly greater than in the semi-structured interview already outlined.

Essentially the interviewer knows the research objectives and knows the individual interview objectives. He is left to achieve these by whatever route is the most suitable for the given circumstance, type of respondent and interview situation. This might well be thought to produce a non-comparable interview yield with the induced biases, not only varying from interviewer to interviewer but between individual interviews of the same interviewer. While it is true that poor interview technique, lack of self-discipline in the interviewers, and ill-prepared questions will produce a far more disastrous effect than these same circumstances using structured or even semi-structured interviews, the survey would in any event be useless if such types of researchers as have been described were to be used.

The success of a non-directive interview rests on the skill and application of the interviewer himself. In describing the essential qualities of the salesman as 'empathy and ego drive'[1] the writers may not have realised they also accurately described the characteristics of the good interviewer. The *Oxford Dictionary* defines empathy as 'the power of projecting one's personality into, and so fully understanding, the object of contemplation'. Transposing what has been said about salesmen in this context, it is also true to say that interviewers cannot achieve their objectives 'without this invaluable and irreplaceable ability to get a powerful feedback'[2] from their respondents.

Thus given the appropriate skills, the non-directive interview is likely to remain the most successful method of interviewing for industrial marketing research, being far more productive of far more usable, validated data than any other method and being less likely to be subject to miscommunication and misinterpretation.

MOTIVATION RESEARCH

Motivation research comprises a group of highly specialised techniques developed by the behavioral scientists to discover the factors influencing human behaviour. Its use is far wider than marketing although it is in this area that it has attracted most notice and most criticism. Almost all marketing studies using motivation research techniques have been confined to consumer research. In a limited form they are neverthelss applicable to industrial situations and can greatly assist in explaining some of the phenomenon present in an industrial market.

(a) *The focused interview*

The principal tool of motivation research is the 'depth' interview, although 'focused' is perhaps a better description of it. It is employed

---

[1] D. Mayer and H. Greenberg, 'What Makes a Good Salesman', *Harvard Business Review* (Cambridge, Mass., July/August 1964).

[2] David Rowe, 'Industrial Selling', *The Marketing of Industrial Products*, op. cit., p. 83.

to elicit the freest possible association of ideas on the part of the respondent. The respondent himself, for the most part, determines the direction, the order and the content of the interview. The interviewer must be skilled in developing rapport, inducing the respondent to express himself and inserting delicate probes where necessary to encourage fuller discussion. It avoids the interruption of the free flow of ideas which other types of interviews necessarily introduce. Instead by giving respondents an opportunity to talk about themselves, listening sympathetically and encouraging further self-exploration, the closest kind of rapport can be developed in the course of a focused interviewing procedure. The mass of information accumulated by depth interviewing techniques is analysed for the purpose of determining the *meaning* of the respondents' behaviour, rather than relying strictly upon their own explanations.

Because broad areas of investigation are mapped out and because there is no fixed sequence to the conversation during a focused interview, it must be necessarily subject to some guidance. But in guiding the conversation it is important that the interviewer avoids accidentally also guiding the answers. 'Funnel' techniques can be used. These, while maintaining the 'open end' approach to questions, keep the respondent within the areas of investigation. For example, in a study of work aids for industrial sewing machines, respondents tended to discuss characteristics of various materials rather than the machines themselves. Questions on fusing and welding characteristics of fibres are directly linked to respondents' interests and indirectly linked to the interviewer's interest. From fusing it was possible to ask for comparisons with stitching and from stitching lead to machine speeds and thus on to work aids, such as thread trimmers. Thus the respondent is held in the mainstream of inquiries without seeming to be controlled.

The focused interview is an intricate technique requiring highly trained interviewers not only to conduct the interview correctly but to make a running interpretation of the replies in order to keep the interview moving in the right direction and to carry out the overall interpretation of the interview and survey.

(b) *Projective techniques*

The projective technique is basically a method of inducing the respondents to talk about themselves in a disguised form. Where, for example, motivation patterns which are socially unacceptable are encountered the projective technique—in which the respondent interprets a deliberately vague story, photograph or design—permits them to attribute their own motives, without feelings of guilt, to some third party. It also enables them to express feelings about external factors which they may not know about themselves but which are extremely revealing of their attitudes.

Projection can be facilitated by presentation of devices which by their very nature are vague and indefinite. A situation clearly depicted, verbally or pictorially with 'little left to the imagination', will generally permit scant projection. But the less structured and less defined the presentation of the situation the more will it allow the individual to project himself and structure it in his mind. The process will receive further stimulation when a person is requested to draw specific conclusions. The situation itself being inconclusive will make it necessary for the individual to produce conclusions out of his own mind. However, responses to devices employed in projective techniques should not be considered as productive of conclusive evidence. Responses can well indicate the existence of feeling. They will not tell much, if anything, about its cause. Psycho-analytically speaking these attitudes in the individual are 'repressed' or 'suppressed' as the case may be, but reveal themselves when 'projected', i.e. attributed to others.

The two commonest types of visual projective tests are the thematic apperception test and the cartoon test. In the former a somewhat vague picture is presented and the respondent is asked to describe the circumstances which led to the pictured situation. In the cartoon test, two figures are usually shown with a minimum of facial expression so that they are neutral. One person is represented as making a statement and the second person has a blank speech balloon which the respondent is asked to complete. Thematic apperception tests actually used in a research project are shown in Figure 20.[1] Salesmen were asked: 'What is the situation depicted?' 'What are the events which led up to it and what will be the outcome? Describe the feelings, thoughts and characteristics of the people involved.'

Verbal projective tests include word association and sentence completion tests. In the former the respondent is presented with a word by the interviewer and is asked to reply with the first word that comes into his mind. It is assumed that by 'free associating' he will reveal his inner feelings about the subject under investigation. The sentence completion is similar to the cartoon test in that the respondent is given an incomplete situation. For example: 'Most trade papers are . . .' Typical completions are:

[1] K. Rogers, *Managers—Personality and Performance*, Tavistock Publications (London, 1963), Appendix C.

'well informed'
'not worth reading'
'full of advertising'
'never read'.

Yet another test, well-known in clinical psychology, is the Rorschach blot test in which respondents are asked to explain with what they associate the shape of blots. This technique is effective in revealing how respondents perceive.

All these and other tests suffer with the same unfortunate disability in industrial marketing research. The major difficulty, other than that of obtaining researchers skilful and trained in the use of these techniques, is to get the co-operation of businessmen and technicians. It is safe to say that whereas it is possible to conduct focused interviews in the majority of industrial situations, projective techniques are not truly suitable for this type of respondent except where the researcher is fortunate enough to come across a particularly sympathetic and understanding person. While housewives and perhaps even businessmen, technicians, scientists and others, in the home environment might enjoy playing these sorts of 'games', within the firm the average subject of an industrial interview is apt to look upon games, particularly psychological games, as rather silly. Hence in attempting to use motivation research techniques, in industrial marketing research it is usually necessary to revert to the focused interview. Nevertheless, just as focused interviewing is slowly becoming a standard weapon in the industrial marketing research armoury, there is every likelihood of greater use developing of the other, more exotic methods using clinical techniques.

(c) *Group interviews*

The high cost of focused interviewing has led recently to attempts being made to conduct industrial marketing research enquiries using motivation research techniques with groups, as is common among consumers. Bearing in mind the methods and objectives of motivation research techniques in industrial marketing research, group interviews are a compromise solution for a situation where the ideal would be individual focused interviews. There are, however, certain advantages in the group interview in that the interchange of ideas and opinions by group members rapidly reduces the resistance, inhibitions and the consciousness of the presence of the researcher, all of which are present in individual interviews. The role of the researcher is to initiate, stimulate and guide the group discussion.

SKETCH 1

SKETCH 2

SKETCH 3

Fig. 20
VISUAL PROJECTIVE TEST

Frequently this role is minimal since groups tend to generate their own dynamic.

The whole problem of group interviews is not connected with the success or otherwise of the method by which they are conducted. Sufficient experience has now been obtained by marketing researchers using these advanced techniques to indicate that they are indeed successful, given the skilful guidance of a trained psychologist to conduct the group and interpret the results. The principal difficulty is to assemble in one place at one time six, eight or ten respondents who fit into the sampling frame. Experience in a number of industries indicates that it is necessary to have as many as forty names from which to draw to obtain six to eight respondents with perhaps two reserves, able to attend an arranged meeting. As a result, in a 'universe' which is itself small it may be impossible to obtain a sufficient number of groups. Further, to fix appointments for this meeting takes the talents of a skilled interviewer though not necessarily in motivation research. Possibly as long as two weeks might be needed to arrange two groups—a factor which adds significantly to the costs. The necessity to explain, usually on the telephone, the purpose and method of the research, to remove suspicion and resistance and to persuade all respondents to attend at a fixed time, calls for considerable talent.

THE INTERVIEW SITUATION

The interviewing situation so far as industrial marketing research is concerned derives from the type of interview being conducted. *Survey* interviews are used most frequently because these are designed to obtain information from authorities and leading opinion in any particular field, or representative groups about which information is required. *Diagnostic* interviews are used to attempt to understand a problem, the causes which gave rise to it, and its present status.[1]

In both these types of interviews the situation will vary because the types of questions and the interview objectives will in themselves produce varying degrees of co-operation, opposition, anxiety or other manifestations of personal reactions. The interviewer must be able to recognise these and avert them, bring them forward in time, or postpone them.

A hypothetical but nevertheless typical situation is illustrated in Figure 21. Here the interview sequence is shown as a vertical bar and the segments of the interview are related to the reaction they produce

[1] *Research Methodology in Business*, op. cit., pp. 95-6.

in the respondent, the degree of tension being indicated by the density of the shading. The interviewer's objective is to narrow the timespan occupied by segments 1 to 3 and at the same time reduce the degree (density) of the tension.

Ideally the interviewer would like to control the interview so that the tension is constantly decreasing towards a completely relaxed

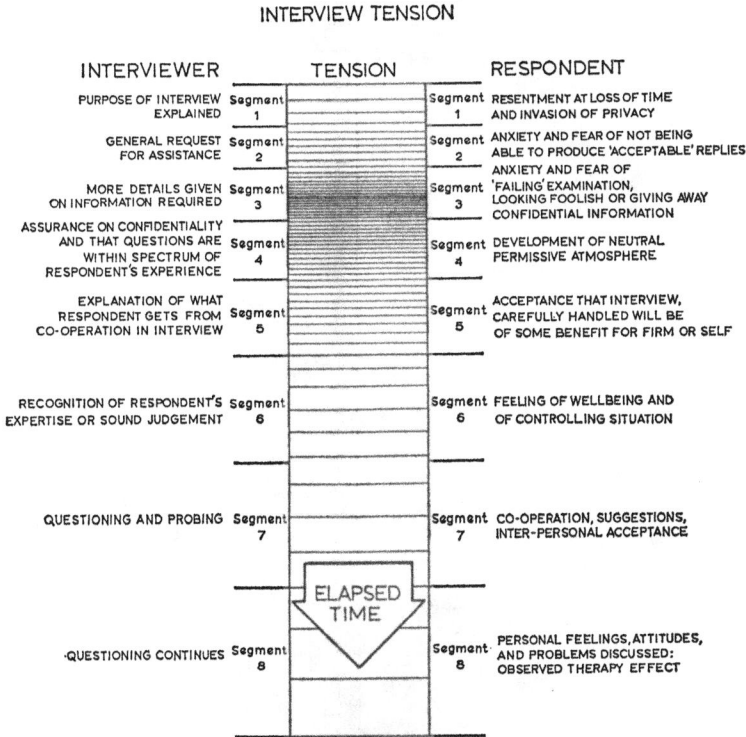

INTERVIEW TENSION

INTERVIEWER	TENSION	RESPONDENT
PURPOSE OF INTERVIEW EXPLAINED — Segment 1		Segment 1 — RESENTMENT AT LOSS OF TIME AND INVASION OF PRIVACY
GENERAL REQUEST FOR ASSISTANCE — Segment 2		Segment 2 — ANXIETY AND FEAR OF NOT BEING ABLE TO PRODUCE 'ACCEPTABLE' REPLIES
MORE DETAILS GIVEN ON INFORMATION REQUIRED — Segment 3		Segment 3 — ANXIETY AND FEAR OF 'FAILING' EXAMINATION, LOOKING FOOLISH OR GIVING AWAY CONFIDENTIAL INFORMATION
ASSURANCE ON CONFIDENTIALITY AND THAT QUESTIONS ARE WITHIN SPECTRUM OF RESPONDENT'S EXPERIENCE — Segment 4		Segment 4 — DEVELOPMENT OF NEUTRAL PERMISSIVE ATMOSPHERE
EXPLANATION OF WHAT RESPONDENT GETS FROM CO-OPERATION IN INTERVIEW — Segment 5		Segment 5 — ACCEPTANCE THAT INTERVIEW, CAREFULLY HANDLED WILL BE OF SOME BENEFIT FOR FIRM OR SELF
RECOGNITION OF RESPONDENT'S EXPERTISE OR SOUND JUDGEMENT — Segment 6		Segment 6 — FEELING OF WELLBEING AND OF CONTROLLING SITUATION
QUESTIONING AND PROBING — Segment 7		Segment 7 — CO-OPERATION, SUGGESTIONS, INTER-PERSONAL ACCEPTANCE
	ELAPSED TIME	
QUESTIONING CONTINUES — Segment 8		Segment 8 — PERSONAL FEELINGS, ATTITUDES, AND PROBLEMS DISCUSSED: OBSERVED THERAPY EFFECT

Fig. 21
CONTROLLING INTERVIEW TENSION

state—something which can happen, particularly when respondent and interviewer are acquainted and like or respect each other. The situation as between friends or persons well-known to each other is one in which tension will usually be low or non-existent. The process of exploring each other's personality will have already occurred so that suspicion, doubt, mistrust and all emotions which manifest themselves at first meetings are avoided.

However, the typical industrial interview will be between total strangers and the feelings engendered will, despite the controlled

manner of their being exhibited, be atavistic and as primitive as those
of Neanderthal man.

The skilled interviewer can use the segments (which it is again
emphasised are entirely hypothetical and are given only for illustrative
purposes) to obtain the maximum interview yield. Each of the reac-

CONTROLLING INTERVIEW TENSION

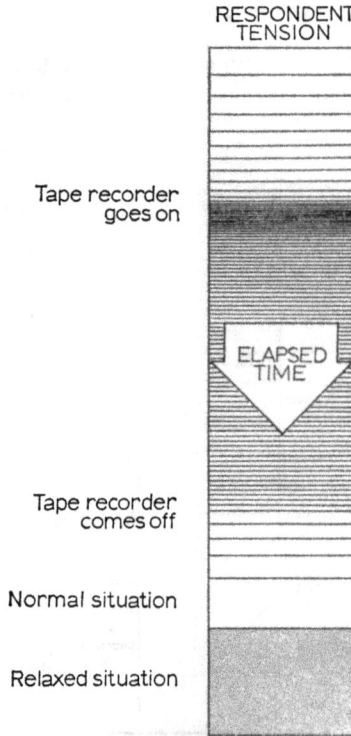

RESPONDENT
TENSION

Tape recorder
goes on

ELAPSED
TIME

Tape recorder
comes off

Normal situation

Relaxed situation

Fig. 22
INTERVIEW TENSION

tions set up in the respondent by the interviewer's statements and
questions can be made to accelerate or slow down any particular sequence of the interview. Thus some aspects can be explored in
greater depth while matters which the respondent may wish to talk
about but which are not relevant to the interview can be covered
quickly and superficially. At the same time this will not give the
respondent the feeling that either his views are of no consequence,
the interviewer has lost interest, or that he is being 'exploited'.

A tape recorder at an interview creates anxiety for many reasons and always inhibits the interview. Ostentatiously switched off, the tension it has created is dissipated and the respondent reacting from that tension becomes far more open because of the sudden removal of the inhibiting factor. He might be said to 'bounce' back from reticence to loquaciousness. This is an example of just one method of using the interview dynamic to produce a given effect. In graphic terms the density representing the degree of tension, instead of increasing quickly and then decreasing slowly will commence suddenly as the recorder goes on and will dissipate almost as quickly as it is switched off but leaving the respondent in a more relaxed condition than that which he was in *before* the recorder was switched on. This is illustrated in Figure 22.

Conversely, a failure to understand the dynamics of an interview can result in the complete loss of the interview. It will be brought to an end precipitously and without warning, the unwary interviewer not even beginning to appreciate precisely what went wrong. The tension will have increased quickly and reached a breaking point at which the respondent will have decided that he can take no more, the situation having become unbearable. The interviewer will have been asked politely, and sometimes not so politely, to leave before the main questions have been reached.

Against this background it can be seen that the first objective of the interviewer must be to gain acceptance and then to put the respondent at his ease. These two factors are both part of the skills of interviewing and of the procedural pattern.

SKILLS OF INTERVIEWING

The *qualities* of the good interviewer have been summed up as empathy and ego-drive. The *skills* of interviewing are less easy to categorise. Any interview must be undertaken with a sense of its functional unity, it must have definite objectives, be well organised, and its results lend themselves to accurate interpretation and the application of judgement. The skills of interviewing must include all these things.

The proficient interviewer must be capable of quickly creating a friendly atmosphere. The best atmosphere can be described as 'cordial' since over-emphasis rapidly produces a reaction in the respondent and being too friendly can be almost as disastrous for an interview as being aggressive. An atmosphere cordial to one respondent may be regarded as over-familiar by another and formal by the third. Thus part of the skills involved in the opening gambits of an interview are to decide just what level of 'friendliness' will achieve the correct effect. 'First name terms in five minutes' may be suitable for some interviewing in the electronics industry in California but is not likely to be regarded as acceptable in, for example, merchant banking circles in the City of London.

It is a truism to say that whenever an individual is placed in an unfamiliar situation he becomes apprehensive. The existence of physically familiar things such as the respondent's own office will only slightly reduce the anxiety caused by the interview situation if it is strange to him. It is important to reduce this apprehension by explaining in some detail the purpose of the interview, the need to take notes, the use to which the information will be put, and in fact all the anxiety-provoking aspects of an unfamiliar situation.

The main skills involved in this part of the interview are to establish a relationship with the respondent which is regarded by him as a meeting of equals. It is unsatisfactory if the interviewer gives the impression of patronisation, or being more expert than the respondent.[1] Since it is impossible to judge in advance if a respondent feels more at ease with an interviewer who knows less or more than himself, equality is the only safe level to aim for. As the interview proceeds it is possible to shift positions but, as in the postal questionnaire, never in any circumstances must the respondent be made to feel he is sitting an examination. The 'third degree' approach can never be successful.

In dealing with the central points of the interview, it is important to be able to formulate questions that will avoid any form of negativism and point-blank refusals. This means that unpleasant associations, emotionally charged topics and personal comment by the interviewer must be avoided. Yet if the interviewer is less than frank this will rapidly be detected by the respondent and induce answers in a like vein. The essential skill is not to move on to the pertinent and key questions until the interviewer is satisfied that rapport has been established. One way of doing this is to discuss areas of agreement, subjects in which the interviewer can, without patronisation, compliment the respondent on his knowledge, activities or form of answers.

It is obvious that questions must always be phrased neutrally. In the majority of interview situations, but particularly with less well-educated respondents or those who will regard the interviewer as of a different and superior class, there will be a tendency to attempt to appraise the answer which will please the interviewer and give this

[1] A discussion on the use of technical interviewers occurs later in this chapter.

answer. Thus the interviewer must not give a clue as to the 'desirable' answer. Indeed the skilful interviewer will convey quite positively that there is no 'right' and 'wrong' answer to any questions put. There are only the respondent's answers.

No interview is likely to be successful if the interest of the respondents cannot be obtained and held. This is one of the main interview objectives. The respondent always wants to know the answer to a number of questions concerning the interviewer although he may not be basically interested in the interview itself. Even if the interview were in the wrong firm, with the wrong person on the wrong subject, the respondent would still want to know: what is the interviewer doing? why? who is he doing it for? why had the respondent's firm been chosen? why had the respondent been chosen? Answering this range of questions is more than sufficient to attract and hold initial attention.

Thus if the interview opens up by establishing a relationship of confidence it is possible to probe quickly areas of mutual interest related to the survey. The essential ingredients for holding the respondent's interest are the same as those in the whole business of life, highlighting the factors of self-interest and the status-raising device of seeking advice of an 'expert', 'pundit', 'knowledgeable' or 'experienced' person. Few people can resist the invitation to give an opinion, offer advice and to generally show that they are of some importance.

The interviewer must reach the point quickly where he can explain precisely how the respondent and the respondent's firm will gain from co-operating in the survey. This way interest is assured and usually held, if there is a genuine gain to the respondent. Figure 21 shows how tension drops from Segment 5 when the 'what's in it for me' factors are revealed and Segment 6 where the 'you are an expert' factors are offered.

An important skill in interviewing is to be able to make a running check on the accuracy of the replies. Sources of error are many: misheard and misunderstood questions, memory attrition and the effects of transfer and interference.[1]

Irrespective of the error source, it is the duty of the interviewer to validate all he obtains to the greatest extent possible. In the first instance the interviewer must convey to the respondent without

[1] 'Transfer' and 'interference' are well-known psychological phenomena. Transfer—the improvement of one mental or motor function by the systematic training of an allied function. Interference—the effect of one piece of learning or one association inhibiting another.

N

lecturing him the need for accuracy in his replies. Asking the same question in two different ways is one method. 'When did you last change suppliers?' and 'How long is it since you appointed your present supplier?' Another method is to ask the same question with a time-lag in between. 'I'm sorry, did I ask you if you had changed your supplier?' 'May I just check back a moment, what did you say about changing your supplier?'

Where inaccuracies can be identified, these should be pointed out with the greatest tact as an indication of more care being required in subsequent answers. This can be done by the interviewer accepting the blame and enabling the respondent to change his statement without loss of face. 'I'm sorry, I misunderstood you. I thought you said you hadn't changed suppliers.'

Interviewers are not infallible. Having ensured the respondent understands the question, it is as well to be quite positive the answer has been understood too. This is particularly relevant when technical terms and trade jargon are used. It is necessary to separate facts from inferences. It has been rightly suggested that facts which contain some measure of emotion are as likely to be a reflection of the interviewer's prejudices as those of the respondent.[1]

Where percentages and fractions are used to express views, it is most helpful to re-state them in a different form and get the respondent to agree them or to disagree. 'About half their deliveries are below specification.' 'Let's see now, that's about 230 units last month, is that about right?' Or 'I spend about 75 per cent of time checking the delivery notes.' By asking if that means six hours a day, a reappraisal will often be made.

One of the most potent interview techniques is the use of silence. Silence except between people with a degree of intimacy in their relationship is generally shunned, indeed feared. The inexperienced interviewer is often much more frightened of silence than the respondent. The developed ability to withstand silence can be used most effectively since most respondents will attempt to fill any silent gaps which is the cause of discomfort and apprehension, either by elaborating further on the last or previous questions, by asking questions themselves, or by trying to anticipate the next question. All these activities can provide invaluable information to the interviewer.

Yet another skill of interviewing and one rarely developed to a high level is that of listening. It is commonplace to try and teach interviewing skills but the course has yet to be devised on the skills of listening. It has been said often enough that people only hear what

[1] *Research Methodology in Business*, op. cit., p. 102.

they want to hear. Although this may be a well-worn cliché, it summarises the mechanics that lie behind poor listening techniques. The individual biases of interviewers and their attitudes as well as role perceptions and stereotyping lead to selective perception. This in turn must lead to inaccurate recording of interviews and, inevitably, inaccurate results.

In order to avoid this situation the interviewer 'must be aware of his own particular filters that tend to impede if not prevent clear and relatively undistorted reception of information. It is possible to hear at the rate of from 110 to 140 words per minute over sustained periods. The thinking or thought projection rate is approximately seven times this figure. The result is surplus thinking time over listening time. The manner in which this surplus time is utilised varies, of course, with the individual. However, it is at this point that the interviewer tends to project his ideas into the interview process, thereby filtering out the interviewee's responses.'[1] The dangers of this are obvious. Thus one of the skills it is necessary to develop in interviewing is the skill of listening and being aware of the distortions which can be introduced by selective perception.

BRIEFING

In industrial marketing research the interviewer and researcher will frequently be one and the same person since the commonest form of organisation of a research project is 'one man one job'. Thus the researcher will conduct the entire enquiry, possibly with the exception of the basic desk research, and thus will not require briefing specifically for interviewing. Where, however, interviewers are used, irrespective of their skills, their performance will be conditioned by the quality of the briefing they receive.

This briefing serves three purposes: (a) to identify and explain objectives, (b) to instruct in the procedures to be adopted, and (c) to motivate to complete the work correctly.

To conduct interviews intelligently the interviewers must understand both the objective of the interview and its relevance to the research objectives. This is particularly important when non-directive interviewing is to take place. The interviewers have no way of checking their own performance and interview yield unless they know what the interview is supposed to produce.

[1] S. G. Trull, 'Strategies of Effective Interviewing', *Harvard Business Review* (Cambridge, Mass., Jan/Feb. 1964).

Clearly instructions on procedure will be required if the interviewing programme is to follow the schedule and the sampling
requirements are to be fully met. Instructions should include the full
sampling procedure, administrative details on timing and reporting,
the use of check lists (if they are to be used), an explanation of any
necessary forms and directions on the use of equipment which might
be needed in the interview. The briefing which generally occurs after
pilot interviews have taken place will be an opportunity to guide
interviewers on the handling of certain questions and to warn them
of the types of reactions they might expect to receive and how to
cope with them. Technical briefing may also be necessary.

Interviewers must understand any technical aspects of the product
or service or the market which are likely to be discussed in the interviews. A familiarity must be obtained with technical terms and trade
jargon. One aspect often overlooked is the common use of abbrevia-
tions in conversations between people in the same industry or
activity. To an engineer 'psi' (i.e. pounds per square inch) requires
no explanation but could leave a non-engineering interviewer confused.

The question of motivation of the interviewers is another purpose
of briefing which is neglected. The interviewers must be satisfied that
the techniques being used are relevant and that their own contribution will produce the required results. If they cannot see the contribution their work will make or if they are doubtful or cynical about
the methodology adopted for the project as a whole or the interview
method itself, it is unlikely that they will produce satisfactory results.
In addition they must see the role they have been allotted as a
reasonable one and that their time schedule and work load are practical. Finally, their remuneration must be related to the extent of the
work to be carried out and to their level of skill as the interviewers.

INTERVIEW PROCEDURE

An unorganised interview is rarely a successful one. Because interviews are described as 'non-directive' or 'unstructured' this does not
imply that they are not organised. It is again possible to see the
similarity in the approaches of the different techniques used in an
industrial marketing research programme when preparing for an
interview. The procedure is (a) to decide who is the correct respon-
dent(s), (b) arrange the interview, (c) plan the interview, (d) conduct
the interview, (e) record the interview, (f) close the interview. Most of
these activities must also be completed in one way or another before

telephone interviews or observations can be conducted successfully and indeed the various actions are also indicative of some of the postal questionnaire processes too.

(a) *Deciding who is the correct respondent(s)*

There is no chance of the interview being completed effectively unless the respondents best able and most willing to discuss the subject under review are identified. It is important for the interviewer to ensure that the people interviewed are representative of the activities, functions or even factions of the groups to be studied.

The concept of the Decision Making Unit was discussed in Chapter 1. It will be obvious from this that it may be necessary within any individual firm to talk with more than one person. A 'visit' may in fact be several 'interviews'.

Thus part of the process of deciding who to interview is also the process of identifying the DMU which can in itself be a complex enquiry. The study of involvement in purchasing decisions previously referred to[1] has shown that in only 4 per cent of cases is only one person involved. In 89 per cent of cases three or more people are involved while in over half the cases between four and six people are involved (Figure 23).

A common failing among interviewers is that they do not devote sufficient time in their questioning to understanding the respondent's concept of his role in the interview. Very often, to take a most common example, a correctly selected respondent will tend to speak as a spokesman on company policy rather than say a member of a DMU. Role perception is a vital part of the interviewer's task and one that is easily overlooked, neglected or poorly applied.

Some guidance can be obtained at the outset by the firm's own experience of the Decision Making Units among their customers, and from the desk research activities. A series of pilot interviews will bring out a pattern of activity even if later this should not prove to be the common pattern. The essentially sequential nature of industrial marketing research is highlighted by the need to shift the respondent criteria as patterns of activities emerge.

Thus preliminary desk research, perhaps combined with pilot interviews, will reveal the criteria by which the correct respondents can be identified. This information will include job title, job definition or job activity, and it must be noted that these will not always correlate. The title of 'Maintenance Manager' can easily include functions such as *purchasing* materials and responsibility for *manufac-*

[1] *How British Industry Buys*, op. cit., Table 5.

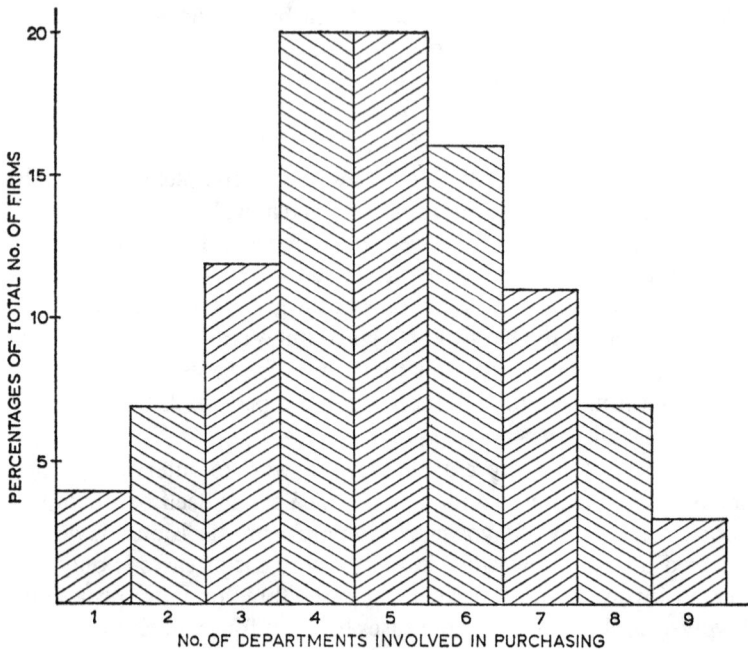

Fig. 23

turing spares. Thus it is essential not only to establish industry practice and nomenclature, but to be aware of the way in which variations from these may manifest themselves.

(b) *Arranging the interview*

By far the quickest and most efficient method of arranging an interview is by telephone. Doubling up in a full interview schedule or the creation of 'blank' spots can be more easily avoided this way. Making appointments by letter leads to delays and dates being held open which are not subsequently filled. The danger of fixing appointments by telephone is to risk the conversation turning into the interview itself. It requires both tact and skill to answer a request: 'Well, why can't you ask me now over the telephone?'

The interest of the prospective respondent must be obtained if agreement to an interview is to be given. In this respect the situation outlined earlier in this chapter applies and the techniques for developing a sympathetic ambient atmosphere must be acquired. The use of the telephone has its own particular problems which are dealt with in the next chapter.

The question of 'cold calling' is one which often arouses quite strong feelings. There are experienced interviewers who believe that the element of surprise and tactful pressure will produce an interview at a higher frequency rate than pre-arranged interviews. This is certainly true for some types of interviews and respondents. At a fairly low managerial or shop floor level and where respondents tend to be immobile, pre-arranging interviews may be more difficult than just walking in. At higher managerial levels and where respondents are mobile—sales managers, service managers, surveyors—the failure rate of cold calling is uneconomically high. Moreover, many respondents in these latter groups would regard it as discourteous, inconvenient and annoying to be disturbed by an itinerant marketing researcher.

In conducting interviews, whether fixed in advance or 'cold', it would be also desirable to be able to arrange the physical conditions. This, however, is rarely possible unless the respondent can be induced to visit the interviewer or is taken to some mutually agreeable location such as a restaurant—something not encouraged either by the respondent's or the interviewer's companies.

The circumstances surrounding the acquisition of information have an important bearing on analysis and interpretation but information given freely may be no more reliable than that extracted with difficulty.

It is useful, if it is possible, for the interviewer to learn in advance something about the pattern of daily business activity so that the interviews can be conducted at the moment most convenient to the respondent. For example, a daily post meeting at 9.30 a.m. may put a quick finish to an interview begun at 9.00 a.m. The rush to get the mail out at 4.30 p.m. will not help quiet and detached thinking. Working hours tend to follow a geographical rather than an industrial pattern. While in the commercial areas in the centres of cities in the United Kingdom lunch tends to be at 1.00 p.m., in factories midday is the more usual time. But then, midday is also the usual lunch hour for many commercial concerns in New York and San Francisco.

When all the environmental factors have been accounted for, if not actually obviated, the interviewer is left with a range of most suitable times and days on which to conduct the interview. This in itself can lead to great wastage and in part accounts for the fact that two interviews per day is a good average for industrial marketing research as against ten times that number in consumer research.

(c) *Planning the interview*

It has already been pointed out earlier in this chapter that non-directive interviews are based on the interviewer knowing the objectives and working towards them by the most appropriate route. In more detailed terms, before an interview commences the interviewer must have a very clear idea of what that particular interview is intended to achieve. Whether pilot interviews have been conducted or not, a range of probes and prompts should be prepared to assist the respondent and to channel the interview. In this respect the types of prompts used in Case Study method have been found to be most effective.[1]

Where any particular reactions can be anticipated, the interviewers' responses must be ready. Thus 'Why do you want to know' from a respondent cannot be countered with: 'It's part of the research,' any intelligent respondent will seek not so much a reason as a justification. 'Who is the survey for?' when it is being conducted anonymously, if countered with a 'Sorry I can't tell you,' will fairly frequently produce a 'Then I can't give you the interview.' Yet anonymity is not a major problem if it is dealt with properly.

The interviewer cannot foresee every eventuality at the beginning of a survey but he can certainly prepare for the obvious ones and be ready to deal with the whole range of them before many interviews have been completed and the survey has patterned.

(d) *Conducting the interview*

There are fairly simple rules which must be followed in conducting an interview:

● Create a friendly and informal atmosphere. The not-too-serious discussions of areas of mutual interst (news, weather, industry events) or identification of mutual acquaintances is a rapid way of doing this. It is unwise to plunge too abruptly into the interview subject. To help the respondent feel at ease, the interviewer must be at ease himself.

● Identify the respondent as the person with whom the appointment was fixed.

● Check, as early as possible, that the respondent fits the selection criteria.[2]

[1] M. P. McNair, *The Case Method at the Harvard Business School*, McGraw-Hill (New York, 1954).

[2] This cannot always be done at the outset of an interview and may only be established during the early phases. The rule, however, is to obtain the information as early in the interview as possible to avoid wasting both the interviewer's and the respondent's time if the latter is not the correct person.

● Explain the purpose of the interview.

● Go over what is required from the respondent so he can orientate himself to the discussion.

● Create an atmosphere of discussion between equals. Neither arrogance nor subservience are good interview attitudes. Showing respect for the respondent and his views, however, is not subservience.

● Avoid 'third degree' type questions and staccato responses. 'Why', 'explain', 'quantity?' worded as 'Can you tell me why you think this?' and 'I'm afraid I don't quite follow that, could you explain it again,' and 'What sort of quantity was involved on this occasion?' are far more conducive to full replies.

● Formulate early questions to produce positive answers. Too many negative replies will make the respondent feel he is being less than helpful and thus he will feel uncomfortable.

● Ask only one question at a time and give the respondent time to answer fully. Do not assume a pause is the end of the answer.

● Be sure the respondent understands the question. If necessary repeat it.

● Observe physical activities, facial expressions, tone of voice and other indirect responses.

● While permitting the respondent a full reply, be prepared to stop him rambling by inserting a new question. However, do not stop him talking about what he wants to talk about if it has any relevance at all to the subject of the interview. If he wants to talk about it, it is important to him and the reasons for this importance will become apparent.

● Avoid the respondent changing the subject and then giving the impression that the subject the respondent introduced is unimportant or foolish. 'Can I just for a moment stay on the question of the change of supplier?' contains no element of brusqueness and implies that the interviewing will be returning to the respondent's digression in due course.

● The interviewer must avoid registering any emotion in relation to the information given, that is surprise, shock, disagreement or agreement. Apart from implying there is a 'right' and a 'wrong' answer, it encourages the respondent to probe what the interviewer wants to hear and then tell it to him.

● If any explanations are needed, avoid patronising or lecturing.

● Avoid embarrassing the respondent by asking questions either in a form which he cannot understand or beyond his intellectual or technical ability to answer.

● Check accuracy of statements as the interview proceeds and as far as possible.

● At the close of the interview go back over the major points to get the respondent's agreement that the answers are in fact what he said and to give him any opportunity to revise, augment, change or withdraw any statements. Present his summary in as neutral a way as possible to avoid the respondent considering he may have been indiscreet.

These points are intended as general guide lines but are nevertheless fundamental to good interviewing and should be observed in all interviewing situations.

(e) *Recording the interview*

The human memory is well-known to be fallible and the memory errors of respondents are neither greater nor lesser than those of interviewers. Possessors of photographic memories are few. For the interview yield to give the maximum value, some record of the interview will be needed.

Tape recorders have been found to be one of the most inhibiting factors in an interview situation and unless they are used as described earlier in the chapter, they have no part in interviewing. Permission to take notes should always be sought. It is far better to make notes but at the same time, impressive clipboards, meticulous writing down of statements verbatim have a 'police' aura. Apart from quickly losing the patience of the respondent it will inhibit spontaneous comments and increase apprehension and thus tension. Note taking should be as informal as the conversation. There is no point in pretending not to take notes by doodling. Few respondents will be fooled by this and will in fact become suspicious of the interviewer's intentions.

However, note taking can be relegated to the backs of newspapers, file covers, business cards and even by asking the respondent to let the interviewer have a few sheets of paper. The purpose is to produce the same informal atmosphere as occurs in a casual discussion when diaries, menu card and even table cloths are called to the aid of the participants. The more ponderous, formal and lengthy the note taking, the less value will the interview yield be.

Writing notes when a respondent is talking may make him stop talking until the interviewer catches up and thus break up his thought process and his statement. It has been suggested writing can be limited by preparing a check list and a range of answers so that the interviewer need only tick or ring the appropriate answers. The disadvantages are obvious, the questions in a semi-structured interview may not, despite funnelling, follow the interview pattern and sequences. The interviewer is left desperately thumbing through his pages trying to find the appropriate question and to check what has been missed.

It is not unusual to offer the respondent a write-up of the interview for him to approve. Apart from giving him confidence and creating trust in the interviewer, it gives him the opportunity to edit what he has said, remove anything he considers indiscreet or undesirable, and to change his statements. This also enables the interviewer to compare the unedited with the edited versions since the changes may give a considerable insight into the thinking, background and experience of the respondent.

(f) *Closing the interview*

The respondent must be left with a friendly feeling towards the interviewer. If the interviewer has done his work properly the respondent will feel his time has been well spent, both for himself and his company, and, more important, will be willing to provide more information should the interviewer need to return.

It is useful for the interviewer to ask the respondent before he leaves if there is anything he, the interviewer, can tell the respondent. Some respondents who may have wanted to ask questions pertinent to the interview subject but have refrained from doing so will at this stage raise a query. 'Well can *you* tell *me* how big *you* think the market is?' 'Do *you* feel that a videophone will have an impact on transportation?' 'Have *you* heard as you've been going round how Trongle's Hypoteneuses are performing?' Answers to these sorts of questions can do much to persuade respondents they have received something in return for their time.

However, the tail-end questions will often highlight the area of interest to a respondent, and certainly any aspects of the interview subject which are causing him personal concern. All this provides more data for the interview so that the opportunity for these last interchanges should not be lost.

Closing an interview can, however, be a difficult thing. At one extreme the respondent might terminate the interview precipitously before the discussion is finished. The obvious course then is to seek another appointment. The respondent may say 'I can give you five more minutes,' and the interviewer has to make a rapid appraisal of outstanding questions and decide which ones to put. At the other extreme the respondent may just want to go on talking—the therapy effect of Segment 8 in Figure 21. In this last circumstance the interviewer must be polite and firm and must not appear to show disinterest once the information he wanted has been given. The plea of another appointment, a train to catch, a car on a meter is understood by most people.

The general rule of industrial marketing researchers is to remain in the interview for just as long as the respondent is prepared to talk. Since the interview rate is usually only two per day, nothing is lost by making interviews longer rather than shorter. It is a truism to say that extra questions in industrial marketing research cost nothing, only extra interviews. Nevertheless, the interviewer with empathy will know when he has reached a reasonable limit in time and will terminate the discussion. The door should always be left open to return.

INTERVIEWING COMPETITIVE FIRMS

It is perhaps appropriate to digress from the main purpose of this chapter to discuss a problem which exercises many marketing researchers, that is the ethics, practicability and desirability of interviewing competitive firms. It was pointed out in Chapter 2 that there is no ethical problem whatsoever, always provided that competitors being interviewed grant the interview in the full knowledge that it is a competitor to whom they are speaking. With this fact before them any decision they take will be what they consider to be in the best interests of the company, and with full knowledge of the circumstances. Thus the ethical problem only exists if unethical practices occur.

For the research sponsor the situation can be clearly set out. Under no circumstances is it ethical or advisable for a firm to interview its competitors using a false identity. No reputable firm would consider doing so and in the past over-enthusiastic marketing researchers who, perhaps with only good intentions and their own firm's interest at heart, have found themselves in trouble with their own employers.

It is, although people who have never done it doubt it, not difficult for a reputable organisation to telephone its competitors and propose a meeting for an exchange of information. This is done formally and informally in parts of the chemical and electronic capital goods and components industry. Had it been done in the polyurethane foam industry in the late 1950s when simultaneous research led to conclusions on market potential which in turn brought about heavy over-capacity, a considerable amount of industrial distress might have been avoided since competitors would at least have been aware of each other's interest in the market. Conversely there is little doubt that if over-capacity exists or develops in the freight container industry, it will not stem from ignorance among the major firms' intentions of each other's marketing research activities.

Nevertheless, firms will often require anonymity in a survey. In these circumstances, and if competitor interviews are needed, there is no alternative but to employ an agency. An agency, however, is just as responsible for revealing that the interview is requested on behalf of a competitor as the competitor is himself, although in these circumstances the agency does not reveal the sponsor's name. It may then be asked why a competitor should grant an interview to a faceless firm behind the agency. The answer remains the same. First a knowledge of the survey will provide important indications of the direction of current thinking in the industry, and indeed may pinpoint areas of specific interest. Requests from three different industrial marketing research agencies to an electronic manufacturer for interviews concerning holography drew attention of the respondent firm to the rapidly spreading interests and business opportunities in this area. Second, if respondent firms expect co-operation in their own surveys, they must be prepared to co-operate. Large-scale sponsors and buyers of research are almost always highly co-operative when interviews are requested, they have learned the importance of *quid pro quo* in research. Third 'A trained interviewer will not expect to get something for nothing, but will be in a position through the knowledge of the market he is surveying to exchange information. An interviewer, after all, has a wider and more recent view of the market than the majority of his respondents and has information, not confidential to the project which he can give in exchange for the data provided by the respondent. That this practice has its merits is borne out by the fact that competitors are normally interviewed during a survey by interviewers who are known to represent a competitor. These interviews are certainly not all one way, and most are conducted with satisfaction to both sides.'[1]

---

[1] Gordon Brand, 'Industrial Marketing Research—Management Aspects', *The Marketing of Industrial Products*, op. cit., pp. 64-5.

USE OF SALESMEN

A further digression from the main subject in this chapter is a discussion on the use of salesmen for marketing research in general and interviewing in particular.

Such a practice is highly undesirable. Salesmen are trained to persuade, not to report objectively on factors which may both reflect on their own performance or which might be against their personal interest and aspirations. It should be obvious that the skills and techniques which have been set out cannot be acquired as 'fall out' from a totally different activity.

A salesman should be enthusiastic and biased about his products. 'If he is able to step outside his job and take a detached view, all too frequently he will be failing in his task of selling. If he is a competent salesman he will have the ability to influence a customer in order to put him in a mood conducive to buying. If requested to put marketing research questions to a buyer, the good salesman will find it difficult not to influence his respondent by putting words into his mouth. The average respondent is easily influenced by an untrained interviewer.

The possibility of bias does not end with the influence of salesmen on the respondent but also exists in the salesman's interpretation of what he has heard. A field salesman will necessarily be detached from the real purpose of the market investigation, however good the channels of communication within the firm. He may well believe that the questions are a method of checking on his own performance, as indeed they might be, and he will be influenced consciously or unconsciously to alter the emphasis of the respondent's replies in a way to present his own position in the best light or to support the views he may have already expressed to management. This danger is particularly true in new product development where salesmen tend to take positive attitudes for or against a new product.

Another drawback in using the sales force for marketing research is the preservation of good relations between the salesman and buyer. There must be an atmosphere of trust which inspires confidence to purchase. It would be unfortunate if, through poor interviewing techniques, a resentment should be built up to spoil a sales association which may have developed over years.

Deliberate errors may be introduced in the answers of buyers interrogated by salesmen. These errors will stem from psychological factors. Buyers often feel that quantitative information given by them in good faith during the marketing research enquiry will lead to sales pressure by the company concerned. The buyer, therefore, tends to give a reply which is less than his real total consumption figures. The salesman being aware of his own sales to the customer will calculate that he has a much larger share of the customer's business than is in fact the case, and thus reduce sales pressure.'[1]

TECHNICAL AND NON-TECHNICAL INTERVIEWERS

The greatest single problem of industrial interviewing and, indeed, perhaps the fundamental difficulty of industrial marketing research is how far technical knowledge of the product is necessary or indeed useful to the researcher. There are two distinct schools of thought on this point and it is worthwhile to state the views of both, since both have some merit.

The first school admits only researchers who can converse freely, and with understanding, with respondents who are themselves not only technically familiar with the product but perhaps among the leaders in the field. At the very least this school maintains that the researcher must be able to understand the products and their applications, and the processes in their manufacture. It is argued that since most industrial marketing research projects involve discussions with technicians or scientists at some stage, it is necessary to be able to communicate with them in a common language. The respondent must respect the technical knowledge of his questioner, or at least be satisfied he is talking to someone who understands his technical world, otherwise there can be no rapport between the two parties to the interview. If is further argued that the attitude of technicians not to suffer fools gladly is sufficient reason to use researchers conversant with the product or process. It is also pointed out that in non-technical interviews, i.e. on commercial matters, the technically trained researcher is no less adequate than the non-technically trained researcher so there is no disadvantage in using the former at all times.

The other school of thought is that which believes that it is unnecessary for the researcher to have more than a superficial knowledge of the product, its manufacture and use in order to communicate at a technical level. The skills of interviewing overcome any such disadvantages and the respondent, provided a rapport is obtained, takes additional care to explain himself. Further, the respondent does

[1] *Ibid.*

not feel himself rivalled in knowledge by the questioner or his security threatened by another technician attempting to wrest his secrets or even his job. A technician respondent may, and often does, test the knowledge of his interviewer who claims, or appears to show, technical competence; and if the interviewer is found wanting, the relationship is likely to be damaged from the outset. It is believed, therefore, that there is more respect for an interviewer admitting little or no knowledge of the product than one with pretensions to knowledge.

The non-technical interviewer may well miss details which, taken together, can make up an important whole. Alternatively, the technical interviewer can develop or possess intellectual and emotional biases in areas where varying opinions exist and thus introduce technical bias into reports. The non-technical interviewer can maintain a detachment and objectivity that frequently escapes the technical interviewer. Examples of this can be found in the period of the controversy between air-cooled and water-cooled engine development. A careful analysis of technical interviewers' reports of that period shows clearly to which of the two schools of thought they belonged. A similar situation prevails now in relation to the use of mechanical, electrical, hydraulic and pneumatic relays, or combinations of them.

The answer, perhaps fortunately, as to which type of interviewer should be used is as often as not dictated by circumstances. Within a firm it is usually possible either to use technicians from the firm trained in marketing research or to train marketing researchers on the firm's products. Within an agency, unless it specialises as a very few do, in limited groups of products, say in mechanical engineering, electronics, chemicals or textiles, there can be no question of using the firm's full time technically trained interviewers for each type of assignment. To do so for each survey, research staff running into hundreds would be needed, all of whom would be either doing nothing or work unsuited to their talents for most of the time.

Given a choice, however, as in so many other areas of decision, a compromise is called for. It is necessary first to demolish the shibboleth that no marketing researcher can interview effectively without technical knowledge at least as great as his respondent's.

To suggest that only technically trained interviewers can interview successfully is to pre-suppose that all the important issues in marketing research are technical ones and of such a nature that they can only be understood by advanced thinkers in the field. The facts are quite different. There are very many other aspects of a product or service and of their markets which will alone and in combination have a decisive influence. It could be argued with equal force that since these non-technical matters are of considerable importance the interviewer must also have an advanced knowledge of accountancy, logistics, pricing strategy and advertising techniques. If such a person existed he would not be employing his undoubted talents in marketing research interviewing. It is only necessary to refer to the techniques and skills of interviewing to appreciate that these are far more important than matching the years of training and experience of the technicians and scientists with whom the researcher will be in contact.

The converse, however, is not to suggest that a researcher can undertake interviewing without studying the product or service. No one respects a salesman who does not understand his product and, equally, a researcher inadequately briefed on the subject of the research soon runs into difficulty. The compromise solution, and one that has been proved by usage, is the expert technical briefing of experts in research techniques, particularly in interviewing. One of the factors which surprises firms using industrial marketing research or being interviewed by industrial marketing researchers is the degree of technical competence that can be achieved by marketing researchers in a short time by complete immersion in the project. For the duration of the survey, a good researcher lives the subject of research and rapidly absorbs all that is needed to be known to conduct the survey. The technical briefing combined with the preliminary desk work gives background information. Discussions with internal technical staff and the preliminary pilot interviews all contribute to the knowledge of the researcher before he reaches the main interviews.

Within a firm conducting research, the technical briefing must be correctly delegated to the person best able to provide and communicate the information needed. This is not a task that can be allocated arbitrarily. The technician must want to contribute his knowledge and, what is more important, must be capable of so doing. Generally within a firm the research sponsor will be part of a management team that includes technicians who will have a vested interest in the success of the project and whose enthusiastic co-operation can be assured. It may even be possible and desirable to conduct the initial interviews with the technicians present and to hold an autopsy afterwards in order to adjust the later interviews. Even if this is not possible the researcher can return as frequently as necessary for guidance on any problems which may arise.

In the independent agency it is rare to employ people who possess

o

high technical skills and knowledge in a range of industries. The usual organisation for the agency is to have a link with a technical research organisation, possibly departments of Universities or Institutes of various types or else with independent technical consultants. Generally the organisations to which the independent agencies are linked will be conducting advanced research in their fields of specialisation and will usually employ researchers of a far higher calibre in relation to the technology being researched, than will be available in the operating management of the sponsor's firm.

Within the context of a discussion on interviewing, the technical consultant's work can be summarised as: designating the technical problems involved in the brief; explaining them to the researchers; indicating the correct approach for the interview; anticipating the direction of the interview (probably by 'pilot' interviews); instructing the research leader and interviewers on the best method of eliciting information needed; and evaluating the information received. A skilled researcher and consultant together form a team which is superior in every respect to the purely technical interviewer or what might best be called ' the professional interviewer'.

DEVELOPMENTS IN TECHNIQUE

Some of the experimental work that has been carried out into interviewing methods has revealed substantial differences in results occurring in investigating the same phenomenon by different methods. Notably the use of 'aided recall' and 'open end' questions has been shown to produce a highly variable yield in replicated samples. Commenting on the findings of an experiment it was stated: ' . . . the sharp difference in the yields from the two systems makes it quite clear that at least one of them can be seriously in error.'[1] Like Lord Leverhulme's dictum on advertising that half of it is wasted but he didn't know which half, it can be assumed that at least one system is inadequate, but which?

This single example illustrates the urgent need for further experimentation and for researchers and particularly their sponsors to make more of their findings available for public discussion.

Nevertheless, although personal interviewing of any type is subject to error, the personal interview is likely to remain the centre piece of any industrial marketing project for a considerable time to come. It can be seen that it has by no means achieved the limits of its potential

[1] William Belson and Judith A. Duncan, 'A Comparison of the Check-List and the Open Response Questioning System', *Applied Statistics* (London, June 1962).

as a method of information gathering and there still remains a considerable amount of research to be done into techniques. The industrial marketing researcher is looking towards the behavioral scientists to push back the boundaries of knowledge in the various activities which together comprise the inputs of a personal interview.

CHAPTER 9

Using the Telephone in Industrial Marketing Research

The previous chapter, concerned as it was with interview techniques and skills, presupposed that all interviews were face-to-face encounters at which the full interplay between the interviewer and respondent could be exploited. Here, certain visual assessments could be added to the armoury of cross-validating methods available to the interviewer.

The majority of the skills and techniques set out are in fact as applicable in the use of the telephone as in a face-to-face interview. However, the moment the partial anonymity of the telephone obtrudes in the interview situation, both checks and balances change and thus the tempo and tensions of the interview.

For this reason but without re-examining the anatomy of the interview, the role, technique and skills of telephone interviewing require separate treatment.

Unless the ownership of a telephone is part of the sampling criteria, telephone interviewing in consumer research creates its own in-built bias since telephone subscribers and non-telephone subscribers form clearly defined and very different socio-economic segments of the population. Moreover, many would-be telephone subscribers are excluded from the sample because of the waiting time for installations (sometimes stretching to years) and restrictions by owners of rented property which they may occupy—particularly furnished apartments.

No such bias obtrudes in telephone ownership in business. Every firm, probably without exception, is on the telephone since the telephone is a vital tool of modern business operations. Ownership in no way signifies a differential although the number of lines owned will, n many cases, indicate a size differential.

ADVANTAGES

The use of the telephone for industrial marketing research has very clear advantages over all other techniques, although its limitations will preclude it in some circumstances. Where however these limitations do not represent a restriction on the attainment of the research objectives, yield and cross validation, there is always a strong case for the use of the telephone.

In terms of cost, the telephone interviewing technique falls between the simple question-and-answer personal interview and the postal questionnnaire. In terms of time, results can often be obtained much more quickly than with other techniques except perhaps observation. In terms of quality, depending upon the skill of the interviewer, it can be almost as revealing as carefully conducted 'face-to-face' interviews. A top grade interviewer examining the purchasing practices of industrial flooring contractors completed 150 successful telephone interviews (a total of 205 calls was necessary to achieve this number) in nineteen working days, including a verbatim write-up of the interviews. Depending on the complexity of the questionnaire and the type of respondent to be interviewed, it is possible to complete seven to ten telephone interviews per day. A good average for industrial personal interviewing would be something less than three interviews per day.

The telephone is very much part of the way of life to most people employed in business and this approach appears to be perfectly normal to them. Psychological studies have shown that no matter how much people may complain about the telephone as an interruption, in fact they like it. 'Most of them will overtly show irritation when they are interrupted in a conversation by the ringing of the telephone; in fact, the more often this happens the more pleased they will be covertly for this proves that they are recognised, that they are an active part of the world, that they are busy people who have a stake in affairs.'[1] This is not to say there will not be times when the intrusion of the telephone is not resented, but objections to it, over a whole range of situations, are neither deeply held nor serious.

This is to a large extent borne out by the fact that the telephone always takes precedence over the person in the room. Again it is true that the respondent may suggest the caller rings at a more convenient time or not trouble him again. The point is, however, that the respondent has, irrespective of his activities in his room, answered the telephone—given it priority over all other activities at that moment. This is an important advantage and will be seen to be true if any single day's activity is considered.

[1] Max K. Adler, 'The Use of the Telephone in Industrial Market Research', *Scientific Business* (Reading, February 1964).

The speed factor in telephone interviewing is an advantage on two counts. Obviously it is quicker in the majority of circumstances in terms of the interviewer's time, to make contact by telephone because of the priority rating it receives. A ringing telephone does not queue. Apart from the obvious advantage in terms of distance or traffic congestion there is also the ability to move quickly and easily from respondent to respondent in the same plant or firm when a journey might take half an hour or more, and expose the interviewer to the whole 'gamut' of screens through which he must pass to the respondent—gatemen, receptionists, secretaries, personal assistants.

Stemming from this it is frequently easier to reach some types of respondent by telephone who cannot be seen personally or who will not reply to postal solicitations for information. Such people, for example, as maintenance engineers moving around a plant, surveyors visiting sites or sales managers can either be 'picked off' at pre-arranged times or else cut off along their route by the aid of their secretaries or others who have knowledge of their location and movement. The cost of a wasted telephone call is never the same as that of a wasted visit.

A further advantage stems from the partial anonymity which the telephone gives respondents. It is true that not all respondents react sympathetically to this and that there are situations when the anonymity is a distinct disadvantage. Nevertheless many people are encouraged to speak more openly on the telephone than face-to-face. The anonymity works both ways. The interviewer has less opportunity and there is less risk, of accidentally intimidating the respondent by his physical presence and different educational or social backgrounds. The mere fact that it is easier for most people to be brusque and even rude on the telephone than in the physical presence of the person to whom they are talking can be an asset in that the respondent does not feel himself at the mercy of the interviewer.

There are many people who find it difficult to an extreme to terminate a personal conversation rather in the manner of Stephen Leacock's apocryphal curate, but can close a discussion on the telephone with much less difficulty. It is in fact the feeling that they, the respondents, are in control of the conversation and can terminate it at will and without embarrassment by replacing the receiver which induces so many telephone respondents to speak so freely. Not to be a 'captive' is everyone's desire.

Another very considerable advantage of the telephone interview is the facility for notetaking not available without risk of the loss of the interview material in the face-to-face confrontation.

As with the personal interview one of the problems of bias is eliminated in that the respondent is faced with only one question at a time and cannot influence his answers by the foreknowledge of later questions. Some biases inherent in the interviewer's presence are also removed. For example, a respondent might in a telephone interview refer to confidential documents which he would not open before a person in the room.

Semi-structured questionnaires can be used more effectively in telephone than in personal interviewing. The problem of the semi-structured questionnaire, it has been pointed out, is that the interviewer may have to make constant reference to his check list which can be both disconcerting to the respondent who tends to watch the list like a bored member of an audience watching for the last page of music or speech notes to be turned over. In a telephone interview the check list can be prominent and closely followed.

A less obvious but distinct advantage can be gained, what might be termed 'name dropping'. A completely 'cold' approach can, by describing the job function of the person who it is required to speak to or the subject of the enquiry, often elicit from the switchboard or person who answers, 'That is dealt with by Mr. Jones.' It has been established by psychological studies conducted by the Bell Telephone Company that attention is always held for several seconds after the respondent's name is mentioned. Thus the conversation opening with Mr. Jones now addressed by name is likely to command full attention. If, as it turns out, Jones is the wrong man most frequently he will refer the caller to who he considers is the right person, also by name. Now a double introduction is possible. 'Mr. Smith, I have just been speaking to Mr. Jones who suggested you may be able to help.' Of course, it is always possible that Smith hates Jones and would not dream of assisting anyone recommended to him by Jones, but by and large intra-firm and inter-personal co-operation is high and the ice is broken for the interview. In short, the telephone interview can be far more satisfactory for identifying the correct respondent and is far less likely to bring about a refusal than a 'cold' personal call will.

These major advantages do not represent the full value of a telephone interview as a technique. Moreover, the advantages will tend to change from survey to survey. Thus, as with all the techniques discussed, it is important to evaluate them against the four research parameters discussed in Chapter 3.

DISADVANTAGES

The disadvantages of the telephone method of interviewing have to be weighed against the advantages if a reasoned assessment is to be made concerning their use.

The most obvious and important disadvantage is the complete impossibility of using visual techniques to add to the information yield. A look, an action, the opportunity to walk round a plant or site and observe numbers, activities, conditions, are all lost.

Stemming from this, the virtual impossibility of assessing the physical conditions of the interview add to the problems of this particular method. For example, it cannot be known except by inference if in fact the respondent is devoting all his attention to the interviewing. There are many people capable of reading a letter, tidying their drawers, tightening a nut, or signing their post while conducting a telephone conversation. The presence of other people in the room, unknown to the interviewer, can change the whole nature of the responses since the respondent may be more concerned in impressing the person in the room with his importance or activities than in providing accurate replies to the questions.

At a personal interview it is often possible to identify environmental factors which may introduce some bias into the responses—noise, interruptions, climatic conditions, health and fatigue of the respondent. The respondent may have answered the telephone with his outdoor clothes on, ready to leave at the end of the day. It would be obvious to a personal interviewer that to delay him may induce-irritation and yield the shortest answers possible so that the interview could be terminated at its earliest moment. On the telephone the fact that the interviewer was keeping the respondent from some other activity is not known, particularly if the respondent is too courteous to mention it. Nevertheless the irritation and the desire to end the discussion is no less. All this is lost in the telephone interview.

A further disadvantage compared to the postal questionnaire only is that the telephone interview can be a relatively high cost operation. The percentage of failed interviews in a telephone survey can be as high as 40 per cent and sometimes much higher for some respondent groups and at some times of the year (e.g. holiday periods). Being held at the PBX can be expensive on trunk and even local calls, call backs reincur the original costs. 'Line engaged' involves the loss of interviewer time.

Another factor is that the partial anonymity given by the telephone will encourage some respondents to be more brusque and even rude than they would be in a face-to-face encounter. It is also possible for them to 'hang up' without warning or apology and without the embarrassment of the effect this produces or any reaction which a rudely terminated interview might evoke when the interviewer and respondent face each other.

Holding the respondent's interest is more difficult without the assistance of visual stimulants, for example the actual product or printed material. The physical presence of the interviewer and his simplest actions such as writing, changing position, opening a brief case, can assist in keeping a respondent's interest or at least to provide a spectrum of minor changes of tone, speed and form in the interview.

It is usual when a massive programme of telephone interviews is to be conducted to work from sampling points—that is geographical locations centred on the main interview area. This reduces the trunk call cost by making the bulk of the calls from a local point. However an offsetting factor may be the cost of sending and locating the interviewer in the area. A minor but nevertheless important problem is that it is often difficult for interviewers to obtain continuous, rather than sporadic, telephone facilities away from base.

Where the interviewer needs to show any material the telephone is ruled out. For example, in image studies it is common practice to ask respondents to rate firms under a number of different headings and on a semantic differential. The options are too many and the concepts too abstract to consider without visual aids and, moreover, such questions require the foreknowledge of all the options if an assessment is to be made in the knowledge of the alternatives. (This point was discussed in more detail in Chapter 7, 'The Postal Questionnaire'.) Thus a card is shown giving the firms' names, the headings and the differentials. Unless the card is sent in advance and then discussed over the telephone, the telephone is an imperfect method for this type of enquiry.

The tendency in summating advantages and disadvantages in the use of different techniques is to end with the impression that one cancels out the other. This in fact is rarely so. More realistically the advantages and disadvantages are not absolute but will change in their importance in accordance with the research objectives and other techniques. Thus in a study of buyer attitudes to heating oil promotional methods, the disadvantage of the telephone interview would be an eliminating factor because reference would need to be made to promotional material. Conversely information from personnel officers on equipment used for staff checking would lend itself to this method of enquiry.

There is little doubt that overall the advantages of the telephone interview far outweigh the disadvantages and therefore it must be a technique that will receive early and careful consideration in almost every research project.

APPLICABILITY

There are a number of circumstances in which the telephone interview will have clear advantages over other methods or which will considerably enhance the value of the other methods.

The major purpose of the telephone interview is to provide wide geographical and industrial coverage at speed and with relatively low cost which nevertheless will give a much greater information yield than the postal questionnaire.

Telephone interviewing to obtain full or limited data will be conducted on exactly the same lines as those of personal interviews, and the same skills, techniques and procedures will be needed.

The interview process follows exactly the same lines as in the personal interview, that is deciding who is the correct respondent and then arranging, planning, conducting, recording and closing the interview.

The method of interviewing, that is structured, semi-structured or non-directive, will be similar to that of the personal interview. The introduction of check and cross-validating questions will be the same and requires no further explanation. However, the weight of importance of the processes may change. For example, the problem of identifying the respondent is just that much more difficult in a telephone than in a personal interview where there is usually visual corroboration of the respondent's job, status, title and other identification characteristics.

The interview may be intended as a major information yielding process or as a support function of other techniques. An example of this latter task has already been mentioned in Chapter 7, that is probing sub-samples of non-respondents to postal questionnaires to ascertain if any common characteristics exist among them. To survey this group by further postal questionnaires is not practical and personal interviews are expensive.

Another support function also in relation to postal questionnaires is to conduct a pilot telephone enquiry to establish the composition of the Decision Making Unit and the job titles or function of the correct person to whom to address the questionnaire. An industry pattern can be revealed very quickly which may take several weeks to perceive by a pilot postal questionnaire.

Another use for the telephone in industrial marketing research which was also referred to in Chapter 7 is to 'warn' respondents that the questionnaire is coming and to request its completion and return. This is then followed by a reminder a few days later. Because a major part of telephone interviewing cost is concerned with 'connection', it will be seen why the pre- and post-questionnaire telephone call is wasteful. The cost of connecting—the process up to the moment of actually speaking to the respondent—taking into account call backs, misconnections, wrong numbers, engaged lines, disconnections and other obstructions—is probably 30 per cent or even more of the total interview cost.

Another support function of the telephone interview is concerned with the use of visual techniques. Observations can only be made when the phenomenon to be observed occurs. It can be highly wasteful to have an observer waiting when the occurrence can be either scheduled or anticipated by preliminary enquiries. For example in a study to determine users' service requirements for rubber-covered rollers for plastic manufacturing machinery, an examination was required of the roller handling method and documentation. It was necessary for the researchers to know when the removal of a roller would occur at the place where the appropriate machinery was located. This information was elicited from each firm by telephone calls.

Probably the greatest support function of the telephone interview is in the sampling process. For example, in a multi-phase non-probability sample the telephone can be used for the first stage to prepare the second stage sample, possibly to be conducted by personal interviews. Because the telephone interviewer is not constrained unduly by distance considerations the first (telephone) sample can be larger and more widespread than the second stage sample, which will in turn be much improved by the scope of the original sample.

Still in connection with the sampling, it has already been noted that finding firms to fit the sample microcosm can be extremely difficult because of the lack of basic information on size, form of organisations, commercial or industrial liaisons, types of equipment installed and whatever else the sample criteria may be. The telephone interview, given a lack of published data, can quickly locate or eliminate companies for personal interview on the basis of the sample criteria. Indeed this is often the only way to ensure accuracy in filling the sampling frame. For this purpose the questions are generally few and can often be answered by a large number of people in a single firm. 'Do you have any petrol pumps on your premises?' can be answered by the service manager, but also probably whoever answers the telephone. 'Do you provide overalls for your engineering staff or do they have their own?' can be answered by the personnel manager and just about anyone on the shop floor. 'Are you an automatic or manual PBX?' is certainly a question which can be answered by the switchboard operators themselves.

One vital support function of telephone interviewing is connected with arranging interviews for personal interviewers. Although 'cold calling' is often practised and can be successful, the bulk of interviews are pre-arranged. When an interviewer fixes these himself he is exposed to the risk of being edged into the actual interview itself and the respondent deciding that he has given all the information he intends to give. A good interviewer can avoid this situation but the fact remains the use of highly skilled personal interviewers in the task of appointment making is an expensive misapplication of talent.

Appointments can be made by good telephone interviewers with no risk of pre-empting the personal interview. These telephone interviews can avoid giving away more of the interview subject than is desirable. Moreover, if needs be, persuasive tactics can be used to get the interview without at the same time biasing the resulting interview itself, as may easily occur if the person who does the interview makes the appointment.

This is not to say that given that on average only two personal interviews can be made a day, the interviewer cannot fill in any available time with interview fixing. The suggestion is that faced with the choice of being out in the field and having someone else fix the interviews or doing it himself, the choice should always be to have the interview arranging carried out by a telephone interviewer.

THE INTERVIEWER

The telephone interviewer is not a particular type of person. Given the necessary physical and personality characteristics, the skills can be learned quickly. Few attempts have been made to define the good telephone interviewer other than that they should have a 'good telephone personality' which is not explicit enough to assist selection of such interviewers. Obviously since the voice is the only personality characteristic which can come through, looks and manner must be substituted by acceptable aural characteristics. A pleasant clear voice, an easily understandable and acceptable accent, a reassuring, confidence-inducing manner, the ability to manipulate pauses in the way the respondent does not think he has been cut off or the interviewer has lost interest, an ability to express himself without the use of visual aids (people who gesticulate and use their hands in talking are often poor communicators deprived of these aids), sincerity and succinct presentation are all basic essentials for the task.

There is no area in industrial marketing research in which women cannot perform at least as well as men, but in telephone interviewing they are often superior. It would be difficult to prove women have a greater aptitude and liking for using the telephone than men—although the preponderance of women telephone operators seems to indicate such an aptitude and liking but, nevertheless, experience has shown them to possess, overall, a greater skill in projecting their personality over a blind medium than men. So much of the subject matter of industrial marketing enquiries is 'men's world' stuff that a woman's voice will frequently attract more attention than that of a man.

To some extent the risk of brusque or even rude replies on the telephone is modified by the use of women interviewers to whom the majority of men would tend to be more courteous. However, against this must be weighed another risk that in a 'man's world' a woman interviewer may not be treated seriously.

Irrespective of the sex of the interviewer, patience and tact are necessary prerequisites. The ability to deal with reluctant respondents is a special skill because it is that much easier for the respondent to terminate the interview. For this reason, aided only by voice and manner the interviewer must be able to maintain interest and, if need be, soothe ruffled feelings without himself losing interest or his temper.

INTERVIEW METHOD

The telephone interview method does not differ materially from the personal interview method. Preparation is just as necessary. Because the use of notes and note-taking is not inhibiting in a telephone interview, it is advisable to have all the points to be covered listed out and an adequate supply of paper, pens and magnetic tape if the interviews are to be recorded, available.

It is always necessary, when the person to be interviewed is identified, not to get sidetracked to any other respondent. Although not always possible, one way of avoiding this is by asking the substitute respondent questions not within his knowledge or authority to answer. Where this cannot be done it is better to terminate the interview with a 'call back' suggestion. There is never any point in continuing an interview with a respondent who does not fit the sampling frame, although such a respondent can sometimes be used to provide a lead towards an acceptable substitute or to obtain information on an exact time when the required respondent can be contacted. If in doubt concerning who the respondent in the individual firm should be, the highest level person who can be reached should be aimed at.

Person to person calls made through the long-distance telephone operator are usually effective in making direct contact with any respondent who can be identified by name or job function, and by using this telephone service facility the intervening screens of telephonists, secretaries, personal and other assistants can be avoided. Since no connection will be made by the G.P.O. telephone operator until the person called is actually answering, this method can be both time and cost saving. Moreover, few people can resist finding out who is making a personal call even if the name of the caller is meaningless. A danger to watch for, however, is the risk that the person called may regard a personal call as impertinent or an invasion of their privacy.

It has been pointed out that each time a person's name is mentioned his attention is riveted for the next ten or fifteen words spoken. It is advisable to get the name as quickly as possible and use it, but sparingly, only preceding key points to be explained or if interest is waning.

As with the personal interview the respondent should be given the opportunity of confirming statements made and they should also be presented back to him in a different form. In some respects this is easier to do on the telephone since the full list of questions and answers can be consulted as the interview proceeds.

In appointment fixing it is important to say no more than is necessary to fix the appointment and not to go beyond this. Information which will help at the interview itself should be watched for and reported to the personal interviewer. Alternative times and places should always be offered if the respondent indicates any difficulty or reluctance to meet. For this reason these alternatives should be at the interviewer's fingertips. As a general rule it is unwise to change appointments already fixed as it may end up in losing both the attempted appointment and the firm one.

In closing the interview it is always good practice to keep the 'door open' by asking that if there are any further questions the interviewer thinks of, may he call back. Very few respondents refuse such a request. A call back can be used to clarify answers given or to extend the questioning at a later phase of the study.

A check list[1] prepared to assist in telephone selling, with modifications also provides a useful basis for telephone interviewing.

- Who is your potential respondent?
- What is known about him (sampling criteria)?
- What is known about his business (sampling criteria)?
- How will you identify yourself and your organisation?
- How will you express your purpose to the respondent or any screening personnel?
- What tactics will you adopt in the event of a refusal by screening personnel to connect you?
- What reasons are likely to be advanced by screening personnel for refusing an interview?
- Will these reasons for refusal by screening personnel be similar to those likely to be advanced by the respondents themselves?
- Will the tactics for dealing with refusals by screening personnel serve to deal with the actual respondents who refuse?
- Are there any fact-finding questions which the screening personnel can answer which will assist either in the interview or in the total research information requirements?
- What is your initial statement to the respondent?
- What other supporting information are you prepared to give him?
- What objections to providing information are likely to emerge after the opening statement or during the research?
- What preparations have been made to deal with these?
- Will the interview closing statement leave the 'door open' for recall?
- (For appointment fixing): are the time and place details clear?
- Are there alternative time and place arrangements available?
- How much information is to be given concerning the purpose of the personal interview?

[1] *Making Appointments with Phone Power*, Bell Systems (New York n.d.).

OPTIMUM MIX

Both in its support functions to other techniques and as a field technique in its own right, the telephone interview is gaining in importance. From being a useful weapon in the industrial marketing researchers' armoury, it has now become virtually indispensable. Even fairly simple desk research is now being commonly supplemented by telephone interviews.

For speed, economy and accuracy it has considerable advantages over the other techniques and because there is no inherent bias in a sample for telephone interviews it is generally more applicable in industrial than in consumer marketing research.

Faced with the problem of interlocking the four research parameters to obtain the optimum mix, it is often the telephone interview which will provide the best time-cost-objective continuum.

CHAPTER 10

Observation Techniques

Many claims have been made that all marketing research—consumer and industrial—owes its existence and its formal appearance to operational research. Certainly many of the techniques are similar. When, however, visual techniques or observations are under discussion the link between the two disciplines is unarguable.

The collection of data by observation is so fundamental a part of scientific research that its separation as a technique is never consciously discussed. In industrial marketing research its use has been so limited or, more frequently, so casual that visual techniques for data collection have tended to be treated in isolation. There is a history of use in consumer marketing research because of the link with social and psychological research where laboratory type techniques have been pursued with vigour and in depth.

Like the telephone interview, visual techniques form both a vital support function for the personal interviewing methods and a technique in their own right. 'Observations' or visual techniques can be defined as the act of recognising and noting factors or occurrences. They can take many forms and have many different purposes depending upon the research objectives and methods. They can be the observations of others than the researchers. In this case the information they yield will be obtained through other techniques. They can also be direct observations of the researcher. Similarly, observations may be the simple recording of phenomena as they occur, or the factors to be observed may be manipulated to obtain information on their behaviour or reaction under, or after, the influence of the manipulation.

Industrial marketing situations rarely permit laboratory type experiments in which single or groups of variables can be altered to permit observation of the effect of the adjustment, although this is always a desideratum of the industrial marketing researcher. Consequently the majority of observations taken in an industrial marketing research project tend to be simple recordings of the

P

phenomena rather than a measurement of the subject of observation under manipulation. Both aspects in studying visual techniques are considered here and also the situation in which the observer himself may be involved in the phenomenon; he can both stand aside and observe or act as a part of the group or activity being observed which will in turn influence the effects.

Because of these various approaches, therefore, it is necessary to establish at the outset a number of important facts before attempting to apply visual techniques for data gathering. A check list comprises the following points:

● What is to be observed?

● If the observed phenomenon is of a recurrent nature, can the occurrence of the phenomenon be anticipated?

● Can access to a point at which observation can be made be obtained?

● What data will the observation yield?

● Can the results be quantified?

● Can a method of rating be devised?

● What contribution will the data make to the research objectives?

● Can the results of the observation be recorded in any way? (written notes, film, tape recorder, instruments, etc.)

● Can criteria for categorising the results be developed?

● What is the role of the observer—non-participant, non-active participant, active participant?

● Will it be possible to repeat the observations under identical conditions?

● Is manipulation of any of the observed factors possible?

● Is the 'freezing' of any of the observed phenomenon possible?

● Can any element of observer bias enter the recording and assessment of the observed phenomenon?

These and indeed many other points require consideration before deciding as to the appropriateness of observation techniques in industrial marketing research.

BIAS

Theoretically at least, visual techniques should be the most accurate of all those available to the researcher since it only requires the occurrence of the phenomenon to be observed for it to be recorded. But the human eye and human mind are extremely fallible. The phenomenon of perceptual distortion, in which people tend to distort reality into conformance with their own values, attitudes and interests, has been recognised for a considerable time. Hearing or reading the conflicting evidence of witnesses in a court of law gives an appreciation that even when prepared, and without intent or malice on the part of the observer, witnesses are not always capable of accurately reproducing information concerning what has been observed. It is necessary therefore to process data obtained by visual techniques with the same care as that obtained by other methods, to be constantly on the alert for bias and errors, and to seek the maximum cross validation possible. In short, a distinction must be made constantly between the observation itself and the observer's interpretation of what he has seen.

EXAMPLES

It is pertinent to examine observation techniques by describing some typical examples of their use in industrial marketing research.

One of the most common uses for visual techniques in industrial marketing research is concerned with the identification of machinery, equipment, materials and components. For example, the market for instrumentation for domestic cookers is easily calculable by simply observing in any shop the makes and types of instruments on each brand of cooker and then examining cooker market brand shares. The correlation, while not being exact, has sufficient precision to provide a figure satisfactory enough for most decision-making purposes. Similarly a serial number of a machine tool and its known date of purchase can sometimes provide almost exact data on numbers made in the intervening period by merely observing the serial number on the latest produced machines. Invoice numbers over a period of time compared with past periods can provide a useful identification of the volatility and, indeed in some industries, the level of business of individual firms. These are all simple direct observations which yield immediate confirmation and, except under the most unusual circumstances, should prove as observations to be highly accurate.

Another use for observational technique is to identify stock levels of materials or components which can then be correlated with lead time data. Similarly stock checks provide knowledge of makes and brands or products purchased which in turn can be correlated with purchasing data obtained by questionnaire and desk research techniques.

Studies of applications of products might be thought to be more properly an activity for applications engineers. The marketing researcher can, however, provide considerable guidance in this field by observation rather than experimentation. The spring balancer example given in Chapter 2 illustrates this position. An adaptation of the balancer was revealed through observational techniques and opened up a whole new market segment for the spring balancer manufacturer. An observation in an African country on the re-use of sacks and sacking material led an importer of materials normally bagged in multi-wall paper sacks to revert to the older bagging material. Because the sack has a 'second-hand' life, greater care was exercised in handling the jute sacks than in handling the paper products which had no second-hand value. Three benefits ensued: for the labourer the sack became a 'perk', for the importers damage of the sack's contents was reduced because of more careful handling by the local labourers not wishing to spoil re-usable sacking material; for the exporter a definite non-product marketing 'plus'.

PREPARING FOR OBSERVATIONS

To obtain the maximum value from any series of observations there are specified procedures which can be adopted under most circumstances.

● Obtain as much knowledge in advance as possible of the phenomenon to be observed, the form in which it will occur, speed or periodicity of the occurrence, recognition criteria, any variations which can be anticipated, assessment criteria (e.g. quantity, speed, weight, colour), environmental factors, any factors which may prevent or hinder the observation.

● Make certain access to the point of observation is either freely available as in the observation of traffic flow in location studies, or is arranged in advance, for example stock checks in factory stores. In the latter circumstance it is important that some form of identification and approval is obtained if the risk of the observations being interrupted by officials checking up on the observer's presence is to be minimised.

● Check the observation point will in fact give a clear and undistorted view of the phenomenon to be observed or that the observed object is or will be in fact at the location chosen.

● Decide what type, if any, of mechanical aids to recording the phenomenon are most suitable, that they are available at the observation point, that they are in working order and the observer knows how to use them. Where possible checking devices on their operation should be incorporated (e.g. transistor indicators for battery strength and sound level meters, light meters).

OBSERVATION TECHNIQUES

Given that visual methods will yield the data required and that the procedures outlined are followed, it is still necessary to decide on the type of technique to be adopted. Like interviewing, it is possible to divide the basic methods into different types. Two have already been mentioned: (a) *participative* and (b) *non-participative*, to which can be now added (c) *structured* and (d) *unstructured observations*.

(a) *Participative observations*

Participative observations, that is when the observer is involved in the activity being observed, are mostly used when experimentation is taking place. For example, observing reactions to various stimuli perhaps provided by the observer are a commonplace check in some types of advertising research. Test marketing is not often conducted in industrial marketing, but where it is, observations can provide some types of data on behaviour of the test market. There are observation situations in which *only* participative activity can be conducted. This is particularly so when the use of mechanical testing techniques such as eye cameras and tachistoscopes[1] which have to be manipulated by the observer are involved. Pre- or post-testing advertising using marking techniques are further examples of participative observations.[2]

One considerable advantage of participative observations is that because the situations are artificial they can often be initiated at pre-determined and convenient times and places, thus optimising the observer's time. Moreover, they can be so organised as to yield the observations of the required type. The disadvantages are nevertheless

[1] An electro-mechanical device for controlling exposure to some visual stimulus for various lengths of time down to fractions of seconds.
[2] See Chapter 12, 'Assessing Advertising Effectiveness'.

also considerable. 'When the situation is artificial, however, and the subject knows he is being observed it is doubtful that the subject will act in a normal manner.'[1] The balance of advantage can only be assessed against the research parameters and the alternative methods available to achieve the same ends.

(b) *Non-participative observations*

Non-participative observations are those in which the observer is involved in the group or with the respondent or activity being observed but takes no part in it; for example, accompanying and observing a salesman while engaged with his customers. In this situation the person observed knows that the observations are taking place. However, non-participative observations can occur without knowledge of the subject of the observations. Concealed observations are those situations in which the observer's presence is not detected by the subject of the observations. These types of observations are particularly important if the phenomenon is to be seen in a natural condition, not in any way influenced by the presence of the observer. It is probably true to say that the majority of observations used in industrial marketing research concerned with human subjects are of this type.

An example of this is the observation of the use of change-giving machines and alternatives available at a chosen site. Who uses the machines, how frequently is the acceptance or options offered at variance with the users' requirements, extent and type of errors in the use of the machine, queueing propensity of users, ergonomic factors, methods adopted to cheat or beat the machine. Another example is the study of methods of securing vehicle cargoes. Under known observation the securing of the cargo is likely to be far more carefully carried out than under normal non-observed conditions, and the degree and extent of care will vary from one climatic condition to another, and between different locations.

An ethical problem arises in the use of concealed observations when mechanical recording devices are used. The invasion of the privacy of individuals cannot be condoned even if the records made are kept confidential and the observed person remains anonymous. The use of hidden recording for observations is unquestionably as unethical as its use in interviewing and is to be strongly discouraged if the technique and marketing research itself is not to be brought into disrepute.

[1] *Marketing Research: Texts and Cases*, op. cit., p. 184.

(c) *Structured observations*

Structured observations can be used when the data to be obtained can be defined with precision and the majority of questions on the check list on page 212 can be satisfactorily answered. Traffic counts when only numbers and types of vehicles are needed, time checks on a process or part of a process, scrap or spoilage rates, are examples of situations in which structured observations can be used to maximum effect.

Like structured interviews, structured observations are far less prone to bias. It has been shown that observers with different viewpoints on a given question will tend to make similar observations under structured conditions.[1] Since it is always important to reduce bias, structured observations are often to be preferred to unstructured. The structured interview for industrial marketing research purposes is recognised as largely useless because it tends to block off important information. Although the same objection can apply to structured observations a stronger case can be made for using them. In interviewing the interviewer has the opportunity to exert a considerable measure of control by use of funnelling techniques and prompts. For observations these alternatives can rarely be invoked even in participative observations, and not at all for non-participative observations. Thus the factors which make the unstructured interview more suitable for industrial marketing research than structured interviews are not applicable in the use of structured and unstructured observation techniques.

(d) *Unstructured observations*

The unstructured observation is the noting of an activity or phenomenon under the natural conditions, the observer recording only what is pertinent as and when it occurs. In the 'systems concept'[2] for new product development the role of the observer is to note existing methods of conducting an operation or carrying out a process so that the research can establish if a demand can be created for a new product which will improve the existing system.

Comparison with the unstructured interview is again relevant since the same problems occur. Not everything can be observed nor can it always be recorded. Inferences stemming from observations can often be incorrect. The use of expensive cargo tie-down systems

[1] H. Thelen and J. Withall, 'Three Frames of Reference', *Human Relations*, Vol. 2 (1949), pp. 159-76. Quoted in *Marketing Research—Texts and Cases*, p. 183.
[2] 'Generation of New Product Ideas', *Marketing of Industrial Products*, op. cit, pp. 26-8.

in a container might imply to the observer the firm concerned is moving expensive or fragile loads. In fact, the cargo tie-down system may well be permanent fitting in a leased container which has been used for other duties. Two hydraulic jacks of different ratings, at different prices and with different trims, may, in fact, be precisely the same capacity but one jack has been derated because it is more economic to sell it at a lower price than make the different rating specially.

The different types of observations are not all mutually exclusive. Structured or unstructured observations can be carried out on a participative or non-participative basis, concealed or open. The 'mix' will vary for different circumstances and the researcher's approach should always be a pragmatic one.

CONDUCTING OBSERVATIONS

To obtain the maximum benefit for observation techniques the observer will need to familiarise and prepare himself in a number of ways. Reference to the check list on page 212 and procedures indicate the areas which require attention. In more detail it has been suggested[1] that the five basic requirements are as follows:

(a) *Research objectives and observation objectives*

As with all industrial marketing research, the researcher must return to the research objectives to see that the intended observations will, if successful, make a contribution towards achieving these and precisely the form this contribution will take. A critical examination of the observation objective is always necessary. It is quite wrong to assume that merely looking at a phenomenon will reveal what is relevant for the purpose of the investigation. It is useful to list out the items on which information is particularly required. These may be related to the physical characteristics of a product or material or applications, to the effect produced by some activity or to human behaviour. The development of an observation schedule ensures that all the relevant factors which can be anticipated and on which information is required are watched for and included. Nevertheless the schedule should not inhibit the observer from noting other factors of relevance. A thorough understanding of both the research objectives and the observation objectives will ensure that both the schedule items and other related data is seen and noted.

[1] *Research Methodology in Business*, op. cit, pp. 82-4.

(b) *Definition and establishment of categories*

The same rules apply for defining and establishing categories as in the handling of any other data generated during a marketing research project. However, the physical circumstances of most observations make precision in defining and establishing categories of greater consequence because of the problems of recording already referred to. The general principles are set out in Chapter 11 'Processing the Data'.

(c) *Observing accurately and critically*

Given that observation has been properly prepared, only the lack of diligence and clearsightedness—literally and metaphorically—and critical abilities of the observer will prevent wholly accurate and unbiased results. 'But whether a researcher can use observational methods in a scientific fashion will depend upon his prejudices and biases, his powers of perception, his outlook, his ability to recognise causal relationships and sequences and his accuracy in recording the results of his observations.'[1]

When the occurrence of the phenomena cannot be predicted and when the phenomena occur for a long period of time, a great strain may be placed on the observer, physically and mentally. The ego drive referred to in discussing interviewers can be translated in an observer to diligence and determination to continue the observations without self-deluding beliefs that the phenomena has patterned or is wholly repetitive.

Only one version of what has occurred during the observation can be accurate, but this accuracy may only apply to the period of the observation. The sampling problem takes on a dual aspect in relation to observations: that is whether the observed sample is typical of the whole and whether the period of the observation was typical of the whole cycle of the phenomenon.

A study of waste in office reproduction work by visual techniques would require first, sampling a representative group of offices and, second, observations *at each point* over a sufficiently long period of time to ensure typicality in machine use had occurred. If for example it was the practice of a company to photocopy certain single sheet documents on a specified day and bound books at another time, both activities would have to be observed as the wastage varies between the two activities. Similarly, an observation of wastage on small litho machine printing in single colour would yield a totally different result when multi-colour printing was taking place.

[1] *Research Methodology in Business*, op. cit., p. 91.

Perceptual distortion, which has already been referred to, is at least as great as the danger of interviewer bias. The other danger is that of inaccuracy (carelessness, poor counts), bad positioning (obstructed or distorted view), optical distortions (speed or direction), environmental distortions (colour, climate). These can only be avoided if a careful watch is kept and the situation is critically appraised.

Certainly the observer should question the accuracy of the observations and wherever possible assess them against any reliable criteria which he succeeds in developing.

(d) *Recording results*

The method of recording the results of observations will, of course, depend upon the type of observation being conducted and the phenomenon or activity observed. For structured and participative observations it is usually possible to devise a form which will enable the results to be recorded quickly and accurately. Forms for recording observational data are much more simple to construct than questionnaires. The aim must be simplicity to aid accurate completion, identification of information correctly, and easy tabulation. Non-quantitative phenomenon represent a particularly difficult problem unless there is adequate time for full descriptions to be given or mechanical means are resorted to. One solution to the problem is the use of two-way tables listing the kinds of phenomenon or activity on one axis and qualitative ratings or interpretations of them on the other axis. The researcher can then easily record data obtained. 'Each category or level of data being collected should be concisely and carefully described by indicating the phenomena the investigator expects to find in each. The description becomes especially important when a team of observers are collecting the information'.[1]

With unstructured observations there are limits to the preparation which can be undertaken to assist recording. These limits are those caused by the lack of forward information on the form in which the observed phenomenon or activity will appear.

The immediacy of most observations, the fact that there may be a long delay before they re-occur or re-occurrence cannot be accurately predicted, make it important to record as much information as possible as quickly as possible, and therefore the development of check lists or other observation schedules is as important as the observation itself. Every opportunity for piloting these should be taken and every reasonable option allowed for. Clearly the check

[1] *Ibid.*

list forms must not be so complicated that the observer is distracted from the observation by the need to record at length. Thus where recording can be made mechanically (i.e. film, video and sound tape recording) it is always preferable to do so, but where it cannot be, observation results should be used in simple code form and kept to the most simple and unambiguous terms.

(e) *Independent rating of specific phenomena*

Rating scales are a condensed method of recording quantitative and qualitative information. In observing non-quantitative phenomena ratings of one type or another will be required but it is not unlikely that the rating of one phenomena may unwittingly influence another. Aesthetic aspects of design may unconsciously influence the rating of performance characteristics. Performance characteristics of a piece of original equipment can easily influence the ratings of components. This can be very damaging indeed to the final results and therefore it is necessary to emphasise the need to separate the ratings of the phenomenon. If it is possible, some transitional observation should be introduced between any two observations where a halo effect is likely.[1] Unlike the transitional statement in interviewing which is used to bridge a gap between a change of subjects, the transitional observation is a deliberate sharp change between two observations, designed to break up the observer's thought pattern and reaction to two observations which might be connected. Separate ratings with or without transitional observations will make a considerable contribution to reducing the bias of the halo effect.

---

[1] A tendency for the impressions or attitudes created by one fact or aspect to influence others.

CHAPTER 11

Processing the Data

It has been noted earlier in this book that in preparing for the field work considerable forethought should have been given to the form in which the data will be analysed. In fact, rather like a critical path analysis, it is better to work from the end back towards the beginning; that is to examine the objectives; how best the inter-pretation might be made of the data collected; the form of analysis required to permit the interpretation; the form in which the field and other data will be presented to assist the analysis programme; the techniques which will yield the data in the way it can be best assimilated and then back to the research parameters themselves.

Thus if these or any of these steps are considered and allowance is made for both preceding and following activities, the form of the final analysis will already be pre-determined to a considerable extent. Certainly it would be very unwise to arrive at the analysis stage without previous consideration of the analyses to be attempted.

Three levels of activity are involved in data handling. First the examination of the material submitted for analysis; second, organising the material; and third the analysis itself.

Each of these activites will reveal different types of error. At the examination stage mostly errors of collection show up—incomplete questionnaires, questions misunderstood by either interviewer or respondent and incorrect recording of answers. When the material is organised it may reveal omissions caused by poor structuring of the interviews or questionnaires and the use of outdated or wrongly classified material gathered during desk research. At the analysis stage contradictions will emerge, relationships will be shown to be spurious, sample biases uncovered, and instability of responses revealed.

Thus at every level of the data handling the researcher must expect to find new evidence of unreliability and must seek to assess accuracy tolerances. Conversely, as the material is worked through the validity of the remaining material becomes greater as that which is dubious or unproved is discarded.

To make industrial marketing research effective, efficient and profitable it is absolutely necessary to process material as it is obtained, to analyse it and to interpret the results. These are integral and parallel sectors of the fact-finding activity. This analysis and the subsequent interpretations are not the end processes of a project; they begin the moment the first facts are uncovered. Without this constant critical appraisal of incoming information all projects would become an untidy mass of facts and deductions in various states of validation. The re-direction of research projects, re-orientations of interviews, redesign of questionnaires and other modifying functions could not take place unless there was a lively awareness of the project, the research process and the implications of the early findings—that is, unless analysis is continuous.

At the end of the fact-finding, however, the major processing, analysing and interpreting activities must take place under totally different conditions. In other words, all the facts that can be found have been obtained and no further research to fill in more details is anticipated.

RELIABILITY ASSESSMENT

The body of information to be analysed usually consists of a large number of disparate and not always apparently related items, some of which are certain to be vital to the research project while some are equally certain to be irrelevant. Reducing the mass of material to be refined to manageable proportions is the necessary next step of the research.

The research yield will comprise a mixture of statistical calculations based on official, unofficial and original sources; information directly or indirectly related to the research objectives or with no apparent relationship to them; information not directly related to the research objectives but indicating significant relationships with other material and data suitable for background and control use. But all the research yield will be considerably modified in its usefulness by the degree of confirmation or validation obtained. This confirmation will in itself range from irrefutable evidence of reliability to single unverifiable statements. Thus the researcher is faced with two problems, first the establishment of the relationship and value of data to the research objectives and to each other, and second, the establishment of the reliability of data.

By the time the processing stage of the project is reached much of the factual material will have already been checked for reliability but there will still remain a body of conflicting information which needs to be reconciled, confirmed or rejected as well as the other group of isolated and perhaps unrelated facts. Material that can be classified as unreliable or in any way speculative in its accuracy can be immediately discarded. The research effort must then be directed to re-classifying the remaining material, perhaps of indeterminate value, into its correct place within the factual structure. There are no rules to enable the researcher to discard or retain unconfirmed material. This process requires the exercise of intelligent judgement and does not depend solely upon the simple correlation of answers.

To grade material of established and unestablished reliability, once again a return to first principles is called for. The significance of each elicited fact cannot be determined unless there is a full understanding of the research objectives and their relationship to the specific marketing or management problem being considered. Further, changes in the research objectives—which occurred because of information obtained early in the survey, and changes in technique which are also likely to have occurred—must be considered by the researcher when facts are being appraised.

Ordinarily a research project yields far more information than is needed or used in the final analysis and interpretation. Some information may have been gathered in the exploration of hypotheses and subsequently abandoned. Hence the researcher must test each fact against the objectives of the research in order to establish what nexus exists between the fact and the research objective and what bearing it has on the research.

A difficulty immediately arises in that facts not apparently important in themselves can and do assume a new significance in their relationship with other facts. Where statistical relationships cannot be established easily, the need to appreciate other relationships becomes greater. Thus the study of relevant data also becomes a study to establish significant links. Only an intimate knowledge of the project in all its stages can guide a researcher in his attempt to identify these. One useful tool in the processing procedure, however, is the use of hypotheses to test relationships. The research initation itself is based upon hypotheses since no market study would be undertaken unless a hypothesis existed concerning aspects of the market to be investigated. Similarly, in preparing the research design and in selecting and modifying the research techniques there is, alongside the continuous analysis that must occur, a continuous setting up of hypotheses and testing of results against them. This may be no more formal than unexpressed ideas in the researcher's mind—nevertheless hypotheses can be used continuously.

BIAS

Before any analysis or appraisal of factual material can occur the analyst must investigate the question of bias. This has already been mentioned as a disadvantage in relation to some of the field techniques and in sampling. Some bias, particularly in the analysis of quantitative data, can be determined more easily than other types occurring in qualitative reports. Because it is difficult to locate and correct bias it is more than necessary to be aware of the areas in which bias is likely to occur and to understand the nature of its effect upon results.

There are many different types of bias that can insinuate themselves into survey results. The important ones are generically: sample bias in both source lists and sampling, question (postal questionnaires or structured interviews) or interviewer (personal or telephone interviews) bias, respondent and analysis bias. So far as is practicable every possible action will have been taken in the appropriate field techniques to reduce or eliminate these. At the data processing stage of the research it will be found that apparent contradictions can stem from bias. The correct method of dealing with the problem where this is suspected is to seek the source of bias and not to attempt to reconcile irreconcilables. It is necessary to distinguish between contradictions which stem from lack of information and those which stem from bias. This is an important differentiation since the former cannot be corrected without further research while the latter can be corrected by a re-appraisal of the material under consideration.

EXAMINING THE MATERIAL

The process of examining the material is essentially the first quick check to remove obviously invalid information. At the later stage of editing more material will be removed. The examination stage is at best a coarse screen to prevent organising and editing material which can be seen immediately to be unusable. The criteria for removal may be simply completed but illegible questionnaire or interview reports, the removal or obscuring of identities by respondents, replies from respondents outside the sampling frames or not qualified to complete the questionnaires. An example of the penultimate disqualification would be users of metal sectional tanks in a survey concerned with user experience of glass fibre tanks. An example of the last type of disqualification is an interview with a purchasing officer when the sample criteria specified the respondent as a maintenance engineer.

When the field work is complete it is possible to develop a check list of the elimination criteria that should apply to the particular survey. If there is a very considerable volume of information, such a list can provide the means of saving both time and money at the processing stage.

In the examination processes each questionnaire is perused as a single unit and then, in the case of interviews, all the reports by each interviewer are examined as a series. By undertaking the examination in this way, incorrect or inconsistent answers are quickly identified. This might be termed a 'vertical' examination of the material. In editing, as is explained below, the examination takes on a 'horizontal' form.

The examination of material, like the anlysis itself, is a continuous process throughout the research, particularly when sequential adjustments are to be made. It is important, however, not to be too hasty about discarding results before all the information which is to be collected is brought together. Without the total picture a negative significance may be overlooked. The example quoted earlier in Chapter 7 on postal questionnaires of the common characteristic on non-respondents is pertinent.

ORGANISING THE FINDINGS

The organisation of the material which has survived the examination stage is itself divided into three steps. These are editing, coding and tabulation. The editing is concerned largely with removing the data which is found to be inadmissable on closer examination and by comparison with the validity criteria set up for the various techniques. It is also the process in which data are converted into comparable form. Coding is the process of allocating groups and selected items or classified information into categories. Tabulation is counting the data by categories, individual or grouped.

(a) *Editing*

The process of separating out relevant material from unsuitable or irrelevant material carried out at the editing stage, is a further refinement of the examination processes. The desk research results, postal questionnaires, telephone and personal interview reports and observation reports are again carefully scrutinised and the material sorted, to ensure that information which can be identified as in any way invalid or unreliable is separated from the acceptable data. At this stage the process is aided by the techniques referred to in the relevant chapters on field and desk work. For example, the 'control' and 'check' questions enable editors to establish relationships between connected questions and to check on the true familiarity or veracity of the respondent.

At the editing stage it is possible to complete missing information based upon data that has already been obtained. For example, if a respondent has failed to indicate which technical journal he reads but in a later question a preference for one particular journal is stated and information is elicited on its contents, it is a fairly safe assumption that this is the paper read. It is not a safe assumption, however, that the paper is read regularly. The researcher editing the data must apply judgement to these matters. The quality of this judgement will depend on the editor's experience and ability, on an understanding of the research objectives and accurate interpretations of other questions asked and other material the research has yielded.

A further task of the editor who in a typical industrial marketing research survey will also be the principal researcher, is the conversion of quantitative data into common values. A magnetic materials survey elicited replies in ounces, pounds, and hundredweights— none of which represented anything more than simple arithmetical computation. However, many replies were also made in feet, cores, pieces and value. The task of the researcher in his role of editor thus became more complex in preparing and computing a conversion of these quantitative data. International statistics on diesel engines will be found to contain data in units, size ratings, weight and value. An attempt to convert weight into values is fraught with dangers because of the highly variable nature of the product, the extent to which it may incorporate accessory and peripheral equipment and how far it is 'knocked down'. Enzymes are another product for which there can be an infinite number of varying relationships between the degree of activity and value. Thus, the editor will require either a knowledge of the relationships, ratios or correlations that can be used, or may have to return to the field workers for more information.

Finally, the ordering of the material for processing takes place.

Q

Information may require to be grouped by Standard Industrial Classification, occupation, size of plant, numbers or age of installed machines, size of circulation or other divisions.

In no sense is the editing function a purely mechanical operation as can be appreciated from the examples given. In fact it requires considerable skill. Without this skill the effectiveness of the later analysis can be seriously hindered and new errors introduced which may at this late stage be difficult or impossible to correct. The editing will, unlike the examination procedure, examine each questionnaire and interview report 'horizontally'. That is, each question will be studied separately on each questionnaire and each subject matter on each interview report, before passing on to the next question or subject. This enables the editing to develop a consistency.

It is obvious that where unstructured interviews are being used it will be necessary to translate what may be rambling, indirect and haphazard answers into a practical sequence. Answers to qualifying questions, answers received to indirect questions, validating answers, probes, funnel questions, transitional questions and other material not yielding direct answers to the main question have to be eliminated and answers formulated from them in a simple form. These answers must then be properly located in the report or questionnaire to enable the editor, coder and the categoriser or classifier to turn straight through without losing time considering extraneous questions.

Qualitative questions are the most difficult to edit and require the highest of editorial skills. Despite the very large number of possible replies to an open-ended question, a pattern does tend to form which enables the editor to select the most appropriate groupings and cluster the remainder. This problem is dealt with in more detail at the end of the chapter.

The editor must, at this stage, indicate the categories into which the replies can be logically grouped and then designate each piece of material into the class to which it belongs. This is a vital editorial responsibility which can spell success or failure of the analysis or the whole survey. As so much material obtained in an industrial marketing research survey is non-quantitative, the importance of accurate, unbiased and skilful editing is paramount.

In handling numerical data it is necessary, if the editor and coder are not one and the same person, to indicate the classes into which the data is to be placed. Once again skills are required over and above those necessary for the tabulation work.

(b) *Classification and coding*

Coding consists of allocating groups, selected items or classified information into categories depicted by a symbol—usually a number. In the interest of clarifying the general picture, the analyst must be willing to sacrifice some of the detail of the individual responses by allocating them to a relatively small number of categories. Thus several hundred answers will be reduced to perhaps ten categories. However, if the method of categorisation is intelligent the basic information which the question coding has been designed to obtain will be clearly indicated. Without the elimination of detail by coding the salient results may be overwhelmed by the volume of minutiae. Coding practice and order are guided by logical principles of classification and by the particular requirements of the project. These have been summarised as follows.[1]

Each individual response should fit into at least one category— that is, the scheme of classification should be exhaustive. This must include categories for 'no answer' or 'not ascertained' as well as 'don't know' and 'would not divulge'. These last categories usually contain a high proportion of the difficult-to-interview respondents who may differ significantly as to the characteristics being studied from the respondents who do answer the question.

Categories must be logical in their content and obviously must be related to the purpose of the study. For example, answers to questions concerning use of conveyor belting could include very widely differing types of operation from the movement of heavy materials to delicate parts, and would therefore relate to belts of different performance characteristics and materials. Categories could be based upon either of these or upon the materials moved, or the type of conveyor system, or the process into which the belting is incorporated. All these could be valid but in relation to the research objectives the most relevant ones will be obvious. Sub-groupings are, of course, permissible to take into account other ramifications which could not be accommodated by the main categories.

Whenever possible each answer should fit into only one category, that is, the scheme of classification should be mutually exclusive. This, of course, cannot always be done—particularly with multiple-choice questions where a valid response may cover more than one answer. Many multiple or ambiguous answers stem from poor question formulation and in these cases treating the response as multiple answers obscures results. Any ambiguity that cannot be

[1] J. H. Lorie and H. V. Roberts, *Basic Methods of Marketing Research*, McGraw-Hill (New York, 1951), pp. 407-8.

eliminated from the questions should be diminished by classifying responses as if, in fact, two (or more) distinct questions had been asked. When this is done any latent ambiguity in the questions is made obvious and the problem of the multiple answer eliminated.

Whatever categories are adopted must be psychologically sound. 'A basic form of behaviour must be indicated in each qualitative category. There should be no possibility of ambiguity of meaning in the categories employed. For example the classification "convenient" could mean many things to many people. However, as general descriptive terms cannot be avoided, in some cases it is good practice to define the meaning as it is employed in the particular study. It is difficult to separate what is psychologically sound and what is logical in content, but the researcher must recognise that there may be two different ways of looking at a qualitative response.'[1]

The detail of classification is a compromise between the obvious need to summarise and the need to know the differences in the individual answers. Too many categories, with a small number of responses in each, obscure the salient findings. Too few categories, with large response rates, obscure the detail and even the broader picture can be lost. If a choice must be made the first alternative is preferable since it is sometimes possible to consolidate the information satisfactorily.

The scheme of classification is determined by the questions being investigated. The reverse should not be attempted—that is, to make coding the Procrustean bed into which the questions must be stretched.

The principles in coding for computer or other electronic data processing methods are precisely the same as for hand analysis. The methods obviously differ to take account of the mechanics of the operation. Generally the code symbols will have been included on the questionnaires or other data forms so that they can be transferred immediately to the computer or machine medium. Obviously the codes and the number of columns must be fitted to the capability of the equipment used.

(c) *Tabulation*

The last step in the preparation of the data is tabulation, or counting that information which lends itself to this process. In its simplest definition it is the determination of the number of admissible items which fall into the established categories.

[1] M. S. Heidingsfield and F. H. Eby, *Marketing and Business Research*, Holt, Rinehart and Winston (New York, 1962), p. 218.

Counting can be accomplished by manual or machine methods. For hand tabulation the edited and coded answers are usually transferred on to tabulation sheets or special forms raised for the purpose. Whichever method is used, the sheet will yield the data to be used in the analysis and must therefore lend itself to its easy extraction, clarity and simplicity of the operation. For example, it is easier and quicker to count groups of dashes than single dashes. Thus it is usual to count in 'gates'. That is four vertical and one horizontal dash to each five replies $\not\!\!\!/\!\!\!/\!\!\!/$. This can be extended to nine + one but beyond this the risk of error through miscounting in the group becomes proportionately higher.

Analysis sheets will be of the straight tabulation, cross tabulation or scale analysis variety. Straight tabulation involves a single dimensional table giving the summation of replies received for each item of information. In cross tabulation the replies to one question are related to replies given to another question. For example, the number of users of intermediate bulk containers falling into each Standard Industrial Classification and taking into account numbers employed by the user firms. This information may have been derived from three different groups of replies from the field research and by desk research. In the case quoted the users might have been located by a postal questionnaire, the Standard Industrial Classifications of the firms by telephone interviews and the numbers employed from directories. The cross tabulation gives a three dimensional count.

Scale analysis is concerned with the data obtained from comparative ratings ascribed to the subject being probed, for example on a self-ranking, comparative or attitude scaling. Appropriate tabulation sheets will need to be devised to present the data. In the case of postal questionnaires this will often be a 'blown up' version of the questionnaire itself to a size large enough to permit the count of the answers to be written in.

Generally tabulated responses are converted to percentages. The appropriate denominators may be the number of completed questionnaires, the number of completed responses to an individual question, or the total number of interviews.

'Percentages are a special kind of ratio and are highly useful in facilitating a comparison between two or more series of data. They can be used to describe a relationship when one figure lacks significance unless compared with another. A further use is for comparing in relative terms the distribution of two or more series of data, when the absolute figure would confuse rather than assist analysis.'[1]

[1] *Marketing Research—Text and Cases*, op. cit., p. 518.

MULTIPLE AND OPEN-ENDED ANSWERS

One of the most difficult problems in the tabulation procedure, whether manual or machine, is that generated by multiple and open-ended answers. Because of the nature of industrial marketing research these types of answers tend to predominate which is why their handling takes on a particular significance. Four approaches have been suggested[1] the most appropriate being decided by the nature of the problem and the research objectives.

(a) Allocating replies by respondent: that is the percentage of respondents found to possess a particular attribute although a number of different attributes may be claimed. For example, in the table opposite[2] each reply for each respondent group has been allocated to the appropriate information source and it is possible to tell the percentage of any one group influence by any one information source.

(b) Summating numbers by respondents. From the same raw data information can be obtained on the numbers in each respondent group obtaining information from one or more sources. While it is possible to deduce from Table 2 that 39 per cent of Board members derive information from catalogues, it is not possible to know how many of these 39 per cent also are influenced by other sources. Figure 24 shows a different analysis of the same material, this time giving the number of Board members receiving information from one, two or more sources.

(c) Duplication analysis. This type of analysis stems from a tabulation which reveals the combinations which result from multiple choices of respondents. To continue with the example, this time it is possible to derive information on the combination of sources of information in each respondent group. Thus Figure 25 shows how many Board members who attend exhibitions also attend demonstrations by manufacturers and receive sales engineers' visits. This type of analysis is particularly valuable in establishing overlap areas. The use of the information is obvious since it reveals the number of Board members not susceptible to the particular influences listed and, conversely, the extent of duplication of information sources.

(d) Answer distribution. This method distributes the answers rather than the respondents. Thus if respondents referred to the ownership of certain makes or types of earth-moving equipment, the number

[1] *Marketing Research: Texts and Cases*, op. cit., pp. 525-6.
[2] *How British Industry Buys*, Table 8, op. cit.

Table 2

METHODS OF RECEIVING INFORMATION

In industry personnel with these functions ⟶ consider, in the percentage shown, these factors to be amongst the two most important when obtaining information on products* ⟶	Board (general management)	Operating management	Prod. engineering	Des. & dev. engineering	Maint. engineering	Research	Buying	Finance	Sales	Others
Catalogues	39	36	45	64	34	64	52	32	44	76
Direct mail	12	9	14	6	31	21	23	14	5	27
Sales engineers' visits	66	61	60	67	78	64	64	60	73	40
Advertisements in trade press	14	32	28	22	21	15	12	23	24	24
Exhibitions	15	17	11	11	47	15	9	19	14	12
Demonstrations by manufacturers	50	41	35	26	37	21	37	38	45	22
Other	6	4		6			5	5	35	

of replies claiming each type would be tabulated. The 'population' and make or brand distribution of equipment can be established by this method and allow for ownership of several types or brands.

Multiple choice questions need not stem from a single question but can be a combination of single answers. With open-ended questions it may be necessary at the editing stage to break the answer

PERCENTAGE OF GENERAL MANAGEMENT RECEIVING INFORMATION FROM ONE OR MORE SOURCES

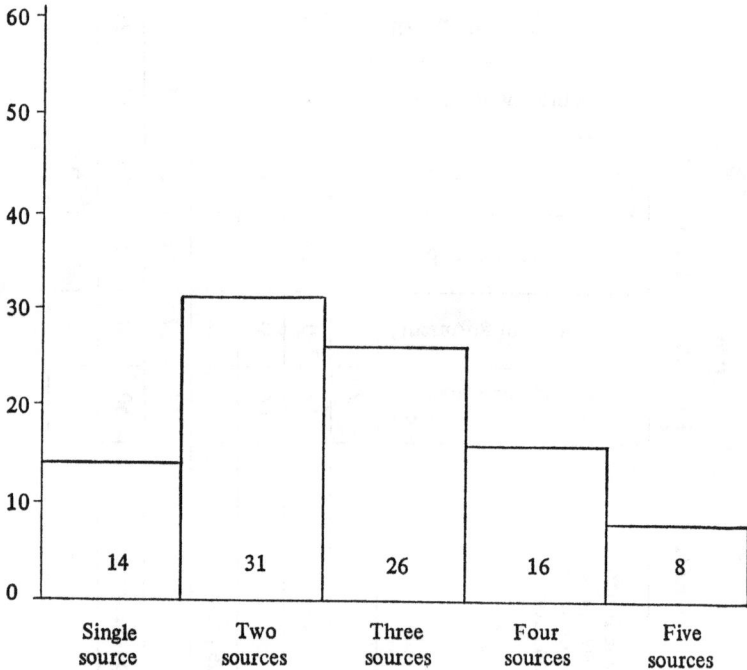

Fig. 24

down into separate parts only one or a few of which can be allocated for any particular analysis.

MACHINE TABULATION

Depending on the size of the sample and the response rate, machine tabulation for the actual analytical process is far quicker than manual techniques. Machine tabulation permits many cross tabulations of multi-dimensional questionnaires and interviews. However, it is necessary in calculating both time and cost to take into account the time that is required to prepare the material for the machine and, in the case of computer use, a programme. This process will consist of either transferring the data onto punched cards or paper or magnetic tape. The cards or tape are then passed through the machine which sorts and counts according to the instructions it has

PERCENTAGE OF GENERAL MANAGEMENT
EXPOSED TO COMBINATIONS OF THREE SPECIFIC INFLUENCES

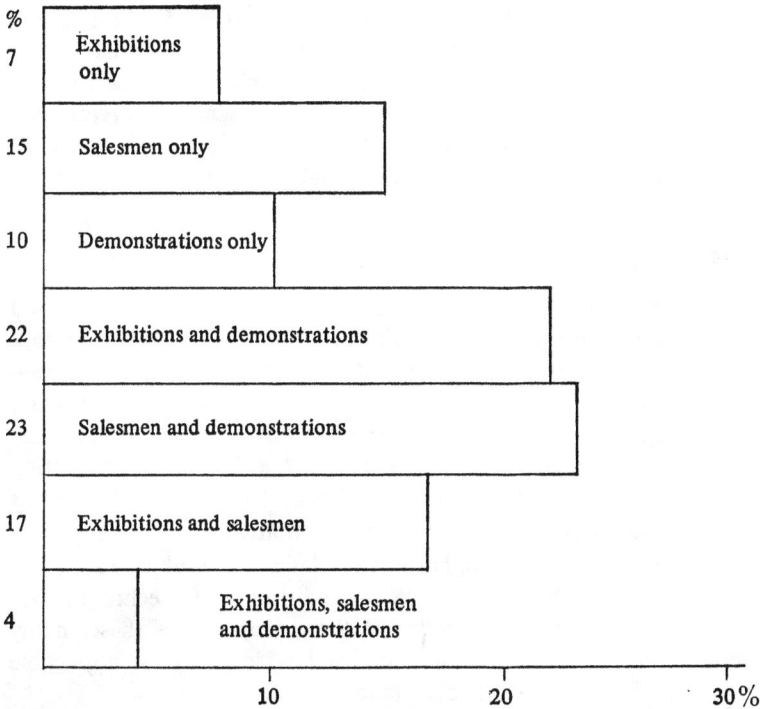

Fig. 25

received from its operator and transfers the results onto tabulation sheets. Many machines will be equipped to verify information and thereby reveal errors which may have occurred in categorising, coding or transfer onto the processing media.

Electronic data processing equipment is not infallible but it is unlikely to be as inaccurate as a clerk. One estimate[1] gives human calculation over a period of time as at best 95 per cent accurate and

[1] Quoted in *Marketing Research—Texts and Cases*, op. cit., p. 524, attributed to R. N. Schmidt and W. E. Meyers. *Basic Programming Concepts and the IBM 1620 Computer*, Holt, Rinehart and Winston (New York, 1962), p. 1.

computer accuracy as 99.99 + per cent. In the latter case a computer also often indicates an error to the operator. Moreover the use of computers makes possible the application of new mathematical techniques to solve complex problems.

The decision whether to use hand or machine tabulation will generally rest on a limited number of clearly definable criteria. These are the number of cross tabulations required, the presence or absence of research continuity, the likelihood of re-runs, the error risk and the comparative time and cost calculations. In the example of the postal questionnaire prepared for computer analysis an extract of which was shown in Figure 16 hand tabulation would have taken very many weeks and then the accuracy would have been open to some doubt. The greater the volume of the data, the more repetitive the tabulation method, the higher the error propensity.

ANALYTICAL TECHNIQUES

There are a multitude of analytical techniques which can be adopted for obtaining information from the data. Not surprisingly, the bulk of them are quantitative analytical methods. It has already been said that a very large percentage of data obtained in an industrial marketing research survey will be qualitative so that, despite the number of analytical tools available, the industrial marketing researcher may in a large number of cases be forced back into his interpretive role. Nevertheless, even qualitative results can give an additional relevant valid and usable yield if they are subjected to some types of quantitative analysis. A limited number of techniques are outlined but it is emphasised that there are, besides these, many others which are worthy of study and which may be applicable under a wide variety of circumstances.

SUMMARY STATISTICS

'Statistical measures which are used to typify the group are referred to as measures of central tendency. Of the several measures of central tendency, the arithmetic mean and median are the most common. Such statistics are of great help to the researcher, but they can also be dangerous'.[1]

This is a timely warning because it is often forgotten that the various 'averages' are only summary statistics and substitutes. They help the researcher to arrive at generalisations about the

[1] *Market Research*, op. cit., p. 127.

universe surveyed but are helpful only if they reflect this universe accurately. Because a measure of central tendency is a number which represents a middle value in a series of data and which conveys the impression of the whole series, it can easily obliterate other equally or more significant information—for example frequency distribution.[1]

Statistical measures which reveal something about the degree to which the values in one or more series vary with respect to a particular characteristic often need to be used. These are called measures of dispersion and of these the standard deviation is probably the most widely used in general analyses. The smaller its value the greater the homogeneity of the data. By establishing a standard deviation it is possible to define with a high degree of accuracy the limits within which the mean of a larger group will fall and it is in this that the value of establishing the standard deviation lies. The techniques for so doing are relatively simple and will be found in all textbooks on statistics, some of which are listed in the Bibliography.

However, in industrial marketing research it is more usual to use standard errors,[2] a variation of the standard deviation. Standard deviation is used when measurements of various types are involved. In marketing research where results are depicted in percentages or proportions, these proportions when dependent on a sample are subject to a standard error and it is this error which it is necessary to measure. Different sample designs will dictate the use of different formulae for calculating standard error so that each case will require separate consideration.

STATISTICAL METHODS

A number of statistical methods and formulae exist to assist in obtaining specific types of analysis. Principal among these are tests to determine whether statistically significant differences exist; these must be established before inferences as to causality can be made. Chi square analyses enable the researcher to determine whether a significant difference exists between two or more sets of data. Analysis of variance determines the relationship between two or more characteristics; basically it is a technique for learning what each of the various factors involved contribute to the total variance.

[1] The relative frequency with which members of a category have the various possible values of the variable quantity.

[2] Standard Error—the inherent variation of a sample or of answers to a particular question, which is measurable and dependent on the size of the sample and the pattern of replies to questions.

Correlation analysis alredy referred to in Chapter 5 'Use of Secondary Sources', determines the degree of relationship between variables and is another aspect of analysis of variance. Multiple correlations take the examination still further to incorporate three or more variables. It has been pointed out[1] that a particular danger to watch for in correlation analysis is the assumption that correlation implies a causal relationship when in fact correlation merely shows the degree to which variables vary together. An error of this type is called a 'spurious correlation'.

In regression analysis the use of a regression equation allows determination of the value of the dependent variable which is associated with a given value of the dependent variable. Regression analysis applications can be summed up as follows:[2]

* to determine the relationship between one variable and a criterion factor while simultaneously removing the influences of other factors.

* to determine which of a set of factors is most related to the criterion factor.

* to match two groups so that they are equivalent in important respects.

* to formulate a predictive equation which allows for the calculation of expected levels of the criterion factor given any combination of values of the independent factors.

* to gain inferences about additional factors which may be related to the criterion variable.

Ratio analysis, also referred to in Chapter 5, is the use of criteria as measures of performance. These criteria may be generated by the field work or provided from internal sources.

All these approaches, however, assume a not inconsiderable volume of available raw data and often a great deal more information about the sample and respondents than in fact exists in the majority of industrial marketing research projects. A further discussion of regression and other analytical techniques is contained in Chapter 13, which is concerned with forecasting procedures.

Perhaps the most complete list of statistical techniques and formulae for use in marketing research has been compiled by Robert

---

[1] *Marketing Research: Texts and Cases*, op. cit., p. 544.

[2] J. B. Landis, 'On Methods: Multiple Regression Analysis—The Easy Way', *Journal of Advertising Research* (New York, March 1962), p. 36.

Ferber[1] and comprises thirty-two separate approaches and is well worthy of study.

PREFERENCE ANALYSIS

Beside these analytical methods which have been mentioned, there are other techniques being developed for use in industrial markets. Preference analysis which was originally rejected by industrial marketing researchers as being applicable only in consumer markets has recently been subject to new thinking.

The preference distribution concept is concerned with measurements of aspects of choice. The idea of estimating frequency distribution of consumer preference can be traced to L. C. Thurstone. The prediction of the outcome of political elections, or the relative consumption of competing commodities, was postulated by him as long ago as 1945. His method was to develop 'estimates of the average effective values of candidates or products, and the discriminal dispersion around these mean subjective values on a psychological continuum'.[2]

While Thurstone's methods do not seem to have been widely used there has been an increasing amount of experimentation in techniques using his concept of frequency distribution of consumer preferences.

Among the methods developed is that of P. H. Benson whose early work was concerned with determination of optimal level of a product attribute. He developed functions which related the degree of like or dislike to the level of product characteristic and the optimum values were then determined by differential calculus. 'Recognising that this model required the highly unrealistic assumption of homogenous tastes across the population, Benson shifted his attention to fitting a distribution curve which would depict the proportions of the population preferring various alternative levels of the product. Benson's recent publications suggest fitting distribution curves to data related to intangible product attributes such as flavour, appearance, style and convenience which cannot be measured directly in the laboratory. He proposed to use scales whose values have no physical counterpart.' Other approaches have been developed, notably by Alfred Kuehn and Ralph Day,[3] both of whom have advanced the methods developed by Benson.

[1] *Market Research*, op. cit., pp. 458-76.

[2] L. C. Thurstone, 'Prediction of Choice', *Psychometrics*, Vol. 10 (Richmond, Virginia, U.S.A., 1955).

[3] R. L. Day, 'Methods of Estimating Consumer Preference Distributions', *California Management Review* (Berkeley, California, Summer 1967).

There is in fact no real reason why preference analysis cannot be adapted to industrial marketing research, even though the barrier which is erected between expressed and real preferences can lead to an analysis of incorrect preferences.

The major blockage in adopting preference analysis in industrial markets has been the still widely held view that industrial buying is rational and circumscribed, whereas the truth is that emotional factors intrude in decision-making. A second objection is that the range of subjects over which preference can be expressed is too narrow to be productive of any information which would assist in marketing decisions. In fact the range of preferences is wide, although ostensibly different from preferences expressed in a consumer buying situation.

QUALITATIVE ANALYSIS

The use of numerical concepts—counting and measurements—is unquestionably the limit which precision in marketing research can reach. However, qualitative concepts, for example, product acceptability or advertising effectiveness—precisely defined, are of equal and not infrequently of greater importance in achieving research objectives where quantification is not always possible. Nevertheless, measurable qualitative data can be presented in quantitative form.

Nowhere is the difference between the importance of qualitative and quantitative data in consumer and industrial research better illustrated than from the opinions of leading exponents of both schools. One view is that 'Information of this kind (qualitative) cannot be treated statistically nor can its accuracy be assessed, but it is often worth highlighting. This should not, however, be done in the body of the report but a comprehensive account of the information and the circumstances under which it was acquired, can be usefully included in an appendix.'[1] The opposite opinion is that, 'although it is essential that analysis should reflect the quantitative weight of market evidence . . . this process requires the exercise of intelligent judgement and cannot be accomplished satisfactorily by a simple tallying of answers'.[2]

While paying lip service to the fact that quantitative and qualitative research are not mutually exclusive, both views do in fact so far limit

[1] A. H. R. Delens, *Principles of Market Research*, Crosby Lockwood (London, 1964), p. 172.
[2] *Industrial Marketing*, op. cit., p. 162.

by both word and implication the value of each of the approaches, that the dual nature of research—qualitative and quantitative—is lost. It is a dangerous kind of dichotomy to make, since research to be valid should be qualitative and to be accurate, should be quantitative. Both approaches are applicable, especially to industrial marketing research, and whereas the 'mix' may vary to a considerable extent they should wherever possible be used concurrently.

The qualitative approach in industrial marketing research is important, not only because quantitative analyses are sometimes impossible to construct but also because even when this is possible they can rarely attain the same accuracy as in consumer research and, therefore, the industrial researcher, it is said, must make a virtue of necessity. The contrary is in fact true, inasmuch as the qualitative approach can by-pass many of the limitations present in the conventional quantitative research procedures.

In a situation in which a respondent is incapable, unwilling or deliberately misleading in answering questions, the qualitative approach is the only method capable of determining the inaccuracies which are likely to occur, and which can guide the situation in a more favourable direction. Industrial marketing researchers have learned to recognise such situations and to adjust the approach accordingly. Qualitative techniques, whether adopted by the question-and-answer type interviewer deeply involved in technicalities of the product, or by the psychologist steering a group along a predetermined course, can produce valid answers in what might otherwise be regarded as unpropitious circumstances.

There are degrees of inability, unwillingness or mischievousnes in respondents and it is possible for the marketing researcher using judgement, experience, technique and skill to appraise these. Even partial success is of value since while one part of an interview may be of little value, other parts can still be utilised. A respondent, for example, may refuse to give information on output but will give facts concerning his own or competitors' market shares which together with other known facts can be of equal value in relation to the original questions. In similar circumstances, information about output may be refused but input or the number of machines in use and even operating times upon which accurate estimates can be calculated are freely discussed.

A useful yardstick for appraising situations for qualitative analysis has been devised.[1] This recognises three dimensions of availability

[1] G. H. Smith, *Motivation Research in Advertising and Marketing*, McGraw-Hill (New York, 1954), p. 18.

of information in terms of what are described as 'levels of awareness'. The *first* level is information or material which the respondent is prepared to discuss or reveal. In industrial marketing research terms, these may be such items as machine uses, advertising media preferences, handling problems, safety. The *second* level is material rarely discussed. Again in industrial marketing research terms, these would be factors such as enlarging a sales force as an instrument of personal aggrandisement in internal power politics, the purchase of new equipment for industrial 'conspicuous consumption', over-inflated research programmes and the use of sub-ethical techniques for obtaining business. The *third* level concerns material that is never revealed or discussed deliberately. Job insecurity stemming from personal inadequacies and ineptitude, inadequate or inaccurate planning as a result of poor judgement and actions taken deliberately to further personal interests against those of the firm are examples.

What is important is that it is now widely recognised that the scope of information completely accessible by the direct approach at each level is far smaller than was once believed. Even at the first level, which is basically discussing material the respondent has no objection to divulging, information over a large area tends to be distorted. There is increasing evidence that unsuspected influences are often active in causing these distortions and thus withholding of information.[1] The problem is less one of respondents being unable to express themselves clearly by the use of the right words and the right concepts, confusing apparent with real determinants, contradictions and changes in attitudes than in the unconscious unwillingness to express certain attitudes and opinions. To this is added the further difficulties of the interviewers of role perception.

At the first level of awareness the researcher can resolve the majority of difficulties either by rephrasing questions or providing explanations of the purpose of the survey which may permit the respondent to answer questions to which the initial reaction was one of rejection. A sophisticated interviewer can penetrate the second level without much difficulty. Respondents tend to develop rationalised explanations and produce 'intellectual discussions, often quite irrelevant to the subject matter of the research and a mass of half truths . . . good training . . . will often enable

[1] Hector Lazo, 'Emotional Aspects of Industrial Buying', George M. Robertson, 'Motives in Industrial Buying', *Dynamic Marketing in a Changing World*, Robert S. Hancock (Ed.), American Marketing Association (New York, 1960), pp. 266-76.

the investigator to spot rationalisations as they show up, formulate hypotheses that can be checked by varied probing and infer general frames of reference and motives from clues that are turned up'.[1]

The third level of awareness is, of course, that about which the main controversy of qualitative research revolves and is the field where motivation research techniques are used. Clearly the analyses of material obtained at this level must be the work of a psychologist since the researcher must be familiar—in the widest sense of the word—with major concepts of psychiatry and abnormal psychology. Further, he must be capable of interpreting indications that appear and utilising techniques such as those described in other chapters and which give direct evidence of information required.

BACKGROUND TO QUALITATIVE INFORMATION

Quantitative data often include within themselves much of their own background. Even so it is still necessary in analysing such information to have full knowledge of the method by which it is obtained, by whom it was obtained and, of course, the type of respondent from whom it was obtained. The fact that researchers using the quantitative approach also need this information emphasises the duality of the nature of marketing research, despite the watertight compartments into which research polemics have tended to force it. Even the most hardened disciples of the 'numerical concept' or, as its exponents in marketing research prefer to call it, 'the scientific approach', admit that there is room for subjectivity in the evaluation of evidence—even of numerical evidence.

Qualitative data, however, must always be viewed against the background of their collection. To this should be added the need to recognise variability of practices between companies and in different markets. An industry which appears to be homogeneous at the beginning of an investigation may turn out to have several different segments of varying importance and characteristics. All this must be within the purview of the researcher when evaluating and analysing qualitative data.

Basically the researcher is concerned with five factors. The technique used to obtain information, the characteristics of the respondent, the characteristics of the interviewers, the characteristics of the markets or companies and the circumstances under which the information was obtained.

The techniques used to obtain the research data provide the back-

[1] *Motivation Research in Advertising and Marketing*, op. cit., pp. 20-1.

R

ground for the evaluation of the other factors. The characteristics of respondents and their accord with the sample will be revealed to a certain degree by the formal information available. What will not be obvious to the analyst will be the realistic position of the respondent within the firm, the amount of time the interviewer received, the rapport between respondent and interviewer and subjective factors—ranging from physical conditions and time of the interview to interruptions and fatigue. Each of these, and others, can materially affect the answers and their applicability and reliability. For the most part only the researcher can interpret the effect of these on the interview. The report should therefore contain the background facts as well as the information interviewers obtained.

The interviewer will not see his own characteristics objectively. Therefore in correcting for interview bias and in analysing reports the analyst, who should know the interviewers, their strengths and weaknesses, their skill and experience (the repetitive pattern of interviewing quickly highlights characteristics peculiar to each interviewer) should view the reports against this background.

The characteristics of the market are another aspect of the evaluation of reports that are virtually produced automatically. However, in analysing results of field techniques not using personal interviews, a very close look is necessary to ensure that any given areas of responses are not conditioned by some internal market or company condition which makes it untypical either in characteristic or time.

An example of this has already been quoted of a postal questionnaire used within an industry being considered for examination before the Restrictive Practices Court. Under these circumstances, responses by members of the industry or their suppliers and even customers was conditioned by the impending decision to investigate. Thus a question on price produced exceptionally 'loaded' answers such as 'they are too high' from a customer industry and 'too low' from a supplying industry. The respondent's real purpose in both cases was not objective reporting on a price situation but a conscious or unconscious propaganda effort.

The analyses of qualitative data stand out sharply from those of quantitative data in their apparent lack of precision and formal techniques. It would be absurd to pretend that considerable developments in the use of qualitative data and their analysis have not still to be achieved. Nevertheless, the skill of qualitative researchers has been proved in the growing body of successful industrial marketing surveys. Qualitative analysis calls for the highest levels of creative judgement, imagination, ingenuity, skill and intellectual honesty. The weight of experience—which by definition cannot always be present—adds to the general ability of the researcher and analyst. The two methods, quantitative and qualitative, which provide a Janus-like approach to marketing research problems, are unquestionably the correct ones for achieving the most accurate results.

INFORMATION BUILD-UP

The description of the various methods which can be used in an industrial marketing research project and the various analytical techniques which are available for processing the data does not on its own explain the contribution of *each* type of activity in *different* areas which is productive of the various parts of the final report. In industrial marketing research it is rare to rely on *one* technique and *one* area to provide information on any *one* section. Thus, a project which examined competitors only by a study among competitors will inevitably lack depth and worse, cross-validation. Information on competitors to be reliable must, in fact, be a build-up from such segments as their customers, distributors, original equipment manufacturers, raw material suppliers, and many other sources. Similarly, the techniques used to obtain this data will also vary, depending on the respondent group.

A simplified form of the technique-areas-results information flow is shown in Figure 26 devised by Hugh Buckner,[1] where the example quoted above can be traced through. Information *from* competitors is obtained by all the methods listed other than postal questionnaires but information *on* competitors is drawn by all the techniques from all the other areas. On the output side, competitive data makes a contribution to each section of the report. Clearly, the weights and value of the information will vary. Competitors' information on user requirements is likely to be governed by the same biases and experiences as that of the sponsor so that it is much more important to check it in the field with users. Competitors' views on technological changes are likely to be far more insightful than users. Raw material suppliers can make a big contribution to the estimate of market shares of their customers but relatively little contribution to information on their customers' customers.

Figure 26 does not set out to show the total information gathering process, but to present, schematically, a number of important inputs and outputs.

[1] Industrial Market Research Limited.

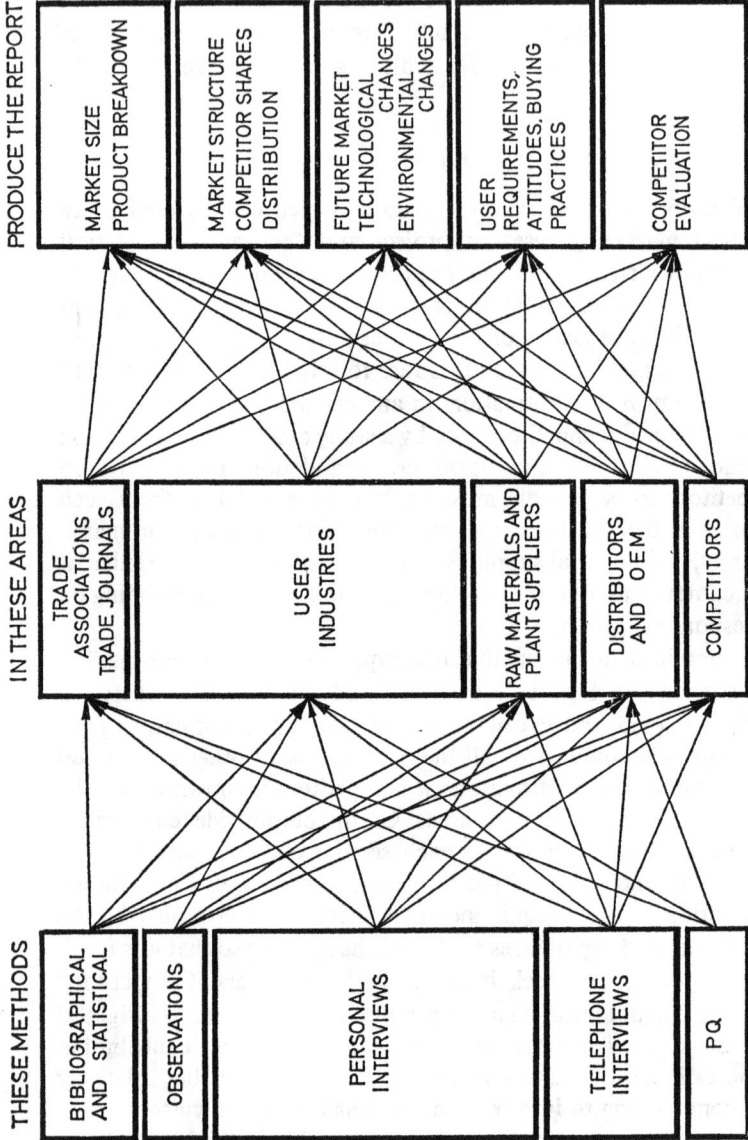

Fig. 26

RESEARCH INPUT-OUTPUT

(PQ = Postal Questionnaires   OEM = Original Equipment Manufacturers)

CHAPTER 12

Assessing Advertising Effectiveness

There is little argument among management that the two areas in which the contribution of industrial marketing research to marketing operations could potentially be the most substantial is in advertising effectiveness evaluation and the identification of 'top out' conditions in product life cycles. In some respects both these facets of marketing are related, since both are subject to an exceptionally large number of variables all out of the control of the individual firm. There is also some similarity in the problems of researching both phenomena.

Advertising in industrial markets has historically represented a smaller proportion of the total marketing budget than is the case for consumer product advertising. Moreover the actual sums of money involved have been and remain relatively insignificant. Thus it is not surprising that research into industrial advertising effectiveness has tailed far behind the work done in investigating consumer products advertising.

Advertising results, even the most enthusiastic supporters concede, are still largely unpredictable. Thus advertising poses one of the most difficult areas for management decisions and, therefore, one in which the accumulation of any knowledge is disproportionately valuable. Mistakes in advertising strategy and technique are costly and difficult, if not impossible, to rectify and expenditure is almost invariably irrecoverable. A misplaced purchase of a machine tool or vehicle will, at worst, yield the second-hand value of the product. Not only can nothing be saved from unsuccessful advertising but often additional monies will be needed to correct the errors made. For these and other reasons advertising research is taking on a new importance as industrial advertising begins to take an increasing part in industrial marketing operations.

Many claims have been made over recent years for having established a method of measuring advertising effectiveness. These range from highly theoretical mathematical models to complex electro-mechanical devices. But if the claims to have succeeded in measuring advertising effectiveness are examined, it will be found in the end that they are a measurement of total marketing effectiveness —a very different story.

It is easy to assume that increased or decreased sales correlate directly with the advertising effort. Such a view is naive in that it takes no cognisance of other marketing activities, environmental factors and all the variables which affect sales, such as distribution, personal selling, pricing, competitors' advertising and economic conditions, among many others. Thus what can be said is that the total marketing effectiveness can be assessed with a high degree of precision but that no single marketing function can be singled out as having alone produced a given result.

It is true that by holding static those of the marketing variables which can be controlled the area of inaccuracy can be considerably reduced and confidence tolerances increased. For example, control of exposure to a particular advertisement can certainly reveal a great deal of information by comparing reactions and activities of exposed and non-exposed groups. However, it is impossible to control other companies' advertising which will also impact on user attitudes, or to control outside events. Thus what has been achieved is a narrowing down of uncertainty but not its elimination.

The difficulty thus revolves around the inability to control variables in any experiment attempting to measure the effectiveness of a particular campaign or advertisement. These variables, individually and combined, have so pervasive an effect upon market conditions that progress towards the development of acceptable tools to measure advertising effectiveness is still slow and hesitant.

Under these circumstances the natural doubt arises as to whether there is in fact any value in advertising research which cannot as yet hope to achieve its objective by any known and generally accepted techniques. The fact that a wholly satisfactory method of measuring advertising effectiveness has not yet been devised does not imply that several promising approaches to achieving a fairly consistent approximate measurement have not been achieved.

Thus while it still may not be possible to assess advertising effectiveness in terms of sales or profits, other relevant criteria can be usefully adopted. For example, advertisements or an advertising campaign can be compared one with another on the basis of readership recall or recognition. Competitive advertising can be compared in content, cost, method and media. It is possible to test, assess and sometimes measure the influence of certain factors, colour, size, repetition, timing, headlines, layout, copy, illustration and appeal.

THE ADVERTISING PROCESS

Before discussing the assessment of advertising effectiveness, it is important to have an appreciation of the advertising process. Advertising can be said to be the communication process which moves the reader or observer through various stages, none of which can be omitted. These are:[1]

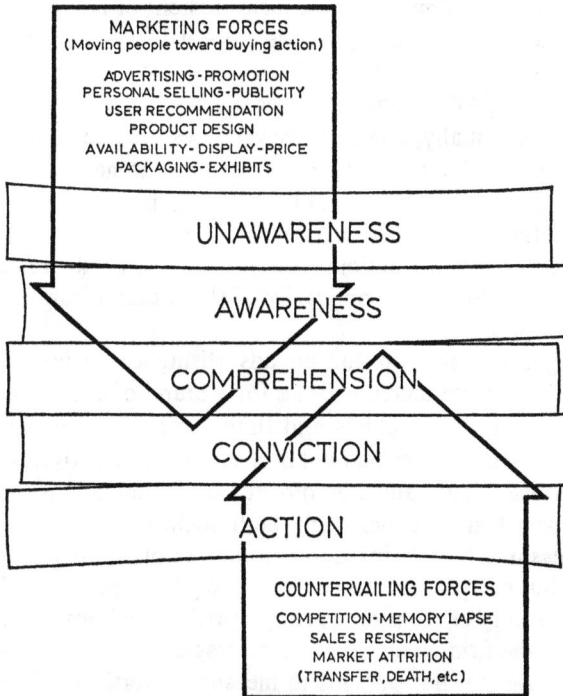

Fig. 27
ADVERTISING PROCESS

This, however, is by no means the only conceptual framework which has wide acceptance as representing the advertising process. Daniel Starch's is equally well-known:

    must be seen
    must be read
    must be believed

[1] A. H. Colley, 'Squeezing the Waste out of Advertising', *Harvard Business Review* (Cambridge, Mass., September/October 1962).

must be remembered
must be acted upon

Yet another view is that the comprehension and conviction stages of the Colley version should be substituted by 'image' and 'rating'.[1]

By the research techniques currently available it is possible to measure with accuracy the extent of awareness and unawareness of the subject matter among given segments of the market surveyed. It is, however, extremely difficult to obtain a measure for comprehension and conviction. Finally a measurement of action, if not the causitive factors, is relatively simple since it is reflected in how far the advertisement objectives are achieved, for example increased sales. Thus the problem viewed vertically is simply defined.

Viewed horizontally, however, the variables become numerous and immeasurable. Taking the prospect from unawareness to action can be accomplished by advertising of various sorts, by public relations efforts, by the inter-personal network, by merchandising techniques, by salesmen, with contributions from pricing and product policy and non-product factors. The complexity of the situation can be seen by giving examples.

It is right to ask how far an advertising campaign aimed at achieving immediate increased sales for a brand of chipboard would have been vitiated if builders and timber merchants had not held stocks or if the sales force had not been efficient and active. Similarly, any Public Relations campaign directed to gaining admission to the list of firms asked to tender might be thought to have its success or failure measured by relating it to the number of 'approvals' the firm received. But entry to the lists may as easily be approved or blocked by the suitability of the product range, pricing methods and physical location of the firm as by the P. R. message.

But because it is not possible to measure advertising effectiveness it does not mean there is not considerable value in measuring that which is measurable and assessing and evaluating that which cannot be quantified. Like marketing research itself, advertising evaluation techniques can be used for reducing the risk even if they cannot totally eliminate it.

For research into the factors which can be quantified, for example measuring awareness and unawareness, the techniques already described will in most circumstances ensure that decisions are taken against a background of factual information. These same techniques

[1] R. D. Godwin and B. Thorogood, 'The Integration of Advertising Research', paper presented at Seminar on Measuring Advertising Effectiveness, Esomar (Munich, April 1965).

have a contribution to make in the second type of qualitative research also, but it is here that the special tools which have been developed are needed and some of which are described in this chapter.

IMAGES IN INDUSTRY

The term 'image' is a useful shorthand form to describe the external views of individuals or series of special publics towards an activity, persons or objects. But its popularisation has lead inevitably to its incorrect use and to it becoming an 'omnibus' term to describe something it was not intended to convey. Moreover, the wrong use of the word 'image' has also led to a belief that under most, if not all circumstances, there is a single 'image' rather than a series of 'images'. In fact every image investigation has led to the uncovering of a whole host of images, many contradictory and with infinite shadings of meaning to the image observers and commentators.

One of the major purposes of advertising and, of course, public relations is to create impressions which lead towards a favourable consideration of the firm and its products. (In this respect the purpose is no different if the image development is for a politician, a country or a cause.) 'The long-term objective is almost invariably one of building the correct image; putting over the right character to suit your product field; or perhaps changing an image of a company that is moving out of a declining field of manufacture into a newer and more vigorous market; or presenting a picture of a united, cohesive company when, in fact, it is a multitude of bits and pieces from takeovers. Whatever the short-term objective, the advertising which attempts to achieve it will have a secondary effect—an effect on the image of the company which can last a very long time.'[1]

Thus image research forms a vital part of advertising research. But image research cannot be successful if it begins with the incorrect concept that the researcher is looking for a single image and its effect upon company performance.

Although images are numerous and variable, they can be conveniently grouped for the purpose of research.

The *current* image—how does the outside world see the particular image subject?

The *mirror* image—how does the company see the image subject?

The *wish* image—what does the company wish the particular image subject to be or to become?

[1] M. Desoutter, 'Industrial Advertising', *Marketing of Industrial Products*, op. cit., p. 96.

This separation permits the adoption of the appropriate research techniques because it provides clearcut objectives for what the research is intended to achieve but it requires little imagination to appreciate how these three types can clash. Not quite so obvious, however, is the conflict between the 'wish' image, whether translated into action or not, and the image which will produce the best impact on the environment into which it is projected; in other words the distinction between how the company *wishes* to be seen and how it *ought* to be seen to improve its operations.

A further complication arises in that images of individual firms are usually formed partly by the image of the industry in which they operate. Thus the current image assessment has to be made with an industry image reference.

If, for example, a study was to be made of a company manufacturing cables and an image emerged of a monopolistic, rigid, protectionist concern, it would be legitimate to seek to find out how far this was the respondent's view of the industry as a whole and not necessarily only of the image subject.

While it is important in image studies to obtain additional validation of the opinions held and the reasons for holding them, it is necessary not to reject opinions because they are formed on the basis of wrong or inadequate information. In image research it is sufficient, from the research point of view, to establish that the opinions are held and not to justify them. Justification or the correction of images is the purpose of the image strategy, not image research.

The research input in an image study is leading towards the identification of an *optimum* image; that is the most desirable image compatible with the company's policy and long-range objectives. It is upon this image that all the others must be brought into focus. The problem of doing so, however, can be particularly complex because images frequently have international connotations. An international corporate or product image is a three-dimensional structure based on three research co-ordinates:

technical-psychological product image research;
national corporate image research; and
international corporate image research

The first research co-ordinate deals with products or services of the company and relates them to the state of the art in the industry, competitive products and users' requirements. The second co-ordinate concerns regional, national and international aspects of image strategy. The third deals with such aspects of the corporate image which have an international common denominator. All three co-ordinates need to be investigated on the basis of the four research areas designated as *current, wish, mirror* and *optimum*. Their relationship and influence on each other will produce the outlines of a range of corporate or company images suitable for projection regionally, nationally or internationally.

The research techniques for appraising each of the images are precisely those described throughout the book, namely desk research, postal questionnaires, telephone and personal interviews of various types and observations. They only require adaptation according to the scope of the enquiry and to the characteristics of the company, industry and market studied. The extent of the adaptations are determined by the depth of the enquiry; whether it is in the corporate or personnel strata, regional, national or international aspects or product or service linked. However, in a typical industrial image study the bulk of the work would comprise non-directive or focused interviews using unaided recall and unprompted attitude questions, preference analysis and scaled ratings.

The creation and maintenance of an image is a continuous operation reflecting the pulse beat of the company. Strategy requires constant supervision and *current* image testing because the image itself changes in the environment into which it is projected.

The data which will have been obtained by the research will enable the firm's marketing management to develop two benchmarks. The first is obtained by bringing the *current* and *mirror* images into focus so that they are superimposed one over the other. The second benchmark—which is where the persuasion comes in—is to bring the *wish* and *optimum* images into focus. These two benchmarks are the agreed point where the company is currently placed and the agreed point towards which it must work. With them the marketing strategists are able to decide on the most suitable means for reaching the goal they have established and much of the data yielded will assist in evaluating the effectiveness of the strategy.

IDENTIFYING OBJECTIVES AND GOALS

The necessary distinction between 'objectives' and 'goals' referred to in Chapter 4, 'Preparing for the Project', is rarely made in the advertising efforts of the majority of companies manufacturing industrial goods or providing industrial services. This is one of the fundamental reasons why advertising effectiveness measurement has been unsuccessful. It is hardly possible to measure or assess how well an advertisement achieved its purpose if its purpose is not defined or else, as is more usual, is so wide that success in achieving one objective spells certain failure in others.

'The sales manager may look on advertising campaigns as a device to move lorryloads of goods in the succeeding months, the advertising agency or advertising manager may be striving to build up a strong dealer loyalty, the Chairman may see the purpose of advertising appropriation as the development of a suitable corporate image and the personnel manager as a means of attracting graduates from University. If the campaign sells the goods but results in a deterioration in distributor loyalty is it successful? If it produced a corporate image of an aggressive marketing organisation but also leaves potential graduate recruits feeling that the atmosphere in the company is not conducive for research and development work, what is the measure of success?'[1]

To take another example, research indicated that users' idealised requirements for open steel flooring are: lighter weight and wider mesh without loss of strength. The flooring offered which was the subject of the research was superior in these aspects to competitive products but nevertheless fell short of the users' ideal. The communication job was to convey information in a convincing manner that the advertiser's open steel flooring was the lightest and most open of any available. This clearly differentiates the advertising from the marketing objective which was to open up new market segments.

There can be no question of success being achieved in the measurement of effectiveness of advertising unless the advertising objectives are clearly stated, non-contradictory and stable. Thus the role of the researcher in relation to advertising effectiveness studies is, as with all industrial marketing research, first to assist the sponsor in identifying objectives. However, this is not just a question of taking vague objectives such as 'to increase profits' (which is in any event a corporate, not an advertising goal) and turning it into a limited and specific goal, 'to create awareness of the product plusses'. Ideally every advertising plan ought to contain built-in methods for measuring or assessing its accomplishments even if in so doing adjustment of goals and objectives are necessary. This adjustment is the premium it is necessary to pay to insure against advertising expenditure being spent in a way that is less than wholly effective.

[1] Aubrey Wilson, 'Myths and Methods in Industrial Advertising', paper read to the Incorporated Advertising Managers' Association (London, February 1963).

Advertising goals can be defined as specific communication tasks to be accomplished among a defined audience to a given degree in a given period of time. This definition is important because of what it does not say: there is no built-in assumption that successful communication necessarily implies success in achieving sales. The belief that advertising must communicate to sell is part of the folklore of advertising and is largely unproved even in consumer markets.

A series of carefully controlled experiments by Du Pont about 1963 provided strong evidence that while awareness was a necessary precondition for sales, recall of facts about the products advertised was not.[1] Similar experiments by other companies revealed comparable situations. Because in a purchasing decision, factors such as product design, price, packaging, personal selling and physical distribution and publicity all have a significant role to play, it is hardly surprising that successful communication—the equivalent of the comprehension stage of Figure 27 does not necessarily imply the 'prospect' will move on to the 'conviction' stage which is a necessary prerequisite for 'action'.

This suggests the futility of attempting with the tools available at the present time to measure the effectiveness of advertising by relating it to sales results. The most successful research into the advertising process, certainly over the next few years, will be that directed to measuring and assessing how far the goals and objectives have been achieved rather than attempting to attribute to any particular part of the marketing activity the results in the form of sales or profits.

THE DECISION-MAKING UNIT

A further problem obtrudes itself in the measurement or assessment of advertising effectiveness in industrial as opposed to consumer markets. Decision-making in consumer markets and over a very large number of products is the function of a single person. Where a unit exists, for example a family, it tends to be stable. In industry the DMU which was defined and described in Chapter 1, is highly variable, often changing in number and composition from purchase to purchase, from time to time and because of the reasons for a purchase. As a result directing advertising to those who participate in a decision becomes particularly difficult.

One of the most vital functions of research in relation to marketing

[1] Charles K. Ramon, 'Must Advertising Communicate to Sell', *Harvard Business Review* (Cambridge, Mass., September/October 1965).

is to identify the typical DMU in an industry or market and to define their responsibilities and interest in relation to the product or service marketed: who initiates a project leading to a purchase, what is needed to be known if a company's product or service is to be considered for purchase? Some of the individuals who will be concerned in the buying decision must be fully informed on technical factors, others on commercial aspects. Some will collect facts and present them. 'Information intended for fact collectors will require particular care in presentation to ensure that it is easily understandable to the *person who will ultimately receive it*. If given to an engineer for example who will pass it on to someone else, possibly not an engineer, the facts may not be understood and the original recipient cannot be relied on to explain them.'[1]

Figure 23 indicates the frequency with which various combinations of individuals participate in purchasing decisions. It shows the complexity of the advertising task in attempting to communicate simultaneously and successfully with all these individuals. It also indicates that researching the effectiveness of an advertisement must also take place among all the individuals involved since comprehension or conviction by one job function does not imply comprehension or conviction by another. It is all too easy in an industrial marketing situation to provide a measure or assessment of some aspect of the advertising among personnel who have no influence or little influence in the subsequent actions.

THE CONTRIBUTION OF RESEARCH

The contribution of industrial marketing research in the advertising field falls into four sections. First the research prior to the development of advertising. Much of this type of research is embodied in a normal industrial marketing research project, although it may be specific to the advertising activities alone. However, the interface between the total marketing strategy and the role of advertising will only come through clearly if the research is designed to reveal it. Research prior to the development of the advertisement will have as its objective segmentation of markets, identification of decision-forming factors in purchasing—both rational and irrational—the location of the buying influences and the identification of those advertising methods and media to which the 'prospect' is exposed. Many of the sub-headings in Chapter 2 are involved in this stage of research.

[1] *How British Industry Buys*, op. cit., p. 24.

The second type of research is that which is conducted during the development of the advertising. This comprises the first evaluations of the advertising idea. Guidance from exploratory studies and surveys will often be needed to turn these first crude approaches into a form nearer the final requirements and to avoid time loss in preparing copy which, however excellent in itself, supports basic concepts which are unacceptable or ineffective. At this stage, in formulating both method and media, more than rough exposure guides will be needed. It may be true that trade journal X has a wide *circulation* among R & D Managers, but what is the extent of *readership* as compared with the professional journals? Having identified likely media detailed analysis of the media will probably be needed.

The third contribution of industrial marketing research is in pre-testing of advertisements. Clearly if an accurate method could be found for determining the effect of any given advertisement before it is in fact used, all advertisers would pre-test all advertisements. Pre-testing—or piloting—which by small-scale activities allow assessments to be made of the full-scale operation, are an insurance policy for the marketer. They cannot always be conducted but it is always worthwhile to see if it is possible to achieve a preliminary assessment by such limited activity. Many of the techniques for advertising effectiveness evaluation can be used in both pre- and post-testing situations, and their applicability in either of these situations will depend upon the specific circumstances.

Basically, pre-testing includes assessment of the responses of the various members of the DMU after the advertisement has been prepared but before it has been circulated in the various media through which it might be exposed to a wider audience. Obviously as the bulk of the cost of advertising is media cost, it is important to discover if any weaknesses are evident in the media coverage or the advertisements so that adjustments can be made.

The fourth type of research for advertising purposes is post-testing. This in fact comprises the bulk of all advertising research and besides giving an accurate guide to the effectiveness of advertising, also provides an additional bonus in the form of a cross check on any pre-testing which may have been done. If both these tests are accurate there should be no significant variations in the major qualitative findings or any such variation should be accountable. The areas in which comparisons can be safely made are the image or impressions communicated by the advertisement and the link between illustration, headline, copy and comprehension. All these should show a minimal variation between the pre- and post-test. Variations are much more likely to occur in such aspects as 'conviction', as in the post-test the user may have had an opportunity of comparing advertising claims with performance and perhaps with the performance of products subject to competing claims and advertisements. Environmental factors may have moved against the product or the form of advertising.

An example of this can be found in the early Nineteen Sixties in the construction industry's attitude towards motor breakers. Although no one could say advertising claims for the original breakers were exaggerated, operationally the machines were found to be less than satisfactory and the poor 'image' of one of the original machines affected not only the succeeding generations but also competitors' products. Post-testing of advertising revealed very different attitudes among users to those shown in the pre-test, all of which were accountable for by the machines' performance, and by reaction to what has been described as the 'brag and boast'[1] school of advertising. Bragging and boasting need not be aggressive to be antipathetic. As in the case of motor breakers, it merely underlines a discrepancy between promise and performance and produces a reaction against the advertisements.

In attempting to evaluate advertising effectiveness two prerequisites for success have been identified: first the isolation and clear definition of the advertising goals and objectives; second the identification of the typical DMU for the product or service to be advertised.

Four circumstances when advertising research can be used advantageously have been listed. Thus with the dimensions of the advertising process identified and the goals and objectives defined, it is now possible to consider the means available to achieve measurement or assessment.

RECOGNITION TESTS

Recognition surveys are, as the name implies, enquiries to indicate where recognition of advertising has taken place and to measure variations in attention and interest of various advertisements which have appeared in publications. The use of recognition surveys determines to what extent advertisements are seen and read, how company advertising compares in attracting and holding interest,

[1] F. R. Messner, *Industrial Advertising*, McGraw-Hill (New York, 1963), pp. 76-7.

and what improvements can be made in the advertising story without increasing space costs.

Recognition surveys are also used to reveal knowledge of the company; to ascertain from respondents whether or not they recognise or remember specific factors and to obtain their impressions. Information can be forthcoming on a company's standing relative to competition, broken down in some detail into, for example, such segments as geographic areas, industrial classification or reader's job function. The company's standing in relation to products can also be discovered as well as information on industry leadership, familiarity with a trademark, slogan recognition and copy platform recall.

Recognition surveys were originally devised and introduced in America in 1932 by Daniel Starch. The technique he adopted was to establish by interview that a given publication had been read, followed by a page by page check with the respondent. Successive interviews commence in different sections of the publication but, nevertheless, cover every page of the issue being measured. The interviewers then determine what advertisements the respondents have seen and read in a particular issue.

'Read' can of course mean many things. Three levels are recognised in the Starch technique: *Noted*, which measures those readers who have seen an advertisement; *Seen-associated*, which is a measure of readers who have seen or read the advertisement sufficiently to recall the product or the advertiser; and *Read Most* which measures the number of readers who read fifty per cent or more of the text of the advertisement. The last stage of the assessment is the determination of the observation and reading of component parts of an advertisement—headline, picture, sub-heading, text units and company's signature or logo. The assessment is then quantified by score numbers which are the 'Starch' ratings of a printed advertisement.

For uncovering specific information questions are posed (either by postal or personal interview) to reveal the extent of recognition or familiarity. These can range from a simple two-question enquiry— 'If you were buying electric motors (two h.p. and over) for your company today, what manufacturers would you consider?' and then a second question to identify the respondent—to complex inter-related and 'control' questions. 'Are you familiar with these company names?' (list follows)—'How would you rate them in terms of their progressiveness in research and product development?' (multiple choices listed)—'How would you rate them in their ability to provide engineering service to customers?' (multiple choices listed)

S

—'What is your opinion of the growth and future earnings potential of these companies?' (multiple choices listed).[1]

All the rules of postal or personal interviewing are of course applicable in carrying out these enquiries. Samples must be as statistically valid as possible and editing, coding and tabulation of replies and interpretation must follow the normal procedures if they are to achieve maximum accuracy.

The basic considerations relating to advertising tests based on memory have been summarised.[2]

All memory tests of advertising effectiveness are necessarily based on two separate reactions to the advertising. To begin with whether or not the respondents *noted* the advertising in the first place. Second, whether or not the respondents *remembered* the advertising. It can never be said with certainty, however, how far the memory tests reflect *noting* as compared with *recall*.

Both noting and recall of advertising are significantly influenced by many factors other than the advertisements which are being studied. These include the respondent's interest, need, or usage of the product type or service or the actual advertised product or service, the frequency of the respondent's exposure to previous advertisements for the product or service, and the similarity of the advertisements studied to advertisements to which the respondents have been previously exposed.

To the extent that the advertisement itself dictates noting or recall of a single advertisement, the major factors in noting and recall are the size, colour and amount of illustration. These factors are often held constant among advertisements being compared by memory measures for any one product or service. Thus the advertising researcher needs to be sure that the measures of memory that he employs are sensitive enough for making the kinds of discriminations called for by the research problem.

All recall is 'aided' to some degree. It cannot be elicited by a blank stare from an interviewer and nothing more. Whatever question is used to assess recall determines the degree of aid given to respondents in stimulating them to remember. Thus recall and recognition measures are relative measure—comparable only when recall or recognition is elicited in exactly the same way.

The use of recognition surveys is much enhanced if they are

[1] *Laboratory of Advertising Performance*, vol. 2, McGraw-Hill Research (New York, 1957).

[2] D. B. Lucas and S. H. Britt, *Measuring Advertising Effectiveness*, McGraw Hill (New York, 1958).

regularly repeated so that previous results can be evaluated against the current position. For example, the first study might show the research sponsor had a high standing in the three industries which held the greatest potential for his product. Advertising and direct mail efforts might then be concentrated on a fourth industry where the position is less favourable. A follow-up study after a period of time using the same questionnaire and a statistically similar sample will then indicate how much progress had been made in becoming known by prospective customers in the lower rated, in this case the fourth, industry. The 'before and after' technique thus enables a company to develop a benchmark and tangible evidence of the effect of its major advertising campaign in a given medium.

Familiarity with a manufacturer's name or reputation and a knowledge of his products and preference for them on the part of prospective buyers is a basic prerequisite for making a sale. An industrial buyer is not likely to consider a company as a source of supply unless he knows and prefers it and also knows it makes a product that may fill his need. Thus the company which has achieved the greatest recognition and preference will, generally, have the best chance of selling successfully. Definite knowledge of how the company and its products are recognised and preferred by potential customers and prospects is vital to manufacturers and distributors since these indicate his selling position.

The recognition survey is a tool which can assist firms to estimate what success or lack of success there has been in making the company and its products known and preferred. Carefully designed and properly interpreted, it is an effective and relatively cheap method for obtaining a general picture of the standing of a company and of its products. Such a study is a useful tool but it is a foot rule not a micrometer.

RECALL AND ASSOCIATION TEST

The major use of recall tests is to assess memorability of advertisements. The recognition method of appraising advertising effectiveness has certain limitations, inasmuch as there is a distinction between recognising an advertisement and gauging its impact and the action it produces. This dichotomy has long plagued researchers of advertising effectiveness because it was realised that an advertisement could simultaneously obtain considerable attention from its readers, yet be ineffective in registering a name or conveying a sales message. The development by George Gallup of 'Impact' research was a breakthrough in overcoming this problem. The 'Impact' research method relies largely upon recall or testimony obtained from advertisement readers who have had no opportunity to refresh their recollections as to the advertisement to which they were exposed, whereas the readership method relies heavily upon recognition.

The technique breaks down into five stages. First, qualifying the respondent as a reader by making him recall and describe at least one editorial feature. Second, proved name recall—presenting to the respondent a list of genuine and composed names of advertisers and requesting an indication of which is remembered both by name and by describing the contents of the advertisement. Third, idea registration, the probing in depth to determine how much the respondent does in fact remember of the advertisement. Fourth, recall after the previous questioning; the advertisements stated to have been seen are shown to the respondent to confirm they were the advertisements thought of. Fifth, identification is sought of any other publications in which the advertisement was seen. This last question is the usual background control question related to identification.

The use of impact techniques presents the identical difficulty as the use of motivation research techniques in industry—namely, the frequent refusal of respondents to be interviewed by this method— particularly where any element of 'right or wrong' answers exists or the risk occurs of appearing foolish, inaccurate or badly informed. Moreover the technique puts a heavy burden on the reader's memory. However, the remembered impression of content is substantial evidence of effective communication (awareness) of the advertising message. That is not to say that either comprehension or conviction have been achieved.

That recall methods of researching advertising are effective is undoubted, but in application they are unpredictable since the problem of sampling generally is added to that of filling the sample with respondents sufficiently acquiescent to accept questioning of the type required by these research techniques.[1]

OPINION AND ATTITUDE RATINGS

Opinion and attitude ratings are the most frequently used of the pre-testing techniques to attempt to assess reader reaction to

---

[1] A full discussion of various recall and association tests as applicable to consumer research will be found in *Measuring Advertising Effectiveness*, op. cit. Many of these tests, with the appropriate adjustments, will be found to be usable in industrial buying situations.

advertisements. Readers of advertisements can be asked to express their degree of interest in an advertisement, how far they believe it and whether they have any desire or requirement for the product or service. In examining the advertisement the respondents can give their reactions at the moment they are exposed to the message. In this the opinion ratings have a distinct advantage over many other methods of advertising assessment.

The major difficulty in using opinion and attitude ratings is that the expressed opinions may not in fact reflect the real feelings of the respondent and may be conditioned by many factors outside the knowledge of the researcher. Attitudes may be formed not only by the interviewer himself but also by certain status aspects of holding given opinions and by a host of other environmental, personality and psychological factors. Thus, unless psychological techniques such as projective tests and focused interviews are used, opinions tend to be overt rather than deeply held views.

Nevertheless, with all the drawbacks of subjective responses something more than crude measures can be developed by good research. The problem of communication, semantic misunder-standings, role perception and varying interpretations have all been dealt with earlier in this book and the discussions apply with particular force in examining the use of opinion and attitude ratings.

The principal types of opinion and attitude ratings are, rank order, single choice, paired comparison and self-selected.

(a) *Rank order*

To place advertisements in league table order of merit is the commonest form of measurement of opinion. The order of merit has, however, to be linked with specific aspects of the advertisement as well as the total effect. For example, the well-known series of Accles & Pollock advertisements for their tubes which makes a play of variations on the name of Accles & Pollock would probably rate high to most respondents for its humorous content and low for the amount of technical information it provides. In asking for an opinion of any advertisement in the series the interviewer would need to be sure precisely what aspect of the advertisement the respondent was commenting on; whether his response to the humorous content was making him particularly favourably inclined towards the advertisement as a whole and as a series, despite the fact perhaps that it did not provide information he would require from other advertisements for the same products manufactured by competitors. Here again the halo effect is apparent in that respondents tend to pick out the best-liked advertisement and rate it highest in all respects.

A timely warning has been made on the likelihood of this method producing a consistent result or patterning with very small samples. 'Users of opinion methods are likely to be lulled into false security by the fact that it usually requires only 40 to 50 people to determine a consistent choice among them of possibly four different advertisements. This consistency is a genuine advantage of the method but it has no bearing upon whether the result of the tests are valid or correct. It merely shows that little can be gained by the use of larger samples. Actually the most difficult problem is that of knowing how to interpret the results'.[1]

Another aspect of this type of research which must be watched for and avoided is similar to that described in relation to the postal questionnaire, namely offering too many choices to permit respondents to make valid distinctions between grades, products or performance aspects. Requests to place in order six aspects of six advertisements on six point scale implies 216 options—far too many to permit accuracy in rating.

One method of avoiding this difficulty is to ask the respondent to identify the top choice first, possibly followed by second choice. The questioning can then be switched to the selection of the last place and next to last. The middle places are then completed. The respondent should not, however, be intimidated into not changing his mind once he has seen the final ranking. Where the distinctions to be made are fine or the respondent holds no strong view, or is more familiar with one aspect or firm or product than another, ample opportunity should be given to permit a change in rating.

(b) *Single choice*

The single preference method of opinion and attitude rating is far more accurate since it focuses the respondent's attention on a single aspect of the enquiry and permits the interviewer to probe in depth the thinking behind the choice. The comparative rating used in rank order assessments cannot obtrude in the answer. The halo effect can be identified and reduced or removed by guiding the respondent across detailed and specific aspects of the advertisements and by breaking up those thought processes which tend to encourage the halo effect.

Obviously the single choice method can be used to identify the east satisfactory as well as the most satisfactory, the interview

[1] *Measuring Advertising Effectiveness*, op. cit., p. 106.

method being precisely the same. It might indeed be said that every item in the league table could be investigated in the same way as in single choice but the moment comparison is asked for from the respondent, a new series of variables comes into play. It is obviously infinitely easier in the majority of cases to establish polarities first and then the total spectrum between them.

In the single choice enquiry it is possible to develop a screen for the various items of performance to be checked, for example copy, headline, illustration, credibility, and seek only the 'best' or 'worst' performance under each heading. It is also possible to weight for importance so that in the final scaling the weightings multiplied by the ratings will give a score for each item investigated.

If it is intended that an advertisement should achieve the highest score on all possible counts, then the single choice approach will show clearly any deficiencies in the advertisement although it will not indicate how far short of the respondent's desiderata the advertisement falls, nor how many other advertisements with a higher score stand between the research sponsors and the top scorer. Nevertheless, because this method tends to produce black and white results it has much to commend it.

(c) *Paired comparisons*

The paired comparison method is an extension of the single choice and offers another variable, namely a comparison between two choices which is another form of polarity. While such a comparison will not necessarily provide a gradation of preference in that there is no indication of the margin by which one of the pair is preferred over the other, it does indicate in absolute terms the existence of a preference. By concentrating the respondent's attention on a very limited number of elements it is possible to obtain a better assessment of preference than when a larger number is involved as in the rank order method.

The respondent is asked to compare each element within a series with every other element in the series. This might be in the form of an illustration in an advertisement. These advertisements might include any of the following: photographs, schematic diagrams, exploded views, isometric projections, and no illustration at all. The photograph could then be compared to the schematic diagram, the exploded view, the isometric projection and the unillustrated advertisement in turn. Then the schematic diagram could be compared with the exploded view, isometric projection and unillustrated advertisement and so on. This approach forces the respondent to select one of two elements, and by elimination a rank order is produced.

Because paired comparisons have the advantage over rank order in that the amount of material which the respondent has to consider at one time is reduced, it makes it possible to use a larger series than is practicable in the rank ordering method. The major advantage of the paired comparison test, however, is that it focuses attention on the intrinsic features of the test items, minimises external influences such as brand names, trademarks and distinctive packaging, and limits the risk of respondent fatigue and confusion which sometimes occurs when simultaneous comparisons of several items are required. The test involves direct comparison, requires an overt choice and places the compared experiences as close together in time as possible. Against this, however, paired comparison tests do tend to magnify minor differences and this danger must be watched for.

(d) *Self-selection*

This method of assessment relies upon the respondent expressing opinions on the advertisements without aided recall. He is encouraged to discuss the advertisement and to verbalise his reaction to it. The interviewer, as in other types of industrial marketing research, assists the respondent in considering important aspects of the advertisement but makes no direct reference to them. Thus if the value of a photograph in an advertisement is in question and the respondent has not made special mention of this, either favourably or critically, the interviewer might interrogate the respondent on the copy and see to what extent the respondent justifies his views by seeking support from the photograph.

'I doubt if the machine could meet the performance claims.'

'Why do you say that?'

'They seem to be exaggerated.'

'In what way do you regard them as exaggerated?'

'I've never seen a machine of this size which could handle those capacities.'

'How big do you judge the size to be?'

'From the picture about two tons.'

'Do you think the picture is exaggerated?'

'No, the camera doesn't lie. I think the advertising men have just got carried away.'

This actual conversation indicates the 'credibility' of the picture to the respondent which is lacking in the supporting copy. Moreover it also indicates that the picture makes a distinct contribution to the comprehension of the respondent. It can be argued, of course, that the situation is totally unreal in the first place and that the attention-getting factors in the advertisement would probably not lead the reader to make a close comparison between the copy and photograph.

The criticisms of the self-selection method are indeed valid if an attempt is made to evaluate an advertisement on every count. However, for limited assessments the method has much to commend it. It has the further advantage of a completely free ranging approach which enables the respondent to identify what is important to *him*, what impresses *him*, what irritates *him*, what *he* finds attention-getting and memorable. None of these may be items which had been considered by the advertisers and when a patterning of responses occurs it can reveal hidden and important aspects of the advertisements which might be missed when using the structured or semi-structured methods inherent in any multiple-choice approach and ranking system.

SCALING

Scaling techniques, which have already been referred to, are the apportionment of values and graduated levels of opinions to answers received. While their use in industrial marketing research is in its infancy, they are perhaps most developed in advertising evaluation techniques. They are therefore most appropriately discussed in this chapter, although they have a wider use than in advertising research.

For qualitative answers the technique has much to commend it, in assessing importance and ranking of the elements scaled. The major difficulty with all scales is to ensure that the individual ratings in the scale carry at least approximately the same meaning to all respondents. It was pointed out in Chapter 7, 'The Postal Questionnaire', that most scales can make a clear distinction between the poles, that is 'very good' or '1' is unlikely to be confused or blurred with 'very bad' or '10'. However, in the middle ranges it is not always easy for respondents to distinguish between 'fair' and 'good' or between 4 and 5. In some types of scaling exercises such as the qualitative screening process errors or blurring are not important[1] provided that the screening team (and thus the

[1] Aubrey Wilson, 'Selecting New Products for Development', *Scientific Business* (Reading, November 1963).

biases) remain reasonably constant, as it is only the final comparison
between product scores which counts, the individual score taking
on a lesser importance.

There are three broad approaches[1] open to the industrial marketing
researcher in using scaling methods.

1. Subject-centred approach. The systematic variation in the
reactions of the subjects to the stimuli is attributed to individual
differences in the subjects.

2. Stimulus-centred or judgement approach. The systematic
variation in the reactions of subjects to the stimuli is attributed to
differences in the stimuli with respect to a designated attribute.

3. Response approach. Variability in reactions to stimuli is
ascribed to both variations in subject and stimuli.

For most scaling exercises it is important to devise a scale that
will minimise blurring. The scale must conform to four major
requirements.[2]

Validity The scale should measure what it purports to measure and
this requires validation against external criterion.
Reliability The scale should continue to yield substantially the same
scores from one time to another so long as what is being measured
remains unchanged.
Equality of scale interval The scale should have what are believed to
be—from a psychological standpoint—equal intervals between the
points on the scale. In the case of descriptive words the values assigned
to the various points on the scale must be reasonably accurate.
Unidimensionality The scale should mean substantially the same to
all respondents and the poles of the scale should refer to only one
dimension of meaning (such as like-dislike, accurate-inaccurate,
rough-smooth, fixed-loose).

A number of standard scaling methods have long been used in
sociological research on consumer goods. The most familiar of these
are the Thurstone, Likert and Guttman scales. However, the one most
used in industrial marketing research is the semantic differential.

The University of Illinois and the survey research centre of the
London School of Economics and Political Science through their
work have added a new precision and have advanced the understanding and use of the semantic differentials to the point where they can

[1] W. S. Torgerson, *Theory and Methods of Scaling*, John Wiley (New York, 1956), p. 46.
[2] *Measuring Advertising Effectiveness*, op. cit., p. 111.

usefully be incorporated in industrial marketing research techniques.[1]

There is little question that of all the scales which can be adopted, one composed of word graduations is the most difficult to compare. The problem is the selection of the polar words and the subsequent descriptive gradations making up the balance of the scale. If, for example, the polar words are 'always' and 'never', between might lie 'frequently', 'occasionally', 'rarely', 'once'. As between 'occasionally' and 'rarely' the possibility of misallocation is high. One approach to avoid this problem has been to use polar words and then symbols to represent the gradations. For example, in simple graphical form a respondent can indicate a response in this way.

SCALE CHART

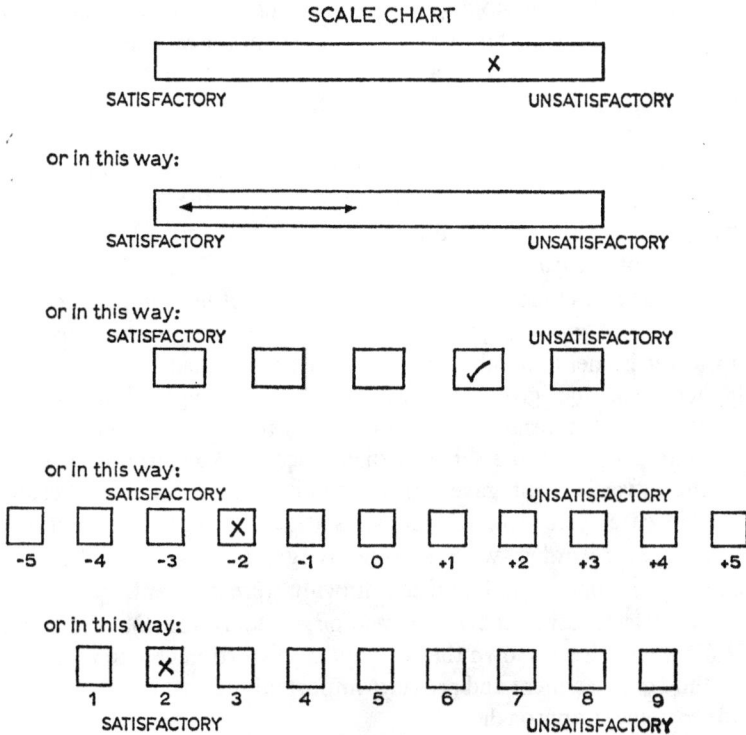

Fig. 28
SCALE CHARTS

Whichever of the several ways available to indicate scale position is used, the development of a satisfactory semantic differential is

[1] C. E. Osgood, G. J. Suci and P. H. Tannenbaum, *The Measurement of Meaning*, University of Illinois Press (Urbania, Ill., 1957). William Belson. *The Semantic Differential Scaling System in Market Research* (Privately published. London, 1967).

always difficult and costly to devise and, more than most of the techniques discussed, requires careful piloting.

PERCEPTUAL DISTORTION

The phenomenon of perceptual distortion has already been referred to in Chapter 10 on visual techniques. That is, the distortion of reality into conformity with a person's own values and attitudes and interest. It has been suggested[1] that this phenomenon can be used to evaluate some aspect of advertising. An experiment using the principle of perceptual distortion was conducted to discern the relative effects of photographs and drawings in advertisements.[2] A full page advertisement for a medium-priced motor car was duplicated with only the art work changed—a photograph in one case and a drawing faithful to the original in the other. Respondents were asked to guess the price of the vehicle. Three groups of respondents were used, one was exposed to the advertisement with the photograph, one the advertisement with the drawing and the third (control) group saw no advertisement at all. Each group was asked to guess the price of the car.

The men respondents exposed to the photograph produced a median price group significantly higher than the groups who saw no advertisement, which group in turn gave a median price result higher than the group exposed to the drawing. With women respondents the results were different again, the photograph and drawing producing the same median price. The group not exposed to the advertisement gave a price significantly lower. The results in this case were not, of course, statistically significant but the differences recorded were sufficiently great to suggest that the effect of the photograph and the drawing were different.

Other tests using the same method, notably for Du Pont and Volkswagen, have shown that perceptual distortion can be used as a method of assessment and provides important indications of desirable advertisement approaches.

Only limited attempts have been used to adopt this technique to industrial advertising, yet it has much to commend it. For one thing the questioning is relatively simple and contains little element of 'playing games' which is so off-putting to many respondents in business situations. Interviewing techniques need not be of the

[1] *Measuring Advertising Effectiveness*, op. cit., p. 120.
[2] J. C. Webster, unpublished thesis, Northwestern University 1961, and quoted by D. B. Lucas and I. H. Britt, *Measuring Advertising Effectiveness*, pp. 120-1.

most sophisticated kind and answers lend themselves to tabulation and quantification. More important perhaps, the results are easy to understand and to communicate to research sponsors.

KEYED ADVERTISEMENTS

Of the purely mechanical methods of evaluation the keyed advertisement in media testing is of considerable importance. This is an advertisement carrying a reference of a type that anyone taking action as a result of the advertisement—writing for sales literature or making a purchase—must reveal the key. This then indicates when and where the advertisement was seen. By inserting various keyed advertisements simultaneously in several publications it is possible to form an opinion of the relative value of the media used. The 'key' itself is usually a code printed either on a coupon to be cut out, as a product reference, or as part of the return address. In controlled circulation journals where enquiries are usually funnelled centrally to the publisher of the journal on a 'ringed number' basis, identification is of course simple. It is necessary, however, in assessing 'keyed' replies not to make any unjustified inferences concerning the total readership of advertisements in the publications used or of the readers themselves because of, for example, duplication of readership, reluctance to cut up what may be valuable technical journals and, conversely, the willingness to cut up newspaper.

SPLIT RUN COPY TESTING

The keyed method can also be adapted to copy testing using separate runs. Different but comparative stimuli are offered to a homogeneous group of readers. The technique involves placing an advertisement in one form in a proportion of the copies of a given issue of a publication and in other forms in the remainder of the issue, or using a different direct mail shot to separate groups which are closely similar in whatever criteria of selection are used. It is then possible to compare the rate of keyed returns or other indicators from the different forms of the advertisement. This comparison in turn provides a basis for judging the relative effectiveness of the forms of advertising adopted. This is basically the same technique for testing postal questionnaires.

ENQUIRIES

It can be argued that only a direct response to an advertisement is an accurate assessment of its 'attention-getting' and 'attraction'. Thus enquiries tend to be the most frequently used criteria of an advertisement's pulling power. Certainly they are a significant measure but in many cases they can be misleading, particularly if used in a limited pre-test. It is necessary as a first step to distinguish between an advertisement designed to solicit enquiries to assist sales, or open the way for a salesman, and that where the enquiries are used as a basis of assessment for a complete campaign or advertisement. Only the latter use of enquiries as a measure of effectiveness is considered here.

The problem that presents itself in assessing the validity of enquiries as a measure of effectiveness is precisely the same as in postal questionnaires, that is the characteristics of the non-respondent are vital. A few tens or hundreds of enquiries are frequently used as the basis of a campaign aimed at thousands and if significant differences exist between enquirers and non-enquirers, it is very likely that the campaign will not be effective.

A number of factors require consideration:

(a) If the inducement to make an enquiry is too great, the inter-personal network may result in a great many enquiries from people who were not exposed to the advertisement. At the other extreme the offer may be so unattractive as to produce no enquiries but that is not to say the advertisement was not effective on some other count. Therefore the reason given to readers to respond to an offer must be neither too attractive nor too uninteresting.

(b) The 'test' advertisement must relate to the actual advertisement. The balance of the offer to the other copy appeals must be realistic otherwise the measurement of enquiries only becomes a measurement of the offer, not the full advertisement.

(c) The use of coupons tends to inflate response in a way which is not necessarily applicable to the main advertisement. The presence of a coupon, the emphasis on its return and, usually, freedom from any implied obligation in returning the coupon, heighten its attractiveness in a way which in no way relates to the basic advertisement.

The other factors governing couponing in 'Keyed Advertisements' referred to, also require consideration in evaluating the relationship of enquiries to advertising.

SALES AS A MEASURE OF ADVERTISING EFFECTIVENESS

It has already been pointed out that, were it possible to isolate the advertising effort from the total marketing activity, then sales would be a perfect measure of advertising's ultimate effectiveness given that that is its function rather than, say, recruiting. However, even though laboratory conditions cannot be produced sales still enable assessments to be made and to provide evidence, to at least some degree, of the work which an advertisement is doing.

If a product or service is advertised by only one method and one media, and sales rise following the appearance of the advertisement, there is usually a *prima facie* reason to assume the advertisement is having a positive effect. This is particularly true in direct mail and catalogue selling.

A series of technical seminars were advertised in a mail shot sent to 25,000 companies No other media was used or announcement made. Within twenty-one days of the first mailing some 242 firm bookings and 146 enquiries were received, the latter for further information on individual seminars. The same 25,000 companies were then mailed over a period of time with a series of separate advertisements for the individual seminars. This resulted in a total of 4,210 firm bookings and 298 additional separate enquiries. The companies from which the bookings came had been subject to no other exposure than the advance notice. Of the bookings about twenty-three per cent were from firms (not necessarily individuals) who had sent participants to the company's seminars previously, so that it could be deduced that while inter-personal factors might have been at work, for the most part seventy-seven per cent of bookings did not stem from purely goodwill or past experience.

Thus it was possible to deduce qualitatively that some non-advertising aspects might have accounted for the response, but overall it could be assumed that the mail shot advertisements were in fact reaching their target, attracting attention and inducing action.[1]

SALES AND EXPOSURE

The techniques for using sales as a measure of advertising effectiveness can be compared by relating purchases to exposure to the advertising and by test marketing techniques.

[1] The figures quoted are by courtesy of *Associated Business Programmes Ltd*. London.

This method is to trace sales of the advertised product and then to interrogate the purchaser, or the DMU., to ascertain what influences were at work in the purchasing decision. It is not sufficient merely to check advertising exposure since this can be notoriously inaccurate. For example, as any consumer researcher knows, far more claims are made to quality newspaper readership than circulation figures show, even allowing for multiple readership. Thus in industrial purchasing it can as easily be a matter of status or declaration of job efficiency to claim readership of particular journals or issue or attendance at an exhibition as to claim readership of a status-giving newspaper.

Only by identifying the pure purchasing decision factors can a correlation be obtained between exposure and purchasing. For example, after qualifying respondents as members of a DMU and the fact that the purchase was actually made, questions can be asked relating to exposure and then to the decision-forming factors. In the purchase of oil for process heating purposes, security of supplies was found to take prior place over both price and quality since both were generally assumed to be competitive. Security of supplies was not, however, a feature of advertising oil for process heating so that a decision to buy based on this could not have come directly from the advertisements. Thus it was necessary to probe how a feeling of 'security of supplies' was in fact built up. In actuality the research revealed that this correlates with size of supply company which is implicit in most oil companies' advertising, but clearly some oil companies are much larger than others either internationally or nationally.

The next stage therefore was to ascertain how far the advertisement concerned communicated the facts upon which the decisions were based and how far this information might have stemmed from other sources. This stage of the research revealed that the impression of size to many industrial buyers was linked with the number of filling stations of the oil companies and the number of tankers seen. Both these aspects were part of the total communication 'mix' and as such made significant contribution to the overall activities of the oil companies, but the advertisements for process-heating oils did not communicate one of the key factors in the decision making process. Essentially probing the relationship of *exposure* to *action* is to work backwards from the purchase, not forward from the advertisement. Thus in the oil example it was necessary to see who initiated the project to purchase the brand currently bought, which other firms were considered, what were the factors which induced either a change in supplier or the selection of the first supplier, how the technical and commercial factors of the product were ascertained, evaluated and the basis on which the decisions were made. Throughout all this it was possible to compare the ostensible reasons given with the advertising exposure and message and, of equal importance, the 'image' of the firms competing for the business.

Needless to say, it is always important to separate out 'status' and other emotional responses from the underlying reasons. A purchasing officer who did not state price to be of key importance might well be thought not to have an accurate conception of his role. Nevertheless the study referred to did in fact reveal that security of supplies and of consistency in quality were of greater importance to the individual in that a failure on either of these counts was likely to have a far more dramatic and public effect on the purchasing officer than the fact that he may have been paying one-eighth pence more per gallon than might have been actually necessary. There is nothing in the normal interviewing techniques of industrial marketing research which could not reveal this situation.

TEST MARKETING

Test marketing is a research technique whose suitability for industrial marketing strategy is now being reconsidered. The present attitudes towards experimentation in marketing make test marketing largely unacceptable but there is little doubt that with improved methods of measurement and assessment and with the increasing sophistication of industrial test marketing methods, this technique will become more widely used in the next decade.

Some confusion exists between test marketing and product field testing, and this inadvertently has led to over-optimism as to its effectiveness. The objective of test marketing is generally the experimental measurement of the effect of single variables. Causal relationships between single factors are extremely difficult to measure in marketing. Most marketing sets out to isolate the factors and stimuli and measure their effects. Thus control markets must be set up. The production equivalent of the test market is the pilot plant. Both have as their objectives scaled down risk taking and are offered as an insurance against the consequences of a number of hazards. Here the resemblance ends. The measurement of performance of pilot plant can be undertaken with far more precision than that of a test market. Unfortunately for many products it is difficult

T

if not impossible to isolate a test market to obtain the controlled conditions of the pilot plant.

But the difficulties are not confined to measurement. The results of setting up a test market are fraught with difficulties and are such that both the product and the firm itself can suffer harm. For example, a test marketing operation can create a disruption of distributors' sales patterns and the supporting services that go with them; differences in the goods or services being tested which can cause production or other hold-ups are likely to induce much bad feeling; the setting up of small-scale marketing support can be hopelessly uneconomic; advance notice is given to competitors and the opportunity suggested to them of entering the field on a national scale is presented. These are only some of the difficulties.

Obviously the situation will differ as between products. A typewriter ribbon is unlikely to be as difficult to test market as, say, electro-mechanical relays. A number of test marketing case studies in the United States have been published[1]—notably plastic pipes, specialised bearings and bar chart recorders—but a study of the research objectives shows they were concerned mostly with product as opposed to market testing and the selection of suitable advertising media.

Given, however, that a test market area can be found which provides a secure base for extrapolation then it is possible to obtain some evidence of advertising effectiveness by conducting a campaign in that area and checking the results against sales.

A manufacturer of loading shovels introduced a replacement scheme by advertising it in a test market. The immediate response was extremely satisfactory and there was little doubt the message was getting through as sales increased by nearly 100 per cent. It was found, however, that the test area sales were in fact partly being 'milked' from the other areas because word-of-mouth information had been passed by branches of firms in the test area to head offices or other branches outside the area and orders were being channelled through the area where the offer was available. In some respects therefore it might be supposed that the test was inconclusive, but in fact it had shown a high success rate since it was obvious that the DMU were being exposed to the advertisement and were acting on it. The advertising message, the only way other than the inter-personal network which anyone could know of the scheme, was making an impact. This is all the experiment was intended to show.

[1] 'How do you Find a "Best" Market?', *Printers Ink* (New York, April 13th 1962).

A useful check list of a number of common faults in using test marketing to evaluate advertising has been devised.[1]

● Failure to decide what is to be tested—each test should aim to find an answer to one major question, for example the most effective weight of advertising, a new creative approach, a new price structure or simply product acceptance. The more elements which a manufacturer tries to test at the same time in a single test area, the more difficult it becomes to identify the real causes of success or failure.

● Failure to base the test market plan on an overall national marketing plan which is both realistic and affordable—the sales target in the test area should be proportionate to the expected national target, and the marketing 'mix' (or alternative 'mixes' if more than one test area is being used) should duplicate as closely as possible that which is proposed for the national launch.

● Failure to make comparative tests—no single test permits the comparative evaluation and choice of the best plan from among a number of possible alternatives.

● Failure to establish benchmarks in the test area—before any test begins it is necessary to establish individual and total sales and/or market penetration of competitive brands (and, where necessary, customer attitudes and preferences) so that subsequent changes can then be compared and evaluated against this base.

● Failure to select representative test areas—the areas selected must be as representative as possible of the country as a whole in terms of geographic location, trade and customer characteristics, media facilities of the type to be used later, in order that the test will serve as a 'projection' model for future national operations.

● Failure to adhere to the test market plan—this applies particularly to changes in advertising weight or content, the media used and pricing; 'changing horses' in mid-market can lead to confusion when it comes to analysing the test results (the need to test the effect of changes in the plan in response to strong competitive counter-measures can be allowed for by choosing another test town within the larger test area for this specific purpose at the outset, in order that results of both the original plan and the changed plan can be compared).

● Failure to consider and get objective and reliable data on all factors influencing sales results in the test area—such as the

[1] *Marketing in a Competitive Economy*, op. cit., pp. 125-7.

calibre of salesmen used, seasonal influences, weather conditions, economic conditions, levels of shop distribution, stock levels and stock cover, out-of-stock ratios, competitors' activities, etc.

● Failure to stay in the test market long enough to get a clearcut stop-or-go decision—slower-moving products require longer test periods than fast-selling products and the temptation to jump the gun and take a final decision should be resisted by the manufacturer until he can be reasonably sure that the sales pattern has stabilised and the results have been properly analysed.

● Reading into test market results more than is supportable by the objective facts—an apparent initial success in test market can all too rapidly turn into a comparative failure as the test market 'matures' due to an over-optimistic reading of the situation based on considerations other than those directly related to the test market findings or due to the failure to recognise danger signals from the test.

READERSHIP

Readership analysis is not a special technique since it can be accomplished by normal field techniques used for obtaining other information. Readership data are important, not only in their own right—since it is always presumed that there is a correlation between the amount of influence an advertisement exerts and the numbers who are exposed to it—but also because in combination with 'Starch' or 'Impact' ratings they can be used to develop another useful yardstick for measurement of effectiveness—a 'cost per hundred' of actual readers. This is a meaningful but not always conclusive figure (the influence of the medium must not be forgotten) in all marketing planning and it is one that cannot be even roughly estimated without first ascertaining readership figures.

However, readership figures need further evaluation. There are clearly classes of readers of any medium, of whom many will not represent potential sales to the advertiser. For example, although all readers of a furniture trade paper can be assumed to be interested in furniture, only a small percentage are potential buyers of varnishes, a further small proportion may buy wood, another woodworking machinery and yet others office equipment and stationery. For the woodworking machinery manufacturers a furniture trade paper may be an excellent medium but for the office equipment firm the cost per hundred may be higher and less effective than, for example, a management magazine.

The development of an efficiency factor is the greatest contribution that readership research can make. It was explained in Chapter 2 that it is, unfortunately, hampered by the reluctance of some publishers to provide readership figures analysed in different ways. There is still a hard core of publishers who will not even provide a total circulation figure (paid and free) and who are not members of the Audit Bureau of Circulations so that it is difficult for many researchers to evaluate the worth of publications by devising an efficiency factor.

MEDIA RESEARCH

The problems of media are no less important for the industrial than for the consumer goods marketing researcher.

In discussing the evaluation of advertising effectiveness, the tendency has been to concentrate on press advertising, largely because this, with catalogues, appears to attract the bulk of industrial advertising appropriations. Nevertheless other methods of advertising, also require evaluation and of course comparison. Films, exhibitions, P.R. demonstrations, sponsored books, gifts and all the activities which together comprise the communication 'mix'. Many of the techniques discussed in this chapter will be applicable to the various forms of advertising media but some will require different methods of assessing audiences. For example, readership in journal assessment; numbers attending an exhibition or visiting a stand. Checking recall on a film will demand of the respondent information on not only what is remembered visually but also aurally, the impact of vehicle livery may be partly a result of numbers of vehicles and partly of design. The appropriate criteria for each method must be developed and the techniques for assessing them adapted from the standard industrial marketing research techniques or those used specifically for advertising evaluation, such as tachistoscope tests.

Because advertising messages and advertising media are inextricably interwoven there is an obvious and important requirement for the copy to fit the media and particularly the media audience. As obvious as this may appear to be, it is evident from the most cursory examination of much industrial advertising that this basic principle is not followed. It is equally obvious that many of the errors stem from shortage of information about the media which could in fact be obtained by the use of industrial marketing research techniques.

The problem commences with a lack of understanding of the

advantages of different media, for example the superiority of direct mail shots over newspapers in obtaining the reader's whole attention and the ability to obtain repetition for the sales message which outdoor posters provide. There is then a frequent failure to appreciate the physical requirements for different media. Colour, movement, the human voice and surroundings all make a distinctive contribution to the effectiveness of the media which can be exploited. Far more needs to be known about the advantages and disadvantages of media types and the methods to maximise the media 'plusses'. This is unlikely to occur while most discussions on media research continue to centre around 'readership' and 'coverage'.

The marketing researcher must look upon an advertising appropriation not as a fixed sum inviolate in itself but as a scarce resource which may be expended on advertising. The alternative to advertising is not necessarily no advertising or reduced advertising but, for example, will the company's funds be better deployed by using other communication methods, by engaging more salesmen or buying more vehicles? The researcher's task is to ascertain how to get fuller value for money.

CHAPTER 13

Industrial Marketing Research as an Aid to Forecasting

Forecasting, or prediction, is as old as man himself. Prophesy, witchcraft, necromancy, superstition, were the trading skills of the Sybils, Old Testament prophets, Merlin, Lilith and Nostradamus, philtres, fire and the entrails of the freshly killed pigeon their materials. The desire to peer into the future, like the desire to achieve a state of invisibility and to fly unassisted by machines, is as fundamental to man's nature as is his need for personal acceptance and recognition.

Forecasting techniques are not yet such as to lead to the belief that a wholly accurate method is yet within the grasp of man even in such well-established and scientifically advanced fields as meteorology. At the present time the tools available have narrowed down the areas of error but not to the extent that a forecast can be developed and safely used without the application of the human qualities of judgement and understanding.

Forecasting is the probabilistic assessment on a relatively high confidence level of future developments in the area or activity under review. Almost everything that is done in industrial marketing research is directed towards this assessment. Current market studies are already historical analyses by the time they are ready. Although the lessons of the past are of vital consequence, it is the course of future events which is of primary concern to managements' planning for and operating their companies.

There is, of course, no natural law which prescribes that forecasting is the function of the marketing researcher, yet most marketing researchers are more frequently engaged in forecasting exercises than almost any other type of activity. There are perhaps two reasons for management allotting forecasting to marketing researchers. First, most of the information inputs for a forecast will have to be generated by the marketing research department and, second, rightly or wrongly, the marketing researcher is thought to bring a less emotional and biased approach to a forecast than others in the firm who may have a vested interest in the result. The marketing researcher is usually capable of distinguishing market goals from forecasts, is able to provide an objective assessment of what his company is capable of achieving and is in closer contact with a wider section of the outside world than many other personnel in the firm.

A small study of forecasting practices in British industry[1] revealed that in some sixty per cent of the firms responding to the enquiry the forecasting function was conducted at least partly by the company economist/market researcher. However, only in three per cent of respondents' firms were the economist/market researchers solely responsible for forecasting.

The contribution of industrial marketing research in forecasting is three-fold: first in providing a sound basis for the forecast by researching historical and current situations and in locating valid correlations, ratios, actuarial and other indicators; second, developing usable hypotheses both in terms of market directions and also as alternative policies and practices; third, testing the validity of the hypotheses.

The purpose of the chapter is not to describe in detail the techniques of forecasting but to relate the role of the marketing researcher to the needs of the forecaster.

THE USE OF FORECASTS

Within a company there are many types of forecasts taking place simultaneously based upon an agreed sales forecast. In the production department output forecasts will be prepared as well as the forecasts for input of raw materials and other logistics, variable and other costs. The financial department will be concerned with cash flow and capital requirements. The major sectors in which forecasting is used formally can be conveniently grouped.[2]

Sales Apart from the obvious implication which sales forecasts have on all other forecasts, they play a vital part in market segmentation, setting targets, quotas, remuneration methods and have an all-pervading effect on planning in relation to product and marketing strategies.

Price Price is interdependent with sales volume. The two co-ordinates are, the demand curve from which estimates can be derived of sales

[1] *A survey of market forecasting practice in Great Britain*, Information Summary No. 115, British Institute of Management (London, 1964).

[2] R. S. Reichard, *Practical Techniques of Forecasting*, McGraw-Hill (New York, 1966), pp. 37-47.

volume at differing price levels and the unit-cost curve which gives the cost levels associated with different sales levels.

Production Forecasts of production levels have an obvious importance in terms of capital, material and labour requirements as well as less directly related opportunities for introducing economies such as optimising transport needs. Foreknowledge of production demands enables work schedules to be efficiently organised to avoid overtime and slack occurring in regular cycles or irregularly.

Purchasing If material supplies can be accurately gauged the security of the operation can be improved and inventory levels can be controlled to a minimum safe level; purchasing officers are given a considerable negotiating weapon.

Financial Accurate financial forecasts are vital for the control of the total operation. Profits, cash flow, dividends, margins, costs, capital requirements, taxation demands and reserves, are all subject to some type of forecasting.

Marketing Sales are inextricably linked with the marketing activity of the firm. Forecasts relating to the marketing effort will provide important guides to such matters as advertising appropriation, the cost and provision of services to customers and depot locations. More important, however, unless accurate forecasts are made in relation to the marketing effort the sales forecast is likely to be unrealistic. In forecasting the total business environment the marketing activities are one of the controllable variables which can change the climate in which the firm operates.

Personnel Suitable personnel are perhaps the scarcest of the factors of production, and of all the inputs of a business the most expensive not to fully utilise. Lack of accurate forecasts of personnel requirements leads to unsatisfactory appointments, personnel gaps and over-staffing. Because it concerns human material, any of these manifestations of poor anticipation of requirements have an immediate, often disastrous effect throughout the firm. Inappropriate promotions or appointments or redundancies can be totally demoralising and create job insecurity which induces resignations of the very type of staff firms most often wish to keep—namely those who have an appreciation of management ability.

Research and Development Forecasts are required to decide on the extent of expenditure of research and development for a product. Thus forecasts of expenditure necessary to bring a new product up to production stage must be combined with forecasts of the inputs necessary to take it to viability.

There is in fact no part of the total corporate activity which is not the subject of some type of forward estimating. So long as the variables are reasonably stable, or correlate with other stable factors, or are to some extent controllable, for example labour, raw material and occupational costs, many types of forecasts can be made with a considerable degree of accuracy.

But although the marketing researcher may be asked to provide forecasts for any of the areas of a business's activity, more generally he will be concerned with two types of forecasts—general economic and business forecasts, and sales forecasting—which are affected by very many environmental and internal factors, some of which are subject to wide and sudden variations.

General and economic business forecasts analyse and predict the future course of developments for the economy and for industries. It is necessary to do this to reduce the risks inherent in decision-making. The impact of government, social, economic and technological change makes it increasingly important to forecast both the qualities and magnitude of change. The prosperity of a firm's customers is bound up with the national wellbeing, therefore any indicators foreshadowing a slackening or acceleration of business activity can be of material help to management and need to be carefully investigated. The problem of the firm is not dissimilar to the problem of an industry or ultimately of the country.

The sales forecast is concerned with the likely reactions of the market environment to changes in the policies of the firm; for example a forecast based upon adjustment in the product use or as a reaction to certain promotional stimuli. The purpose of this type of forecasting is the identification of the most appropriate alternative courses of action which will produce a given sales effect (either maximisation or reduction of cyclical fluctuations).

Between the two types of forecasts, economic and business and sales, there is a one-way link. No sales forecast can be accurate consistently if it ignores the economic or business forecast. The converse is not necessarily true, however. Sales forecasts for the individual firm, except under circumstances of monopoly or oligopoly are unlikely to make any contribution to an economic forecast.

UNPREDICTABILITY IN FORECASTING

The problem of unpredictability in forecasting, either by objective or subjective means, has been summed up thus: 'Whether the relatively subjective methods can be used depends upon the availability of personnel whose judgement has been tested and found adequate. On the other hand, use of objective methods should not be relied on blindly merely because of the fact that they are reached by precise mathematical means and are stated with exactitude.'[1]

Forecasting, it has been pointed out,[2] is frequently practised as a separate exercise by individuals with an imperfect understanding of the economic problems for which the forecasts are required. Moreover it is often difficult for an individual responsible for a contribution in one aspect of an economic forecast, say demand estimates, to be aware of the general significance of his knowledge of his part of the problem. Even when an economic forecast is the work of a team, the same lack of comprehension of the problem as a whole may prevent the full potentialities of the team from being realised. As with all industrial marketing, the relationship and interdependence of the individual segments which make up the whole, marketing or forecasting, has to be recognised and acted upon.

There are many methods of forecasting and of using current data for general business forecasts. The majority of these forecasts tend to be subjective rather than scientific. Many eminent economists have been at pains to emphasise that there is nothing in economic science which enables the foretelling of events. Econometricians who have based forecasts upon mathematical models of the economy have had, despite their more exotic approach, no greater record of success than the 'seaweed' school. However, the use of computers has now brought the mathematical model techniques to a new efficiency and complexity. Results hold promise for more accurate and more detailed forecasts being available to business in the future.

Anticipations of future trends are nowadays more firmly founded than ever before, since better analytical tools, fuller statistical information and more comprehensive intelligence are available. Economic forecasting has taken a long leap forward with the construction of theoretical models of the national economy and its various sectors. There is, of course, nothing new about model building; the novelty is that many more economists are trying to build them today.

In an attempt to chart the future the marketing researcher or economist can only offer indicators and his experience of interpreting these indicators according to the business of the firm. Generalisations about the meaning of the movement of indicators can prove helpful

---

[1] *Basic Methods of Marketing Research*, op. cit., p. 74.

[2] A. J. Merrett and G. Bannock, *Business Economics and Statistics*, Hutchinson (London, 1962), pp. 76–9.

to the businessman in anticipating changes but the adjustment of future plans remains his, and not the economist's responsibility.

For many years a considerable volume of forecasting has been undertaken by government departments to enable annual plans to be drawn up. Well-publicised failures such as the National Plan have had the same temporary effects on the acceptance of forecasting as the failure of the Ford Motor Company's Edsel[1] had on consumer marketing research and the wildly incorrect prediction of the result of the American Presidential election of 1948 on public opinion polling. None of these disasters, however, apart from providing a field day for the critics, in any way invalidated the uses of the techniques, only the shortcomings of those particular exercises.

In the final analysis, no matter how elaborate the techniques, a forecast is a composite judgement of the executives concerned. Just how much this is so is revealed by an American survey of forecasting procedures and which would appear to accord with the situation in most industrialised economies. Table 3 below[2] indicates the

Table 3
FACTORS INFLUENCING FORECASTING

Factor	Companies Using Factor	Rank, By Use	Rank, By Importance	Companies Naming Factor as Important
Past Sales Trends of Firm ..	278	1	1	152
Sales Department Estimates ..	255	2	2	127
Judgement and Hunch	230	3	4	63
General Economic Indicators ..	213	4	5	62
Economic Data on Own Industry	209	5	3	84
Salesmen's Field Reports	199	6	6	60
New Product Plans	182	7	10	26
Competitors' Activities	158	8	11	13
Production Capacity	151	9	7	38
Market Surveys	147	10	8-9	27
Promotion Plans	137	11	8-9	27
Other..	34	12	12	13

extent to which subjective factors, or factual data modified by subjective judgements, play a part in most forecasts.

[1] In fact it was the execution of the marketing plan not the marketing research which was at fault, as W. H. Reynold showed in 'The Edsel Ten Years Later', *Business Horizons*, Vol. 10, No. 3 (Bloomington, Indiana, U.S.A., 1967).

[2] L. Strong, 'Sales Forecasting—Problems and Progress', *Marketing Research— Principles and Readings*, op. cit.

The survey of market forecasting in Great Britain revealed a not dissimilar situation. All firms responding to the enquiry stated they used 'executive judgement' as one of their methods, sixty-five per cent used the sales force composite method described later in this chapter. Only twenty-four per cent used econometric methods.[1]

INFLUENCING FACTORS

Factors influencing direction of business activity can be general, specific or esoteric. There is no more point in listing them all than in trying to compile all possible sources of information. They will include such obvious general factors as population structure and balance of payments position as well as specific aspects such as lead time for a component or a local government planning decision.

A useful grouping has been devised, however,[2] of measures of total activity, individual business processes and financial barometers. The American description of economic indicators is not totally compatible with those available in the United Kingdom; under three broad headings, however, the United Kingdom sources of information can provide:

- Measures of total activity:
    Employment
    Average hours worked
    Gross Domestic Product
    (Components include:
        Consumer expenditure
        Government expenditure
        Fixed investment
        Investment in stocks
        Net trade income from exports less imports of goods and services)
    Bank clearings
    Forecasts of world trade

- Measures of individual business processes:
    Industrial production
    Retail sales
    Stocks—manufacturing, wholesale and retail
    Manufacturers' new orders

---

[1] *A survey of market forecasting practice in Great Britain*, op. cit.

[2] J. R. Stockton, *Introduction to Business and Economic Statistics*, South Western Publishing Company (Cincinnati, U.S.A., 1966), pp. 503-24.

New orders for construction
Raw material prices
Survey of private investment intentions

● Financial barometers:
Bank loans—by industry group
Hire purchase debt
Building society advances
Share issues
Share prices
Corporate profits

These are purely environmental factors which will have to be
investigated or at least considered for each forecast. A second
group will be factors which to a greater or lesser extent the firm can
control and therefore whose effect can at least be roughly predicted.
Among these are: the use of promotional techniques, the ability
of the organisation to satisfy demand—plant capacity (which must
in the short run set an upper limit to sales); availability, cost and
quality of the factors of production; research results and the quality
and confidence of management. With all products, quality and
efficiency are important and with certain products, servicing,
maintenance, repair and replacement facilities. Finally, the level
of selling prices, changes in which depend on the degree of elasticity
of demand for the product and the freedom of manufacturers to
effect them consequent upon variations in the costs of production.[1]

INPUT-OUTPUT ANALYSIS

A major step forward was taken in economic and business forecasting
by the development of input-output analysis. 'Input-output analysis
is the practical extension of the classical theory of general interdependence which views the whole economy of a region, a country or
even the entire world as a single system and sets out to interpret all
its functions in terms of specific measurable properties of its
structure.'[2]

Input-output analysis is based upon tables which show the flow
of goods and services among all the different sectors of a national
economy and therefore indicate what effect any industry's demand is
likely to have on every other industry in the table. This is shown by

[1] *Introduction to Business Forecasting*, op. cit., p. 5.
[2] W. Leontief, *Input-Output Economics*, Oxford University Press (New York, 1966). p. vii.

representing in the tables each industry by a row and a column; each final market by a column; and value added by one or more rows. The row for an industry show the distribution of its output to itself and to other industries and final markets; the column shows its consumption of goods and services of the various industries and its value added. An extract of an input-output table is given in Appendix B.

Applications for input-output analysis are various and diverse. They include evaluating an individual firm's sales potential and probing the implications of broad economic programmes. With supplementary data it is possible to estimate employment required per unit of output, the output requirements from each industry can, therefore, be translated into requirements for employment. Information on capital and capacity can be used to estimate additional plant and equipment needs.

Input-output tables give more than the direct sales effect of an industry activity. They trace through the effect of secondary, tertiary and even further waves of demand initiated by the original activity in both directions. The demand generated can be identified in every industry where an impact is recorded. The tables are the results of massive and complex calculations but are simplicity itself to use. They place in the hands of the forecaster a powerful weapon for improving his own forecasts.

SHORT-TERM FORECASTING

Short-term forecasting is, in many respects, likely to be more accurate than long-term forecasting. Precisely what 'short-term' is will depend very much on the individual firm; anything from three months in many consumer markets to three years in industrial markets.

The types of short-term forecasts most often sought and which can be achieved with a reasonable degree of accuracy and consistency are: stock levels, demand by model type, physical distribution requirements, operating capital requirements, sales targets and quotas, marketing, particularly promotional inputs, and operating supplies requirements.

Short-term forecasting more than long-term forecasting relies upon judgement and surveys and the use of statistical techniques is generally limited to seasonal corrections, smoothing and simple extrapolations.

One major difference in the short-, as opposed to the long-term forecast, is the preoccupation with the fast changing factors such as the length of the order book, stock levels and seasonal considerations. Because of this preoccupation it is usual to revise short-term forecasts frequently whereas long-term forecasts are unlikely to be subject to more than an annual check, unless some change of considerable and unexpected magnitude should occur, for example the devaluation of the pound in 1967, and the 1956 and 1967 Middle East wars which disrupted oil supplies.

Short-term forecasts, given that there will be variations between industries and products, can and should be accurate within a few per cent, even allowing for the fact that some types of analyses, notably those concerned with random series movements, are less accurate for short-term forecasting than for long-term forecasting.

The purpose of monitoring forecasts, however, is to identify error and then to determine the source of error. By this constant surveillance of the forecasting method it is possible to introduce ever-increasing precision into the forecasting methods.

The Long Range Planning Service of the Stanford Research Institute with a build-up of over 350 individual long-range planning reports, has embarked on a considerable programme of monitoring and checking many of the early forecasts as part of an exercise to improve forecasting accuracy. Similarly the National Institute of Economic and Social Research has taken a retrospective view of their forecasts for vehicles, durable consumer goods and energy demand reported on their accuracy.[1]

LONG-TERM FORECASTING

Long-term forecasting requires a far higher degree of skill, insight, maturity, experience and judgement than short and medium forecasts. The major consideration in long-term forecasting is the correct identification of the basic trends which, used in conjunction with the extrapolation of the historical situation, provides a 'band' from which the forecasts can be developed. The data from these inputs can be subjected to a number of mathematical forecasting techniques but it must also be subjected to qualitative considerations. Operational life of equipment, for example, can be extended and shortened, depending upon such variables as the overall economic position, taxation, the climate of competition and technical and psychological obsolescence, and thus move out of line with the

[1] 'Long Term Forecasts of Demand for Cars, Selected Consumer Durables and Energy', *National Institute Economic Review* No. 40 (London, May 1967).

prediction of physical life expectancies. Saturation tables, indicative as they are of market potentials, still require interpretation to obtain a realistic differentiation of the theoretical and realisable market.

Long-term forecasting is conducted for a number of differing purposes; corporate planning being a relatively new but increasingly important application area for the findings. For corporate planning long range forecasts are needed for both divisional activities and environmental factors. Thus whereas it was said as recently as the beginning of the present decade that the major purpose for long-term forecasting was to arrive at a total demand estimate for a firm's products, its ultimate use is now seen as the far more embracing objective as an aid in identifying threat and opportunity in the long term so that a company's activities can be directed to avert and exploit the situations as they emerge. The 'total demand estimate' is far too narrow a concept for business conditions of today.

FORECASTING TECHNOLOGICAL CHANGE

In industrial markets perhaps the most pervasive influence on the course of events is technological change. Its impact creates one of the most intractable problems of forecasting. Technological change affects industrial markets in two ways: changes in the products which are manufactured and sold, and changes in the user industries' processes or methods which require new or adjusted products.

In forecasting technological change it is necessary to revert to the question of durability of products referred to in Chapter 1. It is true to say that rarely will a product be substituted for another identical product. Usually the replacement is of a more advanced design or has improved characteristics. However, if products are kept in use for a period of many years then it is possible they will be replaced, not by an improved version of the existing product but by one which is based on a totally new concept—metal-cutting machines may eventually be replaced by the use of lasers. A non-product example can be found in the service industries. The impact of high definition television telephones on all forms of travel is likely to be considerable. The replacement demand in both the examples quoted bears little relation to the form of the products and services they replace or impact on.

However, although the problem is a real one, within the period of most long-term forecasts it can in fact be largely resolved because really fundamental changes rarely occur at short notice. A Stanford

U

Research Institute Long Range Planning Service Study[1] provided ample evidence of this. The study which covered 10,000 growth products in two periods of five years showed among other things that the concept or theory of the products which became viable in the periods studied were known at least ten years before viability was achieved. If this historical evidence holds good for the future then it can be said that there will be no major technological breakthroughs in the period of most long-range forecasts the theory of which is not known at the time the forecast was made. This is both a comfort and assistance to the long-range forecaster grappling with technological change.

A major study of technological forecasting[2] arrived at three important conclusions.

Technological forecasting emerged as a recognised management discipline around 1960; its modern form has gradually taken shape since the first attempts were made in the mid-1940s to attain 'informed judgement' through systematic and comprehensive evaluation, and it has been adopted on an increasingly wide scale in industry, research, institutes and military environments since the late 1950s.

The value of technological forecasting has been proven, not only in terms of accuracy of specific forecasts (to which numerous positive indications and the general satisfaction of practitioners, though as yet few statistical evaluations, testify) but even more prominently, in terms of its contribution to the definition of long-range strategies.

Technological forecasting is an art, not yet a science and is characterised today by attitudes, not tools; human judgement is enhanced, not substituted by it. The development of auxiliary techniques, gradually attaining higher degrees of sophistication (and complexity) since 1960 is oriented towards ultimate integration with evolving information technology.

The report defined technological forecasting as the 'probabilistic assessment of future technology transfer'[3] including the entire range of vertical and horizontal transfer processes that constitute the advancement of technology and the effectuation of impact in tech-

---

[1] *Characteristics of Growth Products*, a confidential study available to subscribers to the Long Range Planning Service of the Stanford Research Institute, (Menlo Park, California 1966).

[2] E. Jantsch, *Technological Forecasting in Perspective*, O.E.C.D. (Paris, 1966), p. 7.

[3] *Ibid.*

nological as well as non-technological (economic, social, military and political) terms. This is as liberal a definition as any business forecaster could require.

The unusual situation of a discipline acknowledging the contribution of marketing and business research for many of its approaches rather than the reverse is to be found in this field. 'Technological forecasting is one of the latest additions to a family of systematic forecasting activities. If we omit from consideration the very old art of weather forecasting, one encounters as part of this family a number of "precursive" activities such as economic and business forecasting, while forecasting in the political and social areas is more or less developing in parallel to technological forecasting. From a point of view of techniques, there is considerable "crossfertilisation" but perhaps less than one might expect or than would appear feasible. Economic analysis on the basis of discounted cash flow methods is a valuable addition to technological forecasting, as is the use of certain matrix techniques. More elaborate econometric and business models can be adapted to problems of technological forecasting only within certain limits; in general, the economic and business areas have developed sophisticated techniques only for short-range forecasts, whereas the main interest for technology is in long-range forecasts. However, there are numerous refinements which have arisen from the concentrated effort on economic and business forecasting techniques that may be adapted, such as risk evaluation and various forms of probabilistic forecasting.

On the other hand, forecasting techniques developed in the political, social and technological fields—especially those centering on "social technology"—can to a considerable degree mutually benefit from each other. Military forecasting in the non-technological areas may equally produce some "spin off" in the form of techniques.

The two basic approaches that are making the deepest impact on technological forecasting techniques—*operations research* and *systems analysis*—were first explored and developed in response to military incentives. Operations research dates back to World War II developments in the United Kingdom and the United States, and systems analysis has been pioneered by the RAND Corporation in the United States since 1948. Critical path and PERT methods (the latter developed for the Polaris missile programme) also sprang from military planning requirements.

These developments would seem to constitute a vast source of technological forecasting techniques which so far has been exploited only to a small degree. While the possibilities of reasonably sized tasks for operations research and systems analysis are nearly exhausted in the military field—there are almost no problems left in U.S. defence that can be solved with linear programming—technological forecasting is only starting to explore them for its own purposes.

Another very important area of "precursive" activity is *computer development* and the vast evolving field of *information technology*. Technological forecasting has not yet acquired sufficient "status" to inspire developments in these areas, but in a few years it will find a readymade framework for decision-making in business, military, political and possibly social environments, and it will be accommodated without difficulty.

All existing techniques for technological forecasting are characterised by the following three points, which are to some extent interdependent:

> They have been developed for a "man—technique" dialogue and are very sensitive to man's knowledge and his capacity for imaginative thinking, technical and value judgement, and synthesis. Essentially, human forecasting is not replaced but structured and enhanced, by these techniques; in particular the human forecasting potential is extended where large input and complex relationships are involved.
>
> They are partial techniques which cover only a fraction of a complete technological forecasting process; their combination may result in more highly integrated, but not yet in fully-integrated techniques (on the basis of today's state of the art).
>
> They are auxiliary aids to decision-making, which normally has to be based on broader information than can be provided by these techniques.'[1]

The report, quite the most exhaustive yet produced, distinguishes over 100 separate forecasting techniques or elements of techniques.

INFORMATION SOURCES FOR FORECASTING

One explanation why forecasting often falls to the marketing researcher (apart from the fact that they are usually economists and therefore presumed to have derived a knowledge of forecasting and statistics in their training), is because of the very considerable information needs of forecasters, most of which will usually be obtainable from the market research department.

There is little which has been described in the preceding chapters

[1] *Technological Forecasting in Perspective*, op. cit., pp. 110-13.

of this book which will not have some application in forecasting. Clearly the sources of secondary information, and especially the internal analyses described in Chapter 5, 'Use of Secondary Sources', will form one of the chief sources of information.

Field research particularly in the provision of qualitative data will also contribute a considerable amount of usable material. Studies of changing methods and technology, changes in demand patterns, expected level of investment, anticipation of the impact of environmental factors on user and competitor industries, are all typical of the sort of information input which can be obtained from field surveys.

One cheap and reasonably reliable method of generating forecasting material is by a combination of desk and field research. That is, drawing from field research, mostly by interviewing, individual forecasts of firms and then analysing and processing them to provide a composite picture.

FORECASTING TECHNIQUES

There are many techniques for forecasting the likely course of business events, some wholly qualitative and indeed emotional. No one method can claim a record of consistent success and indeed the pursuit of a perfect method for all companies in all circumstances and at all times is not likely to be rewarding. The commitment to any one technique is fraught with hazards and the good forecaster is not likely to fall into the error of adopting only a limited number of methods because they have been reasonably accurate in the past and conversely rejecting others because in some circumstances they have failed. If the forecaster is a marketing researcher there is every chance that his eclectic approach to research problems will induce a similar approach to forecast technique decisions.

The major techniques are summarised but they by no means include all the methods available nor all the adaptations of them. The fact that the OECD report already referred to identified 100 methods of technological forecasting—just one section of the forecast input— is an adequate indication of the great range of methods available to the researcher.

QUALITATIVE METHODS

Table 3 indicated the extent to which subjective judgements are involved in forecasts. Many of these subjective judgements will have a statistical base but in arriving at the forecast estimates, these statistics will have played a relatively minor role. Although the use of qualitative methods in forecasting cannot be regarded as scientific, there is usually a sound methodological approach to it.

Were the users of more scientific methods of forecasting to claim a higher record of success than those achieved by users of qualitative methods, then it might be possible to ignore this approach. However, if the individuals who make qualitative forecasts are experienced, closely in touch with their markets, possess an intimate product knowledge and a knowledge of their own companies, then the views they are expressing are not to be ignored. In another context it was said that the businessman's practical wisdom is of a completely different character than scientific knowledge. While it does not ignore generalities, it recognises the low probability that given combinations of phenomena can, or will be repeated. In place of scientific knowledge the businessman collects lore. Businessmen's lore has that same element of scientific unorthodoxy which makes much country lore accepted by even the most sophisticated. What might be called intuition is in fact the aggregation of past experience unconsciously measured against a current situation. In fact a market or environmental empathy.

Qualitative forecasts are often no more than commonsense checks on more sophisticated approaches which may be statistically immaculate but lack some vital element which is immediately obvious to someone closely involved in the operations which are the subject of the forecast. The main types of qualitative forecasts are: (a) sales force composite, (b) consensus of executive or expert opinion, (c) consensus of independent forecasts, (d) consensus of industries.

(a) *Sales force composite*

Perhaps the most ubiquitous of the qualitative methods is the sales force composite. This method requires salesmen in the field to prepare individual forecasts for their own territories. These are then reviewed by a sales manager or other senior executive with an overview of the marketing operation and the results are aggregated.

The disadvantages are obvious: lack of expertise in gathering data and handling them, bias because forecasts are often used subsequently as a measure of performance and time-effectiveness factors.

The advantages are that it is often possible for salesmen to base their forecasts on the stated forward demand of individual customers within territories so that the aggregation is related to the total customer complex; it provides a sense of shared responsibility, alerts salesmen to opportunities and threats and improves general sales intelligence.

(b) *Consensus of executive or expert opinion*

This method, like the sales force composite, seeks individual opinions as a basis of an aggregation. It has the advantage over the sales force composite method in that opinions sought will span a wider range of activities and contacts with the outside world and it can include the sales force composite, if the contribution of the sales manager or director is included. The aggregated forecast will thus contain the checks and balances stemming from, perhaps, a realistic assessment of price trends from the purchasing department which offsets the ebullience of the advertising department. An overview by the chief executive can do much to introduce some precision into the final results.

Expert opinion reduces individual subjectivity in forecasting and increases the element of collective judgement. It has, however, the disadvantage that it does not bring complete objectivity because subjective judgement often enters into the selection of the executives or experts whose opinion is sought. Other disadvantages of the system are the difficulty or impossibility of weighting the factors which influence the individual forecasts, integrating a forecasting expertise from one individual or department with a crude intuitive approach from another and the cost-effectiveness of the method.

(c) *Consensus of independent forecasts*

This method is an eclectic approach to forecasting. It seeks to uncover existing forecasts, some of which may be pure statistical exercises and others purely qualitative and then to arrive at a composite forecast by adjusting them using the forecaster's own experience and knowledge. The method has much to commend it, given that it is possible to assess and to make a critical review of the individual forecast procedures so that a weighting can be devised. It can be used advantageously to provide base forecasts. For example, the demand for flexible polyurethane foam comes from several industrial sectors, two important ones being the motor and furniture industries. Forecasts for both these industries are detailed and have a history of above average accuracy. These two industry forecasts can form the basis of forecast of demand for these sectors, other components being the amount of polyurethane foam used in each vehicle or each type of furniture, and trends to and away from other filling materials.

(d) *Consensus of industries*

In one respect this is an extension of the sales force composite approach. The sales force composite approach seeks to aggregate demand in each territory. A consensus of industry approach takes the views of the likely direction of the forecast subject right across industry and would include both supply and user industries as well as intermediaries such as distributors, original equipment manufacturers, processors, trade and professional associations, local and central government, consultants and others.

The advantage of this approach is that it allows for the widest possible view and from all vantage points, and often draws in the results of quantitative methods. The disadvantages in working over so wide a spectrum are the high probability of inconsistent or incompatible results, the difficulty of weighting the individual forecasts for accuracy and importance, and again cost-effectiveness factors.

Irrespective of the method of collection or compilation and how much regard has been paid to statistical approaches, qualitative forecasts will always have a part to play, but inevitably as the more elegant methods increase in reliability, less use will be made of the qualitative approach.

QUANTITATIVE METHODS

Even though quantitative methods can vary in complexity from the simple fitting of a trend line to the most complicated and elaborate mathematical models, there is no evidence that a direct relationship exists between the accuracy of a forecast and the degree of complexity of the model.[1] It is always necessary to adopt the forecasting technique appropriate to the objective of the forecast and the quality of the data available. The two basic sections of any forecast will be the industry forecast and that related purely to the firm; in both instances the data can be processed by a number of different methods.

Time series is the most commonly used method. At its simplest, this is essentially a method of plotting historical data as a time series and then attempting to discover and extrapolate a recognisable overall trend in that series. This technique is hardly ever omitted, even if the forecaster proposes to use other techniques.

The objective of time series analysis is to provide a method of measuring changes in individual business related to changes in the

[1] *Marketing and Business Research*, op. cit., p. 110.

economy. Within a business the time series that measure change are provided by the recorded experience of the company; information on changes in a whole industry or economy come from the various external sources, some of which have been listed.

Time series analysis falls into four categories: *secular trend, cyclical, seasonal, random.*

Secular trend is the broad pattern of growth or decline which ignores minor fluctuations. It reflects the effect of forces making for gradual change. Unless a trend reveals a regular pattern its extra-polation will require something more than a free-hand sketch. There are various mathematical formulae and tests which can be applied to determine the 'best' trend relationship.

The major use for secular trend is to derive information about the change in the statistical series being studied. They can also be used to adjust a series to take out the effect of the long-term trend in order to isolate non-trend fluctuations.

Cyclical and *seasonal* influences are those which may move above and below the trend line, sometimes in a more or less regular or predictable pattern or else, although re-occurring, do not conform to a regular pattern.

The simplest method of forecasting these changes is to make direct comparison with a period corresponding to one to be forecast, say the same calendar month in previous years. Sales, if they are the subject of the forecast, can be compared in any given period to a moving average. The moving average has a dampening effect because it takes in the whole of a previous cycle. The ratio of the actual value of any given period to the moving average provides a percentage indication of how the period compares to date with the seasonal influence removed. This method, ratio-to-moving-average, is relatively simple and in fact simplicity is one of its few virtues, since the risks of inaccurate forecasts are high and inherent in the method.

More sophisticated variations on the ratio-to-moving-average method can avoid many of the basic deficiencies of the system. These variations include the process of isolating the cycle, trend-cycle combination approach and exponential smoothing. This is a relatively simple method to use and permits more accurate estimating of seasonal variations and different forms of trends. It has the additional advantage of flexibility. In exponential smoothing the effect of increasingly distant 'actuals' dies away while the effect of more recent 'actuals' is given more importance or weight. A new forecast is made by adding to the previous forecast a certain fraction of the amount or 'constant' by which the 'actual' for the period now ending exceeds that previous forecast.

Variations in business and economic activity which stem from seasonal changes are true periodicities and are reflected throughout important sectors of the economy. Few organisations are not subject to some seasonal variations. Cyclical variations are far less predictable than seasonal variations and secular trend. The cyclical variations in individual series are related to the cycles in the total economy. There are, of course, other periodicities in business besides those that fluctuate with seasons, for example traffic flows at different times of day. Seasonable adjustment is, however, often simple and in some series of statistics commonplace, yet many types of forecast still omit this adjustment in favour of comparison with a suitable period in the past.

Random series movements are intermingled with the other three types of variations and include everything that cannot be catergorised as trend, cyclical or seasonal. These random movements will include a large number of small variables and are derived from an equally large number of factors. They are usually of short duration and of relatively small amplitude.

The trend in business is to require smaller intervals of time for presentation of control data. Yearly data, once considered adequate, is now collected on a half-yearly, quarterly or even monthly basis because it is now possible to obtain and prepare data on machines much more quickly than in the past. This has important implications for forecasting. Over a long period of time irregularities tend to smooth out. Over a short period an erratic fluctuation will influence the series to a significant extent.

Looking at the problem in another way, random irregulars tend to occur most frequently in company data but where a number of companies combine their data once again the smoothing effect is achieved.

Irregular fluctuations require study, particularly when they are of significant proportions. Not only should allowance be made for them but their causes ascertained. However, unless the irregularity is really significant there is little point in pursuing its source because re-occurrence may not occur in a way which aids forecasting. 'The irregular "saw-toothed" effect seen in many time series analyses classified on a monthly or weekly basis usually results from the use of a time unit that is so small that the irregular forces affecting the data were not given an opportunity to cancel out. When it is desirable to use a small time unit as say a week or a month, the irregularities in the data must simply be ignored or some simple method of smoothing should be used.'[1]

Correlations and regression analysis

These are techniques for measuring the degree of association between a criterion (dependent variable) and predictors (independent variables). The procedure can be used to determine the extent to which a set of independent variables are capable of predicting a given dependent variable and to determine the absolute as well as the relative degree of association between each of a number of independent variables and a dependent variable

Industrial market research can assist here in locating the most suitable economic indicators and demand determinants to be used as independent variables. Because of the inter-relationships which exist in the economy, it is important in selecting the independent variables to ensure that it is truly independent, totally unaffected by changes in the other or dependent variable, which will become the subject of the forecast. Similarly, the indicator or indicators selected must have a significant variability during the period of the forecast. Population movement, for example, will be of little use in a twelve month forecast period.

Possible indicators may be screened to assess the extent of their influence on company sales. Variations in consumer disposable income, for example, have different effects on the demand for consumer durables, such as a washing machine and its associated industrial needs, than on more essential products with a relatively inelastic demand.

Once suitable independent variables have been located, correlation analysis provides a measurement of the degree of relationship between the variables. The calculation is complicated by the difference between the units to be related (e.g. the index of industrial production and sales of packaging materials) and their order of magnitude. This is overcome in calculating the coefficient of correlation, by expressing each set of data in terms of a scale, the zero of which is the arithmetic mean of the original data and the unit of measurement the standard deviation of the original distribution.

A more simple relationship frequently used in the early stages of examining the suitability of correlative data is the visual scattergraph in which the variable values are plotted in pairs without any significance to the timing of the relationship in question. A 'line of best fit' can then be drawn between the points on the scattergraph

[1] *Introduction to Business and Economic Statistics*, op. cit., p. 39.

showing a positive relationship between the variables, for forecasting purposes.

The aim in drawing the 'line of best fit' is to minimise the divergence of points from the line. The possibility of too subjective an assessment of the position of the line can be eliminated by regression analysis and particularly by the use of the least squares method in which the points of the line are calculated mathematically minimising the total of the squares of the deviations.

Lead-lag series

In the correlative calculations no recognition is taken of the timing of the relationships but in considering seasonal and cyclical variations, the use of lead-lag series has proved to be of considerable value in improving forecasting accuracy.

If it were possible to find a statistical series which were linked with the forecast subject on a time continuum in a fixed and predictable way, then forecasting would be highly accurate; that is a series of statistics which for example, in showing a rise invariably indicates that a rise will follow after a given period of time in the forecast subject. Any series which rises or falls ahead of the forecast subject are known as lead-series or lag-series.

A direct and unchanging link is, however, still the philosopher's stone of forecasting and certainly so far as total business activity is concerned, no series has been consistently successful in forecasting changes in business directions.

However, as indicators, lead-lag series can provide important inputs for a forecast and their pursuit in relation to specific forecasts is always worthwhile. Certainly the task of identifying relevant lead-lag series has been made simpler by continuous analysis. American studies have identified eighty-seven valid indicators, some fifty-two of which have been classified according to their time relationship. Of these thirty are leading series, fifteen roughly coincident and seven lagging.[1]

Multiple/Discriminant analysis

It has been pointed out that standard regression and correlation techniques, except when dealing with two groups, cannot be adapted to the prediction of other than continuous variables such as market share or total consumption. A technique has been developed for the prediction of multichotomous variables—multiple discriminant

[1] *Business Cycle Development*, Commercial Department, Bureau of Census, Washington, published monthly.

analysis. This analytical method enables the prediction to be made of the assignment of a group or category to one of two or more classifications on the basis of scores on a set of measured characteristics. It also enables tests to be made as to whether sample groups have come from a single population or 'universe' or two or more populations or 'universes'. It can also assist in determining the relative importance of each predictor variable in making 'optimal' assignments of groups or categories to test classifications.[1]

Regression analysis gives a measure of both the absolute and relative importance of a given variable with respect to the degree of its association with the dependent variables. Discriminant analysis provides an estimate only of the relative importance of each independent variable.

Factor analysis

These are a group of analytical techniques to provide information on the intercorrelations within a set of variables. No particular variable is singled out as a criterion or 'dependent' variable. The major objectives of factor analysis have been summed up as:[2]

finding a set of dimensions that are latent in a set of variables
providing valid criteria to segment a market
identifying variables for subsequent regression analysis
creating new variables for inclusion in regression, discriminant, or cluster analysis

Factor analysis is complementary to regression, correlation and discriminant analysis and not an alternative to them.

Canonical and cluster analysis

Two other emerging techniques already used in consumer goods forecasting are worthy of mention. These are canonical and cluster analysis. Canonical correlation procedures are designed to measure simultaneously the inter-relationships between more than one set of dependent variables and a set of independent variables, each consisting of measurements on the same aspects.

Cluster analysis is a method to assess simultaneously the similarity between phenomena, based on 'profiles' of their scores on

[1] P. E. Green and R. E. Frank, *A Manager's Guide to Marketing Research*, John Wiley (New York, 1967), pp. 98–101. (This book provides an excellent summary of both experimental and non-experimental multivariate statistical techniques used in marketing.)
[2] *Ibid.*

a number of measured characteristics. This is quite different from regression, discriminant and canonical analysis in that in these latter procedures the ordering of the phenomena in terms of membership of a category is done in advance through its measured score on whatever variable is chosen as the dependent variable. In cluster analysis no advance assignment of the phenomena to groups is made. Instead one of the principal objectives of the analysis is to find what clusters (groups) of phenomena are similar with respect to their profile. In addition these techniques are used for determining the 'best' number of groups into which a given universe may be divided.

There are a number of different types of these analyses which can be conducted and even the most basic ones are never simple. However, they can be given a considerable elegance and all of them are best left to mathematical statisticians. The computations need not necessarily be difficult to learn but a real understanding of the techniques is rare in marketing researchers who do not usually have the necessary training and experience.

The major deficiencies of all the analyses are the complications of computation which tend to reduce their 'credibility' to non-experts and the need for historical data over a sufficiently long period of time.

CHARTING TECHNIQUES

A study of mathematical statistics in all its facets is helpful for forecasting but by no means essential. A useful and reliable guide to mathematical results can often be obtained by the use of charting techniques. These do not replace mathematical calculations but they are productive of usable working estimates. They are part of a series of graphical presentations which include bar and pie charts, and statistical maps and pictures which are described in Chapter 14, 'The Report'. A chart can, however, be used not merely to present information in an interesting and lucid form but also to analyse data. This can be done by several methods from the construction of simple trend lines on arithmetical grids to increasingly complex approaches which include moving average trend lines, projection trend lines and correlation methods on semi-log, log-log and probability grids.

Arithmetic scales show the *amount* of change. Data plotted on semi-log and log-log grids show *rates* of change. A projection may be the simple extrapolation of a straight line through past data and extending forward into the years ahead or it can be as complex as fitting a standard growth curve such as Gompertz, logistic or exponential curves, to historic data.

There are, however, some inherent dangers in the use of charting techniques for forecasting. Errors occur due to the spread of individual points about the trend which are usually as large or larger than in the past. Moreover no matter how accurately the line has been determined and the spread of points minimised it is still only the best estimate. Just as the forecast is the best estimate and still subject to error, so the trend line itself is subject to error and as a consequence is a source of error for the forecasting purpose. The confidence limit will always depend on the average of the deviations, the number of points of information and the time interval, all of which will require careful consideration.

An understanding of charting techniques has two advantages to the industrial marketing researcher concerned with forecasting; it not only assists him in the construction of the forecast but also makes the presentation more readily understandable and 'credible' to the sponsor.

MATHEMATICAL MODELS AND ECONOMETRIC ANALYSIS

Models consist of a system of equations which attempt to express and to explain the interrelationships among several economic variables. Once the equations are set up, one or more interdependent variables are fed into the system and the equations are solved simultaneously to determine the dependent variables. The technique has the advantage of forcing a systematic organisation of information which is sometimes lacking in other forecasting procedures. However, the construction of a model is expensive, time-consuming and demanding a high degree of technical skill. Almost invariably a computer will be needed to work through an entire model in anything like a reasonable time, and at the end the most complicated model may not adequately describe a situation. Further it may not be possible to express all the basic assumptions as mathematical quantities and no model can be better than the assumptions on which it rests.

Marketing has been one of the last of the functional areas of management to yield to modelling techniques. Model building in marketing can provide guides and sometimes solutions to such recurrent problems as deciding appropriations for the various marketing inputs and their distribution of areas and activities, the optimum 'product mix', deciding and timing the introduction of new products and distribution policy. All these activities require that some assumptions about the future are made and the mathematical model provides important inputs for these assumptions.

The last few years have seen much progress in the development of techniques for coping with the probabilistic time dependent environment of the market. Certainly the next decade will see some spectacular advances in this field and will probably, more than any other forecasting technique, be responsible for increased precision in forecasting. The building and use of models will, however, remain a specialist activity so that in relation to forecasting, the role of the industrial marketing researcher is more than likely to be confined to identifying the problem to be solved and then ensuring the results obtained from the model can make a practical contribution to the forecast at least commensurate with the cost of its building.

CHAPTER 14

The Report

The end result of the work which has been carried out in an industrial marketing research project will almost invariably be a written report which will be presented to the research sponsor. Its purpose is to provide both a working document on which to base decisions and a permanent record of the research project and findings. Although oral presentations are commonplace and in some respects have advantages over the written and illustrated report, no project can be satisfactorily concluded nor make its contribution to the continuing research programme of a firm unless some record of it remains.

The essence of good reporting does not vary from subject to subject and applies equally to scientific, technical, financial or commercial reports. The distinction between different types of reports will be in the ordering and presentation, and not in the fundamentals of report writing.

Readers of industrial marketing research reports will fall into several categories. Two broad groups will be corporate management and operational management. The former can be defined as those who are concerned with major decision-making, particularly forward planning, and the latter as those who implement the decisions and plans. Within these two groups there will be various types of readers; administrators, corporate planners, supervisors, specialists and others.

THE NEEDS OF THE READER

Every report is intended as a communication between the writer and the reader, and to effect good communication requires emphasis on the reader's needs, not those of the writer. Thus a prerequisite for good report writing, irrespective of the subject, is some knowledge of the person or persons who will read it. Generally the industrial marketing researcher will have foreknowledge of the important readers of his report, both by name and job function.

x

This is a considerable advantage since the report can be written with these readers clearly in mind. Some will only be interested in the factual data and be prepared to accept their validity without question. Others will examine the report minutely, weighing each piece of evidence and checking the validity of claimed relationships and will require information on the background to the collection of the material, including details of the deductive processes and an explanation of the interpretation which the researchers have given.

For example, at one extreme a decision to locate a plant at a given geographical point, which will involve perhaps hundreds of thousands of pounds of investment, is not likely to be accepted without ample support for any statements which imply a preference for one location rather than another. At the other extreme an electronic expert will accept without explanation that accuracies required in a vibrating strut transducer to match those which can be achieved by more primitive measuring instruments are, paradoxically, unrealistically high. He will concede without having to spell out the details that a dipstick is more efficient in some situations than a transducer.

The difficulty of meeting the needs of various readers is great; some will be bored by too much detail while to others even minutiae may be inadequate. 'At the highest level little more than the title and evidence that the work is to hand may be enough. At a lower level the manager will want to familiarise himself with the conclusions and recommendations. Further down someone will have to study the argument of the report in detail. At the lowest level of readership the footnotes, authorities, and appendices might have to be checked.'[1]

It is obviously impossible to satisfy all levels of readers and methods of reading but it is possible to structure industrial marketing research reports so as to enable each type of reader to extract what he requires quickly, simply and in a way which is satisfactory to him.

REPORT OBJECTIVES

The need to identify the report objectives is as imperative as the need to identify the ultimate readers of the report. These report objectives are not simply the marketing research objectives. A report can have many different purposes but common to them will be the intention to inform or explain, or both. If the report is to be a record of a situation it will require a very different orientation from one which is to be used to take decisions and choose between alternative

[1] B. M. Cooper, *Writing Technical Reports*, Pelican (London, 1964).

courses of action. A 'benchmark' study is usually only intended for use when the second and later 'benchmarks' have been established. Thus being used for comparison purposes and not standing alone, its ordering and format would vary from a 'one off' report.

COMPILATION

The processes which bring the researcher to the completed marketing research report are:

(a) Collection of material
(b) Selection and editing of material for inclusion
(c) Logical ordering
(d) Interpretation
(e) Presentation

There is, however, no fixed rule which forces the researcher through the stages and the common error of many reports is to omit some of them or unnaturally extend or shorten others. Balance between the stages must be sought.

(a) *Collection of material*

By the time the study is ready for writing up all the material available has usually been obtained. It is, of course, possible that in actually writing the report gaps may be revealed that could force the researchers back into the field. However, such circumstances should be unusual and would in any event indicate a basic deficiency in the analysis which had failed to identify the situation earlier.

(b) *Selection and editing of material for inclusion*

The report is largely all the sponsor sees of the research, although it is by no means all he pays for. Most industrial marketing research reports omit more than they include. They would become largely unmanageable if the researcher attempted to include everything. This is in contrast to most scientific reports. These generally contain the full research yield, details of the research techniques, explanations of the deductive processes and the maximum validation of the conclusions.

In an industrial marketing research report it is the responsibility of the researcher to decide which information shall be included and this is done largely by reference to the research objectives, report objectives and the readers. There are no rules which will guide a researcher on the vexed question of what is to be included. At one extreme it is known for a researcher with a national or international reputation to make a declaration which will be accepted without question. His less fortunate colleagues may have to provide full evidence for even the most marginal comment. Thus in the first case a conclusion or opinion with all validating factors omitted will suffice, while in the second a summary of evidence seems to be called for.

Whatever is included or omitted, the back-up material ought always to be available and the problem of material of a marginal nature is partly solved by reference in the report to its availability. The danger of too brutal an amputation, if not eliminated, is reduced by maintaining carefully indexed and classified back-up material.

The Long Range Planning Service of the Stanford Research Institute with its vast experience of report writing has found that one satisfactory solution is to present the subject findings, often highly technical and complex, in a report of about 7,000 words with minimal validation. The reader is left to decide what back-up information he needs; the evidence for any particular statement is provided as a report follow-up service. This has the inestimable advantage of not boring one group of readers with minutiae of interest only to another group. The disadvantages are that insofar as the report does not contain anything other than the results of the research it is incomplete as a document.

(c) *Logical ordering*

Logic in the context of report writing is that particular type of reasoning which results in the establishment of the facts and drawing conclusions from them. Here again there are no rules which will guide the researcher to a logical presentation; so much will depend upon the report's purpose. In one instance a time sequence will be the logical approach, dealing with for example the marketing history, the current position and the forecast. The same data can be presented as a series of segment reports which in some circumstances—for example where it will be read by product or area managers—is much more meaningful. Yet another approach is to give the conclusions baldly and without validation and separate out into different sections the supporting evidence, hypotheses used and the basis for any deductions which have been made.

If the purpose of the report is kept clearly in mind, that is the decisions which will flow from its acceptance, the logic will also become obvious.

(d) *Interpretation*

Researchers may be simply fact-finders or else may be both fact-finders and interpreters. Like the prophets, the latter not only see the signs but read the auguries in them. The research sponsors will certainly make their own interpretation and test it against that of the researchers, provided always that in the report the researchers have given the information necessary to check its validity—an aspect of reporting sometimes overlooked. A project that does not include interpretation of findings is, to say the least, only partly complete. The researcher has a considerable responsibility in relation to interpretation. No matter how well-founded the report may be, no one but the research leader will be in a position to see in one sweep the whole study from initiation to completion and the background to the various decisions that were taken on techniques, as well as the background to the acquisition of the facts. The interpretative function is thus a vital part of the researcher's work and should not be abrogated.

In interpretation it is necessary for the researcher to keep two objectives before him. First the relationship of the findings to the research objectives and, second, the translation of research findings into clear statements that lend themselves to easy and unequivocal assimilation by the reader. In compiling the report it is as well to remember that the reader has not been immersed for many weeks or perhaps months in the enquiry and will not have the same close familiarity with the subject as the researcher.

(e) *Presentation*

Packaging fulfils a role in industrial marketing research reports as it does in cosmetics. The practical aspects of report presentation require careful consideration and should not be regarded merely as tail-end activities which are frivolous and marginal to the stern stuff of research. Presentation is not trivial and cannot be left to the typist. Attractive layout and ease of handling pre-dispose the reader in favour of the report. Anything in the layout and make-up which tends to irritate the reader—small print, wrongly positioned charts, typing errors and inadequate binding, to name a few common errors —cannot fail to have repercussions on the reader's attitude to the report content. The researcher should make the reader's task as easy and indeed pleasurable as possible. Thus part of the researcher's job is to devise attractive, readable layout and highlight the major findings.

THE ANATOMY OF AN INDUSTRIAL MARKETING RESEARCH REPORT

There is one certain rule which can be adopted so far as the structure of any industrial marketing research report is concerned, namely that it should conform exactly to the structure of the accepted research design except where the research findings have indicated a change of order which has the sponsor's agreement. This at least saves the researcher the considerable time involved in preparing an outline or skeleton of the report—something which is recommended by all commentators and instructors in report writing. If the research design has been based on preliminary research and is sufficiently detailed, there ought to be no major deviation required and the various sub-headings will provide more than adequate guide lines. Reference to the list of headings in Chapter 4, 'Preparing for the Project', in the section on the Research Design gives a very typical ordering. In more detail, however, the report will take the following form:

Title page: This contains the agreed title and any subtitles, the name of the sponsor, the name of the researcher or his organisation, the date of the release of the report and the number of the copy. This last item is important for security reasons.

Contents page: A report ideally should be indexed. This means, however, the report must be completed up to and including pagination before the indexer can start work which involves a further delay while the index is compiled and then typed. Because of this time lapse indexes for reports are relatively rare. Failing an index, however, a detailed contents page is required to assist readers in rapidly identifying sections. It is normal to take the contents page details down to third sub-headings. That is, using decimal numbering, to the third digit, thus:

Section 5. COMPETITIVE CLIMATE

    5.1   *Frederick Trongle & Co. Ltd.*
    5.1.1 Sales Organisation
    5.1.2 Promotional methods
    5.1.3 Distributive network
    5.1.4 In-feeding
    5.1.5 Export performance
    5.1.6 Product range

5.2   *Anthony Edwards & Associates*
5.2.1 Sales Organisation
      etc.

The contents page can also include separately, lists of tables and illustrations. In deciding what should and should not go in a contents page, reference must be made to the likelihood of readers wishing to identify any specific item away from its context.

Terms of reference. The final agreed terms of reference should be restated, at least in a shortened form so that any readers who did not see them or were not part of the original discussions will know precisely what coverage was intended. By stating the terms of reference the researcher avoids the risk of criticisms of omissions which in fact were not included in the work as it was initiated. In giving the terms of reference they should be stated exactly as they were on the day the survey was authorised. Any amendments which might have been agreed during the survey should then be listed separately. Details of these amendments along with the person authorising them and the date of the change must be included.

Summary of Conclusions. This executive summary is the only page of the report many members of the management team may see, so it is vital to extract the most significant conclusions and state them clearly and briefly. The summary requires no explanation or validation; this is for the body of the report and for readers who require them. It is always useful to obtain assistance from the sponsors of the study in deciding which conclusions will be the most meaningful when considering a course of action.

The summary of conclusions is one way of dealing with the problem of variability in readers. It can be a simple five, ten or more point statement of the main findings covering the items in the original 'Objectives' or it can be an extended summary, depending upon the composition of the readership expected for the report.

Recommendations. It is usual for research sponsors to request the researchers, formally or informally, to express an opinion on the correct course of action to take based on their findings. These findings are, of course, only one element of the information 'mix' in decision-making. The researcher's recommendations can only be as good as his knowledge of the overall situation in relation both to the market and the internal organisation and resources of the firm. For obvious reasons the researcher should not be forced against his own judgement to declare himself unless management also make him a confidant to other information which he may not already possess.

For the outside agency to make recommendations can be hazardous in the extreme. The independent agency, more than the internal department, must be ignorant of whole sectors of the corporate economy, activities and politics. Nevertheless, external agencies are asked to produce recommendations with only the outward view of the situation and, in due course, are criticised when recommendations prove to be impracticable or unprofitable. No matter how many times the external researcher may point out that recommendations are based upon market knowledge and without information on the internal organisation and resources of the department or firm, this qualification will be forgotten in the resultant holocaust of failure.

Executive action and management decision should arise from all successful marketing research. The tasks of marketing management and other management begin where the researcher has left off. Frequently and perniciously, managements may act before the full report is delivered to them, and the greater the haste the worse the mistakes that can be made. There is certainly no use in sponsoring the market research survey and then taking action before the report is delivered, because in the course of the enquiry the management has learned some new relevant but limited facts. The report must be considered as a whole—though it may be found that only parts of the recommendations can be implemented—bearing in mind the problems of the firm.

To return to first principles, a marketing research exercise and therefore the recommendations it contains must have as its objective an amelioration in the operation of the firm; it must either increase margins, reduce costs or make possible the better and more efficient use of scarce resources.

Report. The main body of the report now follows and covers the headings already identified as the major research sectors. In a typical market size, structure, trend survey the main headings will include:

Current market
Market structure
Future market
User industry analysis
Competitive climate
Intermediaries (e.g. Original Equipment Manufacturers, Distributors,
    Agents)
Official factors

If the report were an image study the headings would differ considerably:

Composite image of the sponsor
Industry image reference
Awareness of and attitudes towards individual firms
Image of specified aspects of operation, products and personnel.

A multi-national study might follow yet another plan. Beginning with a composite report showing the major findings for the whole area researched, it would follow with a country-by-country breakdown, each area being divided into the relevant sub-sections such as those shown in the examples above. Another approach for a multi-national report to avoid emphasising and perpetuating the deficiencies of national, non-comparable statistics, is to prepare a study of the whole area and then to separate out the non-comparable material. This way all that can be compared is drawn together for interpretation and the exceptions offered separately. Detail within each section will of course vary between reports but should always be sufficient to provide all the information that the sponsor will need in his decision-making.

Whether or not the validation for any statement should be alongside it is both a matter of style and firms' internal practices. It is certainly usual after giving details and breakdowns of a market to explain how the figures were arrived at. This explanation will not only give the facts and the analytical method adopted, but also the steps in the interpretation which lead to the conclusions. Certainly where hypotheses have been used they will be stated at this juncture.

A calculation of the future market for protective devices for machine tools requires an assumption concerning the number of makes incorporating them, usage trends, technical changes in both the devices and the original equipment, the number required per machine during the original equipment's lifetime as well as the life expectancy of the machines themselves. Thus if a figure of 2·5 protective devices per machine during the machine life of 16 years is used as a basis of the calculation not only must these assumptions be stated but also the reasoning behind the adoption of what might seem to be arbitrary figures given. The assessment may have come from an analysis of postal questionnaires, it may represent technical experts' views, or it might be a correlation with some other data or have been derived from data obtained from a universe of original equipment manufacturers. If the report reader is to make his own assessment of validity and reliability of the base figures and subsequent calculations, all this information will be needed.

Once again, to meet the needs of a variable readership which will not be satisfied with the executive summary but is not interested in research methodology, a simple separation in the sections between the market findings and the method of calculation may solve the problem so long as the separate parts are indeed separate and headed as such. The reader seeking only quantitative data and prepared to accept their validity does not want to find himself reading several pages of additional material because there was no indication that no more market findings followed.

The main requirement for the body of the report is that, like the whole report, it should be logically ordered, that the facts given should be relevant to the research objectives and not just interesting in their own right, and that the deductive process should be clear-cut and simple to follow.

Appendices. These will comprise all the remaining related material which does not fall into the major headings already discussed. This information will include, for example, methodology, supplementary data, bibliographies, information sources, glossary of terms, catalogues and prices.

Other types of research information which might find their way into the appendix might be important matter yielded by the research but not specially investigated. For example, a survey of the demand for secondary species of Ghanaian timber in Europe indicated a basically unreceptive market. It did reveal, however, that there was a substantial current demand for carbon which could be made from the species and a long-term developing demand for silva chemicals. Neither product was envisaged as an outlet for timber in the original investigation which was confined to flooring, chipboard, joinery, construction and similar forest product consumption industries. All the additional data was thus contained in the Appendix, separated from that which was required by the Terms of Reference.

Methodological information in an industrial marketing research report will include the full statement of the research procedures and give the quantitative aspects of the research. That is, the sample design, tests of validity and reliability which were carried out, responses and copies of questionnaires. Where the survey is not a closed one (anonymous) it will sometimes be necessary to include names of respondents and their firms where permission has been received from them for these to be given.

Bibliographies in the reports, as in books, provide the reader with a quick and useful source of additional information. They will not often occur in industrial marketing research reports but when they do, appropriately they are placed in the Appendix. This also applies to glossaries but in some surveys it is more convenient to place glossaries or definitions at the beginning of a report to avoid mis-understandings, particularly when overseas readers are concerned. For example 'billion' to a French reader means 1,000,000,000 while to a reader in British industry it means 1,000,000,000,000. It is very necessary to define which 'billion' is used. Turnover will be taken to mean annual sales in Great Britain but capital turnover in the U.S.A.

Some reports may actually contain reproductions of other printed material, competitors' literature, journal features, specifications, maps and correspondence. These too are rightly Appendix material.

The best guide in deciding whether any particular piece of material goes in the Appendix is to assess if it would assist in the smooth flow of the narrative of the report or disrupt it. The major advantage of an Appendix is that it implies no obligation on the reader to study it.

COMMUNICATING THE RESULTS

The two outstanding communication characteristics of a good report might be described as 'readability' and 'viewability'. The former refers to the text and the latter the visual material.

Considerable research has been done on readability, mostly dealing with quantifiable factors—word frequency, number of words per sentence, poly-syllables per hundred words. Style, in the subjective sense, cannot be measured or assessed, it is something far too personal.

But even rules to attain good readability based upon the quantified factors will not necessarily achieve the impact that is required. The now famous 'Fog Index' as a measure of readability which purports to classify written material into an approximation of American school-grade levels of reading difficulty is based upon certain often unjustified assumptions about the reader. The twenty words or less per sentence desideratum can easily lead to monotony, jerkiness in the narrative and the inevitable consequences which a self-conscious contraction can bring about. It only requires an adult's view of children's early reading books to appreciate how boring and indeed ludicrous such a method of writing would be, even though it meets the 'Fog' criterion.

The dangers of adopting either an aseptic depersonalised style which inevitably results from a too slavish compliance with all the rules of 'good report writing' or the over-adjectivised dramatisation of the frustrated novelist forced into report writing, are likely to be avoided if the style most acceptable to the reader is adopted.

It is difficult to formulate precise rules of good report writing which would receive general acceptance. It is not difficult, however, to highlight a number of common errors which can mitigate against acceptability. If these are not avoided the results will be misunderstandings, cynicism and hostility.

● Failure to express precisely what is meant—ambiguous statements.

● Lack of 'flow' in the narrative.

● Failure to take a posture—over-qualification of statements as an insurance policy against being wrong.

● Over-elaborate sentence structures which are difficult to follow.

● Mechanical flaws—spelling mistakes, incorrect grammar and calculations and typographical errors.

● Too much inaccurate, illogical or irrelevant cross-referencing.

● Incorrect positioning of charts and tables.

● Meaningless headings and sub-headings.

● Lack of purposeful organisation in the report.

● Use of unfamiliar words.

The last point is perhaps the one which causes greatest criticism. The recommendation that report writers should use words with which the readers will be familiar but which will provide variety and change of pace to the report is sound advice indeed. 'The prime purpose of the report is to communicate the results of the study—not to impress the reader with the erudition of the writer.'[1]

It cannot be said that jargon should not be used because it is not commonplace. Jargon, however deprecatory the nuance, is a convenient form of shorthand for anyone who is familiar with the subject. Thus for a report to be read by marketing researchers there is no reason whatsoever for not referring to 'sampling frames' or 'skew distribution'. If, however, the readership is to be wider than just marketing researchers, obviously these terms, if they are to be used, will require definition. Those who complain loudest about 'jargon' are generally only complaining about the use of jargon and trade terms they themselves do not use.

[1] *Marketing Research: Texts and Cases*, op. cit., p. 571.

The advice to choose simple rather than complex words and the familiar rather than the unfamiliar word completely embraces the policy to adopt in relation to jargon.[1] If the so-called jargon word is simple and familiar it should be used. One word of warning is necessary, however. The shorthand words of the industry or activity should not be confused with slang words or colloquialisms which will create an impression of superficiality and indeed frivolity. While it is completely acceptable to talk about 'software' in relation to systems, it would not be appropriate to use such phrases as 'a bucket of worms' to describe a circuit diagram or to use school or Service slang such as 'gen' for 'information'.

For the sophisticated reader the report can be sophisticated in content and style and will be regarded as a recognition of his ability to assimilate it. The less well-informed (on the subject being re-searched) will require a simpler explanation and will accordingly be grateful for it. Once again the risk of appearing either patronising with over-simplifications or unnecessarily obscure can only be avoided by having some foreknowledge of the types of readers for whom the report is intended.

A report must be an accurate description of the total project but it is a fact of life that the researchers will have to make efforts to gain its acceptance. Report writing can be likened to the 'empathy' attribute of the salesman and marketing research interviewer. An empathy with the reader will prevent the introduction of nuances which can predispose the reader against the report. If, for example criticisms have to be made they must appear as criticisms, but gratuitous insults are not likely to assist the acceptance of the report. 'It is obvious that the basic skills which are totally lacking must be acquired,' can hardly be expected to receive a rapturous welcome by many of those to whom the deficiency is attributed. 'The basic skills for these developments must be acquired,' conveys exactly the same thought without being likely to arouse the same reactions since it has not 'written off' the possibility of other, if not necessarily appropriate, skills being possessed. Findings and recommendations which are unpalatable to some sections of a management may be criticised by them on totally different grounds in order to destroy the credibility of the report as a whole. Thus while the report must be wholly truthful and accurate, it must nevertheless very often be made acceptable to management if it is to become the action document which was intended.

Report writers are usually urged to write objectively and indeed

[1] A. B. Sklare, *Creative Report Writing*, McGraw-Hill (New York, 1964), p. 100.

this advice should be followed when the researcher is reporting his findings and not his opinions. Thus in respect of the findings, the methods of the research and the analyses, it is necessary that objectivity should be sought and conveyed. Where, however, the researcher is giving an opinion or an interpretation or applying 'best judgement', objectivity ceases to be desirable. This does imply a somewhat harsh change of style but, just as the transitional questions or statements in interviewing can be used to bridge a difficult gap and assist the respondent's thought process, a change from the impersonal to the personal pronoun can be used deliberately to break up a thought process, reducing the halo effect of previous statements. The change from objective to subjective can thus provide an additional indication to the reader that the standpoint of the reporter has changed.

Writing in the passive voice is claimed to indicate greater objectivity than the use of the personal pronoun. Whether this objectivity is real or pseudo depends not only on the writer but the viewpoint of the reader. While some readers will find a report which includes a good sprinkling of self-effacing 'it is apparent that', 'while there is no evidence to show', 'it was noted during the research', 'in the opinion of the researcher', 'the writer received similar indications from . . .' boring and coy, a fulsome sprinkling of 'I's' can build up an omnipotent image of the researcher which may readers will take great pleasure in destroying.

There can be no hard and fast rule for any aspect of style. The needs of the readers are paramount but the report writer cannot be expected to so alter his style and method so as to make his final submission totally objectionable to himself. No research project is better than the report which presents the findings. The report itself will have been envisaged from the beginning of the project. The allocation of the research project to the researchers will have certainly taken into account their talents both in the field and at at the desk, and their compatibility with the readers. If it has, then differences in the style, provided the basic rules of good report writing are observed, should cause little difficulty.

TABLES

Inevitably reports which are concerned with quantifications of any sort will require tables. These cannot, and indeed the researchers should not want them to be avoided. What a table conveys can rarely be communicated in writing in any detail with the same precision, although they can usually be summarised adequately. The effectiveness of a table depends entirely on its arrangement and titling.

Like the text itself, tables should be as simple and as attractive as possible and still present the data in a way to make the evidence they contain obvious and easy to assimilate. The clarity of a report is enhanced if tables in the text are confined to those essential for an understanding of the report. All others can be more conveniently grouped in an appendix and cross-referenced in the report. Although it is not always possible, tables should be presented next to the first reference to them. If they happen to be long and complex it may be better to include a summarisation table at the point of reference and the full table in the Appendix. The main points for consideration in table construction are ordering, titling, ruling or format, spacing and structure.

The order of tables, whether it is alphabetical, chronological, numerical or any other designation should be obvious. For quick cross-referencing the sequence should be easy to follow and identify.

Each table requires a fully descriptive title of what it is intended to convey and, where relevant, the date of the compilation. It is vital to indicate what the figures represent (for example, 'establishments', 'visits', 'entries') and the unit and quantity of measurement (for example, 'dollars' '000', 'ton/miles'). Percentage bases must always be given. It is usual to quote sources including those generated by the research itself (for example, 'Source: Postal Questionnaire').

The format of a table is important. The eye can follow a vertical column of figures more easily than a horizontal line, particularly a horizontal line broken up by vertical rulings. The exclusion of rulings should always be considered and where the same effect can be achieved by spacing, they should be omitted.

The use of different type faces or colour can heighten the interest of a table, emphasise key data and relegate secondary data. By breaking up the monotony of a regular type face it is possible to present considerably more data in a table without significant loss of clarity or impact. The tables should of course be in large enough type to make reading easy.

HEADINGS, FOOTNOTES, ACKNOWLEDGEMENTS

Headings, footnotes, and acknowledgements all have a role to play in report writing and make the task of the reader very much simpler if they are used correctly.

On completion of a first draft every heading should be listed. This will immediately reveal if the headings are correct and meaningful, or if the material is illogically ordered or the report subject inadequately covered. At this stage these types of error can be corrected.

Headings and sub-headings not only serve as signposts to the report but provide a visual break on the page and prevent monotony. A glance at any newspaper or journal will show the importance placed on headings and sub-headings of all types. However, they should not be used as they often are in journals, merely to break up the page, being often meaningless in themselves. Too many headings are as ineffectual as too few.

Footnotes should be used with care. It is tiring and irritating to have to constantly refer to the bottom of a page or a separate list at the end of a report for information which relates to the body of a report. Footnotes are most often used for reference sources and as such are legitimate; as explanations to textual material they are less frequently justified. Critical consideration should be given to all footnotes to ensure that they cannot in fact be incorporated into the text without disturbing the flow of the report. Footnotes should always be used sparingly and presented with brevity.

A device for incorporating important but not directly related material is the use of 'boxes'. That is, secondary material is shown in a box actually set in the text. An example from a Stanford Research Institute Long Range Planning report will be found in Figure 29. This method has the advantage of keeping the material close to the text to which it is related but gives the reader the option of passing over it. Unlike the footnote, it does not drag the reader's eyes down from the top or middle of the page to the bottom and then force him back to find the part of the text to which it is related and to resume his train of thought. The 'box' can be taken in with the sweep of the eye and the decision to read it or pass it can be made without breaking up a train of thought.

Acknowledgements and other documentation, although often glossed over in marketing research reports, are a moral requirement and reproduction invokes legal obligations. External sources should be acknowledged either in the text or as a footnote using the methods generally adopted in books and which the footnotes of this book exemplify.

The first reference should contain the author's name, the full and correct title of the source, place and date of publication and page number(s) where the original which is quoted can be found. Later references to the same source can be in shortened form such as *op cit* (*opere citato*—in the work quoted) followed by the page number. If high performance plastics will be the major components of this growth.

Stimulated partly by improved coating materials and better application methods, surface coating expenditures will reach about $1.5 billion annually by 1975, up from $1.1 billion at present. This prospective increase — about 35% — is comparatively modest, partially because of emphasis on competitive corrosion control methods.

LET IT RUST?

The "Let It Rust" school has support based on several practical considerations. First, the rusting piece of equipment may already be fully depreciated and written off. Replacement or repair may have its most obvious effect on the debit side of an expense ledger. Further, the economic advantage of measures taken to control corrosion may not be predictable (particularly in the marine and process industries). In addition, rapid obsolescence may encourage a *laissez-faire* attitude toward corrosion.

Tax considerations also encourage the "Let It Rust" philosophy. It is sometimes cheaper to continue replacing a corroding item rather than to install a corrosion resistant substitute. This is particularly true when cost of replacement, for tax purposes, is considered an operating expense fully deductible in the year the expenditure is made. On the other hand, a resistant substitute may be considered an investment in capital equipment that must be depreciated over a long, useful life.

Among developments running contrary to the "Let It Rust" tendency are increases in the costs of down time and labor. These make corrosion more costly and narrow the circumstances in which the lack of control measures will be economic. Changes in tax regulations could also have an important effect.

Inhibitor sales — aided by the development of new agents and growing realization of the savings they offer — may double by 1975 to $200 million yearly. Because inhibitors are themselves expensive, however, they will lose out in some instances to corrosion resistant materials.

Sales of electrochemical anticorrosion systems could rise from roughly $25 million currently to $75 million or more by 1975. Cathodic systems, now accounting for the bulk of electrochemical system sales, will remain the most important as advances in applications technology broaden their commercial usefulness. Relatively more spectacular advances will occur in anodic passivation systems, which are just reaching the commercial stage; these will probably represent $5 million in sales during the early 1970s.

Removal of corrosive materials from the environment will continue to be a significant means of corrosion control but will probably do little more than "hold its own" during the coming decade. The newer techniques — for example, use of industrial enzymes to remove oxygen from packages — may gain in special applications.

GENERAL IMPACTS ON USERS

Users of corrosion control materials and methods have previously depended heavily on suppliers for innovations, but competitive self-

Fig. 29

(EXTRACT FROM A LONG-RANGE PLANNING REPORT
OF THE STANFORD RESEARCH INSTITUTE SHOWING
THE USE OF A TEXTUAL BOX)

the second reference immediately follows the first and is in the same work and on the same page *ibid* (*ibidem*—in the same book, chapter or passage) is an accepted form.

It is always useful to append a Bibliography where sources are not specifically quoted but provide a general background. Bibliographies by and large are more useful if grouped under subject headings rather than alphabetically.

VISUAL AIDS

Many studies of memory have shown that the retention of information and impressions is very considerably higher when they are conveyed both visually and orally rather than either on their own. A study conducted by the Socony-Vacuum Oil Company showed that using speech alone after 3 hours only 70 per cent recall occurred while after 3 days the residual recall was as low as 10 per cent. Visual communication showed a 72 per cent recall after 3 hours and 20 per cent after 3 days. A combination of both methods produced 85 per cent recall after 3 hours and 65 per cent after 3 days. This very conclusive result bears out numerous other studies in the field of communication. There is little doubt that apart from improving the appearance and focusing attention, the use of visual methods of presentation is an extremely efficient way of communication research results.

The standard methods of illustration only require summarisation since they are well-known. These are:

Charts of various types which are generally used to depict quantities. Typical of this group are plain and pictorial bar and pie charts.

Diagrams which are adopted to show effects or mechanics, for example organisational charts and flow charts.

Maps are of course used to indicate location but they can also be used statistically both by differentiation in colour or shading or by distortion to show relationships. Figure 30 illustrates this last type.

Graphs are the commonest and often the most useful form of visual presentation in a report to depict in a concrete form the abstract ideas embodied in numerals.

Other illustrative methods include pictorial diagrams, schematic diagrams, various types of drawings (isometric, orthographic, perspective and exploded line) and photographs. All of these can often be used to make a point more tellingly than the written word.

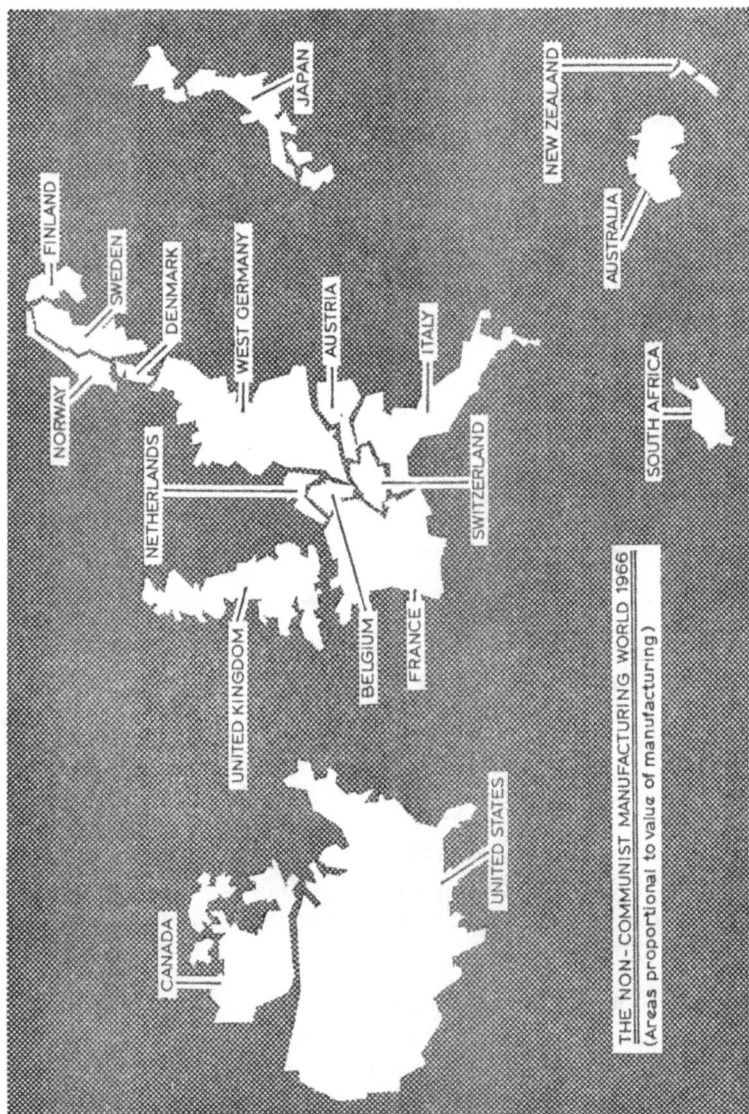

Fig. 30

PROPORTIONALLY DISTORTED MAP

CANADA

UNITED KINGDOM

NORWAY

FINLAND

SWEDEN

DENMARK

WEST GERMANY

AUSTRIA

ITALY

NETHERLANDS

BELGIUM

FRANCE

SWITZERLAND

UNITED STATES

JAPAN

NEW ZEALAND

AUSTRALIA

SOUTH AFRICA

THE NON-COMMUNIST MANUFACTURING WORLD 1966
(Areas proportional to value of manufacturing)

But the use of illustration does not automatically guarantee clarity, unambiguousness or emphasis. Many illustrations, whatever form they take, are duller than the written description and sometimes more obscure. To turn a mass of figures quickly into intelligible data with emphasis on key factors takes imagination and skill. The most frequent mistake, however, is to attempt to transfer all the data into a single chart or else to depict the findings in a manner which makes no more impact than the figures themselves.

HEAT CONTENT OF AIRCRAFT FUELS

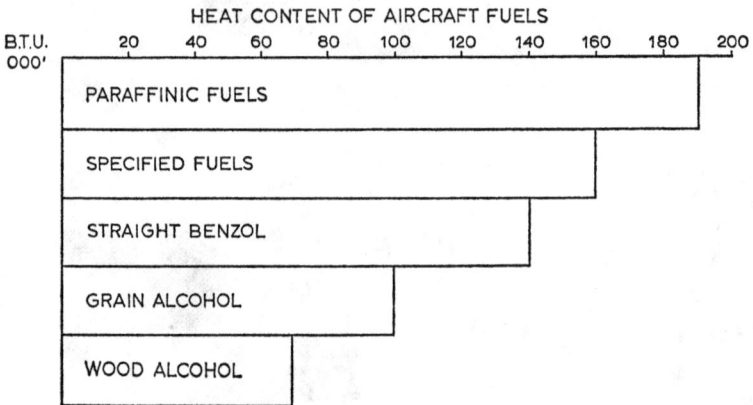

Fig. 31
HEAT CONTENT OF AIRCRAFT FUELS

The above chart accurately illustrates a finding but lacks impact. Re-interpreted the salient facts can be drawn out even from the most cursory study, as Figure 32[1] clearly shows, and which was originally printed with the exhaust lines in red.

A check list of points to be considered in introducing and using illustrative material will quickly reveal conceptual and mechanical errors.

● What is the objective of the visual?

● Is the point worth making? Is it essential to the understanding of the report—does it assist comprehension or does it merely repeat what has been written?

● Has the subject been chosen because it adds to the comprehensibility and emphasis, or because it is easy to illustrate?

[1] C. Hardesty, *Making More Effective Graphic Presentations*, Industrial Education International (London, 1966).

● Will the emphasis given by the use of graphics be out of proportion to the balance of emphasis in the text?

● Does the text give an additional meaning to the visual?

● Has the visual a unity and is it free from incompatible ideas?

● Has the reaction of the reader been considered and are the symbols meaningful to him?

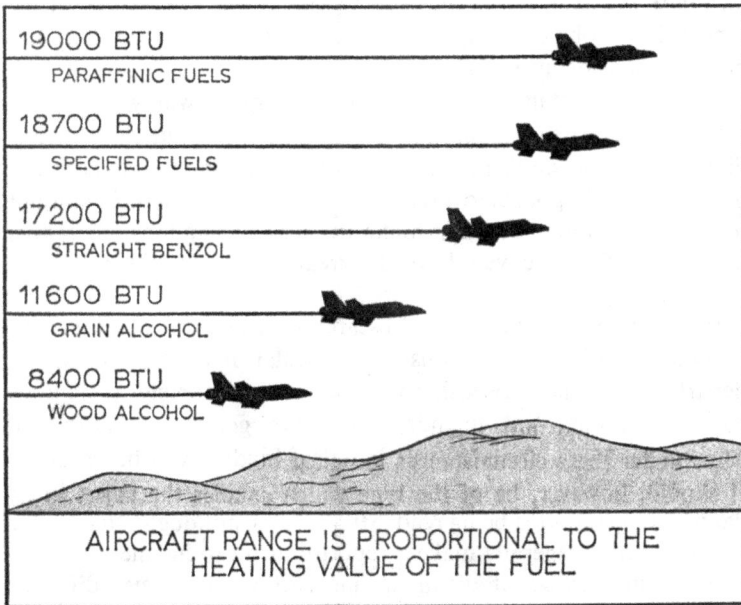

19000 BTU
PARAFFINIC FUELS
18700 BTU
SPECIFIED FUELS
17200 BTU
STRAIGHT BENZOL
11600 BTU
GRAIN ALCOHOL
8400 BTU
WOOD ALCOHOL

AIRCRAFT RANGE IS PROPORTIONAL TO THE HEATING VALUE OF THE FUEL

Fig. 32
HEAT CONTENT OF AIRCRAFT FUELS

● How many separate ideas does it combine? Are they clearly separable?

● Does it reveal the facts in an unbiased way? Is there any unconscious element of distortion caused, for example, by the scales used?

● Is it completely readable?

● Has the legend been given? Is it understandable?

● Was the artwork designed for the printed medium or adapted from some other medium?

● Would it be more effective if colour were used?

The use of visual material is of very considerable value to support the text but it does not in any way compensate for weaknesses in textual material nor should it be used to conceal poor reporting.

MAKE-UP

The actual physical make-up of a report is an important aspect of presentation that often belies the amount of work that has gone into both the project and the report writing. The appearance of the report is of obvious importance in assisting its acceptance but practical considerations must not be forgotten.

The life expectancy of the report document will govern how substantial covers, binding and paper must be. Thin card covers, flimsy paper and stapled binders do not usually stand up to constant or rough handling. Moreover, covers pick up a considerable amount of dirt and staining and can make the task of handling the report unpleasant. Plastic covers have the great advantage of being easily cleaned.

It is also very useful to some research sponsors to be able to split a report to circulate sections of particular relevance to various departments without releasing the whole report, or else to remove confidential data not intended for more general consumption. Thus under these circumstances looseleaf binding will be required. It should, however, be of the type which enables the pages to lie flat when the report is being read. Stud fittings, although often neater in appearance, generally make a report difficult to handle.

A useful method of distinguishing sections is to use different tinted papers. It enables readers to identify specific parts of a report. For example, if all the factual evidence in each section is on one colour and the methodology on another, this will save referring back to the contents page.

The report from the moment it is presented in its pristine state up until the time it is removed from the archives and destroyed will be the image of the researcher and the research. If this thought is kept in mind in devising presentations there is every likelihood it will do justice to the research and the researcher long after it has ceased to be anything more than of academic or historical interest.

ORAL PRESENTATIONS

It is usual, after the research sponsors have had time to consider the report, for a presentation meeting to take place at which the research team can be interrogated on the report's contents and asked for further explanations.

Although these meetings may be highly informal and possibly only involve the sponsor and researcher, on occasions they will be more akin to a lecture with the researcher facing a largely passive audience. To a skilled public speaker this presents no problems but to the unskilled and nervous an oral presentation can be an unpleasant ordeal. Under such circumstances it is not surprising that excellent reports are unappreciated and much first-class material is lost.

An agenda should always be circulated in advance so that both speakers and audience can know what is expected of them. Sponsors should submit their major points in writing in advance and the researchers should then answer these. This gives the researchers an opportunity to consider their replies and to re-work any material which is necessary. It also makes sure that time is not wasted perusing marginal or unimportant aspects in depth, because it is not known by those attending the meeting which important points remain to be discussed.

At the presentation meeting many sponsors will expect the researchers to give a résumé of the report findings and methodology. The researchers are then questioned on specific aspects of concern to the individuals attending the meeting.

Alternatively or additionally, it is not unusual to go through the report document page by page, everyone present raising any points or queries they may have as they are reached. This type of approach is notorious for taking about 80 to 90 per cent of the time available to cover the first few pages and then the remainder of the report has to be concentrated into only ten or twenty per cent of the time available.

The use of visual aids will materially assist an oral presentation in the same manner as they aid the comprehensibility of the report itself. Very often the same graphics can be made to serve the double purpose although transfer from one medium to another can be less than effective. Flip boards, overhead projectors, 35 mm slide projectors, blackboards, flannel and velcro boards can all be used to add interest to the meeting and to hold the attention of listeners. For oral presentations it is possible to use free-hand drawings and graphs and touches of humour, and a generally 'humanising' effect will greatly assist the acceptance of the report.

The rules for attaining the mastery of any audience apply equally to oral presentation meetings. The presenter must make every effort to be at ease and to be natural. He must introduce variety into the presentation. Apologies rarely receive the sympathy they are supposedly made to obtain. Reading should be avoided at all costs. This is incompatible with the very necessary quality of 'expertness' the researcher must project if he is to obtain the confidence of his audience.

The best of speakers, however, can sometimes fail to prevent oral presentation meetings from deteriorating into a display of internal politics when they should be a constructive inter-management consultation. Any marketing research report that overtly or covertly suggests a change is certain to meet opposition of a more intense type than one which leads to a conclusion that no change need be made. Change itself is a threat and in any event is regarded by many as a less comfortable situation than a continuation with the old methods, products, customers or techniques. For this reason the marketing researcher may find himself fiercely attacked by the protagonists of the *status quo*. It is necessary for him to be absolutely sure of the research techniques, the findings and the interpretation, as any weaknesses can and will be seized upon under such circumstances to discredit the report and thus the recommendations for the changes. A marketing research report can be used as a justification for a long desired course of action, as an excuse for no action, or as a 'hatchet job' for finding a scapegoat.

Consequently the marketing researcher will sometimes be in the centre of an internal political storm and it would be eschewing the realities of the business situation as it is today in large and small firms to pretend that all management teams are of such quality that research reports are always treated objectively, on their merits. The facts of corporate life are otherwise, and most experienced marketing researchers are ready enough to concede this point. An understanding of, and a feeling for, internal strengths, dispositions biases—not to play one off against the other but to make the presentation in the most acceptable manner—can be an inestimable advantage. There must nevertheless be no move away from objectivity and truthfulness to which all reports must conform.

The presentation meeting is generally the last action the researcher will take on a report unless he is called upon to revise a forecast, make adjustments to take account of changed conditions or otherwise modify it. The meeting ought therefore to be attended by all the researchers whose special knowledge of any aspect of the research will contribute to the discussion. Similarly, all relevant working papers must be available for immediate reference. Points which cannot be cleared at the meeting should be investigated as soon as possible afterwards. Subsequently a supplementary report or clarification note must be sent to all those present at the meeting who required the information or, if necessary, a further meeting should be called.

RE-USE OF MATERIAL

The final report which after the meeting will have become a document for appropriate sections of the firm, never ceases to be a child of the research department.

Once the report is accepted all the working papers which are ever likely to be of further use require classification and then filing to form the back-up of the report itself. The title of each document filed should be included in classified lists of the research material so that it is possible to identify what the back-up contains without going through all the papers.

If it is intended to monitor or up-date the report, then the method of classifying and sorting the back-up material will require adjustment. In any event, since today's report is an item in tomorrow's bibliographical research, it is always worthwhile recording any major changes which might occur. These can probably be most conveniently recorded on a copy of the report kept specifically for that purpose. Regular monitoring, however, will mean adding additional material to the files and classification lists and, if the back-up is not to become unmanageable, culling the files regularly to remove papers which are no longer required or which are replaced by updated material.

A study by National Cash Register Company suggested that much additional value could be obtained from original research if it could be adapted to provide information on a closely related project. A saving of about twenty-five per cent on the original research might be achieved on average. If, however, the original data could be combined with other results then it is likely a new research project could be completed for half the original cost. Finally, if it is possible to make direct reference to a report or its back-up material for the information required, the cost of the later survey is likely to achieve an economy of seventy-five per cent over the original research appropriation. This example highlights the very great value to be obtained from the re-use of material.

SURVEY INQUEST

Because of the essentially one-off nature of many industrial marketing research reports, it is a most useful exercise to evaluate the research procedure after each report is completed. It is also useful for the researchers to compile a check list of questions which can be asked after each survey is completed. An outline list would include the following questions:

- Could the same results have been achieved more cheaply or quickly by other means?

- Could accuracy tolerances have been improved by the adoption of other or additional methods?

- Did the later phases of research reveal secondary sources which ought to have been identified in the early stages?

- Would a phased approach have permitted the project to be terminated sooner?

- Was the sampling method satisfactory?

- Was the sample too small or too large?

- Could the sample source lists have been improved?

- Was the analytical technique correct?

- Could the analyses have been carried out more effectively (cost-time) by machine/hand methods?

- Was the research team of the right composition, calibre and background for the tasks they were allotted?

- Were the D.M.U. correctly identified?

- Did the hypotheses in the original phases prove to be accurate?

- If not, could the inaccuracies have been identified at an earlier moment?

- Were the check lists sufficiently precise? If not, could they have been made more precise at the outset?

A critical examination of the survey methods on these and other points will reveal not only methods of improving future research but any basic recurrent weaknesses in the research department and its organisation.

This, however, begs the question of whether the research methods, irrespective of their effectiveness, achieved the research objectives. A critical appraisal of the total project is also a very necessary activity. Chapter 15 discusses evaluating the research results.

CHAPTER 15

'Make or Buy' in Marketing Research

The growing use and acceptance of industrial marketing research has led to a rapid increase both in the numbers of firms with industrial marketing research departments or employing industrial marketing researchers, and also the number of agencies offering industrial marketing research services. These increases have permitted a great deal of specialisation inside firms and among agencies and have also resulted in users of industrial marketing research being faced with a proliferation of services of varying degrees of exoticism. Today firms have not only to make such basic decisions as whether to create and operate their own marketing research departments or to purchase research from outside; they must also decide between the employment of researchers of various types, the specialisations of different agencies, and the combinations which are appropriate from working with both inside and external personnel simultaneously.

It is clear that while there are circumstances which make the use of an external researcher appropriate, this does not automatically exclude simultaneous use of the internal researcher. For a company with no research department the decision to 'make or buy' can be materially assisted by using certain criteria (discussed on pages 340–3) against which to compare the alternative situation. The position is, however, complicated by the fact that in setting up an internal organisation it is usually impossible to create such a section complete in every respect, as can be done with a production unit. It is both possible, and feasible, to evolve a department and to shape it exactly to the emerging circumstances of the firm's requirements. An industrial marketing research department has to be planned like any other business activity. From a point of no research, setting up a department will almost invariably follow the purchasing of external research which it ultimately replaces or controls.

Indeed the extent of sophistication within the firm is an important determinant of when to use marketing research and whether or not it is desirable to establish an internal section. It is top management which gives the lead; if the firm's managers want to have recourse to additional facts and information, both to audit performance and/or aid the planning functions, as well as explore market potentials, test products or check on advertising efficiency, then in due course the need for an internal marketing research section is likely to ensue. As soon as this need for information supplemental to existing sales data is felt, the necessity to have someone to provide a flow of information can be taken as the forerunner of establishing an internal section, if only for the reason of auditing the outside agency's work, interpreting the firm's requirements to the agency and explaining the agency's reports to the firm.

It would be idle to pretend that every sizeable or large firm needs the facilities of an internal marketing research department. Nevertheless, the broad marketing and, in a sense, marketing research function cannot be abrogated; it has to be performed by someone. In the small firm this person may be the entrepreneur himself or the sales or marketing manager. In the medium-size firm, and particularly in the large firm, marketing and marketing research will tend to become more specialist functions.

THE WORK LOAD

The volume and type of research to be undertaken is the most significant factor for consideration in deciding to set up an internal department. All other factors such as anonymity, the need to achieve complete objectivity, the existence of special skills or resources and the reasons for conducting research are not on their own inputs for a go, no-go decision on setting up a department. To meet these latter criteria the combination of internal-external research can often produce better results than either method on its own.

Past use of research services, expected departmental demands, the likelihood of external developments within markets, competitors' activities and the need for marketing and economic intelligence engendered by the growth of the firm, are all guides to anticipated work loads. A research department will, however, tend to generate its own work inasmuch as an intelligent researcher working in the interests of his firm can always see useful and profitable sources of employment for his skills. It is a characteristic of marketing research departments that they generate a two-way flow of ideas. For every research idea that emanates from management in the firm, the marketing research department can generally match it with another. In some of the largest organisations, with fully equipped and staffed marketing research departments, it has been found that half of the research department's time is occupied by research sponsored on its own initiative and that this research is often more relevant than that which is initiated by other departments in the firm.

The difficulty of optimising the work-load is the problem of maximum demand for services and minimum staff for efficient operation. Control of growth can engender a smooth build-up. Uncontrolled growth not only produces the research philosophy and techniques which are basically just staggering from one crisis to another—it is the antithesis of good project planning and execution.

OTHER CRITERIA

Another useful guide to the possible establishment of an internal department—irrespective of whether or not the firm already uses an outside marketing research agency—are *commercial factors* prevalent in an industry. Rapidly growing firms, rapidly developing products and growing competition within an industry are conditions usually requiring extensive use of marketing research by the firm and for the earlier rather than later establishment of internal marketing research sections. It cannot be said that organisations selling into markets which are highly concentrated such as to computer manufacturers, have less informational needs than those selling into widely dispersed markets. The requirements of the former are often of a nature which allows their needs to be met most economically by using external research organisations, perhaps with a higher degree of specialisation.

Size of an operation is not necessarily significant. Firms with a turnover as low as £250,000 per annum have found it profitable to employ a researcher while companies with turnovers running into many millions of pounds have found it equally satisfactory to make use of an industrial marketing research agency to satisfy all their information requirements. Information needs will vary both in content and frequency depending on the types of markets firms are operating in. Markets subject to only slow change, such as sea freighting, obviously require less surveillance than the highly volatile electronics industry.

The *method of operation* is another determinant in a 'make or buy' situation. Intermediaries in the industrial distribution channels only rarely believe that it is their responsibility to probe the user markets. Such activities, they consider, are more suited to the suppliers' role. There is some justification for this view because although probing their customer requirements, practices and attitudes could benefit intermediaries very considerably, their control of many of the factors necessary to meet their customers' wishes is limited. This is because they are, for the most part, in their suppliers' hands so far as products are concerned.

The *method of organisation* will also condition decisions to undertake research internally. It is not always economic for a division or subsidiary of a firm to undertake its own research perhaps duplicating the work taking place in another part of the organisation. The opposite can apply equally. The parent company may maintain a small advisory industrial marketing research unit but leave the research to be undertaken by the subisdiary or divisional unit acting under the general guidance of the central unit.

The *disposition of management* is a very clear signal as to whether a research department should operate. The concept of the role management wants research to play has a considerable influence on its company-wide acceptance. There is little point in setting up a department that does not have management's support. For the management which does not believe in research, research is a very costly activity indeed.

If the circumstance of the firm in relation to the criterion outlined are such as not to warrant setting up an internal department or employing an industrial marketing researcher, then the decision must be either not to do research, to undertake it on an amateurish unskilled basis, or to purchase industrial marketing research services.

THE EVOLUTION OF A RESEARCH DEPARTMENT

Initially a firm which has not carried out industrial marketing research projects would be advised to commission the work it requires from an *independent* agency *specialising* in industrial marketing research. The importance of *independence* and of *specialisation* cannot be over-emphasised and is dealt with at some length later in this chapter.

An experienced agency can without difficulty carry out the entire process of defining the problem, devising the brief, drawing up the research design and terms of reference, setting up the project, carrying out the work and guiding management towards the correct recommendations and their implementation, in fact all the internal department would do if it existed. By entrusting the agency with the overall responsibility for the project, the firm is saved from the danger and expense of making a marketing research appointment while still not yet being in a position to appreciate the marketing research needs and the type of researcher required to meet them.

The next stage of the plan is for the firm to appoint a suitably qualified marketing research executive to be responsible for the marketing research requirements of the firm. This is a key appointment because the researcher is generally the nucleus of the section to be built. The amount of research one researcher can undertake on his own is limited and the purpose of this first appointment is mainly to liaise between the firm and marketing research agencies. The researcher's function is to appreciate the research requirements of the firm and to translate them into research terms for the agency. At this stage the brief can be written for the agency and the agency's research designs can be checked, modified and adjusted by the internal researcher. At the end of the project the internal researcher is the arbiter for the firm on the satisfactory completion of the research assignment.

Such liaison work does not, of course, preclude the researcher from carrying out simultaneously other valuable work for the firm—including advising management on where research can help to solve problems, preparing regular intelligence reports, laying the groundwork for a full marketing research section and undertaking some types of research enquiries. As the section builds up with research assistants, statisticians, specialists of various types and in various subjects, the need for the outside agency can diminish. At this stage a new pattern of internal department-agency relationships is established.

In some instances the company research section assumes the major initiative in designing and interpreting research projects and delegates the routine research tasks to external agencies. Between one extreme of the internal section only acting as liaison and the other of conducting all but routine work which is contracted out, there are infinite variations, any one of which can be justified by prevailing circumstances. As an internal section enlarges, so do the research needs of the firm and vice versa. As a result the need for outside agencies does not necessarily tend to diminish.

Surveys of industrial marketing research in the United Kingdom and the United States show that if anything, the amount of commissioned work increases as internal departments are set up and develop. It is certainly the experience of the leading industrial marketing research agencies in the United Kingdom that their most important clients, in terms of research appropriations, are sizeable firms with internal departments. In other words, the need for research, the value of research and opportunities for the profitable use of research are perceived more easily and quickly by firms with research units than those without.

ORGANISATION—THE INTERNAL DEPARTMENT

Before an internal marketing research section is established management must decide to whom this new section is to report. In practical terms there are only two possible areas in which it can operate successfully and efficiently. These are either by allocating responsibility for the marketing research department to general management or to marketing management.

To make the marketing research department responsible to some line aspect of marketing—for example advertising or selling—is bad organisational practice. The marketing researcher should not be made responsible to any person or department upon whose activities, however obliquely, he may have to report. Moreover, by placing marketing research in this relationship its activities will be restricted by its very lack of prestige and status.

A useful screen for assisting in decision making in relation to the location of a marketing research department has been suggested.[1] This screen requires the consideration of the scope of research activities, the level of acceptance of research within the firm, the efficiency of the research operation and research quality, special company characteristics, the stature of research and, finally, the use of the results. Overall, the consideration of these factors tends to lead to the view that general management is the most appropriate place for the department to report to, although in practice, and perhaps for understandable reasons, the majority of marketing research departments report to marketing management.

Once established the internal marketing research unit will want to show its appetite for work. It is at this stage that it often begins to store up trouble for itself. A plethora of work may delay the completion of reports on time and soon the inevitable cry for additional staff will be heard. If the work load increases too fast and the build-up is too rapid, the criticisms of mounting overheads will be made, especially from those quarters which marketing research has placed under scrutiny.

In a large industrial organisation the marketing research function once accepted is likely to be divided into several autonomous or semi-autonomous parts. In such firms several groups or usually divisions

[1] A. B. Blankenship and J. B. Doyle, *Marketing Research Management*, American Management Association (New York, 1965), pp. 65-71.

exist, each manufacturing widely divergent product groups or providing services even if they loosely form parts of the same industry.
Some of the divisions or groups of giant companies are indeed
sufficiently large to rank as major companies in their own right.
Given such a situation, efficient marketing research from the centre is
an unattainable objective. Economic research, the interpretation of
national and industry statistics, however, can be performed from a
central section. Marketing research for the wide variety of products
made by the several divisions of subsidiaries of a large company
cannot be successful unless the research work is restricted to the
continuous examination, and that from a distance, of a very narrow
range of output. No marketing research section in the firm can be
all things to all people. The cardinal rule for successful industrial
marketing research must be for its practitioners to be in close
touch with line management and to live as near the product as
possible.

But the accountability of the divisional marketing research section
for its efficient functioning does not stop there. Peripheral marketing
research sections must have access to the central section for advice.
The central section may well have several functions in relation to the
divisional marketing research departments. It is part of their function
to be familiar with the latest techniques and to be aware of experimentation which is occurring. They should be able to assist divisional
departments to prepare briefs for the external commissioning of
research, advise on suitable agencies for specific assignments, make
recommendations for the improvement of the form and content of
reports to management as well as to actually initiate research and to
examine reports produced by the peripheral sections.

The size of the budget of an internal marketing research section
hinges on the volume of work it is expected to perform. If little or
no outside work is commissioned, then the budget comprises salaries,
overheads and purchases of source material. But once the work gets
beyond the desk research stage and information must be obtained
from the field, then costs can climb steeply. While the extent of the
budget is a matter between the marketing research section and the
management, if there is a central marketing section the draft budget
of peripheral units should be submitted to it, so that the central
guiding section has a general idea of the extent of the work, type of
assignment and estimated costs of the group or divisional section in
any one year. The central unit may be able to save money or obtain
better results for the same expenditure by combining the research
efforts of two or more sections.

z

The marketing researcher, as it has been repeatedly emphasised, should be well aware of the problems of the firm; this does not happen automatically and the aspiring candidate must be trained. For this reason it is useful to recruit market research assistants both from inside the firm as well as from outside. Furthermore, it is helpful if an established internal marketing research section is not a monopoly of economists or statisticians but uses, for example, engineers as well. As marketing research enquiries become increasingly complicated, it is necessary to call on the talents of non-economists or non-marketing researchers to enlarge on the technical implications of the problem. It seems, therefore, that as regards the composition of staffs the successful internal marketing research sections may be more and more microcosms of the firms which have brought them into being.

FACTORS AFFECTING A DECISION TO BUY RESEARCH

The aspects to be considered in purchasing research can be grouped under a number of headings. The major ones are: lack of specialist skills, the reasons underlying the decision to do research at all, the need for anonymity, difficulties in achieving objectives and the absence of specific resources. Their relative weightings in a research purchasing decision will vary from project to project and from time to time.

Special skills

The many aspects of industrial marketing research covered in this book indicate the unlikelihood of any single person being an expert in all its branches. The industrial marketing manager and the internal researcher, particularly in a one-man department, both tend to be generalists, not specialists. If the research requirements are for special skills not possessed by the firm, then the need for external help is obvious.

The circumstances when these factors might apply could be in the design and execution of a multiple image study which is a highly specialised research approach in which few firms have experience or the necessary team of psychological or sociological trained interviewers to conduct the field work. Research needing advanced statistical techniques might well be outside the scope of a department of a company staffed with economists, sociologists or engineers with only limited knowledge of statistics.

On a different level, a firm moving into a completely new field of activity may lack research staff with a knowledge of even the basic technology concerned in the project. Whereas a company engaged wholly in chemical engineering research could without much difficulty adapt the experience and knowledge of its research staff to grapple with problems of metal fabrications, it might be more difficult for a chemical manufacturing company to do the same.

Reasons for conducting research

Another factor to be considered in deciding whether to 'make or buy' is the reason for undertaking the research. The nature of research is such that long-term operation is always more efficient and profitable than an *ad hoc* enquiry. In some respects business intelligence is not unlike military intelligence in that it is not usually organised on an *ad hoc* basis. Both types of information should be planned as a continuous but changing operation. If a firm's research requirements are of a sporadic or 'one off' nature, for example a market check prior to taking up a licence to manufacture—the chance of the economic operation of an internal department is small. Thus if the reasons for conducting research are to satisfy a non-recurring or very short-term need, external research will be more satisfactory.

Anonymity

The consideration of anonymity is one where the option of choice between internal and external research is narrowed. If it must not be known—perhaps because such information would be an 'early warning' to competitors of the direction of the firm's product policy —that research is taking place, the internal department cannot carry out the research function. It is rarely possible to disguise research objectives over a period of time except by the most costly methods of diverting attention and interest. If the bulk of a firm's marketing research needs are for confidentially acquired information, then there can be no case for a substantial internal department even if it is technically capable of doing the work. It cannot be successful nor prudent for a firm to attempt research with its own staff while at the same time it refuses to acknowledge sponsorship of the survey. Customers, suppliers, shareholders and competitors resent, and resent both rightly and often bitterly, a firm sending its own staff to investigate and interview under false pretences. It can do considerable harm to the sponsoring firm's reputation and image for a researcher to be found 'sailing under false colours'.

Objectivity

It has been said that it is possible to obtain a greater objectivity by using external researchers free from the internal pressures and politics within the firm. While this is true over a wide range of circumstances, it is not true in absolute terms. It may be difficult, indeed hazardous, for an internal researcher to report critically on management, but an outside agency no more wishes to risk losing a client than the internal researcher wishes to risk losing his job or being passed over for promotion.

What can be said about objectivity so far as the agencies are concerned is that if they are not made aware of internal differences, vested interests in a development, strongly held views, or past performances, then they are unlikely to be biased in their own reporting to either meet the supposed wishes of management or to avert difficulties.

On major issues there is in fact little to choose between the internal and external researcher in terms of objectivity. Both will undoubtedly strive to present their findings as objectively as possible. But in a host of minor circumstances the outside agency may have the advantage since they will not, consciously or unconsciously, manipulate the results of their findings to produce any given effect.

By its very nature marketing research—consumer or industrial— is far less objective than physical research. The marketing researcher has more opportunity to project himself into his findings. Thus it is necessary for the researcher to make an extra effort to achieve objectivity in both his results and in the manner in which they are presented. A good researcher, whether he is employed or commissioned by the sponsor, will always keep that important objective in view. The only difference between the internal and external researcher may be that the latter in being physically and commercially separated from the sponsor in many circumstances has a freedom from implicit or explicit pressure generated in the research sponsoring firm.

However, when the research is concerned with arriving at decisions made impossible by internal divisions of opinion, then there can be little doubt that the external researcher has a considerable advantage if the brief is that the research will provide data to enable a decision to be made one way or the other. Moreover, as an impartial judge gathering up the facts, weighing the evidence and arriving at a decision, the external researcher's findings are more likely to be accepted as in a sense the 'referee's' decision, than his internal colleague's findings who might have been, according to the losing side, 'got at'.

Special resources

One outstanding reason for purchasing research from outside bodies is the availability of special resources. It is obviously cheaper to 'hire' these than develop them, particularly when the type of project or research subject is unlikely to be repeated.

A research company with a history of successful research in, say, the chemical industry, will have built up very many contacts and have a wide knowledge of the industry structure, the composition of its typical DMU, its dynamics and its particular problems.

Some agencies have developed specialised sampling frames, created panels of users, tabulated the existence and location of certain types of equipment or studied particular areas or trade flows. Similarly the absence of some special resources, data processing equipment, mailing room machinery, mechanical or electronic testing devices such as tachistoscopes, could easily lead to a decision to purchase research from organisations possessing such facilities.

All these are special resources which can be tapped into and can save a very considerable amount of time and money for the sponsor. Reference to the 'Resource' parameter in Chapter 3, 'Parameters of Research', will indicate how wide the specialities can be.

CHOOSING AN AGENCY

Buying research is just as much a skill as buying any other service but, like the purchasing of all services, it is far more difficult to carry out successfully than buying a product. For the latter it is possible to set out the commercial, technical and performance characteristics of a product with exactitude and often to pre-test their conformity with the specification. For services, while it is possible to detail methods and expected results, it is not possible to pre-judge their effectiveness and successful achievement. With industrial marketing research the buyer's role is additionally complicated in that the research yield is problematical until the end, the methodology often empiric and the applicability of the results not foreseeable.

There are, however, certain guide lines which can be followed to assist in the selection of an appropriate agency. The first rule is for would-be research sponsors to always use an agency of which satisfactory experience has been gained in the past. The sponsor not only benefits by the agency's previous knowledge of his type of business but will have the advantage of knowing something of the agency's strength and weaknesses. Shopping around for agencies is a commonplace practice which is wise in moderation but can be time-consuming, confusing and wasteful to both sponsor and agency if carried to excess. If, however, the project is a first attempt at marketing research, then it is necessary to check all the available services that appear suitable. In the United Kingdom, industrial marketing research services are centred on London. When the market under enquiry is overseas, it is also advisable to check on local research agencies on the spot before deciding whether or not to have the assignment undertaken from the United Kingdom.

It is always useful to discuss proposed research with business associates who may have had experience of particular agencies and can advise on their competence. Banks, trade associations, trade papers and particularly market research departments of other organisations are usually willing to advise based on their own experience or on that of their clients or members.

A number of professional organisations, for example the Institute of Marketing and the British Institute of Management, can provide a short list of firms they consider suitable to handle a particular assignment.

Directories of market research agencies are not a reliable guide to services or companies. As with most trade directories, many more claims are made by companies appearing in them for the ability to provide services than can in fact be substantiated. Moreover, since the majority of directories require paid entries they are rarely exhaustive. Directories produced by marketing research associations are simply lists of firms which employ a member of that Association and as such provide little guidance on the suitability of agencies for the project.

Once a list of agencies has been obtained the next step is to narrow down the lists to those which appear most likely to meet the need of the project. To do this agencies should be asked to submit their literature and any published material, and to explain the scope and extent of their services and resources. A careful study of this literature will provide further clues to the agency's suitability.

Points to be watched for are the degree of specialisation both in industrial marketing research and in the types of research conducted. The wider the scope of the services offered, the larger the staff of the agency might be expected to be. Links with overseas organisations and membership of overseas consortia will also provide an indication of the extent of an agency's interest in foreign marketing research. Client and job listings again provide further clues, albeit often unwitting ones, to the prospective purchaser of the agency's services.

The most suitable agencies, on paper, should then be visited to establish both how far their claims are borne out by the physical evidence of their activities and also to get the 'feel' of the agency. An organisation claiming to employ thirty researchers might be expected to occupy more than two or three rooms. Commercial status symbols are not necessarily indicative of top quality work, but then neither is the use of very old machinery and furniture likely to invoke the feeling of a successful organisation to any prospective purchaser of the agency's services.

Information on the qualifications of research staff should always be asked for. In most agencies all but the most junior of researchers will hold a degree or equivalent qualification. A market research agency offers a service for sale which depends to a large measure upon the qualifications and experience of its staff. There are many kinds of businesses which can be operated without formal training but industrial marketing research is not one of them.

No reputable agency will object to a quick tour of its offices, nor refuse the opportunity to the research buyer of a conversation—however brief—with researchers who are working in the offices at the time. It is no breach of confidence to indicate the type of work each researcher is dealing with at the present time and often it is possible to show something of the researcher's actual work. The use of observation techniques by the would-be research buyer can be applied very tellingly in a visit to an agency.

This is also the time for asking penetrating questions about the agency's organisation. A check on background, and performance, should be attempted, preferably with clients for whom the agency has worked. How, for example, does the agency deal with the need for expert technical guidance in any particular technology? If from internal staff, the researchers themselves should be quizzed, and if from external experts the name, qualifications and background of the expert should be sought. In seeking overseas research the name of the associate organisation in the countries concerned should also be asked for.

The links of the agency must be subject to the most careful scrutiny to establish if it is independent or if it is in any way controlled or influenced by other organisations, for example an advertising agency. Cross-directorships are another important aspect of agency checking. Because an agency director may also sit on the board of another company does not imply that the agency and its clients' confidences are likely to be divulged. But the potential research buyer should at least have the opportunity of assessing just how much at risk he will be if such external links do exist.

A most important check can be made by returning to the agency's client list. The agency can, of course, rightly refuse to reveal the names of clients but it is usual for most agencies to be able to mention at least some clients for whom they have worked and who are prepared to give a reference as to the effectiveness of their work. Prospective clients of agencies should not hesitate to ask for references and to take them up.

When negotiating with the larger agencies it is a useful precaution for the sponsor to ascertain which executive will be responsible for the project. This serves the dual purpose of removing the faceless aspect of the agency where responsibility is difficult to pin down, to that of a personal contact. It also ensures that if the project is successful and further work is commissioned, the same executive can again be asked to handle the new assignment. Agencies may have a continuous corporate life but the individuals in them change and there is no guarantee of a consistently high standard merely because the same firm carries out a project.

The last step in choosing an agency is based on the submission of a research design and costs. It is unfair to ask more agencies than necessary to prepare these, but it is wise in many circumstances to obtain more than one quotation. Comparison of prices is difficult because no two designs are strictly comparable. The final decision must depend upon the quality of the research design, how far the price and time conforms with the research needs and the rapport that had been built up in the initial appraisal stage of the agency.

To reiterate, agencies have nothing to sell but their reputation. By the time the client has the end product he has paid for, the choice of agency has long been made. For this reason there is a good deal of subjectivity in the choice of agencies. Few independent agencies spend time and money in advertising themselves on a large scale because the majority of business stems from personal recommendations and from continuing business from past clients. This itself is proof that it is reputation and image rather than 'hard selling' and publicity which count.

DANGER SIGNS

The positive aspects of selecting an agency have been given. There are a number of danger signs that can be detected by an observant, potential sponsor. These have been summarised[1] and they are well worth restating.

● '*Overselling*. Be on your guard against those marketing research organisations that: try to "high pressure" you into buying their

[1] William C. Gordon, Jr., *Selecting Marketing Research Services*, Small Business Administration (Washington, D.C., 1960).

services; or try to sell you a research "package" which is more than you need or can afford; or make exorbitant claims about their experience and qualifications which you know or have reason to believe, cannot be fully substantiated. A reputable marketing research firm will not "balloon" a research project out of proportion to the needs of the problem or the client's pocketbook. To protect its professional reputation, it will not take an assignment it is not equipped to handle. It will usually be the first to tell you so.

● *Disparagement of competition.* Avoid marketing research organisations that tend to "run down" their competitors. Not only is this a poor selling tactic in the professional field but also a highly questionable business practice. If your interests can be better serviced by using the facilities of a competing organisation, most responsible marketing researchers will tell you so. They may even recommend someone.

● *Price cutting.* View with scepticism organisations which say they are quoting a price "at below cost" and whose competitive bid for a research job appears abnormally lower than others. Chances are that the statement is not entirely true; costs can be padded. An unusually low bid may be genuine but may also indicate a weakness in research methods. Be sceptical, too, of the organisation that tries to find out from you what prices competitors have quoted before submitting their own.

● *Extravagant promises or guarantees.* Much marketing research work, like scientific experiment, is exploratory. Results may some-times be inconclusive. There is always the danger in designing a research project with a pre-conceived idea of what results should be. Any marketing research organisation that sells its services by guaranteeing precise answers to a problem is on shaky ground. It should be viewed with suspicion.

● *Vague ideas of approach and results.* Exercise caution, too, in employing a marketing research firm that is overtly vague con-cerning the approach and probably results of the project. Such an attitude may reflect an uncertainty about how to attack the pro-blem. A responsible marketing research organisation should be able to say, within reasonable limits, what procedures will be used and what their capabilities and limitations are.

● *Reluctance to be specific.* Beware of a research organisation that refuses to put on paper the specifics about a job. It is, to be sure, general practice not to require a formal contract for marketing research services. Most commitments are entered into in good faith by mutual agreement of both parties. Authorisation for the work to proceed is given by letters. So, if an organisation insists on a contract satisfy yourself that the demand is reasonable.'

AGENCY CHARGES

All projects outlined in research designs submitted by an agency to a sponsor should carry a firm costing. Where difficulty is experienced in giving such a costing the sponsor might suggest that the survey should be phased to enable it to proceed sequentially. For example, in a survey of plastic pipes it is difficult to know in advance just how many pipe materials in given applications are likely to prove significant and therefore how much time must be devoted to each product and user section.

A first-stage survey would identify each application by material used and provide the framework for the study. It will not indicate the relative uptakes but it will reveal the total number of different applications for each material. The second phase could then be directed to uncovering the relative quantities taken up by each application for each material. The third stage would be to probe in depth those applications and materials found to command a considerable demand. Each of these stages can be costed with precision because the factors which govern the cost of the later stages will be revealed by the results of the first stages.

The possibility can arise from time to time, when it can be as expensive to uncover if the research can be completed as to actually accomplish it. In these circumstances research sponsors must accept that the cost given is for carrying out the enquiries and not a guarantee that the objectives can necessarily be achieved. In these circumstances it is common practice to offer a 'not more than' figure as an upper limit if the objectives are achieved, and then a graduated reducing scale for the amount by which the project cannot be completed. This scale, however, includes a payment to the agency even if no information is obtained. The acceptance of a cost is not *ipso facto* a guarantee by the agency that the research can be completed.

Practice in relation to charging for research designs varies. Research sponsors should consider where an agency does not charge for preparing a full-scale research design, clients who do provide business for the agency are saddled with the costs non-clients have incurred. In other words, if one design in three is converted into agency business, the third client is paying the costs of the other two designs. Thus a charge for research designs is in fact a guarantee that research costs quoted are research costs and that they do not include a substantial element of the agency's development costs.

Research design charges by agencies should not be levied if, in fact, it is accepted and the project is commissioned. The costs of preparing a design are part of the research costs. This preparatory and pre-study work itself makes a valuable contribution to the research proper. The agency only seeks to recover these initial costs if the project is not initiated. Thus there should be no such thing as a charge for research design—only a charge for the work carried out on preliminary project work which cannot subsequently be used as part of the research proper.

If all agencies made a nominal charge for designs not proceeded with, a new and perhaps not insubstantial cost element would enter into the research sponsor's budgeting since, presumably, only one of several designs would be accepted, hence the other charges would be, in a sense, waste. For this reason many research sponsors will not agree to a charge being made.

From an agency viewpoint, charging for designs eliminates frivolous enquiries and indicates the client's seriousness. Sponsors should, however, realise that in agreeing not to charge for an unsuccessful design the agency will also be agreeing either not to carry out all the necessary pre-study work or else to subsidise potential clients by existing clients. On balance, a charge for a design is a guarantee to a research sponsor of realistic costs for his project.

ORGANISATION—SPECIALIST AGENCY

External marketing research organisations vary widely both in organisation and in the type of work for which they are specially equipped. Broadly three types of specialisation occur in marketing research. The first and fundamental division is between the consumer and industrial marketing research agency. Rarely is an agency equipped to accomplish both types efficiently. To protect its professional reputation, a reputable marketing research firm will not undertake an assignment which it is not fully competent to carry out.

The second type of specialisation is based upon *technical* capabilities within the agency and upon its concentration on certain industries. For example, an agency may operate almost continuously within electrical or mechanical engineering fields or concentrate its activities upon the textile or plastics industries using engineers, physicists or chemists.

The third type of specialisation is based upon *research* skills, resources and experience. Here an agency may have made special studies of, and have wide experience in, personal interviewing of high level executives, motivational research techniques or even postal surveys.

The first division, between consumer and industrial marketing research, is obviously fundamental and clearly a choice of which kind of agency to use will be self-evident. The secondary specialisations are not fundamental, although it is advantageous to use an agency with specialist knowledge and experience of industries in which the research sponsors are interested. The specialist agency is organised in a way which permits the maximum efficient deployment of its resources and hence most probably gives best value for money. That is, if its interviewers are all engineers it will seek engineering assignments and the technical quality of its staff will be an important asset. Similarly, if an agency includes experts in sampling techniques the assignments of the type it is best equipped to carry out will be the most attractive to it in terms of return and, indeed, job satisfaction and will be expressed to the sponsoring firm by submitting keen quotations.

The question must be asked how can any industrial marketing research agency operate effectively over wide-ranging fields without technical expertise in any of them? The answer to this springs from the organisation of the agency. It is mandatory for the general agency to work with at least some technical consultants who guide the research through the technical stages. Many agencies are organised on the basis of a research team consisting of various skills and experiences; in economics, statistics, librarianship, market, commodity and international affairs specialists and others. Most technical aspects of research are then funnelled through the consultants who, apart from conducting pilot interviews, briefing interviewers, pinpointing the sources of published and other technical information and setting up the enquiries in relation to technical aspects and their commercial implications, also liaise between the client's technical staff and the agency.

Reference was made in Chapter 8, 'Interviewing', to the fact that the leading independent agencies have gathered about them panels of technical consultants or have established links with universities or research institutes, conducting physical research to create a consortium of formidable knowledge and experience which probably not even the largest client firms can hope to rival. Such technical consultancy arrangements have proved by experience to be efficient and profitable to both agency and client.

Consultancy used by independent agencies is not confined to technicians and scientists. Many agencies find it worthwhile to retain the services of marketing specialists whose unique skills could not, for the most part, be used on a permanent basis. Thus a research sponsor using an independent agency is as likely to find that the research team has not only included the services of leading technical consultants but also of economists of international repute and pioneers and exponents of new research techniques.

RESEARCH ETHICS

The existence of a body of independent consultants operating with the agency can lead to a conflict of interest between the agency's clients and the independent consultant's clients. This is something which can be anticipated and avoided if a declaration of interest by both agency and consultant is sought at the outset. This particular risk, however, is only one of several which can arise in using external researchers. Another equally important one stems from the commercial links which research agencies may have. Industrial marketing research agencies which are a part of other organisations are involved in relationships which are fraught with pressures that might easily lead less scrupulous people to unethical behaviour.

'The risks are greatest where the parent company has large, continuing accounts, common with advertising agencies and media. Potentially there could be tremendous pressure by an aggressive and unscrupulous executive to obtain information from the research subsidiary about a new market for a competitive product or the marketing plans of a competitor. A complex of firms including an agency for a publishing house and research firm might have personnel transfers that could invite leakage of confidential information. Such personnel transfers, of course, can occur without such a tie-up. But why not discourage a structure which encourages the possibility?'[1]

Why not indeed? Short of legislative interference which would hardly be desirable, the best discouragement is for research buyers not to purchase research where information is likely to be at risk and to insist on full disclosures of all other interests of, and holdings

[1] A. B. Blankenship, 'Some questions of ethics in Marketing Research', *Journal of Marketing* (New York, May 1964).

in, the agency, and of interlocking directorship which also offers the same risks.

A perhaps new thought suggested in the same feature is that research firms in public ownership whose first responsibility is the shareholders' interest, may well sacrifice quality and client service for profits. Moreover, a large shareholder it is thought could bring the same pressures to bear for the release of the agency's client's information as perhaps the parent company of a research subsidiary.

The other aspects of the ethical considerations is the problem of an agency handling competitive assignments. From the extreme of the agency which sells its services or a project to all comers willing to pay the fee and makes this clear to each client, to the company that will only accept one client in each field of activity, the combination of arrangements to meet conflicts of interest is very great.

While it can be argued that prior experience in a field helps each successive client, it is equally true that information paid for by one firm should not form a windfall profit for the agency by selling it to a competitive organisation. Certainly the prospective research buyer should probe an agency's policy on the handling of competitive assignments. Generally it will be found that a commonsense approach is taken in preserving the interest of clients.

In a reasonably fast-moving market most agencies will provide a two year lead time before repeating a study but where the subject of research is either a new product or a product in a slow-moving market a longer period would be adopted.

It is difficult to set down a rule for handling competitive assignments. The research firm is behaving ethically if it accepts a competitive account, or assignment when the sponsor knows the agency's policies on such matters and its client list.

EVALUATING RESEARCH

It has been said that it is difficult to assess the research offer and that much has to be taken on good faith. It is therefore all the more important to assess the research results. The ability to appreciate excellence and recognise mediocrity is required in assessing research. The research buyer must ask a number of questions:

● What was the research attempting to achieve?

● How did the research attempt to achieve what it set out to do?

● Are there a sufficient number of facts and are they satisfactorily validated?

- Was the methodology correct?
- Did the research succeed or fail in its objectives?
- How 'hedged' was the reporting?
- What degree of confidence can be placed on the results?
- How far do the final results depart from the agreed research design?
- Are the reasons for any departures valid?
- Could they have been foreseen before the research began?
- Was the researcher suitably qualified and experienced to carry out the project? How much reliance can be placed on his judgement?
- Is the report intended to inform? Does it do this?
- How far is the report an explanation or a plea? Are these justified?
- Has the research coverage been adequate?
- Have all secondary sources of information been tapped?
- Is the research taken to the most recent date possible?
- Is the project logical, complete and well-designed?
- Are the conclusions justified by the facts?
- Are the recommendations reasonable and do they take account of internal factors?
- Is the reasoning correct and without fallacies?

A critical approach to reports is of inestimable value in improving the purchasing techniques for research and in identifying weaknesses in a research organisation. Lessons from external research can be applied to the internal department to improve their own operations.

It is fairly safe to prognosticate both an increasing sophistication in the operation of internal departments and in the purchasing of research services, and a higher degree of specialisation in industrial marketing research agencies. These two trends will together be productive of greater precision in research results and a greater tendency to experimentation. However, there will be little advantage to be obtained from improved operations and more reliable findings unless there is a parallel improvement in management skills in appreciating the meaning of research findings and applying them to the operations of the firm.

It is true to say that skill in carrying out research and skill in using it have never kept in step for long, first one going ahead and then the other. The lead-lag between these twin activities must be shortened if the fullest advantage is to be obtained from the use of industrial marketing research and if the benefits of experimentation are to be exploited quickly and effectively.

Conclusion

Marketing research is problem orientated research which seeks to assess, on the basis of facts, the effect of alternative business decisions and to search out additional profit opportunities. Its main functions therefore are risk reduction and need identification. Nevertheless, it cannot alone guide businessmen to the correct alternative or outstanding opportunities. Sound marketing based on intelligent interpretation of the research yield is only one of the major responsibilities of management. But its absence today in a world of rapid technological obsolescence can place the continued successful existence of large and small firms alike in jeopardy.

In attempting to describe the processes and techniques of industrial marketing research in this book, it has been necessary to treat many activities and functions in isolation from others when in practice they are, of course, closely interconnected. Similarly marketing research which, like Public Relations and distribution, is just one of the activities within the total marketing effort, has been separated from other essential activities. Both these situations are unreal and there is a continuous and important interface between the different marketing research activities and between marketing research and other marketing functions.

In many projected courses of action industrial marketing research is the opening move in a long and complex process, but not necessarily the most important move. Any attempt to elevate any one marketing function to a dominating role is as unwise as it is impractical. Industrial marketing research must be part of the marketing mix and used in correct proportion to the other elements in that mix.

Throughout this book the emphasis has been on the importance of establishing goals and objectives: survey objectives, interview objectives, advertising objectives, report objectives. It is only by designating these that marketing research can be brought into the marketing plan and activities at exactly the right moment and with the correct

2A

emphasis. The vital need for management to lay down broad corporate and divisional objectives and specific marketing goals is a function which is still not wholly accepted. These are, however, management exercises in which industrial marketing research has an increasing role to play.

Industrial marketing research to some degree continues to occupy an emergency or junior role in the marketing activity of very many organisations but it is bound to have an increasing participation in marketing decisions for industrial goods manufacturers and traders. The current difficulty in ensuring its wider influence over marketing policy is its frequent collision or fear of collision with the hunches and inspirations of entrepreneurs and their senior managers. For the future perhaps the greatest changes will be less in the methods and skills of industrial marketing research than in the change of attitudes towards its use in business. The marketing concept of a customer-creating, customer-satisfying organism is a challenging adjustment for firms to make, and it is one that is unlikely to be made without the contribution of industrial marketing research. The true measure of marketing effectiveness is to be found not in sales volume or percentage profit alone but in the return on all the resources employed in an organisation. Research executives will be increasingly charged with the task of providing a better combination of means and methods to ensure the satisfaction of needs in the market.

Business requirements in future will not only be for more information on marketing conditions, but also for improved methods of checking the effectiveness both of the marketing effort and of marketing research itself. More often researchers will face a total marketing situation, not just narrow segments of fact-finding apparently unrelated to the total corporate activity and development. The battle for greater recognition and acceptance of industrial marketing research will be won by the development of a unified concept of marketing research, and by the researchers being able to see the marketing problem and the problems of the firm as a totality in the competitive struggle for survival, profit and growth.

APPENDIX A

Industrial Marketing Researchers Check List

MARKET SIZE

1. What is the size of the total market for the product?
2. How durable is the market?
3. What is domestic consumption (volume or value)?
4. What proportion or amount (volume and/or value) is met from domestic production?
5. What proportion or amount (volume and/or value) is met from imported sources?
6. What are the main export markets from (a) domestic production (b) re-exported imports?
7. What factors limit the size of the total market?
8. What are the sizes of the various market strata?
   by geographical regions
   by size of user
   by industry
   by type, quality, design or price of product
   by type of distributor.
9. What is the size of the total market for a substitute product?
10. What are the export possibilities?

MARKET STRUCTURE

1. Who are the main domestic suppliers to the market?
2. Which countries are the main sources of imports?
3. Which importing firms are the most important?
4. What is the export performance of main competitors?
5. Which are their main markets?
6. What are the geographical variations in the domestic market?

7. What are the seasonal/cyclical variations in the domestic market?
8. What factors currently favour the emergence of new competitors?
9. What factors are currently likely to lead to the reduction of competitors?
10. Which are the main user industries?
11. Which are the subsidiary user industrues?
12. Is in-feeding significant in the user industries?
13. Do reciprocal trading practices exist?

Market Trends

1. How does the market size compare with
   10 years ago
   5 years ago
   last year?
2. How does product demand differ from
   10 years ago
   5 years ago
   last year?
3. What trends are revealed indicating a shift in demand over the
   10 years
   5 years
   last year?
4. In what ways are market changes likely to manifest themselves?
5. What changes are occurring in the user industries likely to induce a change of demand?
6. What changes are occurring in the non-user industries likely to induce a new demand?
7. What changes are occurring in the firm's products and processes likely to induce a change in demand?
8. What changes are occurring in the economy likely to affect demand for the firm's products?
   levels of employment
   levels of income
   level of industrial investment
   level of industrial profits
   industrial dividends
   rates of corporate taxation

wholesale prices
level of indistrial production
consumers' expenditure
personal savings
rates of personal taxation
retail prices
population trends
rates of interest
credit restrictions
hire-purchase debt
export trends
import trends
balance of payments.

9. What trends are likely to attract new entrants into the industry in future?

10. What trends are likely to reduce the numbers of competitors in future?

11. Are changes in materials or production methods likely to reduce the need for the product?

Market Share

1. What share of the market does the firm command?

2. What are the main competitors' shares?

3. What is the firm's share of the market broken down?
   by industries
   by size of firms
   geographically.

4. What are the main competitor's shares?
   by industries
   by size of firms
   geographically.

5. What share of the market is held by imported products?

6. What factors support the market share of imported products?

7. What percentage of business is from:
   old customers
   new customers?

8. How concentrated or dispersed are sales?

THE FIRM

1. What is the reputation of the firm within the user industries?
2. What is the reputation of the firm's products within these industries?
3. What is the firm's 'image'?
4. What are the firm's individual 'brand images'?
5. Is the name and reputation of the firm established?
6. Do the firm's suppliers form potential markets for its products?
7. Can the firm absorb any of its own products?
8. What services are provided by the firm?
9. How do these relate to market requirements?
10. What guarantees are offered?
11. How advisable is it to brand own products with private brands?

SALES METHODS

1. What are the usual personal selling methods adopted for the product?
2. What is the history of the firm's personal selling methods?
3. What is the user industry structure, organisation and geographical division for the sale of the product?
4. How does this compare with the firm's usual structure, organisation and geographical division for the sale of the product?
5. What is the sales history of the product in value and volume?
6. How specialised is selling among competitors?
7. If the product is seasonal, can fluctuations be evened out by balancing sales of varying types of products or by buying inducements?
8. What aids do salesmen need?
    advertising support
    technical advice
    marketing data
    catalogues
    drawings
    samples
    educational slides or films
    demonstrations

offers of credit
offers of H.P. facilities.

9. How effectively are tenders handled?

10. What proportion of inquiries are converted to sales?

11. How does this compare with:
    5 years ago
    last year?

12. What is the image of the firm's salesmen?

SALES PROMOTION METHODS

1. What is the history of the firm's advertising expenditure in value, and per unit sold?

2. What is the cost of sales promotion?
   annually
   per enquiry
   per order
   per salesman
   by media.

3. What is the expenditure on sales promotion broken down?
   by media
   seasonally
   by geographical area
   by industry towards which promotion is directed.

4. How does the firm's sales promotion history and performance compare with competitors'?

5. What is the copy strategy used on the firm's products during the last 5 years?

6. What are the major changes and causes of change in copy strategy which have occurred in the last 5 years?

7. How does budget percentage in each of the following media compare with competitors'?
   newspapers
   journals
   outdoor
   direct mail
   exhibitions
   educational campaigns
   catalogues and brochures
   public relations campaigns

point of sale
films
sampling.

8. To what type of advertising and media are users and potential
   users most exposed?

9. In what way does competitive advertising differ from the firm's?
   media
   frequency
   space
   copy
   strategy.

10. What is the audience (in numbers) for specific advertisements?

11. What is the extent of recall?

12. What percentage of enquiries are from:
    old customers
    new customers?

13. How are these proportions changing?

DISTRIBUTION METHODS

1. How effective are the distributive methods used?

2. How do they compare with competitors' distributive methods?

3. What alternatives exist?

4. What is the division of the firm's sales by:
   each type of distributor
   size of distributor
   geographical location of distributors
   industrial concentration of distributors?

5. What percentage of total sales for each product is directly
   transacted with users?

6. What is the history of the introduction of the product and the
   sequences of marketing steps which led to its present distribution?

7. What is the replenishment lead time?

8. What is the history of 'out-of-stock' situations?

9. What stocks are normally held at the plant?
   average
   seasonal.

10. What stocks are normally in the distributive pipeline?

11. How far do distributors handle service, maintenance, spares, etc.?
12. How far do distributors handle competitors' service, maintenance, spares, etc.?
13. How technically competent are distributors?
14. Are franchise and exclusive dealing arrangements prevalent?
15. Are the distributive outlets the most efficient available?
16. How effective are distributors' selling efforts?
17. What aids do competitors give to distributors?
18. How do the firm's aids to distributors compare with those offered by competitors?

SHIPMENT AND PACKAGING

1. How is the package shipped?
2. How do the firm's physical transport methods compare with competitors'?
   cost
   speed
   liability to damage
   liability to pilferage.
3. What are the comparative shipping costs and times using alternative methods?
4. Would standard crate dimensions affect cost of shipment?
5. Is the package destroyed, returned or re-used?
6. Is the package used to hold contents until empty or is it immediately emptied?
7. Should the package have a dispensing device?
8. What is the average amount of contents used on each occasion?
9. Is other material subsequently stored in the package?
10. At what distance must the package be identified?
11. How is identification of contents achieved?
12. How is the package handled in the stockroom, on the factory floor and elsewhere?
13. How long is a package held in stock?
14. What stock protection measures are necessary?
15. How are empties stored?

16. What protective measures are required against damage in transit and storage by vermin, moisture, temperature, pilferage?

17. How is the package handled in storage and shipment?

18. What is the history of delayed deliveries?

19. Are customers informed when product is despatched and by what route or carrier?

20. How far are late deliveries caused by delayed despatches and how far by slow transport methods or handling?

21. Are customers made aware of delays caused by carriers?

PROFIT

1. What is the profit history of the product?

2. What is the unit profit history?

3. What is known about profits of other manufacturers in the same field?

4. What contribution to profits of other products does the product make?

5. What non-profit advantages does the firm derive?

6. What changes in profits have changes in marketing strategy achieved in the last 5 years?

COSTS

1. What is the cost history and structure of the firm's product?

2. What information is obtainable on competitors' cost structures?

3. Does the firm have any advantages in production costs over the competitors?

4. Does the firm have any advantages in marketing costs over the competitors?

5. Does the firm have any advantages in procurement costs over the competitors?

6. How does R. & D. expenditure and results compare with competitors?

THE PRODUCT

1. What are the major uses for the firm's product?

2. How do the major uses for the firm's product compare with the major uses for competitors' products?

3. What is the width of the firm's range?

4. What is the depth of the firm's range?

5. Under what conditions are the firm's products used?

6. What is the extent of these additional uses?

7. What is the idealised 'profile' for a product of the type being marketed?

8. How far does the firm's product accord with the users' idealised conception of the product?

9. What are the product's unique qualities?

10. What are the product's 'plusses'?

11. What are its weaknesses?

12. How does the product differ from
    10 years ago
    5 years ago
    last year?

13. What changes have been made in the product since its introduction?

14. What were the reasons for changes?

15. What technical changes have occurred in the processes in which the product is used?

16. Have ranges been extended or reduced since they were introduced?

17. What were the reasons for range changes?

18. What is the reputation of the firm's product in its principal applications?

19. What changes in materials, products, processes or end-use products are likely to limit or increase demand for the firm's product?

20. How do proposed modifications in product or product range measure up to market demand and trends?

21. What is the percentage of the firm's and competitors' sales broken down by quality range?
    high
    medium
    low.

22. What is the image of the product?

23. What is the quality spread?
    great
    small.
24. How far beyond the buyer is the product known in the user firm and how far is it associated with the supplier's name?
25. How far can special orders be handled or undertaken?
26. How strong are patents?
27. Can raw material purchases be bulked?
28. What standards exist for the product, and does the product conform to them?
29. What new standards are likely to be adopted?
30. What guarantees are offered and what is guarantee claim record?
31. Is it possible to achieve a high 'break cost'?

SERVICES

1. What design services are required?
    physical planning
    pre-sale service and advice
    prototype fabrication
    equipment design and checking
    facilities advice
    packaging advice.
2. What pre-start up services are required?
    assembly
    installation
    engineering and inspection and testing.
3. What negotiation services are required?
    resolving complaints
    warranty adjustments including exchange of product
    liaison between customers and production department.
4. What education services are required?
    guidance on application use and adaption of products to customers' needs
    on-site demonstration, instructions, training and in-plant lectures
    handling and safety advice
    library service
    technical literature
    general industrial advice.

5. What visiting services are required?
   general and specific purpose visits to customer's plants
   customer visits to service and production departments.

6. What maintenance and repair services are required?
   periodic testing and adjustment
   cleaning and repairing
   rehabilitation and reconditioning.
   is loan equipment required.

7. What product adaptation services are required?
   modifications
   applications research.

8. What emergency assistance is required?

9. What standby facilities for emergency and peak load periods are required?

MARKETING RESEARCH

1. How does marketing research expenditure compare with competitors'?

2. What marketing research has been accomplished in home and export markets?

3. How effective has it been?

4. How efficient are the firm's information sources?

5. How comprehensive are the firm's statistical data?

6. Which methods of marketing research have been found to be most effective?

7. What experimentation in marketing research is taking place?

8. In what circumstances is the use of independent agencies preferred to the firm's own research?

9. What methods exist for obtaining product intelligence?

OVERSEAS MARKETS

1. Can earnings be remitted to the exporting country?

2. How narrowly based is the economy and what are trading conditions for principal exports?

3. What is the local taxation position on:
   products
   profits
   labour
   turnover?

4. What is the import duty for each of the main exporting countries?

5. Do quotas or licensing arrangements exist?

6. Are local producers protected?

7. Do specific countries and/or firms have official or unofficial preferences in seeking supplying countries?

8. What are local charges?
   dock dues
   landing charges
   clearance charges
   weighing and measuring
   shipping agents
   local transport.

9. What production under licence from foreign competitors is taking place?

10. What development schemes are taking place or are planned which will affect demand for the product and business conditions in general?

11. What physical conditions call for product and packaging modifications?

NEW PRODUCTS

1. What industries will use the new product?

2. Has the product a potential market among institutional and government users?

3. Will the new product round out the firm's lines?

4. How will the new full line compare with competitors?

5. Will the new product fill idle time of plant and equipment?

6. Will the new product contribute to long-term growth and security of the business?

7. Will the new product contribute to a lessening of the effects of business cycles?

8. Will the new product put excess capital to work?

9. Will the new product be accepted because it satisfies some need and sells at a price prospective buyers will pay?

10. Will the new product have to penetrate an already developed field?

11. Does the new product offer some important competitive advantages in a developed field?

12. Will the new product, even without competitive superiority, penetrate a developed field by virtue of the firm's reputation or other factors?

13. Will marketing agreements, franchises, etc., in any way limit production, sales, or the use of the product?

14. Is there any element in pricing policy or trade practice which may be a violation of law or accepted trade practice?

15. Are buyers of the new product accustomed to purchasing ahead of need or do they order for immediate delivery?

16. What is the structure of the raw and processed material and equipment supply industries for the manufacture of the new product?

17. How secure are material and components supplies?

18. What stocks of materials and components are necessary and usual?

19. What substitutes are available?

20. How deep seated are existing loyalties and how receptive are buyers to new products?

21. What are user preferences in relation to distributive channels and methods for the products of the new product type?

22. What standards (official or unofficial) exist or are likely to be adopted?

23. Can 'top out' signs be identified?

COMPETITIVE CLIMATE

1. Which firms make competitive products?

2. What are their respective market shares?

3. How firmly entrenched are competitors?

4. What specific advantages do the main competitors have?
   geographical
   industrial
   size
   related products
   commercial and industrial associations and liaisons
   protection—official and unofficial.

5. What is the reputation of the leading competitors?

6. What methods of distribution are used?

7. Are franchises used?

8. What is their sales structure?

9. What sales promotion techniques are used?

10. What services do competitors offer?

11. What are the usual credit and discount practices?

12. What guarantees are offered?

13. What is the firm's and competitors' policy in relation to the use of technical and non-technical salesmen?

14. What is the sales history of the firm's and competitors' technical and non-technical salesmen?

15. What is the extent of competitors' product research and development?

16. What is the quality of personnel and management?

17. What is the manufacturing potential of principal competitors?

18. What are competitors' appropriations for advertising and sales promotion generally?

19. Are changes in materials or methods likely to increase present competitors' sales?

20. What proportion of competitors' output is sold for export?

21. Which are their principal export markets?

22. What is the extent of competitors' marketing research?

23. What is the image of competitive firms?

24. What is competitors' guarantee policy?

25. Have competitive firms built in a 'break cost' element?

26. Do competitors offer loan equipment?

27. What is the extent of manufacturing for private brands?

COMPETITIVE PRICES

1. How does gross price compare with strictly comparable products?

2. How does net price compare with strictly comparable products?

3. How does gross price compare with substitute products?

4. How does net price compare with substitute products?

5. How does the firm's discount structure compare with competitors'?

6. What hidden discounts are offered by competitors?

7. What other 'off-setting against price' factors exist?

8. What is the price history of the most popular unit of sale?

9. What is the price history of the least popular unit of sale?

10. How do distributor margins allowed compare with those granted by competitors?

11. How do distributors' profits actually obtained compare with those obtained on competitors' products?

12. What are the reasons for fluctuations in price?

13. Is price used as part of competitors' marketing strategy?

14. How do spares/service/installation/maintenance/technical advisory charges compare with those of competitors?

15. Is price fixing practised?

16. How sensitive is the market to price changes?

COMPETITIVE PROCESSES

1. Do processes not incorporating or using the product offer significant cost advantages?

2. Do processes not incorporating or using the product offer significant production advantages?

3. What technological developments are occurring or being explored which may lead to product obsolescence in particular processes?

4. What technological developments are occurring or being explored which may lead to new demands for the product in new processes using or incorporating them?

5. What is the reputation and record of success of processes not using the product?

6. What is the reputation and record of success of processes using the product?

7. What is the reputation of the firm's product in its principal applications?

COMPETITIVE PRODUCTS

1. How do competitive products closely similar in characteristics compare?

2B

2. How do competitive products, dissimilar but substitutable for the firm's product compare?
3. What are competitive products' 'plusses'?
4. What additional products in competitors' ranges give them sales advantages?
5. What sales advantages does availability of products in depth give competitors?
6. To what extent do unrelated products or processes compete with the new products?
7. How far do competitors' products accord with the idealised 'profile' for the product?
8. What is the reputation of competing products?
9. How does the product compare on:
       price
       quality
       performance
       finish, design
       length of service
       packaging or methods of packing
       guarantees
       other characteristics?
10. What are bases of the purchasing decision in relation to competitive products?
       price
       technical specification
       other physical characteristics
       delivery and services
       packaging or packing method
       supporting services provided
       company's reputation and guarantees
       brand or product reputation
       reciprocal trade agreements
       company affiliations
       personal relationships.
11. What stocks are normally held?
       at the plant
       by distributors
       by users.
12. What is the history and cause of sales fluctuations over the last few years?

13. What is the history of firm or brand leadership over the last few years and what were the reasons for changes?

14. Under what manufacturing conditions are competitive products used?

15. How far beyond the buyer are competitive products known in the user firms and how far are they associated with competitors by name?

16. What uses do the products have other than those promoted?

17. To what extent are these uses practised?

18. What changes have competitors made in their products since their introduction?

19. What were the reasons for changes in products?

20. Have ranges been extended or reduced since they were introduced?

21. What were the reasons for range changes?

22. How strong are patents?

23. How closely do competitors' products conform to official and unofficial standards?

DEMAND

1. What is the demand history for the product?

2. How well is demand met by current suppliers?

3. What are the limitations to demand?
   technical characteristics
   availability of purchasing power
   availability of products
   substitutions
   obsolescence
   fashion
   seasonal or physical factors
   price
   availability of services.

4. How do the firm's products fit within acceptable style/quality price range?

5. Are the product characteristics acceptable to the majority of purchasers?

6. How does demand vary between the various strata of the market?
   industrial
   geographical
   by size of firm
   in specific uses.

7. What conditions in the end-user markets are affecting demand?

8. How many potential users are there of the product in terms of:
   industries
   firms
   geographical areas
   in specific uses?

9. What is the average rate of consumption?
   by industry
   by size of firm
   by process
   by season
   in specific uses.

10. What factors affect consumption rate?

11. What characteristics identify the largest customers?

12. What characteristics identify the smallest customers?

13. How stable would demand be in time of depression?

14. How stable would demand be in time of war?

15. What requirements are there for hire facilities and loan equipment?

USER ATTITUDES AND BEHAVIOUR

1. What are the decision-forming factors in purchasing, broken down by:
   industry
   size of firm
   geographical areas
   job function of buyers
   season?

2. What emotional factors are important in buying decisions?

3. Who comprise the decision-making unit in customer firms?

4. How far is buying a function of a committee?

5. What is the usual method of negotiating orders and contracts?

6. What inter-personal factors exist affecting sales by the firm and by competitors?

7. What preferences exist among users for specific methods of selling and sales promotion?

8. What is the frequency or periodicity of purchase?

9. What is the extent of user knowledge of the firm's products?

10. What is the extent of user knowledge of identical competitive products?

11. What is the extent of user knowledge of competitive substitute products?

12. What is the extent of mis-use of the product?

13. How does the user judge the end of the useful life of the product?

14. How do decisions concerning the end of the useful life of the product vary between industries and firms?

15. Are the same criteria for judging the end of the useful life of the firm's the same as those applied to competitors' products?

16. What is the usual status and job definition of buyers of the firm's and competitive products?

17. What size orders should be expected, broken down by:
    industry
    size of firm
    geographical location
    job definition and status of buyers?

18. What are the history and the reasons for lost orders?

19. What are the history and reasons for cancelled orders?

20. How postponable is purchasing?

21. What commercial conditions are required?

22. What requirements exist for products to be supplied under 'own brand'?

23. Have user preference distributions been studied?

24. Does buying responsibility change at discrete points, which may alter the product's acceptability within an industrial firm?

GOVERNMENTAL FACTORS

1. What is the current tax structure on:
   the product
   the end products?

2. What is the history of taxation of the product and end products?
3. What is the import duty?
4. What restrictions on imports exist?
5. What restrictions are imposed on credit terms?
6. What would be the effect of tax changes on demand?
7. What is the position in relation to protection, subsidies and support prices?
8. What is the government attitude to price agreements and restrictive practices?
9. What legislation exists on safety, quality control and weights and measures?
10. What is the extent of government participation in purchasing?
11. What is the role of international agencies?

IMAGE

1. What is the industry image reference?
2. How does the firm's image compare with industry image?
3. How far does the industry image affect the firm's and its competitors' image?
4. To what extent is the industry image compared with the image of other industries?
5. How do the competitive firms' images compare?
6. What is the product or service image of the firm and its competitors?
7. What is the image of the firm and competitive supporting services?
8. What is the image of the firm's and competitors' personnel—sales, administrative, technical, service.
9. What is the image of the firm's and competitors' premises?
10. How do the images vary between different classifications of customer?
    regular
    sporadic
    single transactions
    discontinued customers
    failed quotations
    no contact.

11. How far are the images uncovered based on:
    direct experience
    known by reputation
    heard of by name?

12. What is the 'mirror' image?

13. What is the 'wish' image?

14. Has the 'optimum' image been identified?

15. Is there any image variation within the DMU's?

16. What factors are influencing image perception?

APPENDIX B SUMMARY INPUT-OUTPUT TRANSACTIONS MATRIX (1963)

Purchases by / Sales by		Agriculture, forestry and fishing	Coal mining	Other mining and quarrying	Food, drink and tobacco	Mineral oil refining	Other chemicals and allied industries	Metal manufacture	Vehicles (including aircraft) and shipbuilding	Other engineering	Textiles, leather and clothing
		1	2	3	4	5	6	7	8	9	10
Agriculture, forestry and fishing	1	—	5	—	571	—	—	—	—	—	28
Coal mining	2	1	—	1	14	—	156	12	5	9	16
Other mining and quarrying	3	—	—	—	3	2	9	19	—	19	—
Food, drink and tobacco	4	315	—	—	—	—	35	—	—	—	2
Mineral oil refining	5	19	1	1	9	—	78	20	6	14	7
Other chemicals and allied industries	6	91	9	12	156	48	—	95	69	140	34
Metal manufacture	7	—	48	—	8	—	23	—	374	781	
Vehicles (including aircraft) and shipbuilding	8	10	1	1	4	—	3	8	—	41	2
Other engineering	9	26	42	14	100	2	83	98	545	—	40
Textiles, leather and clothing	10	10	8	—	10	—	8	1	21	27	—
Other manufacturing	11	42	49	7	143	12	83	21	198	289	28
Construction	12	30	18	—	12	—	11	8	11	22	7
Gas, electricity and water	13	16	25	3	42	5	60	60	40	93	35
Services	14	281	40	51	404	84	232	212	247	510	148
Public administration, etc	15	—	—	—	—	—	—	—	—	—	—
Imports of goods and services	16	151	5	1	507	284	284	315	107	221	436
Sales by final buyers to one another	17	—	—	1	8	—	5	66	22	22	8
Goods and services (1 to 17)	18	992	251	92	1,991	437	1,070	935	1,645	2,188	793
Taxes on expenditure less subsidies	19	−252	9	10	59	7	32	37	28	73	28
Income from employment	20	353	535	47	546	25	388	502	890	1,877	771
Gross profits and other trading income	21	601	117	34	473	29	312	249	244	714	286
Total input (18 to 21)	22	1,694	912	183	3,069	498	1,802	1,723	2,807	4,852	1,878

National Income and Expenditure, 1967. **Table 19, H.M.S.O. (London)**

£ million

Other manu-fac-turing	Con-struc-tion	Gas, electri-city and water	Services	Public admin-istra-tion, etc.	Total inter-mediate output (1 to 15)	Final buyers					Total final output (17 to 21)	Total output (16 plus 22)	
						Current expenditure		Gross domestic capital formation		Exports			
						Pers-onal sector	Public authori-ties	Fixed	Stocks				
11	12	13	14	15	16	17	18	19	20	21	22	23	
9	—	—	4	—	617	987	14	9	24	43	1,077	1,694	1
51	—	345	37	—	647	208	26	21	—23	33	265	912	2
58	54	—	2	—	166	—	—	—	—	17	17	183	3
3	—	—	76	—	431	2,290	49	—	56	243	2,638	3,069	4
18	20	30	64	—	287	61	15	8	2	125	211	498	5
156	96	22	124	—	1,052	244	135	—	—19	390	750	1,802	6
18	127	29	14	—	1,424	—	5	40	—27	281	299	1,723	7
7	9	2	313	—	401	484	598	437	67	820	2,406	2,807	8
128	192	68	217	—	1,555	353	284	1,322	81	1,257	3,297	4,852	9
76	5	—	42	—	208	1,145	37	—	15	473	1,670	1,878	10
—	465	25	647	—	2,009	631	151	42	13	318	1,155	3,164	11
14	—	8	118	—	259	387	303	2,170	21	10	2,891	3,150	12
83	9	—	236	—	707	653	81	158	—	4	896	1,603	13
410	202	160	—	—	2,981	6,787	742	437	2	1,473	9,441	12,422	14
—	—	—	—	—	—	1,440	2,732	—	—	—	4,172	4,172	15
451	143	17	680	—	3,602	1,656	186	242	16	262	2,362	5,964	16
13	—	—	74	—	219	167	—366	—95	—	75	—219	—	17
1,495	1,322	706	2,648	—	16,565	17,493	4,992	4,791	228	5,824	33,328	49,893	18
70	55	69	412	—	637	2,648	91	112	—	—	2,851	3,488	19
1,169	1,364	373	6,242	3,063	18,145	—	—	—	—	—	—	18,145	20
430	409	455	3,120	1,109	8,582	—	—	—	—	—	—	8,582	21
3,164	3,150	1,603	12,422	4,172	43,929	20,141	5,083	4,903	228	5,824	36,179	80,108	22

APPENDIX C

Glossary

Actuarial techniques: Analytical methods using life expectancies of, and replacement demand for, industrial products.

Back-selling: A sales effort directed beyond the immediate customer, for example adhesive manufacturers selling to building firms, although the products are only available through builders' merchants.

Bias: Systematic error running through the whole or part of the sampling operation, the essence of which is that it forms a recurring component of error.

Bibliographical research: Research into sources of published data.

Brief: Statement by the research sponsors of research requirements.

Business indicators: Selected statistics, sensitive to changes in the state of industry, trade and commerce. There are three types: 'leaders'—offering advance pointers; 'coincidents'—moving in tandem with business conditions; and 'laggers'—showing delayed results.

Capital goods: Products (facilities) for production, distribution, transportation, communication and commerce.

Check list: (1) List of alternative answers to a set question (Multiple choice); (2) List of points upon which information is required in relation to a study or any particular aspect of a study.

Chi Square Test: A test to determine whether observed frequencies in a distribution differ significantly from the frequencies which might be expected according to some assumed hypothesis.

Classification: Reduction or rearrangement of data into groups for analysis purposes.

Coding: Equating of groups or items of information and representation by a symbol—usually a number.

Components: Manufactured articles which are incorporated into the product without further processing.

Consumer goods: Products in the final form in which they will reach domestic consumers.

Control question: Question against which the validity of other questions can be assessed.

Controlled sample: Sample which is controlled in accordance with the known characteristics of the universe or population.

Correlation: Method of measuring relationships between two or more variables, the analysis indicating whether or not a relationship exists.

Cross-tabulation of replies: Establishment of the relationship between various questions.

Cybernetics: Science of communication and control mechanics and processes.

Data Processing: Rearrangement and refinement of data into a form suitable for further use.

Decision Making Unit (D.M.U.): A number of individuals who are participants in the decision making process, who share common goals which the decision will help to achieve and the risks deriving from the decision.

Depth interview: See 'Focused interview'.

Desk Research: Survey techniques not involving field work.

Dichotomous question: Question framed to produce two possible answers, usually 'yes' or 'no'.

Econometric model: Type of 'mathematical design study' with certain in-built economic assumptions; models can be constructed for static or dynamic economic situations and the interaction of forces (i.e. assumptions) can be isolated and studied.

Economic indicators: See 'Business indicators'.

Editing: Questionnaire and interview report checking to ensure accuracy and comparability for the purpose of data analysis.

External research: All research which is conducted externally to the firm.

Field work: Survey activities carried out externally to the firm.

Focused interview: A method of interviewing to elicit the freest possible association of ideas on the part of the respondent.

Forecasting: Use of collected and analysed data to foretell economic business or sales developments.

Frequency distribution: The relative frequency with which members of a group or category have the various possible values of the variable quantity.

Funnel techniques: Technique of interviewing which, while maintaining the 'open end' approach to questions, keeps the respondent within the area of investigation.

Group interviewing: Focused interviewing conducted with groups of individuals.

Halo effect: A tendency for the impressions or attitudes created by one fact or aspect to influence others.

Image: The way in which a product, company, activity or any other manifestation of human or corporate activity is perceived by individuals or a series of special publics.

Impact Testing: Method of evaluating advertising effectiveness by measuring recall of advertisement by respondents who have had no opportunity of refreshing their recollections of the advertisements.

Industrial goods: Products for industrial users—primary materials, fabricated parts, fabricating materials, process materials, packaging materials, capital equipment, accessory equipment and operating supplies.

Industrial Marketing: All those activities concerned with purchases and sales of goods and services in industrial markets and between organisational buyers and sellers.

In-feeding: Supply of goods and services from within an organisation.

Input-Output Analysis: A means for characterising and analysing economic activity. A tabular organisation of transactions in which the sales (outputs) of a producing sector are distributed across a single horizontal row, while its purchases (inputs) are distributed down a single vertical column.

Internal research: Research into sources of information available within the firm.

Inter-personal network: Communication of attitudes held by individuals forming part of a market, usually by word of mouth.

Interview: Discussions between two or more people structured, semi-structured or non-directive, in which information is exchanged, values and attitudes explored and standards established. A number of such meetings can take place during a single 'visit'.

Keyed advertisement: An advertisement identifiable by means of coding.

Lead-time: Elapsed period between placing an order and receipt of goods.

Least Square Test: A method of fitting a straight line to a set of variants.

Life cycle: The period between the development of a product and its final withdrawal from the market. The life cycle is generally taken to include periods of 'introduction', 'growth', 'maturity', 'saturation' (or 'top-out') and 'decline'.

Market: (1) Aggregate of forces or conditions within which buyers and sellers make decisions which result in the transfer of goods and services. (2) Aggregate demand of the potential buyers of a commodity or service.

Marketing: Performance of business activities that direct the flow of goods and services from producer to consumer or user.

Marketing research: Systematic gathering, recording and analysing of data about problems relating to the marketing of goods and services.

Mathematical model: See 'Econometric model'.

Media analysis: Evaluation of publicity media in respect of a particular product or audience.

Merchandising: The planning and supervision involved in marketing particular goods or services, at the places, times and prices and in the quantities which will best serve to realise the marketing objectives of the business.

Motivation research: Group of techniques developed by the behavioural scientists which are used by marketing researchers to discover factors influencing marketing behaviour.

Multiple choice question: Question framed to produce an answer from among a list of alternatives.

Non-Directive Interviews: See 'Unstructured interviews'.

Observational method: Research technique in which factual information is obtained by observation.

Open-end question: Question phrased to permit the respondent a completely free answer expressed in any manner chosen.

Perceptual distortion: The distortion of reality into conformance with a person's own values, attitudes and interests.

Pre-coding: Reduction of questions and possible answers to a numerical code before a survey takes place.

Primary information sources: Data obtained by the use of original research and not previously published.

Projective technique: An indirect testing technique creating a specific stimulus situation.

Qualitative screening process: A method of assessing marketing characteristics of a product, service or a market by apportioning values and weightings to a series of important factors or variables.

Quota sample: Sample which is broken down into quotas according to the factors it is intended to use as controlling factors and in accordance with their known incidence in the universe.

Random sample: A sample in which every item in the universe has equal chance, with all other items, of being selected.

Ratio: Relationship of one quantity to another sometimes expressed as a fraction.

Reciprocal trading: An 'agreement, formal or informal, between a supplying company and a customer to purchase requirements which can be met by the customer firm (e.g. a steel manufacturer in return for placing all or the bulk of its oil requirements with an oil company receiving that oil company's orders for pipe and structural steel).

Recognition survey: Enquiries to discover where recognition of advertising occurs.

Replenishment lead-time: See 'lead-time'.

Research design: A statement of research objectives, methods and time and cost estimates.

Role Perception: An individual or group's interpretation of their own or other's role in a specific situation.

Sales Analysis: Sub-division of marketing research which involves an analysis of data obtained from internal sales records of a firm.

Sales Forecast: Estimate of sales, in value or physical units, for a specified future period under a proposed marketing plan or programme and under an assumed set of economic conditions outside the unit for which the forecast is made.

Sample: Representative group drawn from the defined universe.

Sampling frame: A specification of the information available relating to the population to be studied in sufficient detail so as to make possible the location of particular units should they be selected for the sample drawn.

Secondary information sources: Data drawn from previous published sources.

Segmentation: The division of a large market into a number of smaller segments each homogeneous in respect of some common characteristic or characteristics.

Semantic code: Numerical weighting of subjective adjectival ratings.

Semantic differential: Apportionment of numerical values to subjective adjectival ratings.

Semi-structured interviews: Interviews with a pre-arranged series of questions but in which the interviewer has discretion to alter their form or order.

'Split run' copy testing: An advertising evaluation technique which depends upon the advertisement having several forms in the same media. By keyed returns or other indicators it is possible to measure the effect of the copy for each run.

Standard error: The inherent variation of a sample or of answers to a particular question, which is measurable and dependent on the size of the sample and the pattern of replies to questions.

'Starch' rating: Quantification of recognition factors in advertising evaluation based upon the method devised by Daniel Starch.

Stock turn: Average rate at which stock is turned over in a year calculated by dividing sales by stock at selling price.

Store audits: Regular (periodic) physical checks on shop or warehouse stocks including goods received during the period of review.

Stratification: Division of the universe into strata representing the possession of various characteristics and their incidence.

Structured interview: Interview, personal or telephone, in which the questions are formulated in advance and asked in a prearranged manner and order.

Tabulation: Process of consolidating research information into segregated and annotated tables.

Tachistoscope: An electro-mechanical device for controlling exposure to a specific visual stimulus for various lengths of time down to fractions of seconds.

Terms of reference: Accepted statement of research objectives and methods.

Test marketing: Experimental measurement of the effect of single variables in a marketing situation.

'Throw away' or 'pilot' interview: Interviews in which the technique can be tested irrespective of the results.

Top-out: The point in a product life cycle at which demand levels out before declining.

Trade relations: See 'Reciprocal trading'.

Transition statement: An interpolation by the interviewer to assist respondents move from one subject to another.

'Triangle' clause: Technique for using multiple checks on respondents by seeking answers to questions in varying forms.

Unstructured interview: Interview, personal or telephone, in which the form and order of questions is not predetermined.

Visit: A call on an organisation during field work to obtain research information; a visit may include a number of interviews or none.

Weighting: Process of giving numbers their due values according to their individual importance, real or estimated.

Work Plan: Statement of the overall research activity, phasing and allocation of resources and priorities.

Bibliography

There are few books which deal exclusively with industrial marketing activities of any sort and books concerned wholly with industrial marketing research are almost non-existent. Recognising this deficiency the bibliography includes a number of books and articles on consumer marketing and marketing research which have relevant and adaptable material in them and can be used by the industrial marketing researcher. Those items which do deal specifically with industrial and business research have been marked with an asterisk.

CHAPTER I

Characteristics of Industrial and Consumer Markets

*Jacqueline Marrian. 'Marketing Characteristics of Industrial Goods and Buyers'. *The Marketing of Industrial Products.* (Ed. Aubrey Wilson). Hutchinson. (London, 1965).

*R. S. Alexander, S. C. Cross and R. M. Cunningham. *Industrial Marketing.* Irwin. (Homewood, Illinois, 1961) Part 1.

P. Bliss (Ed.). *Marketing and the Behavioral Sciences.* Allyn & Bacon. (Boston, 1963). Chapters 19, 25, 27 and 29.

J. A. Howard. *Marketing: Executive Behaviour and Buyer Behaviour.* Columbia University Press. (New York, 1963). Chapters 1, 4 and 5.

Leslie Rodger. *Marketing in a Competitive Economy.* Hutchinson. (London, 1965). Chapters 1 and 2.

CHAPTER 2

Objectives for Profitable Research

*Mary Griffin. 'Generation of New Product Ideas'. *Marketing of Industrial Products.* (Ed. Aubrey Wilson). Hutchinson. (London, 1965).

*Hugh Buckner. *How British Industry Buys.* Hutchinson. (London, 1967).

A. R. Oxenfeldt. *Pricing for Marketing Executives.* Wadsworth. (Belmont, California, 1966).

*W. T. Diamond. *Distribution Channels for Industrial Goods.* Ohio State University. (Columbus, Ohio, 1963).

A. B. Blankenship and J. B. Doyle. *Marketing Research Management.* American Management Association. (New York, 1965). Chapter 1.

*M. S. Heidingsfield and F. H. Eby. *Marketing and Business Research.* Holt, Rinehart and Winston. (New York, 1962). Chapter 1.

*R. S. Alexander, J. S. Cross and J. M. Cunningham. *Industrial Marketing.* Irwin. (Homewood, Illinois, 1961). Part II.

'Uncovering your Competitors' Costs'. *Chemical Engineering.* (New York, November 26, 1962).

CHAPTER 3

Parameters of Research

Lee Adler. 'Phasing Research into the Marketing Plan'. *Harvard Business Review.* (Cambridge, Mass., May/June, 1960).

A. B. Blankenship and J. B. Doyle. *Marketing Research Management.* American Management Association. (New York, 1965). Chapters 6 and 7.

CHAPTER 4

Preparing for the Project

Harper W. Boyd and Ralph Westfall. *Marketing Research: Texts and Cases.* Irwin. (Homewood, Illinois, 1964). Chapter 6.

*M. S. Heidingsfield and F. H. Eby. *Marketing and Business Research.* Holt, Rinehart and Winston. (New York, 1962). Chapter 2.

A. B. Blankenship and J. B. Doyle. *Marketing Research Management.* American Management Association. (New York, 1965). Chapter 6.

CHAPTER 5

Use of Secondary Sources

*D. E. Davinson. *Commercial Information*. Pergamon Press. (Oxford, 1965).

*William A. Bagley. *Facts and How To Find Them*. Pitman. (London, 1962).

*Bernard Houghton. *Technical Information Sources*. Bingley. (London, 1962).

*T. D. Wilson and J. Stephenson. *Dissemination of Information*. Bingley. (London, 1966).

*Bernard Houghton (Ed.). *Information Work Today*. Bingley. (London, 1967).

*Keith Davison. *Theory of Classification*. Bingley. (London, 1966).

*R. J. P. Carey. *Finding and Using Technical Information*. Arnold. (London, 1966).

*J. Barzun and H. Graff. *The Modern Researcher*. Harcourt Brace. (New York, 1962).

CHAPTER 6

Sampling in Industrial Markets

R. Ferber. *Market Research*. McGraw-Hill. (New York, 1949).

W. E. Deming. *Sample Design in Business Research*. Wiley. (New York, 1960).

M. J. Slonim. *Sampling*. Simon & Schuster. (New York, 1966).

J. R. Stockton. *Introduction to Business Economic Statistics*. South Western Publishing Company. (Cincinnati, 1966). Chapter 8.

*R. D. Mason. *Statistical Techniques in Business and Economics*. Irwin. (Homewood, Illinois, 1967). Chapter 14.

*J. F. Rummel and W. C. Ballaine. *Research Methodology in Business*. Harper and Row. (New York, 1963). Chapter III.

CHAPTER 7

The Postal Questionnaire

*Hugh Buckner. *How British Industry Buys*. Hutchinson. (London, 1967). The Appendix of this book provides a complete case history

2c*

of an industrial marketing research project using postal question-naire method only.

There is no other substantial published material on the use of postal questionnaires in industrial marketing research but the detailed study by Christopher Scott is particularly well worth studying.

Christopher Scott. 'Research on Mail Surveys'. *Journal of the Royal Statistical Society*. Series A. (London, 1961). Vol. 124, Part 2.

Harper W. Boyd and Ralph Westfall. *Marketing Research: Texts and Cases*. Irwin. (Homewood, Illinois, 1964). Chapter 5.

D. Wallace. 'A case—for and against—Mail Questionnaires'. *Public Opinion Quarterly*. Vol. 18. (Princeton, New Jersey. Spring, 1954).

W. F. O'Dell. 'Personal Interviews or Mail Panels'. *Journal of Marketing*. Vol. 26. (Chicago, October, 1962).

CHAPTER 8

Interviewing

*J. F. Rummel and W. C. Ballaine. *Research Methodology in Business*. Harper and Row. (New York, 1963). Chapter V.

*M. S. Heidingsfield and F. H. Eby. *Marketing and Business Research*. Holt, Rinehart and Winston. (New York, 1962). Chapters 11 and 12.

H. V. Kincaid and M. Bright. 'Interviewing the Business Elite'. *American Journal of Sociology*. Vol. 11. (Chicago, 1957).

E. Sydney and M. Brown. *The Skills of Interviewing*. Tavistock. (London, 1962). (This book is concerned with selection interviewing but contains some information which is relevant for industrial marketing research interviewing.)

CHAPTER 9

Using the Telephone in Industrial Marketing Research

*Max K. Adler. 'The Use of the Telephone in Industrial Market Research'. *Scientific Business*. (Reading, February, 1964).

Although not specifically concerned with the use of the telephone in industrial marketing research, Bell System's various guides to the use of the telephone, particularly related to telephone selling, contain many useful ideas for the industrial marketing researcher.

Making Appointments with Phone Power. Bell Systems. (New York, n.d.).

Opening New Accounts. Bell Telephone Company. (New York, n.d.).

Tele-Marketing Programme. Bell Telephone Company. (New York, n.d.).

CHAPTER 10

Observation Techniques

*J. F. Rummel and W. C. Ballaine. *Research Methodology in Business*. Harper and Row. (New York, 1963). Chapter IV.

J. H. Lorie and H. V. Roberts. *Basic Methods of Marketing Research*. McGraw-Hill. (New York, 1951). Part IV.

M. S. Schwartz and C. G. Schwartz. 'Problems in Participant Observation'. *Americal Journal of Sociology*. Vol. 60. (Chicago, January, 1955).

A. J. Vidich. 'Participant Observation and the Collection and Interpretation of Data'. *American Journal of Sociology*. Vol. 60. (Chicago, January, 1955).

H. J. Leibowitz. *Visual Perception*. Macmillan. (New York, 1965).

CHAPTER 11

Processing the Data

*S. R. D. Mason. *Statistical Techniques in Business and Economics*. Irwin. (Homewood, Illinois, 1967).

*M. J. Moroney. *Facts from Figures*. Pelican. (London. Revised Edition, 1965).

*J. R. Stockton. *Introduction to Business and Economic Statistics*. South Western Publishing Company. (Cincinatti, 1966).

*A. J. Merrett and G. Bannock. *Business and Economic Statistics*. Hutchinson. (London, 1962.)

Robert Ferber. *Market Research*. McGraw-Hill. (New York, 1949).

P. E. Green and R. E. Frank. *A Manager's Guide to Marketing Research*. Wiley. (New York, 1967). Chapters 2, 3, 4 and 5.

CHAPTER 12

Assessing Advertising Effectiveness

*F. R. Messner. *Industrial Advertising*. McGraw-Hill. (New York, 1963).

D. B. Lucas and S. H. Britt. *Measuring Advertising Effectiveness*. McGraw-Hill. (New York, 1963).

C. E. Eldridge. *The Management of the Marketing Function*. Association of National Advertisers. (New York, 1966). Section 11.

Papers for the Seminar on *Measuring Advertising Effectiveness*. European Society for Opinion Surveys and Market Research. (Munich, April 1-13, 1965).

D. Starch. *Measuring Advertising Readership and Results*. McGraw-Hill. (New York, 1966).

CHAPTER 13

Industrial Marketing Research as an Aid to Forecasting

*F. Hummel. *Market and Sales Potentials*. Ronald Press. (New York, 1961).

*R. S. Reichard. *Practical Techniques of Sales Forecasting*. McGraw-Hill. (New York, 1966).

*W. Leontief. *Input-Output Economics*. Oxford University Press. (New York, 1966). Chapter 1.

R. M. Carpenter. *Guide List for Marketing Research and Economic Forecasting*. American Management Association. (New York). (Originally published 1957, revised edition n.d.).

R. S. Hancock (Ed.) *Dynamic Marketing for a Changing World*. American Marketing Association. (Proceedings of the 43rd National Conference). (Chicago, 1960). Part 4, Section C.

Introduction to Business Forecasting. Institute of Costs and Works Accountants. (London, 1959).

W. F. Butler and R. A. Kavesh (Eds.). *How Business Economists Forecast*. Prentice Hall Englewood Cliffs. (New Jersey, 1966).

CHAPTER 14

The Report

*B. M. Cooper. *Writing Technical Reports*. Pelican. (London, 1964).

*A. B. Sklare. *Creative Report Writing*. McGraw-Hill. (New York, 1964).

*E. Gowers. *Plain Words:* A guide to the use of English. HMSO (London, 1948).

W. Boyd and Ralph Westfall. *Marketing Research: Texts and Cases*. Irwin. (Homewood, Illinois, 1964). Chapter 13.

*J. F. Rummel and W. C. Ballaine. *Research Methodology in Business*. Harper and Row. (New York, 1963). Appendix B. (Although this Appendix refers to academic research reports it is directly relevant to industrial marketing research.)

*R. D. Mason. *Statistical Techniques in Business and Economics*. Irwin. (Homewood, Illinois, 1967). Chapter 5.

*J. Barzun and H. F. Graff. *The Modern Researcher*. Harcourt Brace. (New York, 1962). Part Three.

CHAPTER 15

'Make or Buy' in Marketing Research

A. B. Blankenship and J. B. Doyle. *Marketing Research Management*. American Management Association. (New York, 1965). Although almost wholly concerned with consumer marketing research, this most comprehensive marketing research management study contains much that is appropriate for the industrial marketing researcher.

*R. S. Alexander, J. S. Cross and R. M. Cunningham. *Industrial Marketing*. Irwin. (Homewood, Illinois, 1961). Chapter 5.

William C. Gordon Jnr. *Selecting Marketing Research Services*. Small Business Administration. (Washington, D.C., 1960).

How to get the best results from Management Consultants. Association of Consulting Management Engineers Inc. (New York, 1964).

S. Dietz. 'The Art of Using Marketing Research'. E. Konrad and R. Erickson (Eds.). *Marketing Research—A Management Overview*. American Management Association. (New York, 1966).

*Gordon Brand. 'Industrial Marketing Research—Management Aspects'. Aubrey Wilson (Ed.). *The Marketing of Industrial Products*. Hutchinson. (London, 1965).

Leslie Rodger. *Marketing in a Competitive Economy*. Hutchinson. (London, 1965). Chapter 3.

Index

For Product Safety Concerns and Information please contact our EU
representative GPSR@taylorandfrancis.com
Taylor & Francis Verlag GmbH, Kaufingerstraße 24, 80331 München, Germany